Statistics for Sports and Exercise Science

Visit the *Statistics for Sports and Exercise Science* Companion Website at **www.pearsoned.co.uk/newell** to find valuable **student** learning material including:

- Software guides for Minitab, SPSS and R
- Complete data sets for use with Minitab, SPSS and R

PEARSON

We work with leading authors to develop the strongest educational materials in sports science, bringing cutting-edge thinking and best learning practice to a global market.

Under a range of well-known imprints, including Prentice Hall, we craft high quality print and electronic publications which help readers to understand and apply their content, whether studying or at work.

To find out more about the complete range of our publishing, please visit us on the World Wide Web at: **www.pearsoned.co.uk**

Statistics for Sports and Exercise Science

John Newell

Tom Aitchison

Stanley Grant

Prentice Hall
is an imprint of

Harlow, England • London • New York • Boston • San Francisco • Toronto
Sydney • Tokyo • Singapore • Hong Kong • Seoul • Taipei • New Delhi
Cape Town • Madrid • Mexico City • Amsterdam • Munich • Paris • Milan

Pearson Education Limited
Edinburgh Gate
Harlow
Essex CM20 2JE
England

and Associated Companies throughout the world

Visit us on the World Wide Web at:
www.pearsoned.co.uk

First published 2010

ISBN: 978-0-13-204254-3

100612530X

British Library Cataloguing-in-Publication Data
A catalogue record for this book is available from the British Library

Library of Congress Cataloging-in-Publication Data
Newell, John.
    Statistics for sports and exercise science / John Newell, Tom Aitchison, Stanley Grant.
       p. cm.
    Includes bibliographical references and index.
    ISBN 978-0-13-204254-3 (pbk. : alk. paper)   1. Sports sciences—
Statistical methods.   2. Sports sciences—Research.   I. Aitchison, Tom.
II. Grant, Stanley.   III. Title.
    GV558.N475 2010
    613.7'1—dc22

                                                        2009016104

10 9 8 7 6 5 4 3 2 1
13 12 11 10 09

Typeset in 9.25/12.5 pt Stone Serif by 73
Printed and bound in Malaysia (CTP-VP)

The publisher's policy is to use paper manufactured from sustainable forests.

Contents

| Introduction | ix |
| Acknowledgements | xi |

1 Discovering statistics — 1

1.1	Why bother with statistics in sports and exercise science?	1
1.2	The basic approach	2
1.3	Some basic vocabulary	2
1.4	More on variables	4
1.5	Some underlying ideas	6
1.6	Examples of illustrations	7
	Summary	10

2 Designing a study — 11

2.1	Introduction	11
2.2	Collecting the data (sampling)	12
2.3	Sources of variability	21
2.4	Other important issues in designing a study	28
	Summary	33

3 Summarising and displaying data — 34

3.1	Introduction	34
3.2	Numerical summaries for continuous variables	35
3.3	Graphical methods for continuous variables	37
3.4	Single-sample problems (independent data)	38
3.5	Between-subject designs (independent data)	42
3.6	Within-subject designs (dependent data)	48
3.7	Designs with between-subject and within-subject factors	57
3.8	Between-subject designs incorporating a covariate	60
3.9	Modelling relationships (correlation and regression)	64
	Summary	72
	Technical appendix	72

4 Estimating parameters   78

4.1   Introduction   78
4.2   Interval estimation   79
4.3   Interval estimation for a population mean   80
4.4   Comparing two population means (the simplest between-subject design)   83
4.5   Interval estimation for paired data (the simplest within-subject design)   90
4.6   One between-subject and one within-subject factor (each at two levels)   92
4.7   Prediction and tolerance intervals   97
4.8   What if the Normality assumption is questionable?   102
Summary   113
Technical appendix   113

5 Testing hypotheses   116

5.1   Introduction   116
5.2   Introduction to the null and alternative hypotheses   116
5.3   Comparing two population means: the two-sample t-test   118
5.4   Paired data (the simplest within-subject design)   122
5.5   One between-subject and one within-subject factor (each at two levels)   123
5.6   Testing for Normality   127
5.7   The misuse of P-values: significance and importance   130
Summary   131
Technical appendix   131

6 Modelling relationships: regression   135

6.1   Introduction   135
6.2   Simple linear regression   135
6.3   Using simple linear regression to make predictions   145
6.4   Multiple regression   149
6.5   Variable selection techniques   157
6.6   Incorporating categorical explanatory variables into a multiple regression model   164
6.7   Regression trees   169
Summary   171
Technical appendix   172

7 Investigating between-subject factors: independent observations   175

7.1   Introduction   175
7.2   One-way ANOVA: a general linear model with one between-subject factor   176
7.3   Two-way ANOVA: a general linear model with two between-subject factors   185
7.4   ANCOVA: correcting for a covariate in ANOVA   197
7.5   Allometric scaling   201

Summary 207
Technical appendix 208

8 Modelling categorical data 213

8.1 Introduction 213
8.2 Interval estimation for categorical variables 214
8.3 Hypothesis tests and categorical variables 222
8.4 Association and categorical variables 229
8.5 Paired data and categorical variables 237
8.6 Modelling relationships with a categorical response variable 241
8.7 Logistic regression in more complex problems 246
8.8 Classification trees 257
Summary 259
Technical appendix 259

9 Investigating within-subject factors: dependent observations 261

9.1 Introduction 261
9.2 Analysing dependent observations: paired data 263
9.3 Analysing dependent observations: a single within-subject factor
at three or more levels 269
9.4 Analysing dependent observations: two or more
within-subject factors 276
Summary 292

10 Investigating studies with between-subject and within-subject factors: more on dependent observations 293

10.1 Introduction 293
10.2 One between-subject factor at two levels and one within-subject
factor at two levels 294
10.3 One between-subject factor at two levels and one within-subject
factor at $K > 2$ levels 299
10.4 One between-subject factor at $K > 2$ levels and two within-subject
factors each at two levels 306
10.5 Two between-subject factors each at two levels and one within-
subject factor at two levels 313
10.6 Two between-subject factors each at two levels and two within-
subject factors each at two levels 318
Summary 323

11 Handling linear mixed-effects models: more on dependent observations 325

11.1 Introduction 325
11.2 One within-subject covariate 327

11.3 One within-subject factor and one within-subject covariate   336
11.4 One between-subject factor and one within-subject covariate   342
11.5 More complicated designs involving within-subject covariates   348
Summary   356

12 Measurement error and method agreement studies   357

12.1 Introduction   357
12.2 Measurement error   359
12.3 Testing for agreement   374
Summary   382
Technical appendix   382

13 Speculating on the sample size required   385

13.1 Introduction   385
13.2 Using interval estimation   385
13.3 Power and sample size determination   392
Summary   409
Technical appendix   410

Appendix: Table of illustrations and exercises   411
Index   423

Supporting resources

Visit **www.pearsoned.co.uk/newell** to find valuable online resources

Companion Website for students
- Software guides for Minitab, SPSS and R
- Complete data sets for use with Minitab, SPSS and R

For instructors
- Powerpoint slides
- Solutions guide

For more information please contact your local Pearson Education sales representative or visit **www.pearsoned.co.uk/newell**

Introduction

Many sports scientists and students look on statistics with a certain disdain, typically the course they least look forward to as part of their formal training. One of the inspirations for this book arose from the fact that biostatistics textbooks currently available really do not engage with sports and exercise science and invariably do not include relevant examples and case studies similar to the research undertaken by such people. The present authors consist of a sports scientist of thirty years' standing and two (relatively tame) statisticians who have been analysing data from sports and exercise science as well as many other areas for thirty and twelve years, respectively. The shared experiences of all three over this period are utilised in this book to display the practical nature of statistics and to facilitate an understanding of its usefulness and importance in analysing data from studies in sports and exercise science.

This book assumes no previous knowledge of statistics and the main emphasis will be on getting the reader to think statistically about:

- asking appropriate (and answerable) questions;
- designing a suitable study to answer these questions;
- choosing an adequate number of subjects for the study;
- producing appropriate graphs to describe the study data;
- carrying out a proper analysis of these data;
- presenting clear and justifiable conclusions based on the data.

Chapter 1 introduces the basic ideas and definitions required while Chapter 2 covers some of the considerations for good study design. It is essential in any study to have a clear 'picture' of what the data are saying about the question of interest, and this is covered in Chapter 3. The key ingredients of statistics are the concepts of interval estimation and hypothesis testing, which are introduced in Chapters 4 and 5, respectively, with the main emphasis throughout this book on the former. Chapters 6 and 7 cover the specific areas of regression and analysis of variance, while Chapter 8 deals with all areas for categorical data problems. Chapters 9 and 10 deal with the procedures known as repeated measures and this is extended in Chapter 11 to cover linear mixed models. The notion that the measurement of a characteristic of a subject needs to be both reliable and valid is discussed in Chapter 12. The final chapter deals with the eternal problem of how many subjects are required for a study.

Through a series of carefully chosen illustrations this book intends to help the reader better appreciate the role of statistics in sports and exercise science from designing a study, through the formal analysis, to the writing of a final report. The extensive use of illustrations helps to simplify and clarify the somewhat esoteric mathematical ideas underpinning statistical analyses. Each illustration includes graphs and output mainly from the Minitab statistical software, with additional output from SPSS (Statistical Package for the Social Sciences) and also from computing freeware known as R.

Almost all of the illustrations are from the authors' own research consisting of over thirty years for the two veterans and twelve years for the new boy on the block. Hopefully, this marriage of young and old(er), Scottish and Irish, sports scientist and statistician, will provide the building blocks to the reader's discovery of how useful and interesting statistics can be to the sports and exercise scientist. Perhaps 'interesting' is stretching it a bit but read on and discover how common sense can go a long way in statistics.

Acknowledgements

We would like to thank our colleagues, students and friends for supplying the contexts and data used throughout the illustrations and exercises. In particular we would like to thank the following people for their valuable comments, criticisms and suggestions: David Borchers, John Bradley, Mary Byrne, Richard Davison, John Hinde, Domenico Piccolo, Lindsay Jack, Jim Kay, Roddy Macdonald, Kenny McMillan, Colm O'Riordan, Viki Penpraze, Marco Reale, Irene Riach and Carl Scarrott.

We are grateful to Julian Partridge, Owen Knight and Rufus Curnow for their valuable contribution to this book.

We would especially like to thank Anne, Karen and Margaret for their patience and support throughout the project.

Publisher's acknowledgements

We are grateful to the following for permission to reproduce copyright material:

Text

Illustration 3.3 adapted from Can Relaxation Enhance Running Performance?, *Scottish Sports Council Research Report* 44 (Ashley, E., Mutrie, N. and Hayes, C. 1996); Illustrations 6.3 and 6.4 adapted from The relationship between strength, power, flexibility, anthropometry and technique in predicting 2000m and 5000m rowing ergometer performance, *Kinanthropometry: Proceedings of the 10th International Society for the Advancement of Kinanthropometry Conference, Held in Conjunction with the 13th Commonwealth International Sports Conference, Melbourne (Marfell-Jones, M. and Olds, T., eds)* (Graham-Smith, P and Ridler, A. 2006); Illustration 6.7 adapted from The relationship between plasma lactate parameters, Wpeak and endurance cycling performance, *Medicine & Science in Sports & Exercise*, 30, pp. 1270–1275 (Bishop, D., Jenkins, D.G. and Mackinnon, L.T. 1998); Illustration 8.6 adapted from MacPhail, A. (2001), The social construction of higher grade physical education : teacher curriculum decision making and pupil subject choice (PhD thesis, Glasgow University); Illustration 10.5 adapted from Dudley, C., Moran, S. Penpraze, V., The effectiveness of cognitive-behavioural intervention in golf (University of Glasgow sports science student project); Illustration 11.2 adapted from Baxendale, R. (supervisor),

University of Glasgow student project 2005; Illustration 11.4 adapted from Ommer, J. (1987), Motor ability in children (MSc thesis 7650, Glasgow University); Illustration 12.1 adapted from Sports Performance Unit, Scottish Premier League Club; Illustration 12.6 adapted from Archibald, S., Bibby, C., Henderson, L. and Baxendale, R. Comparison of different methods of predicting percentage body fat. Glasgow University student project 2006.

In some instances we have been unable to trace the owners of copyright material, and we would appreciate any information that would enable us to do so.

1 Discovering statistics

Why bother with statistics in sports and exercise science?

Sports and exercise science, as well as sport in general, depends upon variability. Imagine a world with no variability between athletes. Every race would end in a dead heat, every game in a draw. Variability is the essence of sports and the sports scientist must know how to study and interpret it. No two athletes always perform exactly the same; variability is inherent and fundamental in sports. Statistics is the study of such variability.

Assuming that a researcher has carried out a study (or survey or experiment) with specific questions in mind that he/she hopes the study will answer, then statistics or data analysis attempts to provide an **objective** framework to provide such answers. Without at least an attempt at an objective look at the data, then all that is left is personal opinion.

> **Statistics** is the science of collecting, analysing, presenting and interpreting **data**. It provides the logical framework which enables the **objective** evaluation of research questions of interest.

Some examples of study (key) questions of interest are:

1 What is the average survival time of avalanche victims who breathe through a soda lime container when buried under snow?

2 By how much, if at all, is the knee extension strength of the average professional soccer player greater than that of recreational soccer players?

3 Does the use of walking poles significantly reduce, on average, the energy expenditure of a typical two-hour gentle hill walk for a healthy, middle-aged male?

4 Will a twice-weekly customised exercise regime significantly improve, on average, the mobility of the institutionalised elderly (as measured by a timed stair ascent) over two months compared with the 'natural change' over that period?

These are examples of one-sample, two-sample, paired-sample and two-paired-sample contexts, respectively (introduced in more detail in later chapters) and the last of these is probably the most common type of problem encountered in sports and exercise science. The other three are among the simplest contexts encountered in data analysis but this book covers many other contexts and techniques in varying degrees of complexity throughout the following twelve chapters.

1.2　The basic approach

For every part of every context where a statistical analysis is carried out, the basic approach involves the following integral steps:

1 *Specify* clearly each question of interest.
2 *Design* a suitable means of gathering appropriate data to answer the question posed.
3 *Collect* such data in as unambiguous and organised a manner as possible.
4 *Plot* or *tabulate* the data in an appropriate form to provide a subjective answer to the question posed.
5 *Build* a mathematical model to describe how the data actually collected were generated.
6 *Analyse* the data using this mathematical model.
7 *Report,* in simple English, the answers from such an analysis, exploiting graphical displays of the data to allow ease of interpretation of the conclusions of your analysis.

Throughout this book each of these steps will be discussed and highlighted. Although the formal role of statistics is concentrated on steps 5 and 6 (i.e. the formal analysis), the role of a practical statistician is to be involved in all aspects of an experiment or study. In particular, the ability to communicate effectively and simply with his/her collaborators in the sports (or agricultural or industrial or economic or . . .) world is essential.

Indeed, because of years of poor quality data analysis in many medical and biological studies most academic journals have statistical referees and insist on clear and sensible statistical analyses. Look at any of the articles in the sports and exercise science literature and appreciate the 'statistical content' of many sports and exercise science papers nowadays.

1.3　Some basic vocabulary

When someone thinks of the word 'statistics', what comes to mind? More often than not 'statistics' is taken to mean numerical summaries (e.g. the average $\dot{V}O_2$ max of soccer players in La Liga; the range of percentage body fat of children in Slovakia), while in fact the word 'statistics' exists as both a singular and a plural noun:

Statistics *is* the science that involves collecting, summarising, analysing and interpreting data, whereas statistics *are* numerical summaries calculated from a sample of data. The phrase **data analysis** is often used to refer to the use of statistics in practice.

In research in sports science, industry, commerce or the academic world, statistics is an integral part of every analytical study as a means of providing effective and objective analyses of the problems that the study was designed to address. Statistics, as in all areas of science, comes with its own jargon and terminology and some definitions of this essential vocabulary are given here to ensure that everyone is 'singing from the same songbook'.

A **variable (of interest)** is a single aspect or characteristic associated with each of a large group of 'individuals' under consideration.

Example: The cardio-respiratory fitness (as measured by the $\dot{V}O_2$ max) of all 18–25-year-old females in the West of Scotland (roughly 40,000).

A **population** is the large group of 'individuals' under consideration.

Example: All 18–25-year-old females in the West of Scotland at present.

A **sample** is a subset of the population – 'selected' as being representative of the population – in which each subject will have the variable of interest measured.

Example: 20 females in Glasgow University hockey club in 2007.

A **parameter** is a single number summarising in some way the values of the variable of interest in the *population* of interest.

Example: The *average* $\dot{V}O_2$ max of *all females* at present in the age range 18–25 years in the West of Scotland.

A **statistic** is a single number summarising in some way the values of the variable of interest in the *sample* actually collected.

Example: The *average* $\dot{V}O_2$ max of the *20 females* in the hockey club in 2007.

The major aim of the subject of statistics is to draw inferences (i.e. make conclusions) about the value of such Parameters in the Population of interest based upon the observed values of the Summary Statistics from the actual Sample obtained.

Usually, the target population is large, and so it would be impractical to study the whole population without access to substantial resources (e.g. time, money, staff, computing equipment).

Some examples of these definitions for studies covered in this book are:

1 One-sample problem (Mont Blanc Ascent Time study)

This is the simplest type of problem where a single sample of subjects is investigated.

Question:	What is the average time taken to climb Mont Blanc in summer?
Variable of interest:	The Ascent Time to the summit of Mont Blanc (from the Gouter Hut)
Population:	All successful climbers of Mont Blanc during summer (July and August) across many years
Sample:	197 successful climbers in August 2002
Parameter:	The average Ascent Time of all successful climbers over many years
Statistic:	The average Ascent Time of the 197 successful climbers sampled in August 2002

2 Paired-sample problem (Ice Baths and Blood Lactate study)

This is a type of problem where a single sample of subjects is taken and each subject investigated under two distinct 'conditions'.

Question:	Do ice baths significantly increase Blood Lactate Reduction immediately after exercise?
Variable of interest:	Reduction in Blood Lactate 25 minutes after exercise
Population:	All club-standard oarsmen who currently use ice baths or intend to do so in the future
Sample:	Ten club-standard oarsmen from a local club
Parameter:	The average Difference in Blood Lactate Reduction between use and non-use of ice baths 25 minutes after exercise across all oarsmen
Statistic:	The sample average Difference in Blood Lactate Reduction between use and non-use of ice baths 25 minutes after exercise across the ten oarsmen

3 Two-paired-samples problem (Osteoporosis and Exercise study)

This is a type of problem where two distinct samples are taken and each subject in each sample is investigated under two distinct 'conditions'.

Question:	Does exercise significantly improve the balance of females suffering from osteoporosis?
Variable of interest:	The change over two months in Balance (as measured by a functional reach test)
Population:	All female osteoporosis sufferers in Scotland capable of regular exercise
Sample:	Sixty such women in the Glasgow area divided into two sub-samples. The women in one sample exercised and those in the other sample did not change their current exercise pattern
Parameter:	The Difference in average Change in Balance over two months of all female osteoporosis sufferers on regular exercise compared with not doing this form of regular exercise
Statistic:	The Difference between the sample average Change in Balance over two months of the thirty female osteoporosis sufferers and that for the non-exercisers

1.4   More on variables

There are two types of variable encountered in practice, namely **qualitative** (non-numerical) and **quantitative** (numerical) variables.

Qualitative variables can be subdivided into:

- **Categorical** (or nominal) variables where an individual can fall into one of a small number of categories, but these categories do not have a natural ordering.

    Examples: Sex (male, female)

    Source of Leg Injury (hamstrings, quadriceps, other)

- **Ordered categorical** (or **ordinal**) where an individual can fall into one of a small number of categories but these categories have a natural ordering.

  Examples: Back Pain (mild, moderate, severe)
  Shivering (none, slight, substantial)

Quantitative variables can be subdivided into:

- **Discrete** variables which can take only integer values.

  Examples: Number of Sit-ups achieved in 30 seconds
  Number of Goals scored in a soccer match

  Note: the term 'discrete' is used sometimes to include qualitative variables.

- **Continuous** variables which can take any value at all across a wide range.

  Examples: Body Mass, 10 m Sprint Time, $\dot{V}O_2$ max

In practice, the values of many continuous variables are measured to a reasonable degree of accuracy such as the nearest whole number, so that an actual height of 179.281 cm might well be recorded as 179 cm.

The two major types of variable are *continuous* and *categorical*, with continuous variables more common in sports and exercise science than categorical.

There is another key distinction between variables which it is essential that the researcher is able to recognise. Study questions will concern a key variable of interest which is referred to as the **response variable**, e.g. Mont Blanc Ascent Time, Reduction in Blood Lactate (for the Ice Baths study) or Change in Balance Score over two months (for the Osteoporosis study). This will be the outcome for each subject which will be investigated in the key question(s) of interest.

Other variables may well play an active role in an analysis, not as the key (response) variable of interest but rather to adjust or correct for their (possible) effect on the response variable. These are referred to as **explanatory variables**. For example, body mass is likely to influence grip strength, so, for a study using Grip Strength as a response variable, Body Mass would be a (possible) explanatory variable. These appear mostly in the material from Chapter 6 onwards concerning techniques known as regression, analysis of covariance and linear mixed models.

One final piece of terminology used throughout the book concerns qualitative variables known as **factors**. Again, these are not response variables but a collection of different interventions or procedures or conditions which could be applied to members of a single population, and it is the possibly different effect on the response variable of these so-called **levels** (i.e. the different interventions or procedures or conditions) of the factor which is of interest in the study. When a single sample is taken from the target population and each subject in the sample is allocated to one and only one of these levels, the factor is referred to as a **between-subject factor** since comparisons are made between subjects on different levels of the factor. When it is practical to have the same subject undergoing (at different times) each of the 'conditions' corresponding to each level of the factor, it is known as a **within-subject factor** since comparisons can now be made across the same subject (and hence constitute a more efficient study).

An example of a between-subject factor would be types of possible treatment for chronic back pain such as *outpatient physiotherapy, spinal stabilisation classes* or *pain management classes* (i.e. three levels) and the effects of these assessed over six months by a response variable such as percentage time off work. An example of a within-subject factor would be different conditions for carrying a rugby ball such as *in both hands, in the dominant hand only, in the non-dominant hand only* or *not carrying a ball at all* (four levels) and could be assessed by 10 metre sprinting time from a running start. A special case of a within-subject factor common in sports and exercise science is that of time. Here, rather than distinct interventions or conditions, the within-subject factor will consist of the response variable being measured at specific times from the start of the study. For example, a study looking at the effect of regular exercise classes for pregnant women could assess subjects in *early, late* and *post pregnancy* (three levels).

It is worth noting that the basic idea of between-subject factors can be used in analysing studies where a number of different populations are being compared (e.g. grip strength across *elite, recreational* and *non-climbers*, again three levels).

1.5 Some underlying ideas

In general, a study will involve collecting data/information on a sample from a (target) population. Hopefully, the sample will be **representative** of the population, but it must be recognised that another sample from the same population would produce different data. It is therefore important to be aware that, unless the whole of the population of interest is 'sampled' (almost certainly impossible to achieve), then only **inference** can be made about the population (parameter) from the sample (statistics), with a degree of uncertainty depending on aspects of the study such as the number of patients in the sample, the consistency of response of subjects, and so on. A schematic representation of the underlying process is given in Figure 1.1.

One of the first steps in a formal statistical analysis is to decide upon a suitable assumption for the general form of a **mathematical model** by which the sample has been generated from the population of interest. This is called a **probability model**, or sometimes a **statistical model**, but regardless of the term used, this can be a crucial assumption and, throughout this book, attention will be drawn to the choice and assessment of such assumptions. The most common assumption for continuous response variables is that based on the family of **Normal** (or **Gaussian**) **distributions**; the

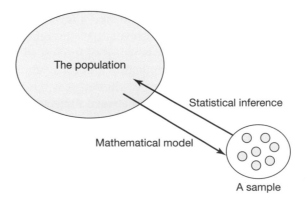

Figure 1.1 **The process underlying statistical analysis.**

distribution of a random variable is basically a mathematical representation of all the possible values of the variable with the word 'random' being used to denote when all members of the population are equally likely to be included in the sample. (See the technical appendix to Chapter 3 for more information on the Normal distribution.) One property worth noting here is that the key parameter of the Normal distribution is the **population average** or **population mean**. Almost all questions relating to so-called Normal data involve the comparison of population means.

Remember, though, that in practice the true underlying population is unlikely to be 'exactly' described by a Normal distribution. All that is looked for is that the assumed model is an adequate (but approximate) representation of the 'true' underlying distribution.

When the study involves **explanatory variables** and/or **factors**, the effects of these on the response variable are usually modelled through the population mean, often in a linear form. There is then a crucial choice of which, if any, of these explanatory variables and/or factors are required in the final model. The techniques of **model choice** are essential to statistical modelling and are covered in detail from Chapter 6 onwards. Be careful, though, not to be fooled by the huge number of so-called **match statistics** that TV companies throw at their viewers. These are simple summaries of the actual match itself but bear no relation to any sample or indeed population and hence cannot be used to infer anything outside the context of the actual match covered.

Occasionally there will be 'strange' observations in the data which may be simple mistakes in data recording or may be observations which are not compatible with the population under investigation. Care must be taken with such potential **outliers** and it is better to repeat the analysis with and without any such outliers rather than arbitrarily to remove dubious observations without due cause. Examples of how to handle outliers will be interspersed throughout the book.

1.6 Examples of illustrations

This book relies heavily on illustrative examples of all the statistical ideas and techniques covered. The illustrations in this section give some flavour of the types of problem dealt with in the book and appear in later chapters with appropriate analyses. All illustrations are written up in a style intended to give the reader an impression of what motivated the study as well as a brief description of the study itself. All of the datasets used in the illustrations are provided on the relevant webpage to encourage the reader to tackle the problems themselves.

Illustration 1.1 Overweight women and exercise

[*See also Illustration 10.1*]

Background
Obesity is an ever-increasing problem in the western world. Problems associated with obesity include a greater incidence of diabetes and coronary heart disease. One problem often encountered by the obese and substantially overweight is limited mobility. Exercise programmes have the potential to enhance mobility by decreasing body mass and by improving strength and endurance.

Study description

Twenty-six overweight middle-aged females were randomly allocated (see Chapter 2) to be either an Exerciser or a Non-Exerciser. The 13 Exercisers were asked to carry out two (aerobic and strength) exercise sessions per week for 12 weeks while the 13 Non-Exercisers were asked not to alter their usual lifestyle (such a sub-sample is often referred to as Controls). Among a battery of measurements, one key variable used to investigate the efficacy of the exercise programme was the time taken for a woman to walk 20 metres from a standing start.

Aim

To investigate whether such an exercise programme can significantly improve, on average, the 20 m Walking Time of overweight women over a 12-week period of this form of exercise over any 'natural' improvement of Controls.

Reference: Grant, S., Todd, K., Aitchison, T.C., Kelly, P. and Stoddart, D. (2004). 'The effects of a 12 week group exercise programme on physiological and psychological variables and function in elderly obese women.' *Journal of Public Health*, **118**: 31–42.

Comments on Illustration 1.1

1 The *target population* to whom the results of this study will apply are 'all overweight middle-aged women in Scotland in the early part of the twenty-first century', although clear definitions of 'overweight' and 'middle-aged' will have to be provided. Since all women in this sample were deemed able enough to undergo the exercise programme, then the target population must be reduced by excluding all such women who, for whatever medical, physical or emotional reasons, are unable or unwilling to undergo such an exercise programme.

2 The *response variable* used in the aim of the study is 20 m Walking Time (in seconds). This is a continuous variable since it could effectively be measured to any degree of accuracy over a fairly wide range of potential values, say from 5 to 50 seconds.

3 There is one *between-subject factor,* which can be labelled Exercise Regime, with two levels, namely Exercisers and Controls.

4 There is one *within-subject factor,* which can be labelled Time, and there are again two levels, namely immediately Pre and Post the 12-week period of the study.

5 Although not explicitly included in the description of this study, it might prove useful to consider the Body Mass of each woman as a possible *explanatory variable* of such women's 20 m Walking Times.

6 Since the key question is to consider any improvement in 20 m Walking Time, the analysis usually reduces to investigating the *change* in 20 m Walking Time for each subject over the 12-weeks (e.g. 'Pre-Study minus Post-Study' to allow positive values of this to be an improvement and negative values to be a worsening in walking time).

7 The formal analysis will then become a comparison of the *population mean change in 20 m Walking Time* for Exercisers with that for Controls and will be based on the samples of changes in 20 m Walking Time for the 13 Exercisers and the 13 Controls, respectively.

8 If each of these samples can be assumed to have arisen from *Normal distributions*, then the sample mean change in 20 m Walking Time for the Exercisers will be directly compared with that for the Controls, taking into account the sample variability for each as well as the respective sample sizes.

9 The phrase 'significantly improve'* used in the aim of the study denotes a set of data where the result of the appropriate analysis rules out, beyond reasonable doubt, that there is no difference in population mean changes in 20 m Walking Time between the two populations (i.e. Exercisers and Controls).

*The word 'significant' is used extensively in data analysis and refers to situations where the results of the data analysis allow a clear and objective conclusion to the question of interest.

Illustration 1.2 Bubble Wrap

[*See also Illustration 3.7*]

Background

Anecdotal reports from Norwegian mountain rescue teams suggest that a layer of Bubble Wrap around a casualty requiring evacuation from a mountain is useful in preventing loss of body heat. Scottish mountain rescue teams currently use casualty bags which are bulky and fairly heavy and thus are awkward for such teams to transport to any accident.

Study description

Twelve male subjects each participated in two tests to compare the performance of Bubble Wrap with a Casualty Bag currently in use by Scottish mountain rescue teams. Tests simulating weather conditions met in mountain rescue were carried out lying on a stretcher for 25 minutes in a cold ($-10°C$), windy (wind speed 2.7 m.s^{-1}) environment, separately for each type of protection (i.e. Bubble Wrap and Casualty Bag). The design of the study was such that half of the subjects were randomised to try out the Bubble Wrap first and the other half the Casualty Bag first. Reductions in Skin Temperature (averaged over four body sites) from the start of the study were recorded at 5-minute intervals throughout the test.

Aim

To investigate whether there is any difference, in general, in the Reduction of Skin Temperature between the two levels of Protection over the test duration under these simulated mountain weather conditions.

Reference: Tsianos, G. (2004). 'Human responses to cold and hypoxia: implications for mountaineers.' PhD thesis 13784, Glasgow University.

Comments on Illustration 1.2

1 The *target population* to whom the results of this study will apply are 'all males likely to venture into the Scottish mountains in winter conditions'.

2 The *response variable* used in the aim of the study is Reduction in Skin Temperature (ST) in degrees centigrade, taken for convenience in the form 'ST at 0 minutes into study minus ST at any other time' into the study.

3 There are two *within-subject factors*. One of these is simply Protection, which has two levels: Bubble Wrap and Casualty Bag. The other is Time, which has five levels, namely 5, 10, 15, 20 and 25 minutes into the study. Note that each subject has his Reduction in ST recorded at all ten combinations of Protection and Time.

4 Although not necessary, it may be reasonable to *model the profile* of Reduction in ST *across Time* (on either or both levels of Protection) by modelling Time as an *explanatory variable* exploiting the fact that all five times are equally spaced (i.e. 5 minutes apart).

5 The analysis is likely to assume that the population distribution of Reduction in ST at *each of the ten combinations* of Protection and Time can be adequately described as a *Normal distribution*. A further assumption here relates to how consistent the shape of the Reduction in ST profiles are across subjects, with, naturally, the more consistent the profiles, the more precise the conclusions of the analysis about the underlying population mean Reduction in ST profiles.

Summary

Statistics is the mechanism by which variability across subjects, all too common in sports and exercise science, can be allowed for in any study and provides, through suitable mathematical modelling, objective conclusions to the key study questions of interest.

There is essential jargon in statistics, as in any science, and the reader must acquaint him/herself with the definitions of variable, population, sample, population parameter and sample statistic(s). One essential idea is that the sample observed by the researcher is only one of many possible samples that might have been observed from the target population. Other concepts that are required for understanding statistical ideas are those of response variables, between- and within-subject factors and explanatory variables. Finally, the Normal distribution is a key element in the analysis of most continuous response variables in order to model how the sample may have arisen from the underlying population.

2 Designing a study

2.1 Introduction

The enthusiastic researcher almost always wants to 'get on with carrying out' the study and consequently might not take sufficient time to design it properly. Such an approach can easily render the whole study useless. No amount of 'fancy data analysis' can save a badly designed study – no matter how complicated or how many data are collected. Beware the temptation of multiple repeat measurements on the same subject unless interest lies in the variability of that subject only. The competent researcher must give as much time and thought (and basically common sense) as are necessary to ensure that the study will not be a waste of time. Easily said, easily paid lip service to, but much harder to practise. This chapter offers some basic ideas and practices to help sports and exercise scientists improve the design of their own studies, with particular reference to comparative studies as defined in the first chapter.

The key step is to have clear and simple aims for the study. Do not be tempted to try to do too much in the study. Simple, short studies will generally be the most efficient and worthwhile approach to even the most complicated problem. Trying to push as much as possible into a study will almost certainly reduce the effectiveness of all parts of the study, sometimes even rendering parts useless – possibly after a lot of hard work. It is always advisable to discuss any proposed study with as many and as varied people as possible. A first tentative step is often to carry out some form of trial or pilot study to assess whether what is being suggested is practical and feasible, never mind considering whether or not it is capable of answering the key questions posed in the study. Remember, though, to keep the aims/questions which are the basis of the study as simple as possible and to frame them in a scientific/statistical form using the appropriate terminology (introduced in Chapter 1).

The major aim of statistics is to draw inferences (i.e. make conclusions) about the value of specific **P**arameters in the **P**opulation of interest based upon the observed values of the **S**ummary **S**tatistics from the actual **S**ample obtained. In practice, **population means** are the parameters most commonly investigated in all types of study – not just those in sports and exercise science – when the **response variable** of interest is **continuous** in nature.

2.2   Collecting the data (sampling)

2.2.1   Observational studies

If the aim of the proposed study is **observational**, e.g. simply to investigate or summarise an interesting response variable in a single population, then the first question is how to obtain an appropriate sample. The words **representative sample** are likely to spring to mind in such a circumstance and the one phrase that most people have usually heard of is that of a **random sample**, i.e. a sample where each member of the population has the same chance of being included in the study sample as any other member. Hence the random sample is likely to cover the full range of the population and therefore be, in some sense, representative of the population. In reality, it is almost always impossible to find a truly representative or indeed random sample in sports and exercise science studies because that would necessitate having a list of all members of the population from which the random sample could be drawn. Finding or creating such a list is usually either impossible or prohibitive – even in the simple example covered in Chapter 1 defining the key vocabulary. Obtaining a list of all 40,000 18–25-year-old females in the West of Scotland might, in theory, be possible but accessing a random sample from it would take a huge amount of time and effort – try contacting an opinion polling organisation to see how much that would involve and cost. So, in reality, random samples are very unlikely to exist and sports and exercise scientists generally use **convenience samples**, i.e. a selection of subjects from the population under consideration gathered often from appropriate subjects locally available and willing to take part in the study – friends and students are often the basis of such. In consequence, there is little or no justification in claiming such samples are representative of any population and extreme care should be taken in interpreting/generalising results from convenience samples. If there is no alternative, then such samples may have to be used and should perhaps then be thought of snapshots of the population rather than true reflections of it.

2.2.2   Comparative studies: independent samples, between-subject designs

Fortunately, most sports and exercise science studies tend to be **comparative** in nature and here the composition of the actual sample of subjects is less important if some of the ideas introduced in this chapter, such as randomisation and balance, are adhered to in the study design. This is not true, however, if the comparison is of two or more distinct populations (e.g. elite climbers compared with recreational climbers and with non-climbers). Once again, the almost insurmountable problem is how to obtain representative samples for each population.

Many studies involve the *comparison of two or more different interventions* on a single population (e.g. comparing the effect of strength training (ST) against calcium supplementation (CS) on bone density in post-menopausal women with osteoporosis). If subjects are allocated to one and only one of these interventions for physical/economic/application reasons, then this type of design is comparing interventions only *between* subjects and this would be referred to as a **between-subject design**.

The most common of this type of study is when two interventions are involved and this is often referred to as a **two-sample problem**. The key aim of such designed studies will be to compare the population means for the response variable among the different interventions where there will be a target population to whom all of the interventions could, in theory, be applied (e.g. post-menopausal women with osteoporosis).

Here the key element of any good design is to **randomise** the allocation to subjects of the two or more interventions as they enter the study. First, for the case of two interventions (i.e. the two-sample problem), obtain a list of random digits from a computer or random number table (i.e. a list of integers from 0 to 9 where, for each integer in the list, all possible integers are equally likely regardless of what integer comes before or after it). For example, such a list might be 3, 7, 6, 0, 4, 6, 5, 1, ... Next, in the Osteoporosis and Exercise study comparing the effects of strength training and calcium supplementation, the randomisation could be as follows. Allocate the five integers 0 to 4 to intervention ST and allocate the five integers 5 to 9 to intervention CS. So, using the list above, the first subject receives intervention ST since she corresponded to the first integer 3 while the second subject is allocated intervention CS since she corresponded to the second integer, i.e. 7, and so on. Hence subjects 1, 4, 5, 8 etc. are allocated to ST while subjects 2, 3, 6, 7 etc. are allocated to CS.

For three interventions, allocate any three integers to each intervention ignoring the remaining integer if it appears in the list (or use only nine integers, e.g. 0 to 8, if the statistics package being used can do that, e.g. Minitab), and so on for four or more interventions.

A key question ignored so far is, how many subjects are required for this study? For the statistician, the answer is simple: as many as possible. However, for the researcher, the real question is often, how few subjects can I get away with? The compromise has to be the calculation of the minimum number of subjects required to give a 'realistic chance of sensibly answering' the question of interest for the study. But what does that mean in practice? Basically, this requires the researcher to make some 'educated guesses' – hopefully based on previous research or at least a pilot study – about various aspects of the underlying situation and then the statistician can work out the minimum sample size based on ideas of the power of a study (covered in Chapter 13 for some common scenarios in sports and exercise science). There is really no escape from this; the researcher must 'come down off the fence' and provide both information and choices on which this minimum sample size can be assessed.

In most studies it is imperative to have a **control** sample to compare the effect of any real interventions with the effect of doing nothing at all to the subject population. To conclude that any intervention is significantly better than another without knowing the effect of no intervention can only be described as poor practice.

The set of interventions is often referred to as a **factor**, and, as in the instances described here where subjects are allocated to one and only one intervention, that factor is usually called a **between-subject factor** (or **grouping factor**). An example of the use of randomisation for a study involving a single between-subject factor with three levels is given in Illustration 2.1.

Illustration 2.1	Chronic low back pain

Background

Chronic low back pain is a common problem in western society. Each year in the UK the National Health Service provides treatment for around 1.3 million low back pain sufferers. There are a number of treatment options available and it is important to establish which treatment, if any, is most effective. Information on the most clinically effective treatment may help reduce pain and may reduce NHS costs. One key outcome variable from an economic viewpoint is 'time off work'.

Study description

Patients referred to orthopaedic clinics with chronic low back pain were to be recruited from Glasgow hospitals. Based on power calculations (see Chapter 13, Illustration 13.4), a sample size of 96 subjects was found to be the minimum required for this study. Each of these 96 subjects would be allocated to one of three treatments: usual outpatient physio-therapy (OP), spinal stabilisation classes (SC) or physiotherapist-led pain management classes (PM). Compliance to each of the three treatments would be monitored over the period of the study. The time off work for the after six months after the end of treatment would be taken as the response variable of interest.

Aim

To investigate any differences, on average, in Time Off Work among the three treatments for chronic low back pain patients for the six months after the end of treatment.

Data

Response variable: Time Off Work (days)
Between-subject factor: Treatment (3 levels: OP, SC, PM)

Design

Order the 96 subjects (randomly by picking names out of a hat or using random digits or, less preferably, the order in which they enter the study) and label the subjects as S1, S2, . . . , S96.

Allocate that a subject will be on outpatient physiotherapy (OP) to digits 0, 1, 2.
Allocate that a subject will be at the stabilisation classes (SC) to digits 3, 4, 5.
Allocate that a subject will be on pain management (PM) to digits 6, 7, 8.

Provide a list of (more than 96) random digits such as:

6 7 3 0 7 5 1 4 3 3 1 9 4 8 5 . . .

So the allocation of diets is:

PM PM SC OP PM SC OP SC SC SC OP (ignore) SC PM SC . . .

Thus subjects S4, S7, S11 etc. will receive outpatient therapy for the study, subjects S3, S6, S8, etc. will be at spinal stabilisation classes and subjects S1, S2, S5 etc. will be at pain management classes, making sure that only 32 subjects are allocated to any one treatment (i.e. stop allocating to that treatment after 32 subjects are randomised to it).

2.2.3 Comparative studies: dependent samples, within-subject designs

Another common type of study in sports and exercise science involves the use of a *single sample* from a population of interest for the *comparison of two or more* methods of measuring a physical characteristic (such as densitometry or electrical impedance for percentage body fat 'measurement') or two or more apparatus (different makes of automated oxygen uptake systems for measuring $\dot{V}O_2$) or two or more easily exchangeable and/or short-term interventions (using or not using an ice bath after exercise in an attempt to reduce blood lactate). The key feature in designing a study for such scenarios would be that it is possible to measure the response variable on every subject on every method/apparatus/intervention. The key design aspect of this is to ensure that there is a **balance** over all subjects of the order in which subjects receive all the methods/apparatus/interventions (henceforth referred to as **conditions**). The simplest form of such a study involves two conditions and this is often referred to as a **paired-sample problem**.

Since each subject will receive all the conditions, this type of design allows the comparison of conditions within the same subject and is known as a **within-subject design**. Furthermore, the set of conditions is called a **within-subject factor** and the key aim of the study will be to compare the population means of the response variable among the levels of the factor (i.e. among the set of conditions). Clearly, as will be illustrated later in this chapter, designs can incorporate both between-subject factors and within-subject factors, with the most common type of design in sports and exercise science involving *one between-subject factor at two levels and one within-subject factor also at two levels,* which, in terms of analysis, often reduces to a two-sample problem on the differences of the response variable across the two levels of the within-subject factor.

Why is it important to have a balance across subjects regarding the order in which subjects receive the conditions? Simply, because issues such as fatigue, boredom, familiarisation and learning effects may influence subjects' performances in tests/trials and, in order to allow as far as possible for such effects, it is advisable to achieve a 'balanced design' with respect to the order in which subjects undergo the various conditions. In one study, rugby players sprinted 20 metres with no resistance or when pulling weights from 5% of body mass to 30% of body mass. The aim of the study was to determine the impact on running speed of the resistances. If all subjects towed the resistances in the order from no resistance, 5% body mass to 30% body mass, it is possible that fatigue or perhaps boredom would result in a relatively slower time with those resistances that were pulled near the end of the test session. Additionally it is advisable to allow for sufficient time between trials on the same subject to reduce, if not remove, such effects – usually called wash-out periods in clinical trials.

If there are only two conditions (A and B) – the paired-sample problem – then ensure that the number of subjects who are given condition A first (and hence condition B second) is equal to the number who are given condition B first (and condition A second). The actual allocation of which subject receives which condition first would then be carried out by random allocation as described in Illustration 2.2.

Illustration 2.2 Ice baths

Background

Ice baths are sometimes used in aerobic sports after training and competition. One of the supposed benefits of this practice is a reduction in blood lactate. There is little, if any, direct evidence that the use of ice baths really does lower blood lactate.

Study description

It was calculated that ten club standard oarsmen were needed for this study (see Exercise 13.2) and each would have his Blood Lactate Concentration (over a 25-minute cool-down after exercise) recorded at regular intervals after successfully completing a 2 km row in under 7 minutes on two separate occasions three days apart. On one occasion each rower would cool down 'normally' (i.e. a Control) while, on the other occasion, the oarsman would be immersed in an ice bath immediately after completing the row.

Aim

To investigate whether ice baths significantly reduce, on average, Blood Lactate Concentration at any stage in a 25-minute cool-down after exercise.

Data

Response variable: Blood Lactate Concentration (mmol.L^{-1})
Within-subject factor: Condition (2 levels: Control, Ice Bath)

Design

Order the ten subjects (randomly by, say, picking names out of a hat) and label these as S1, S2, . . . , S10.

Allocate the event (C) that a subject is a Control first (and then uses the Ice Bath three days later) to digits 0 to 4.

Allocate the event (B) that a subject uses the Ice Bath first (and then is a Control three days later) to digits 5 to 9.

Provide a list of (more than ten) random digits such as:

4 8 7 4 2 2 9 4 6 5 6 5 4 1 4

So the corresponding list of first conditions is:

C B B C C C B C B B (and ignore the other digits)

Thus subjects S1, S4, S5, S6 and S9 act as Controls on their first visit and have Ice Baths on their second visit while subjects S2, S3, S7, S8 and S10 have Ice Baths on their first visit and act as Controls on their second visit.

As it turns out here, it was lucky that the first ten integers contained five integers between 0 and 4 as well as five between 5 and 9 otherwise, when the required five Cs had been allocated (but not yet five Bs), then any further integer between 0 and 4 would simply have been ignored.

The reader should try generating random digits in any package, say Minitab, and see how 'non-random' these might well appear.

2.2.4 Comparative studies: within-subject designs with three or more conditions

When there are three or more conditions and each subject is to be measured for the response variable on all conditions (sometimes referred to as a dependent-samples problem), then the key aspect of the design of such a study is to ensure **balance** in the following ways:

- All conditions should be the first condition for the same number of subjects.
- This should also apply to the second and further conditions.

- Each condition should follow each other condition the same number of times preferably for each pair of conditions (i.e. first and second, then second and third etc.).

These balance requirements imply that the total number of subjects should be a *multiple* of the number of conditions/levels of the within-subject factor. The crucial question of 'how many subjects?' is dealt with in Chapter 13, but if there are too many conditions being compared then the above balance requirements become 'subject expensive', e.g. for five conditions, 120 subjects would be required. Thus, the third requirement is sometimes watered down by ignoring it for 'every pair' of conditions. The basic design needed here is called a **Latin squares** or **Latin rectangles** design. (In fact, these are the basis of the Su Doku craze.)

For three conditions (labelled here as C1, C2 and C3), there are two basic designs each of three subjects (i.e. two Latin squares of order 3) neither of which is itself balanced, but when they are combined as in Table 2.1 then every condition appears twice as the first condition etc. and every pair of conditions (e.g. C1 and C2) appears once in every pair of positions (i.e. first and second conditions then as second and third conditions).

So, for a within-subject design with three levels/conditions, use at least 6 subjects or a multiple of 6 all based on Table 2.1. For within-subject designs with four levels, then at least 4 and preferably 12 (or more) subjects are required, as can be seen in Illustration 2.3. If the researcher insists on more than four conditions, then many subjects are required to achieve any form of well-balanced design and this is probably best carried out in consultation with someone well experienced in the mathematics of design.

Table 2.1 Two Latin squares of order 3

Subject	Condition number		
	1st	2nd	3rd
S1	C1	C2	C3
S2	C2	C3	C1
S3	C3	C1	C2
S4	C1	C3	C2
S5	C2	C1	C3
S6	C3	C2	C1

Illustration 2.3   Rugby ball carrying

Background

Different methods of ball carrying can be used when a player sprints with the ball in rugby union. The following three methods of ball carrying may influence sprint speed: using both hands, under the left arm and under the right arm. These methods would be compared to running without a ball.

Study description

Twelve Scottish National League rugby players (all of whom were backs) would be recruited from local clubs in the West of Scotland and each would undertake a set of four sprints, each time using one of the four different methods of ball carrying (i.e. not carrying a ball (N), left arm only (L), right arm only (R) and both hands (B)). Each subject on each sprint would have his 20 m Sprint Time recorded from a 'rolling start'.

Aim

To investigate the differences, if any, in average 20 m Sprint Times across the four different methods of carrying a rugby ball among club-standard rugby players.

Data

Response variable: 20 m Sprint Time (seconds)
Within-subject factor: Method (4 levels: N, B, L, R)

Design

The twelve subjects should be allocated a label (S1, S2, . . . , S12) in a random order. In Table 2.2 is a set of three so-called balanced 4 × 4 Latin squares where:

- each condition (C1, C2, C3 and C4) appears three times in the first trial and three times in the second etc.;

- each pair of conditions appears in order the same number of times at each pair of trials (i.e. first and second, second and third, third and fourth).

Table 2.2 **Three balanced 4 × 4 Latin squares**

Subject	Sprint/trial number			
	1st	*2nd*	*3rd*	*4th*
S1	C1	C3	C2	C4
S2	C2	C4	C1	C3
S3	C3	C1	C4	C2
S4	C4	C2	C3	C1
S5	C1	C4	C3	C2
S6	C2	C3	C4	C1
S7	C3	C2	C1	C4
S8	C4	C1	C2	C3
S9	C1	C2	C4	C3
S10	C2	C1	C3	C4
S11	C3	C4	C2	C1
S12	C4	C3	C1	C2

Now allocate (randomly) each of the methods (i.e. N, L, R and B) to the four conditions above. For example, using random digits yet again, allocate N to the digits 0 and 1, i.e. {0, 1}, L to {2, 3}, R to {4, 5} and B to {6, 7}, say. Now produce a list of random digits, e.g. 6, 8, 3, 5, 4, 9, 0, ... Therefore B (carrying with both hands) is allocated to C1 (corresponding to the first digit, i.e. 6, in this list), L to C2 (corresponding to third digit of 3 since the '8' is ignored), R to C3 (since the third digit is 5) and hence by default N to C4 since it is the only method left unallocated.

Replace C1 by B, C2 by L, C3 by R and C4 by N in Table 2.3 to produce the balanced design with, for example, subject S1 using both hands (B) on his first sprint/trial, right arm only (R) on his second, left arm only (L) on his third and not carrying a ball (N) at all for his fourth sprint/trial since the allocation in Table 2.2 for S1 was C1, C3, C2, C4.

So, in words rather than symbols, the first subjects in the design are allocated to the orders of ball-carrying methods set out in Table 2.3.

Table 2.3 **Allocation of methods to the first six subjects**

Subject	Sprint/trial number			
	1st	2nd	3rd	4th
S1	Both	Right	Left	No
S2	Left	No	Both	Right
S3	Right	Both	No	Left
S4	No	Left	Right	Both
S5	Both	No	Right	Left
S6	Left	Right	No	Both

Additional comments

1 *Order effects.* When the same subject carries out a number of trials in the same manner but under different conditions, there is always the possibility of the subject's learning how to 'perform' better or of their becoming 'fed up' or 'fatigued' with the effort of each successive trial – regardless of which condition applied at each trial. If this happens to a sizable fraction of the sample, then this may manifest as an **order effect** where, for example, subjects may on average do better in the response variable on the first trial than on the second than on the third, and so on. Such an order effect must be investigated in any analysis and reported and corrected for, if significant.

2 *Carryover effects.* The researcher must try to ensure that there is sufficient time between trials to eliminate the effect on the response variable of possible **carryover** of benefits (e.g. in giving ergogenic aids too soon after one another) or deficits (e.g. in having successive sprints too close together). For example, if drugs are involved in the study (e.g. amlodipine, a calcium antagonist), it is advisable to allow sufficient time between interventions on the same subject for possible effects from the drug to be eliminated. These are usually called wash-out periods in clinical trials. In one study, three weeks was allowed as a wash-out period in a study involving amlodipine. The staging of successive sprints too close together can result in fatigue from a previous sprint influencing speeds in succeeding trials. Again, the careful researcher will consider these as possibilities in the analysis, and confirm (or otherwise) their non-existence.

3 *Blinding.* If it is at all possible, ensure that the subject does not know what condition is being applied on any trial (a **single-blinded study**). While this is clearly impossible in some circumstances (e.g. which arm the subject carries a rugby ball in), in other studies, such as those which involve the use of dietary supplements, it can be useful to negate the effect of the subject 'knowing' that this condition is 'useless' or the data collector giving the benefit of the doubt to a 'clearly useful' condition. For example, the colour and taste of both treatment and control fluid supplements should be as similar as possible. A study in which neither subject nor data collector knows which condition is being applied is called **double-blind**. The placebo effect in medicine is well documented,* and generally accepted as an important aspect in study design which should not be ignored. One study known to the authors involved a series of 'maximal' tests comparing the effects of beta blockers and sweets as a placebo. It wasn't too hard to realise which was which and put much less effort into the beta blocker trial, knowing it would be 'much harder'.

*See A.J. de Craen et al. (1999). 'Placebos and placebo effects in medicine: historical overview.' *Journal of the Royal Society of Medicine*, **92** (10): 511–515.

4 *Controls*. As remarked earlier, it is essential to have a baseline condition, which can often be the population at large left to their own habits (or even a standard procedure), in order to be able to claim the usefulness of any condition. For example, a group of middle-aged women are asked to take part in a 6-month training programme. Aerobic fitness tests and blood lipid tests are administered in January and July, respectively. It is then found that aerobic fitness and lipid levels have improved greatly. Reasons for this apparent increase in aerobic fitness and enhanced lipid profile may be attributed to season (the subjects are more active in summer and eat more fruit and vegetables in summer) and/or the subjects enjoyed the social interaction with other subjects and experimenters and thus were highly motivated to improve scores in the second (July) aerobic test. Thus it is not possible to state that the training programme was the sole reason for aerobic fitness and lipid profile improvement without a control sample 'chosen by randomisation'. Beware of 'historical controls' measured earlier (and perhaps therefore under different circumstances or by differently calibrated equipment) as these can often be wholly misleading. Also, do not consider post-study controls measured at a later date where a seasonal effect may influence scores resulting from climatic and/or dietary differences. Randomisation is the key to using controls although the effect of subjects 'improving' just by taking part in studies is possible – never mistake the power of the human mind, conscious or not.

5 *Data collection*. This may seem trite but it is well worth ensuring that the measuring and recording of data are carried out as systematically and as simply as possible. Data collection should be precise, ritualistic and almost robotic. It is stating the obvious that a study is likely to be fatally flawed if the data collection can be described as haphazard and sloppy. Students sometimes have claimed that they do not need study procedure or data collection sheets, but they usually learn better the hard way. Attempts to collect data without a procedure sheet are usually characterised by chaos. All studies should have a procedure sheet which is followed to the letter. Strict adherence to the procedure sheet ensures that any differences in test results cannot be attributed to differences in test administration or calibration techniques. It is all too easy to jumble bits of paper or record dubious values in a spreadsheet and/or mix up or lose information on individual subjects.

Having clearly labelled and marked forms (electronic or paper) is essential and, if a computer is used, having some form of data checking (e.g. based on acceptable ranges of the response variable) might prove useful – not to mention 'independent' data recording and double entry by different data collectors.

Experimental Design for the Life Sciences by G.D. Ruxton and N. Colegrave (Oxford University Press, 2003) is a simple introduction to basic ideas of study design written in a clear and non-mathematical style.

Exercises

2.1 Being overweight, if not obese, is an ever-increasing problem in the western world. Problems associated with obesity include a greater incidence of diabetes and coronary heart disease. One problem often encountered by the obese and substantially overweight is limited mobility. Exercise programmes have the potential to enhance mobility by decreasing body mass and by improving strength and endurance. Twenty overweight (i.e. body mass index BMI > 25) middle-aged females are to be randomly allocated to be either an Exerciser or a Control. The Exercisers are to be asked to carry out two (aerobic and strength) exercise sessions per week for 12 weeks. One key variable used to investigate the usefulness of the exercise programme is the time taken for such a woman to walk 20 metres from a standing start. Provide a suitable design plan as to which Treatment (i.e. Exercise or Control) each of the 20 women should be allocated to ensure 10 women in each sub-sample.

2.2 A sample of 30 recreational distance runners is to be taken and randomised into one of three possible Relaxation Regimes, i.e. either Meditation (M), Progressive Muscular Relaxation (PMR) or Control (C), as a potential way of reducing the oxygen cost of running and of lowering exercise heart rate. The steady-state Heart Rate in a standardised (running) exercise bout is to be taken as the response variable. Provide a suitable design plan as to which Relaxation Regime (i.e. M, PMR or C) each of the 30 women should be allocated to ensure 10 women in each sub-sample.

2.3 The sight of hill walkers using walking poles has become more common over the last few years. Manufacturers claim that walking poles provide benefits for the (hill) walker such as enhanced stability, less strain on the lower limbs and lower ratings of perceived exertion. A sample of 14 physically active males are to undergo a simulated short hill walk of 10 minutes, once using walking poles and once without using walking poles, with a 15 minute rest between the two 'hill walks'. Each subject will walk for 10 minutes at 3.7 km.h^{-1} on a 12.5% gradient and have his VO$_2$ measured (in ml.kg^{-1}.min^{-1}) using Douglas bags during the last three minutes of each walk. Provide a suitable design plan as to which order of Use of Poles (i.e. Use/Not Use) should be applied to each of the 14 subjects to ensure that half of the sample use the poles first.

2.4 Major athletic events can be held in cities where high heat and humidity are prevailing weather conditions (e.g. the 1996 Olympics in Atlanta, USA). High heat and humidity have the potential to reduce athletic performance in a number of events. Researchers are to carry out a study comparing three distinct Conditions. One is in effect a control involving a warm-up and intermittent supra-maximal running performance test (ISRPT) in cool (UK) conditions (CC). The second involves a warm-up in cool conditions but an ISRPT in hot and humid conditions (CH). The third involves a warm-up and ISRPT in both hot and humid conditions (HH). Twelve athletes will have their performance in an ISRPT monitored in each of these three Conditions (i.e. CC, CH and HH). Provide a suitable design plan as to which order of Conditions should be used by each of the 12 subjects to ensure that all three Conditions are 'balanced' across the study.

2.3 Sources of variability

2.3.1 Introduction

In general, sports and exercise sciences are concerned with comparing the typical value (i.e. the population mean) of the response variable across the interventions or conditions (i.e. across the levels of the factor of interest regardless of whether it is a between-subject or within-subject factor). However, in virtually every study involving humans or animate beings, there will be **between-subject variability** so that, no matter how careful or precise the study, subjects are likely to record different values of the response variable under even exactly the same stimuli or conditions. This natural phenomenon can be due to a variety of sources, often aspects of the subject's physiognomy. For example, grip strength may increase with increasing body mass, and sprint time may rise with increasing body fat.

Even for the same subject the recorded value of the response variable may not be the same on every occasion it is measured due to a number of reasons, including **within-subject variability** from day to day or minute to minute or even changing physical conditions (e.g. ambient temperature). Indeed, different observers may record different values (e.g. two experimenters may have different scores for skinfold thickness resulting from measuring technique differences. Their method for lifting up the skinfold may be different and the length of time before they record the reading from the skinfold caliper may vary) or different apparatus may give different measurements for the same subject at the same time (e.g. different types of blood lactate analysers may provide different blood lactate values). Ideas on reliability, repeatability and reproducibility of measurements are investigated in detail in Chapter 12. The conscientious researcher should at least be aware and take cognisance of these different sources of variability in any recorded measurement. He/she may not be able to do anything except record a single value for any subject in a study but he/she should at least be aware of the magnitude of any effect of these sources, as the key requirement of any study is that it should be reproducible by any other competent researcher with adequate resources to replicate the full study. If the study is not in that sense reproducible, then there is almost no purpose to carrying it out in the first place as it will be biased by the peculiarities of the experimental set-up. Good, clear reporting of a study is essential in order for another researcher to be able to carry out the same study and, while this repeat study will obviously not return exactly the results of the first study, it should produce effectively the same conclusions and hence reinforce what has been learnt from the experimental context.

Medical science has often gone down the path where small biased studies resulted in conclusions later proved false, and now the trend is for all published studies to be notified in advance to a central register (current controlled trials are available at http://www.controlled-trials.com/) and often to be multi-centre studies so that an individual researcher's results do not produce distorted or unrepeatable conclusions. Researchers in sports and exercise science would be well advised to throw aside unhealthy personal competition and collaborate with colleagues across a wide variety of competent centres in order not to try to achieve 'international fame as a researcher' but instead to further the advance of his/her areas of scientific interest.

2.3.2 Between-subject variability

Returning to the sources of variability, what can good study design offer in identifying, measuring and correcting for such sources? For **between-subject variability**, one simple procedure would be to allow for any known (or suspected) component of subject-to-subject variability by ensuring that the study sample incorporates a wide range of subjects covering the full spectrum of this component (often a characteristic of the subject him/herself such as body mass, height, percentage body fat). On the basis of this component, divide the sample into as many subgroups as seems viable (at least four, say) and randomise any conditions or levels of the factor of interest *within* each of these subgroups (sometimes called **blocks**, and these ideas are also closely related to the technique of **stratified random sampling**). For example, if the study is comparing strength after a course of one or other of two dietary supplements among the population of amateur male rugby union players, then ensure that sufficient players with a body mass between, say, 80 and 120 kg are included in the overall sample. Now divide the sample into four sub-samples of players with body mass between 80 and 90 kg, 90 and 100 kg, 100 and 110 kg, and finally between 110 and 120 kg. Then, *within each of these sub-samples*, randomise the players to one or other of the supplements. In such a study, the response variable could be the improvement in strength of the players (i.e. each player would perform strength tests both immediately before and immediately after a three-month course of his allocated dietary supplement).

If the subjects and their details are not available prior to the study (e.g. the study consists of treating the next 40 tennis players with a particular type of wrist injury), then the simple solution is to set up **randomly permuted blocks** for each sub-sample/block and allocate subjects as they 'enter' the study (see Illustration 2.4). A randomly permuted block is defined by the number of conditions being randomised and the size of the block (chosen somewhat arbitrarily but usually between 4 and 8 and a multiple of the number of conditions). For example, to compare two conditions, C and P say, in blocks of four subjects then the order of each set of four subjects could be from any one of the following six possible blocks:

$$\{C, C, P, P\} \quad \{C, P, C, P\} \quad \{C, P, P, C\}$$
$$\{P, C, C, P\} \quad \{P, C, P, C\} \quad \{P, P, C, C\}$$

Next, allocate a digit to each of these possible blocks (e.g. 1 to 6) and then generate a random digit to dictate the relevant randomly permuted block for each set of four subjects. Illustration 2.4 shows this in practice for a 'stratified or blocked' design.

Illustration 2.4   Golf psychology

Background
There has been much written on the mental strength and focus required to play good golf. Nowadays, there is considerable material available intended to aid the club golfer, and a package of such material has been compiled at Glasgow University for a study of its practical usefulness in improving golfers' performances.

Study description
Twenty-four male golfers, each with a club handicap, were to be recruited as Controls or to a 6-week course intended to improve psychological aspects of golf performance. Golfers' handicaps would be used to collect golfers into subgroups of roughly similar ability, and randomisation of condition (i.e. Control or the 'Psycho' course) would be carried out in each subgroup separately. Each golfer would then be tested and measured on his performance both before and after the study (see Illustration 10.5 for details).

Aim

To investigate whether an intervention of a 6-week course focusing on psychological techniques intended to aid golf performance has any significant effect on improving golfing performance on average.

Data

Response variable: Distance from Hole (centimetres)
Between-subject factor: Condition (2 levels: 'Psycho', Control)

Design

From studying club records spiced with a modicum of experience and common sense, it was decided that a reasonable representation of handicaps among 24 club golfers would consist of:

4 golfers with handicaps between 1 and 6
4 golfers with handicaps between 7 and 12
8 golfers with handicaps between 13 and 18
8 golfers with handicaps between 19 and 24

These choices are slightly arbitrary but not unreasonable, and indeed a bigger question is whether 24 golfers are enough to satisfactorily answer the key question. This latter issue will be tackled in Chapter 13.

Given the choice of multiples of 4 for the sample size of each handicap subgroup, the choice of randomly permuted blocks (RPBs) of four subjects to two conditions seems 'natural' and so one RPB is required for the two lowest handicap subgroups and two RPBs for each of the two higher handicap subgroups. The steps needed to do this are as follows:

- Allocate each of the six possible blocks of four subjects to two conditions a digit, e.g. 1 as {C, C, P, P} etc. as above.

- Use the letters C to denote a golfer allocated to be a Control and P to denote a golfer allocated to the Psychological-based course.

- Produce a list of random digits such as

$$3\ 7\ 2\ 8\ 3\ 0\ 9\ 0\ 5\ 6\ 6\ 2\ 1\ \ldots$$

- Since the first digit is a 3, allocate this RPB, i.e. {C, P, P, C}, to the subgroup with handicaps between 1 and 6 inclusive so that the four golfers recruited to this subgroup are given, in order of recruitment, the conditions C, P, P and C, respectively, i.e. the first and fourth golfers are to be Controls while the second and third low handicap golfers are given the Psychological-based course.

- Since the next digit between 1 and 6 is a 2, the next handicap subgroup (i.e. 7 to 12) is allocated the RPB of {C, P, C, P} and hence the first and third golfers with handicaps between 7 and 12 are Controls, etc.

- The two RPBs allocated to the golfers with handicaps between 13 and 18 are {C, P, P, C} and {P, C, P, C} requiring, therefore, the first, fourth, sixth and eighth golfers with handicap between 13 and 18 to be Controls, etc.

- Finally, the last two required digits are both 6 so the two RPBs allocated to the golfers with handicaps between 19 and 24 are {P, P, C, C} and {P, P, C, C} requiring, therefore, the first, second, fifth and sixth golfers with handicap between 19 and 24 to be Controls, etc.

The full design can be neatly summarised in Table 2.4.

Table 2.4

Handicap subgroup	Order of allocation of condition
1–6	C, P, P, C
7–12	C, P, C, P
13–18	C, P, P, C, P, C, P, C
19–24	P, P, C, C, P, P, C, C

2.3.3 Within-subject variability

The idea that a single measurement of a variable on a subject under given conditions is sufficient to describe the 'true value of the variable for that subject under these conditions' is appealing in terms of cost and effort, but is it always enough to do so? Would two biceps skinfolds taken almost simultaneously from the same subject give the same result? Would two blood samples from the same subject taken at the same time yield identical blood lactate concentrations? Would the skin temperature of a subject be the same regardless of which part of the chest area it was measured from? The answer to all of these is 'probably not'. Taking two or more measurements on the same subject provides no problem for the easily repeated variables above, but what if the time, resources and effort involved in recording the measurement was substantial (e.g. repeat $\dot{V}O_2$ max tests)? It is very appealing then simply to duck the issue!

At the very least, it is clear that many variables associated with human beings exhibit considerable variability from day to day and even from minute to minute within the same subject. Physical, mental and emotional stimuli, even of a mild nature, can alter many physiological variables, including heart rate and blood pressure. Any subject, over a length of time, will have some 'average' for a physiological variable which may remain almost constant throughout that time (e.g. arm length) or vary considerably depending on external and internal stimuli (e.g. heart rate). In general, the researcher hopes that a single measurement on a subject will 'capture' this 'average'/true value, but that is an expression of hope and not of expectation. Before embarking on any study, a researcher should have as clear an understanding as possible not only of the *short-term variability* in his/her variables of interest *within a single subject* but also of whether there is additional variability due to *different observers* not being fully consistent with each other and indeed whether changing the *measuring apparatus* would likely give a different value. If a researcher uses a response variable where the between-subject variability is not much larger than the within-subject variability or the between-observer or between-measuring-apparatus variability, then he/she is really just wasting time and effort. Only a carefully designed study allowing for all these extra (and unwanted) sources of variability will offer any hope of sensible and sustainable conclusions.

So, what can be done in practice to investigate these extra sources of variability? Using the same measuring apparatus and same measurer on all subjects on all occasions under effectively standardised conditions will go some way to reducing these effects, but can the researcher guarantee that a similar study using a different piece of apparatus or a different measurer will give the same overall conclusions? Probably not. Using a balanced design incorporating different measurers and different measuring devices (allegedly measuring the same thing) would be the only real approach to assess these sources of unwanted but potentially significant systematic bias and extra variability.

To allow for within-subject variability, **replication** is the order of the day. Simply make sure that multiple (preferably at least three) measurements are taken from each subject under each condition, but do not fall into the trap of thinking 100 observations on the same willing subject is worth 1 observation on each of 100 differents subjects. This is clearly not so and the researcher must still ensure that sufficient different subjects are measured (see Chapter 13). For studies involving single samples and for comparative studies using between-subject designs (see Section 2.2.2), it is advisable to ensure that at least three replicates are taken for each subject to ensure that a single 'rogue' observation does not distort the overall results. Whether to use the mean, median, maximum or whatever summary of the replicates depends on the particular context, and any decision on how to define a rogue observation can be contentious.

What constitutes a replicate? For some studies it could be measurements taken quickly one after the other (e.g. arm length), while for others there will have to be a suitable interval between replicates (e.g. between sprints). The characteristics of an individual study will dictate what can constitute a replicate but the overall message must be that, regardless of the additional effort, time and expense involved, replication will ensure a more reliable and scientifically valid study. However, be aware of the notion of so-called pseudo-replication which creeps into the literature. This, consciously or unconsciously on the part of the researcher, involves the use of observations which are not independent of each other and which should be avoided as far as possible. Multiple measurements on the same individual under the same conditions are much less valuable than the same number of single replicates on different individuals. Do not be fooled or swayed by convenience, no matter how difficult it is to obtain suitable subjects for a particular study.

For comparative studies involving within-subject designs (see Sections 2.2.3 and 2.2.4), there are a few simple ideas that can allow for the incorporation of within-subject variability into the design and hence analysis of the study. For example, in comparing two levels (called A and B) of a factor, such a design would involve half the subjects being measured under level A first and the rest under B first but every subject would have two measurements taken. If it were thought practical to take only three measurements per subject, then one simple procedure would be to allocate subjects in blocks according to the following:

Subject	1st condition	2nd condition	3rd condition
1	A	A	B
2	B	B	A
3	A	B	A
4	B	A	B
5	A	B	B
6	B	A	A

Overall again there is a balance here with two observations per level on the first condition etc. as well as the fact that both between- and within-subject variability can be estimated.

If four measurements could be taken per subject then a corresponding design could be based on:

Subject	1st condition	2nd condition	3rd condition	4th condition
1	A	A	B	B
2	B	B	A	A
3	A	B	A	B
4	B	A	B	A
5	A	B	B	A
6	B	A	A	B

The choice of the number of measurements per subject depends on many aspects of the study not least how easy it is to take a single measurement as well as the availability and willingness of subjects, not to mention the durability of the researchers. No easy answers are available to suit all studies but common sense and scientific veracity should guide the researcher in such decision making. Talking through a study with as many and as varied persons as possible (certainly including other professionals expert in the area, statisticians, potential subjects and indeed any man or woman out walking his/her dog or cat) will never be time wasted.

This section ends with an example of a slightly more complicated design involving the use of multiple measurements and incorporating the ideas of balanced designs and Latin squares introduced in Section 2.2.4.

Illustration 2.5   Zig-zag sprinting

Background
Speed is vital for success in rugby. However, it is not just speed in a straight line that is important. The ability to change direction quickly is of great importance. It may be that sprint performance varies on one or other of both a straight run and a zig-zag sprint as well as differing between amateur and professional players. Playing position (i.e. forward or back) may also influence sprint performance.

Study description
Six male rugby players of each combination of Status (Professional/Amateur) and Position (Forward/Back) will be recruited for this study. Subjects would perform three sprint tests on each day and would be available for subsequent sprint tests on three successive days. The sprint tests involved three different Directions of running – a 30 m sprint in a straight line (S) and two zig-zag sprints (one with a right/left (R) sequence and the other with a left/right (L) sequence).

Aim
To investigate any effects of Status, Position and Direction in terms of average 30 m Sprint Times.

Data
Response variable:	Sprint Time (seconds)
Between-subject factors:	Position (2 levels: Forward, Back)
	Status (2 levels: Amateur, Professional)
Within-subject factor:	Direction (3 levels: Left, Right, Straight)

Design

For the sample of six members of each sub-population of Status and Position, use the following pair of balanced 3×3 Latin squares introduced in Section 2.2.4:

C1	C2	C3
C2	C3	C1
C3	C1	C2

C1	C3	C2
C2	C1	C3
C3	C2	C1

Now allocate (randomly) one Direction (L, R, S) to each of the conditions (C1, C2, C3) above and then allocate at random each of the six subjects in that sub-sample to one of the six rows above. These will constitute the first day's sprints for that particular subject as in the table below so that, on the first day's testing, every Direction will be the first sprint twice and will follow every other Direction of sprint twice – once for each pair of sprints i.e. {1st, 2nd} and {2nd, 3rd}.

Subject	Day 1	Day 2	Day 3
1	L S R	S R L	R L S
2	S R L	R L S	L S R
3	R L S	L S R	S R L
4	L R S	R S L	S L R
5	R S L	S L R	L R S
6	S L R	L R S	R S L

Next, allocate the second and third day's sprint test order by the same Latin square used to define the first day for that subject in order that, for each subject, each Direction of sprint is the first for one of the days, etc. This will ensure that the properties described at the end of the previous paragraph for the first day are also relevant to the second and third days. So, for example, based on the first row of the table below, one of the subjects undergoes the sprints in order L, S and R on the first day, in order S, R and L on the second day and finally R, L and S on the third day.

The same procedure is then repeated for each of the four samples of six subjects from each combination of Status and Position of the rugby players.

2.4 Other important issues in designing a study

Pilot study

Carrying out a small pilot study (even on only three or four subjects) may help identify problems that are not apparent on paper despite the fact that a great effort has been made to compile a comprehensive procedure sheet. It is useful to ask subjects in the pilot study for feedback on explanations they received and on test procedures. Valuable information can be gained and possible misunderstandings prevented in the main study. It is almost certain that new experimenters will need time to learn how to collect data. Time must be allocated so that new experimenters can become proficient in their specific data collection tasks. It is often desirable that the same experimenters carry out the same tasks so that there is consistency throughout the whole study. This may be particularly true for some techniques. For example, skinfold measurement scores may vary from experimenter to experimenter. If possible, the experimenters should be subjects in the pilot study as they may be able to identify possible problems and can also appreciate the experiment from the subject's perspective.

Despite the fact that all aspects of the design have been scrutinised, it is still important that a pilot study is carried out to confirm that all of the procedures operate as planned. Experimenters owe it to their subjects, themselves and their institution to be highly skilled in their tasks before they begin data collection.

Familiarisation

There is no point throwing subjects in at the deep end and expecting them to undergo a series of procedures without their being aware of what is involved. A procedure that is straightforward and simple to the researcher may prove the exact opposite for some subjects. Examples include the need to allow novice subjects to practise with walking poles, to allow subjects to experience the test treadmill, to give subjects practice of climbing finger specific endurance tests which involve high levels of concentration as the subject keeps the force within predetermined levels while blood pressure and blood oxygenation levels are measured. It is always a good idea to allow subjects a run through of any parts of the study which involve any degree of complexity. These may become obvious in the first place through a pilot study.

Sample size

'What should the sample size be?' is a key question asked by all researchers, (with the implication that it should be as small as possible!). There are no easy answers and no statistician can give any answer without some assumptions or guesses as to a number of quantities such as the variability in the response variable of interest or the minimum population average difference between, say, an intervention and control which would be of scientific or practical value. Some basic approaches to guiding a researcher in coming to terms with an adequate sample size are given in Chapter 13. It is true in general to say that a researcher should try to involve as many subjects as possible, of as varied a nature as allowable by the context and to repeat a few measurements at least on a number of subjects.

Choice of variable

When replicates from the same subject under the same condition are involved, they are usually fully incorporated into the analysis, but, on occasions, interest may lie in some function of these, such as the maximal response across the replicates. In that case, all but the highest value of the replicates will be thrown away and the analysis carried out on the maximal response (e.g. using the best of three Counter Movement Jumps as a response variable to measure the jumping ability of a soccer player.)

Intention to treat

Intention to treat is an idea used widely in clinical trials; it can also be appropriate in sports and exercise science. If a subject drops out from a study then their doing so may be due to the intervention/condition that he/she is undergoing and hence reflects on the applicability of the intervention or condition. The idea of intention to treat requires that any analysis should involve all subjects randomised to an intervention/condition and, as such, all subjects should be followed through for the full study and their data included in the final analysis. Excluding subjects who have not fully complied with a training regime is considered by many to be unethical and unfair. Every effort should be made to assess all subjects (even those who drop out) at all scheduled study times and an analysis of the full set of data should be included in any report to summarise the effect of the intervention/condition on the full target population along with an analysis of those who actually completed the intervention to summarise the effect for the subset who comply with it.

Data checking and storage

If the study involves even a moderate amount of data, it would not be good science to allow the possibility of wrongly entered data. Always try to ensure that data are entered independently by two persons and that even that is backed up by some automatic checking using 'sensible ranges' of the variables involved as well as programming routines to identify any odd or inexplicable series of results where, say, the heart rate of a subject suddenly rose by 50 beats per minute over one minute then fell back the next. In addition, make sure that there is at least one back-up copy of the data on a different computer or storage device (convenient, safe and cheap data storage such as USB flash drives is readily available).

Limitations

The perfect study has still to occur. It is important to avoid built-in limitations. For example, failure to include a control group in a training study or to consider an order effect in the analysis is likely to limit the study findings.

The researchers need to decide before the study whether the limitations or constraints are so great that it is not worthwhile proceeding with the study. Limitations with subject recruitment may present difficulties. For example, the aim of the study may be to describe the characteristics of an 'elite' group of athletes. First, a definition is required of what constitutes elite. The number of elite athletes available for testing may be small and may not be representative of any sensible target population. It may be necessary to enlarge the sample and to target the population of elite and intermediate athletes.

Further, it is often difficult to verify that subjects have complied with an intervention. Training diaries can provide information on frequency, duration and intensity of training but some subjects may not be honest. In some training studies, the authors have asked the subjects to train in a laboratory or gymnasium and it has been possible to determine accurately the compliance to the study and the training intensities of the subjects. The above strategy is very time consuming for experimenters. Thus, there may not be resources available to allow training sessions to be monitored, so training information may have to be provided by subjects, with all the inherent question marks that entails.

In one study of the authors, blood pressure of subjects was measured at the end of a finger endurance test. The blood pressure measuring device could not be activated until it was established that the test had been terminated. As the blood pressure device needed time to inflate the arm cuff pressure, there was a time lag between the end of the test and the actual blood pressure measurement. Thus, the values measured may not be representative of those at the end of the test, but represent blood pressure as close to the end as possible, given the constraints imposed by the measuring device.

Before the study begins, the researchers should review the methods as if they were journal reviewers and identify possible flaws and suggest improvements to the design. It is important to recognise the limitations in a study and to highlight these limitations in the discussion section of any publication. This strategy highlights to the reader that the authors are aware of the limitations and indicates that the results may be influenced by the limitations.

More complicated designs

There is a whole mathematical science covering the subject of experimental design. Some of the most useful and simplest procedures have been illustrated here but other aspects of design can prove esoteric in the extreme and are perhaps best left to consenting adults in private. Again, though, collaboration with a compliant statistician is the way forward if the study to be carried out does not seem to be covered in this chapter.

Reliability studies

A researcher must take reliable and relevant measurements or the study will be a complete waste of time. It is essential therefore, if the variables used in the study are not well tried and tested, that, prior to the full study, the response variables undergo checking for at least reliability if not validity. It is always desirable to carry out a study based on a suitable number of subjects, at least two measurers or observers, at least two different measuring devices (if possible – but try!) and multiple 'independent' measurements per subject/measurer/device. Such a study will allow investigation of any systematic biases or differences between observers or measuring devices as well as allow estimation of the magnitude of different sources of variability across subjects, observers and measuring devices. Some basic ideas on how to judge whether measurements are 'accurate and reliable' are given in Chapter 12.

Exercises

2.5 Pregnancy can often result in major psychological trauma for the mother. A midwife in a West of Scotland local hospital believes that regular exercise would benefit expectant (and recent) mothers not only physically but also mentally. She has devised a simple questionnaire to measure various aspects of a mother's mental health with respect to how she coped both during and just after the pregnancy. Thirty-two expectant first-time mothers are to take part in the study and are to be randomised to one of two Exercise Regimes, i.e. to be a Control (who carried on with their natural lifestyle) or an Exerciser (who attended twice a week specially designed exercise classes for pregnant women). The researcher thought it prudent to randomise within each of four Age strata (i.e. >20, 20–25, 25–30 and >30 years old). Using randomly permuted blocks of four mothers-to-be, provide a design plan to allocate each of the eight mothers-to-be in each Age stratum to one of the two Exercise Regimes.

2.6 In a study of three nutritional supplements for 1–2-year-old children in Third World rural communities, a sample of 24 such children are to be randomised to one of three Supplements (i.e. a High Energy (H) or a Mineral (M) or a Placebo (P) supplement). If six children in each of four age groups (12, 15, 18 and 21 month olds) are available, use randomly permuted blocks of six children to allocate the three Supplements and provide a design plan for the study. The key response variable to be analysed here is the motor activity level of the child after two months of daily supplementation.

2.7 Deep water running (DWR) is performed by some athletes who wish to reduce the number of training sessions on land where the high impact of foot strikes may result in injury over time. Despite the fact that lactate threshold (LT) is sometimes used to provide training intensity guidance, no comparison has been made between LT in DWR and during track and treadmill running. As some athletes use DWR, track and treadmill training, it would be useful to compare, say, the heart rate at LT for DWR and track and treadmill running. Information relating to the above will help the athlete to adjust his/her training heart rate (if necessary) for a given exercise setting. Eighteen well-trained male endurance runners are to be recruited to perform incremental tests using three-minute stages once for each of DWR, track running and treadmill running. Tests will take place at the same time of day at least one week apart. The key response variable is Heart Rate at Lactate Threshold. Using pairs of balanced 3×3 Latin squares, provide a design plan to allocate the order in which each of the 18 subjects should take the three tests (i.e. one for each of DWR, Track and Treadmill).

2.8 Some rugby union coaches have recognised the value of players carrying out sprint training while pulling sledges. While players have pulled sledges with varying resistances (dependent upon the specific player's body mass), there is no consensus on what is the most appropriate resistance to pull. At some percentage of body mass there may be a breakdown in the supposed linear relationship between sprint time and percentage of body mass being pulled. For example, the resistance becomes so heavy that there is a marked decrease in running speed which is allied to a change in running mechanics and thus a loss in training specificity. Thirty-two rugby union players are each to undergo a series of four 20 m sprints while pulling a sledge with a range of 0% to 30% of their Body Mass in steps of 10% (i.e. 0%, 10%, 20% and 30%). Each player will have his mid-sprint 10 m time recorded under each Resistance over a 30 m sprint. Using balanced 4×4 Latin squares, provide a design plan to allocate the order in which each of the eight subjects – available for each of the combinations of Position (Back/Forward) and Status (Professional/ Amateur) – should sprint using each of the four Resistances (i.e. one for each of 0%, 10%, 20% and 30% of Body Mass).

Summary

Basic definitions of the necessary building blocks for a scientific study were introduced in Chapter 1. These included the vital notions of *population* and *sample* as well as population parameter and sample statistic.

The simplest studies are *observational* in nature but, often, the results of such studies may not be sensibly generalised to any target population. More commonly, sports and exercise science is concerned with *comparative* studies involving samples from distinct and different populations – so-called *between-subject designs* of which the most common is the two-sample problem. Here the essential ingredient of a good design is *randomisation*.

When subjects can undergo more than one intervention, then the key ingredient of a good design is *balance* through ideas such as Latin squares – so-called *within-subject designs* of which the most common is the paired-sample problem. This type of design attempts to ensure that hidden biases due to order or carryover effects have only limited effect on an analysis.

To allow for different *sources of variability* in a study, the ideas of *balance* and *replication* can be employed to estimate the different components of variability within subjects, between observers, etc.

Common sense and meticulous planning play the essential roles in the good design of a study. Simple ideas such as carrying out a *pilot study,* use of *controls,* allowing for the possibility of *order effects* and assessing *limitations* can be used to enhance a study but the essential ingredient is to discuss the proposed study with as many and as varied people as possible. Remember, though, that if a study has a flawed design, then not even the most imaginative and creative statistical analysis can rescue it. Time spent on the production of a well-thought-out design is time well spent.

3 Summarising and displaying data

3.1 Introduction

Once the data have been collected and electronically recorded, the starting point in all statistical analyses is to provide useful and meaningful **numerical** and **graphical** summaries of the data. The importance of providing such summaries as a prerequisite of any formal analysis cannot be underestimated. This process will allow a subjective opinion to be formed regarding the key question of interest and provide an indication of the statistical model that was likely to have generated the data. In addition, a thorough investigation is needed to assess numerical accuracy, i.e. were the data correctly entered and do the data 'make sense' given the subject matter (e.g. no heart rates of 1000 beats per minute).

Typically, too much emphasis is placed on the formal analysis and not enough on gleaning information from the sample at hand. Techniques useful in looking critically, but subjectively, at data are provided in this chapter across a wide variety of common contexts encountered in sports and exercise science. These should be thought of as complementary to the 'statistical techniques' on which the 'formal analysis' of the data is based.

Recall from Chapter 1 that data typically consist of two variable types: **continuous** and **categorical**. Continuous variables can take any value within a wide range, for example Body Mass, Sprint Time or $\dot{V}O_2$ max, while categorical variables typically represent binary characteristics such as Sex (Male/Female) or indeed characteristics with a small number of levels (e.g. Controls, Treatment A, Treatment B). This chapter deals solely with continuous response variables, although categorical variables do appear in terms of between- and within-subject factors. Chapter 8 provides graphical and numerical methods for summarising categorical responses.

One example of a continuous variable in exercise related areas is the $\dot{V}O_2$ max of a human being. Useful summaries of this variable might include the $\dot{V}O_2$ max of the 'typical person' in the population of interest (e.g. elite female hockey players), as well, perhaps, as some indication of the variability in $\dot{V}O_2$ max across this population. A reference range to cover the vast majority of the population for the variable (sometimes called a 'Normal range') might be required in order to highlight any present or future observations that would be considered atypical of this population.

This chapter concentrates on appropriate numerical and graphical summaries from data consisting of samples of continuous response variables.

3.2   Numerical summaries for continuous variables

3.2.1   Sample centre: sample mean and sample median

The most commonly used sample statistics to numerically summarise a continuous variable from a single sample are the sample mean (i.e. the sample average) and the sample median. These describe the 'centre' of the sample in (slightly) different ways.

The **sample mean** is undoubtedly the most reported summary statistic. It is calculated by adding up the observations and dividing the total by the sample size. It is easy to calculate but also easy to misinterpret. Care must be taken when using the sample mean to summarise a sample, as the following example illustrates. Consider a random sample of English Premier League soccer supporters in Stamford Bridge, London, watching Chelsea Football Club. Say the average salary of ten randomly sampled supporters in attendance at a match is £30,000. What would happen if Chelsea club owner Roman Abramovich (11th richest person in the world with an estimated fortune of £13 billion) turned up in the sample? The sample mean would rise dramatically and football supporters in Stamford Bridge would now appear to be millionaires 'on average'. A nice prospect but it is clearly false. What has happened? Consider a simple dataset with the five observations 1, 2, 3, 4 and 5. The sample mean or average is

$$\frac{1}{5}(1 + 2 + 3 + 4 + 5) = 3$$

Increase the final observation to 50 and the sample mean becomes 12 which is clearly not a good measure to describe the 'typical' value in this small set of numbers. In this situation a more 'sensible' measure of the typical value is given by the **sample median**, the middle 'observation' if all the observations in the sample are arranged in increasing magnitude. The value of the sample median is 3 in both cases above and is a more sensible (and stable) summary statistic to use when describing the typical value in this context. This example highlights the fact that the sample median is **robust** to extreme values in a sample, unlike the sample mean. This property of the median is particularly important in small (≤ 20) samples.

Note that if the number of observations is even, the sample median is the middle of the two middle observations once the data are arranged in order e.g. for 4, 2, 1, 3 the median is midway between 2 and 3, namely 2.5.

Accordingly, for any sample of data involving a continuous variable, the most obvious sample statistics are the sample mean and the sample median where the sample median is more appropriate if the data exhibit some extreme values.

3.2.2   Sample spread

Once a sensible summary statistic representing the typical value of the sample is chosen, the next step is to provide an indication of the spread of the values in the sample. Are two golfers each with a handicap of 16 the same? In some 'average sense' the answer is yes but the variability about their handicap may determine who is the more successful. The golfer who can score fairly close to his or her handicap on most rounds will be more consistent than a golfer whose scores vary considerably but the latter might just pull out a 'magic round' to win a competition. Consider two 100 m sprinters with sample mean times over a season of 11.1 and 11.5 seconds, respectively. Is it possible that the slower runner could have beaten the faster in any of the races in question? To assess this an indication of the variability in each athlete's individual race times is needed. If the slower runner had considerably more variability in her times, it is entirely possible that she could have beaten her opponent in several races during the season.

The simplest measure of spread is the **sample range**, i.e. the maximum value in the sample minus the minimum value. One disadvantage of the sample range is that it will be influenced by extreme values or 'wild' observations. A better approach is to consider the **sample lower quartile** (often given the label Q1) – the 'middle' of the numerically smaller half of the sample – and the **sample upper quartile** (often given the label Q3) which is the 'middle' of the larger half, i.e. these are in effect the medians of the bottom and top halves of the sample if all the observations are arranged in increasing magnitude. The distance between the **sample upper and lower quartiles**, the so-called **sample interquartile range** (IQR) represents the range containing the middle 50% of the data.

The usual summary statistic quoted in sports and exercise science literature to describe sample spread is the **sample standard deviation**. This quantity is often misunderstood as it is much less intuitive than the sample range or sample interquartile range. The sample standard deviation is tedious to calculate by hand and is best left to a statistical software package. What is more important is an understanding of why and when the sample standard deviation is used and how it should be interpreted.

If the variable of interest appears to be distributed in a symmetrical manner in the sample, it is plausible that the population from which it arose was symmetrical. Why is symmetry so important? The foundation of most statistical inference is based on an important symmetrical distribution called the **Normal distribution** and identifying whether data are likely to have arisen from a population with a Normal distribution for this variable will become crucial in later chapters. Furthermore, the sample standard deviation is essential to any analysis if the underlying population can be adequately assumed to follow a Normal distribution.

One useful result to note at this stage is that if the data really have arisen from a Normal distribution then the set of values comprising

Sample mean $\pm$ 2 * Sample standard deviation

will cover effectively the vast majority (approximately 95%) of the sample and hence by inference the underlying (Normal) population. However, *this result applies only to the Normal distribution.*

3.2.3 The five-number summary

Probably the five most useful numerical summaries to use when summarising a continuous variable of a single sample of data are (in sample order):

- sample minimum
- sample lower quartile
- sample median

- sample upper quartile
- sample maximum.

This collection of numbers encapsulates the range, spread and middle of the sample for the variable of interest and will provide a useful overall summary of the sample. Indeed, such a summary is used as the basis of the most informative graphical representation of the sample, as demonstrated in the next section.

This section concludes with a reminder of the more common summary statistics and their general uses as outlined in Table 3.1.

Table 3.1 **Summary statistics for continuous variables**

Sample statistic	*Basic use*
Sample *mean*	To describe the typical value (i.e. the centre) of a sample of data but can be influenced by 'wild' observations
Sample *median*	To describe the typical value (i.e. the centre) of a sample of data
Sample *extremes* (minimum and maximum) and hence sample *range*	To describe the spread of a sample but can be influenced by 'wild' observations
Sample *quartiles* and hence sample *interquartile range*	To describe the spread of a sample and are not unduly influenced by 'wild' observations
Sample *standard deviation*	To describe the spread of a sample but can be influenced by 'wild' observations

3.3 Graphical methods for continuous variables

Providing suitable summary statistics is a useful and necessary first step in describing the typical value and accompanying variability present in a sample of data. Arguably, a more important step is to provide some graphical representation of the data. The use of appropriate plots will help greatly in identifying features about the population from which the data were sampled.

That a picture paints a thousand 'numbers' is almost self-evident in data analysis. Rather than staring at a batch of numbers, drawing an appropriate graph or diagram may:

- throw up an unsuspected view of the data such as a pattern or odd observations;
- allow a subjective answer to the specific question of interest;
- give an indication of the likely shape of the population distribution from which the sample arose;
- provide a way of assessing at least parts of any assumed statistical model before engaging in formal analysis;
- aid the presentation and understanding of results and conclusions in subsequent conference presentations and publications.

One of the tasks in this exploratory stage is to investigate the likely shape of the **population distribution** using the available sample. A population distribution gives the relative frequency of the different values of the response variable in the population of interest. Almost all statistical analyses make certain assumptions regarding the population distribution from which a sample has been generated and these assumptions must be investigated and found to be adequate in order to justify the analysis.

Some of the most common graphical methods for use with continuous variables are given in Table 3.2 in addition to the types of context in which these methods are used. These methods are then introduced and illustrated throughout the next few sections.

Table 3.2 **Common graphical methods for continuous variables and the contexts illustrating their use**

Graphical method	Context	Basic use
Box plot	Single samples	To illustrate and summarise a single sample
Box plot Labelled scatter plot	Between-subject designs	To compare samples from two or more distinct populations
Labelled scatter plot	Between-subject designs with a covariate	To compare samples from two or more distinct populations while adjusting for a covariate
Scatter plot Box plot	Within-subject designs	To compare *changes* across samples from two or more distinct populations
Case profile plot	Within-subject designs	To investigate the pattern of response across different conditions for the same subject
Scatter plot Labelled scatter plot	Modelling interdependence relationships	To investigate the dependence between two variables

3.4 Single-sample problems (independent data)

Recall from Chapter 1 that data are termed **independent** if the observed values of the random variable in the sample are not influenced by each other. In order to present a graphical summary of independent data involving a single response variable of interest measured on a single sample of subjects, the following steps must be carried out:

1 Provide summary statistics such as the five-number summary introduced in Section 3.2.3.

2 Provide a box plot of the variable of interest using an appropriate axis scale and including a suitable title and axis labels.

If the plots show a general pattern of points (i.e. subjects) that are quite symmetrical about the sample median – but possibly widely spread about it – consider using the sample mean and standard deviation as suitable summary statistics. If the data look far from symmetrical, use the sample median and interquartile range.

An example now follows where a single continuous variable (Ascent Time of Mont Blanc) is measured for a sample of 197 subjects from a single population of interest (Alpine climbers).

Illustration 3.1   Mont Blanc ascent time

Background
Many people aspire to climb Mont Blanc (4807 m), the highest mountain in western Europe. A key component when a climb of Mont Blanc is planned is the likely time for a successful ascent.

Study description
In August 2002, physiological tests were performed on 285 climbers passing through the Gouter Hut as they prepared to climb Mont Blanc and the Ascent Times of 197 climbers, known to have succeeded, were recorded.

Aim
To provide adequate graphical summaries of the sample of 197 Ascent Times and to estimate the typical Ascent Time for successful climbers of Mont Blanc (at this time of year).

Data
    Name of data file: *Mont Blanc Ascent*
    Response variable: Ascent Time (hours)

Analysis
The first step in any statistical analysis is to calculate summary statistics for the response variable of interest and, more importantly, to provide a suitable plot of the data to subjectively assess the 'typical' value and the likely variability in the population of interest. Summary statistics for the Ascent Time variable are given in Box 3.1.

Box 3.1

```
Descriptive Statistics: Ascent Time

Variable       N    Mean   StDev  Minimum      Q1  Median      Q3 Maximum
Ascent Time  197  4.2589  0.8209   2.8330  3.5000  4.2500  4.7500  6.6660
```

Note that the fastest (i.e. lowest) Ascent Time recorded was 2.83 hours whereas the slowest ascent took 6.66 hours, giving a reasonably wide sample range. The sample median is 4.25 hours which is nearly identical to the sample mean. The spread in Ascent Times can be summarised by the sample quartiles (3.50 and 4.75 hours). Although this information is interesting, a clearer view is provided by plotting the data. By far the most common method used to summarise continuous variables is a plot of the five-number summary, a so-called **box plot**. Thus the box plot highlights the 'middle half' of the sample and places less weight on each of the end quartiles.

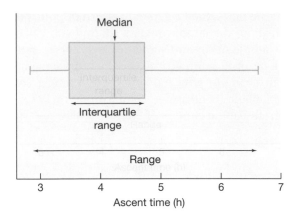

Figure 3.1 **Box plot of Mont Blanc Ascent Time.**

A box plot is a line plot of the sample's five-number summary made up by the sample median, sample quartiles (Q1 and Q3) and sample extremes (minimum and maximum). The simplest version is to denote the sample median by a line, surround it by a box to the sample quartiles and draw tails from this box to the sample extremes.

A box plot of the Ascent Times for the sample of Mont Blanc climbers is given in Figure 3.1. The plot is useful as it gives an indication of the typical Ascent Time (through the 'robust' sample median), the spread (through the 'robust' sample quartiles) and the overall sample range.

If there is evidence of symmetry in the box plot and the sample mean and median are similar then the Normal distribution is likely to be a reasonable assumption as to the process which generated the data. For example, although the box plot of Ascent Times has a slight lack of symmetry in that the box is not exactly in the middle of the range and the median is not quite in the middle of the box, these departures from symmetry are not severe. Given this graphical evidence, a rough estimate of the likely range of Ascent Times for 95% of the population of interest (i.e. those who successfully climbed Mount Blanc) is available by calculating:

Sample mean $\pm$ 2 * Sample standard deviation

i.e.

$$4.2589 \pm 2 * 0.8209 = 2.6 \text{ to } 5.9 \text{ hours}$$

Conclusion

For those who made a successful ascent of Mont Blanc, the typical Ascent Time was around 4.3 hours. The vast majority of climbers who successfully climb Mount Blanc should take between 2.5 and 6.0 hours.

Reference: Tsianos, G., Woolrich, L., Watt, M., Peacock, A., Aitchison, T., Montgomery, H., Watt, I. and Grant, S. (2005). 'Prediction of performance on the ascent of Mont Blanc.' *European Journal of Applied Physiology,* **96**: 32–36.

Additional comments on Illustration 3.1

1 Once a suitable measure of spread has been decided upon, a difficult question to answer is 'How far away from the bulk of the sample does an observation have to be to be declared dramatically unusual?' In statistical jargon such an observation is termed an **outlier**. One simple rule of thumb employed (by Minitab) is that an observation is

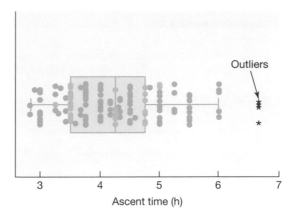

Figure 3.2 **Box plot of Mont Blanc Ascent Time (with data points and outliers included).**

considered an outlier if the observation is either at least 1.5 * IQR (i.e. one and a half times the interquartile range) greater than the upper quartile or 1.5 * IQR less than the lower quartile. Using this rule, three climbers in the sample have Ascent Times that have been flagged as atypically long as they are considered 'too far' away from the bulk of the data. Typically outliers are often displayed in the box plot using an asterisk, as the box plot of the Mont Blanc Ascent Times in Figure 3.2 demonstrates. Note also that the individual data points have been included in this box plot. This is often a sensible thing to do when generating a box plot as it highlights the sample size (which is not at all obvious in a box plot) as well as other important aspects of the sample that will be discussed in later chapters.

2 Three observations are highlighted as outliers in Figure 3.2, suggesting that there are three climbers with atypically long climbing times when compared with the rest of the sample. The sample mean Ascent Time *without* these climbers is still close to 4.3 hours, which suggests that these longer climbing times are not overly influential in terms of their effect on the sample mean in this illustration, presumably due to the large sample size (i.e. 197).

3 This sample is considerable in size as evident by the number of data points in the box plot. Observations with identical values of the response variable (i.e. identical Ascent Times) are impossible to distinguish as the data labels 'lie on top' of each other. One method to counteract this is to add a 'jitter' (a small amount to each response) in order to make observations more easily distinguishable, and this was done in Figure 3.2.

Exercises

3.1 Regular physical activity has been shown to have potential health benefits, including an enhanced aerobic fitness and a reduction or maintenance in body fat levels. One such form of exercise is a Popmobility aerobic dance class. As part of an assessment of Popmobility classes, ten 18–21-year-old female students had their Energy Expenditures measured (in a laboratory) for such a session. Use these data to provide numerical and graphical summaries and a subjective impression as to the typical value and range of Energy Expenditures in such a Popmobility session. The dataset is called *Popmobility*.

> 3.2 Samples of male and female elite distance runners had their Haemoglobin Concentrations measured and these are contained in the dataset *Haemoglobin*. Using these data, provide numerical and graphical summaries of Haemoglobin Concentration for each sex separately. Identify any female or male athlete who has a haemoglobin concentration below the World Health Organization values for anaemia of less than 12 g per 100 ml for non-pregnant women and less than 13 g per 100 ml for men.

3.5   Between-subject designs (independent data)

Armed with the summary statistics and graphical techniques introduced in the previous section, it is time to look at extensions of the single-sample problem. Between-subject designs – comparing a response variable of interest across independent samples from two or more different populations – are commonplace in sports and exercise science research. Such studies can be of two types (see Chapter 2): an **observational** study where samples are selected from different populations and compared with respect to a response variable of interest (e.g. comparing the grip strength of recreational and elite climbers), or a **designed experiment** where a single random sample from a target population is taken and then each subject is randomised to one of two or more different levels/conditions as defined by the between-subject factor. The response variable of interest is measured on each subject in each sample (e.g. from a target population of professional soccer players, the change in $\dot{V}O_2$ max for a sample undergoing a high-intensity training programme for three months is compared with that experienced by a sample of controls across the same period).

Three examples of between-subject designs are now illustrated graphically starting with a single between-subject factor at two levels (i.e. a two-sample comparison) followed by a single factor at three levels and finally a design with two between-subject factors.

The approach needed for summarising data from between-subject designs is as follows:

1   Provide summary statistics such as the sample five-number summary separately for each sample and, if appropriate, the sample mean and sample standard deviation.

2   Provide box plots of the response variable for all samples on the same graph using a suitable axis scale, title and axis labels.

Illustration 3.2   Soccer fitness

Background
Many professional soccer clubs use a physiological test battery to assess their players on a regular basis. Testing can be of benefit to the players and coaches for a variety of reasons, including the identification of strengths and weaknesses in individual players and the monitoring of players throughout the season. Jumping ability is considered to be important in soccer as players often have to compete for the ball in the air. A comparison of this variable across Senior and Youth players may provide players and coaches with information on whether the Youth players have attained the levels of the Senior players.

Study description

As part of a fitness test battery in a Scottish professional soccer club, 37 elite Senior and Youth soccer players performed a counter movement jump (CMJ) test. This test is similar to some jumping movements carried out in a game. Counter Movement Jump Height was measured using a contact mat and the highest value from three attempts (after familiarisation) was recorded.

Aim

To provide numerical and graphical summaries to compare CMJ Height across the populations of Senior and Youth professional soccer players.

Data

Name of data file:	*Soccer Fitness*
Response variable:	CMJ Height (centimetres)
Between-subject factor:	Squad (2 levels: Senior, Youth)

Analysis

A useful starting point is to generate summary statistics and box plots of the response variable (CMJ Height) separately by Squad.

Box 3.2

```
Descriptive Statistics: CMJump

Variable  Squad    N   Mean   StDev  Minimum    Q1    Median    Q3     Maximum
CMJump    Senior  14  55.08   5.52   46.48    49.97   57.28   58.74    65.02
          Youth   23  48.492  4.059  40.132   45.720  48.514  50.800   58.166
```

The summary statistics (Box 3.2) and box plot (Figure 3.3) suggest that Senior players tend to have a higher CMJ Height when compared with Youth players by approximately 6.6 cm on average. The variability in CMJ Height is slightly larger in the sample of Senior players as assessed by the sample standard deviation and the interquartile range.

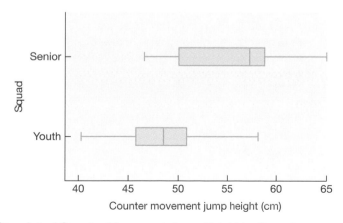

Figure 3.3 **Box plot of Counter Movement Jump Height by Squad.**

The CMJ Height distribution for the Youth players appears symmetric and may well be summarised adequately by (separate) Normal distributions. There is evidence of a right skew in CMJ Height distribution for the Senior players as the median is not in the middle of the box.

Conclusion

The subjective impression from the plot is that, typically, CMJ Height is higher in the population of Senior soccer players than in the population of Youth players. The estimated difference in mean CMJ Height is 6.6 cm in favour of the Senior players. The higher scores for the Senior players may reflect differences in maturational status and training background.

Source: Sports Performance Unit, Scottish Premier League Club.

A natural extension of this between-subject design with two levels (or two-sample problem) is to consider data involving a single response variable measured on three or more independent samples of subjects, i.e. a between-subject design with one factor at three or more levels. Such a study would involve a random sample from a single population which is randomised into three or more samples. The equivalent graphical techniques can, of course, be used for an observational study involving random samples from three or more distinct populations.

Illustration 3.3   Relaxation and running performance

Background

Relaxation techniques could reduce the oxygen cost of running and lower heart rate during exercise. A reduced oxygen cost has the potential to improve endurance running performance. It is also of interest to examine the effects of relaxation techniques on exercise heart rate. A reduced exercise heart rate may result in a lower myocardial oxygen consumption which may be of value to some cardiac patient groups.

Study description

A sample of 28 recreational distance runners were taken and randomised into one of three Treatments (Control, Meditation or Progressive Muscular Relaxation (PMR)) as a potential means of reducing their heart rates during exercise. The steady state heart rates during a standardised running test of all 28 athletes (13 Controls, 8 on Meditation and 7 on PMR) were taken both before and after two weeks of 'treatment'. The Reduction in Heart Rate over this two-week period (i.e. pre-study heart rate minus post-study heart rate) was taken as the response variable.

Aim

To determine which, if any, of the relaxation methods (Meditation or Progressive Muscular Relaxation) significantly reduce exercise heart rate on average compared to Controls over a two-week period.

Data

Name of data file:	*Relaxation*
Response variable:	Reduction in Heart Rate (b.min^{-1})
Between-subject factor:	Treatment (3 levels: Control, Meditation, PMR)

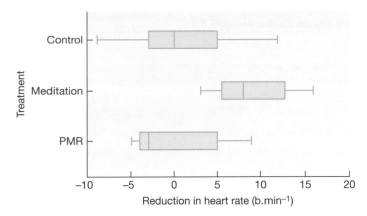

Figure 3.4 **Box plot of Reduction in Heart Rate by Treatment.**

Analysis

Box plots and summary statistics of Reduction in Heart Rate by Treatment are reported in Figure 3.4 and Box 3.3, respectively.

Box 3.3

```
Variable    Group          N    Mean  StDev  Minimum      Q1  Median      Q3
Reduction   Control       13   0.846   5.55    −9.00   −3.00    0.00    5.00
            Meditation     8   8.75    4.33     3.00    5.50    8.00   12.75
            PMR            7   0.429   5.47    −5.00   −4.00    3.00    5.00

Variable    Group        Maximum
Reduction   Control        12.00
            Meditation     16.00
            PMR             9.00
```

It looks obvious from the box plot that there are differences (in terms of the sample medians at least) among the three treatments and in particular that Meditation produces larger Reductions in Heart Rate than either of the other two Treatments.

Note the higher sample mean reduction for the Meditation group (8.75 b.min^{-1}) when compared with the sample mean Reduction in Heart Rate for the other two Treatments. Indeed, the sample mean Reduction in Heart Rate for the Control and PMR Treatments are both practically zero, suggesting no improvement for either on average.

It is difficult to make a subjective impression as to the likely underlying distributions in each Treatment given the small sample sizes. The variability within each Treatment looks fairly similar.

Conclusion

It appears that Meditation tends on average, to reduce, heart rate during a standardised running test among recreational distance runners, unlike the other two treatments where there is not only virtually no overlap with the Meditation Treatment but also what looks like a random scatter about zero reduction for both these other Treatments.

Reference: Ashley, E., Mutrie, N. and Hayes, C. (1996). '*Can Relaxation Enhance Running Performance?*' Scottish Sports Council Research Report no. 44.

A simple extension of the between-subject design with one factor is to incorporate two or more factors of interest, each with two or more levels.

Illustration 3.4 Exercise and well-being

Background

It is often suggested that regular exercise has a positive effect on a person's well-being. There are a number of possible reasons why regular exercise may enhance well-being. When people take part in exercise, they take time out from the stresses of life. Regular exercise has been shown to reduce anxiety levels, improve mood and enhance self-esteem in some populations.

Study description

A random sample of 285 Glasgow University students filled in a questionnaire detailing the amount of exercise they undertook each week. From this questionnaire, subjects were classified as either Regular or Non-Regular Exercisers based on whether they had undergone a minimum of three sessions per week of at least 20 minutes aerobic activity at, or above, 65% of maximum heart rate. Each student filled in a visual analogue scale of 0 to 100 (where 100 represents exceptional Well-being) as a measure of their current feeling of physical Well-being.

Aim

To determine if regular exercise has, in general, a positive effect on a student's self-perceived physical Well-being, and if any such effect is the same for both Males and Females.

Data

Name of data file:	*Wellbeing*
Response variable:	Well-being (0 to 100)
Between-subject factors:	Regular Exerciser (2 levels: No, Yes)
	Sex (2 levels: Male, Female)

Analysis

Box plots of Well-being grouped by Sex and Regular Exerciser are given in Figure 3.5 and suggest that a positive effect of regular exercise is noticeable for both Males and Females.

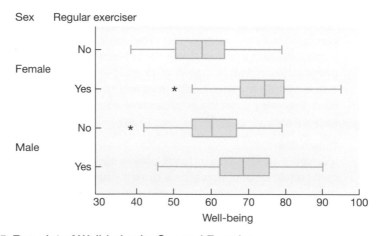

Figure 3.5 **Box plot of Well-being by Sex and Exercise.**

The distribution of Well-being scores is quite symmetrical for all four sex and exercise combinations with similar spreads in each sample. An estimate of the typical difference in Well-being between Regular and Non-Regular Exercisers is available from the summary statistics in Box 3.4 for each sex separately.

Box 3.4

```
Female

              Regular
Variable      Exerciser   N    Mean   StDev  Minimum     Q1  Median      Q3  Maximum
Well-being    No          80  57.27    9.55    38.03  50.47   57.39   63.40    78.95
              Yes         60  73.17    9.20    49.30  67.50   74.29   79.45    95.24

Male

              Regular
Variable      Exerciser   N     Mean  StDev  Minimum      Q1  Median      Q3
Well-being    No          95  60.361  8.800   37.035  54.765  59.952  66.533
              Yes         50   68.63  10.26    45.51   62.13   68.43   75.31

              Regular
Variable      Exerciser   Maximum
Well-being    No           79.032
              Yes          90.16
```

The sample mean difference in perceived Well-being (for Regular Exercisers over the others) is 15.9 units among Females and 8.3 units among Males. These results suggest that general Well-being may indeed be higher in the population of Regular Exercisers and that such a difference in Well-being may well be *larger* in Females than in Males.

Conclusion

Based on the sample provided, Regular Exercisers typically have a greater sense of self-perceived Well-being than Non-Regular Exercisers. The beneficial effect of exercise on self-perceived Well-being appears to be nearly twice as large in Females as it is in Males.

Reference: Glasgow University, Sport and Recreation Service Student Survey.

Exercises

3.3 Investigate whether there is likely to be a difference in average Multi-Stage Shuttle Test Score between Youth and Senior players in the soccer study described in Illustration 3.2. The variable of interest is called Bleep Test and the data are located in the file *Soccer Fitness*.

3.4 A change of diet (e.g. a reduction in the proportion of protein ingested) may influence the energy expenditure of a human being. The basal metabolic rate (BMR) measures the energy expenditure of an individual in a standardised resting situation. Twenty-four 20–30-year-old women were randomised to either a 'Normal' controlled diet or a Protein-Reduced diet. After three months on the specific diet, each woman had her BMR measured. Using summary statistics and a box plot, make a subjective comment as to whether the Protein-Reduced diet led, on average, to an increased BMR. The data are in a file called *BMR*.

3.6 Within-subject designs (dependent data)

The previous section was concerned with studies where a sample of subjects from a population of interest were randomised into two or more treatments i.e. a between-subject design. Another common form of design undertaken in sports and exercise science research is to measure the same variable under different conditions ('levels') for each individual in a single sample, i.e. a within-subject design.

The simplest case involves a within-subject factor with two levels – the same variable is measured twice (once each under two different 'conditions' or levels) on each subject in a single sample from the target population. Each response has *two* observations (e.g. under different 'conditions' such as *before* and *after* some intervention), which will likely to be dependent upon each other. Typically, the analysis relates to assessing the population mean difference between these two conditions/levels under the usual assumptions of Normality. This type of design is often referred to as a **paired design** as there is a pair of observations per subject. Note that, although two measurements are taken for each subject, the data consist of a *single* sample of paired observations from the population of interest.

Graphical procedures for such studies again include box plots as well as scatter plots and case profile plots, while numerical summaries are also useful. Three examples of within-subject designs are now illustrated graphically starting with a single within-subject factor at two levels (i.e. a paired-sample comparison), followed by a single within-subject factor at three levels and finally a design with two within-subject factors.

Illustration 3.5 Exercise and the elderly

Background

Regular exercise has the potential to help limit the deterioration in mobility in the elderly as well as maintain or improve their aerobic fitness. Aerobic dance and walking are two possible modes of exercise that can be carried out by the elderly. Comparison of these modes of exercise at a self-selected pace will determine if they have the potential to maintain or improve aerobic fitness in the elderly.

Study description

Twelve subjects performed both an Aerobic Dance exercise session and a Walking session individually on an indoor track. The order of sessions was balanced, with half the subjects performing the Aerobic Dance first and half the Walking session first. Gas collection was carried out during the 18 minutes of each session and the gas samples were collected in Douglas bags in 3-minute periods. The subjects also performed an incremental treadmill test to volitional exhaustion. During the treadmill test each subject's peak $\dot{V}O_2$ was determined so that the Relative Intensity (the average % Peak $\dot{V}O_2$ over the 18 minutes) of the Aerobic Dance and Walking sessions could be established.

Aim

To compare Relative Intensity during the Aerobic Dance and Walking sessions.

Data

Name of data file:	*WalkDance*
Response variable:	Relative Intensity (% Peak $\dot{V}O_2$)
Within-subject factor:	Exercise Regime (2 levels: Walking, Aerobic Dance)

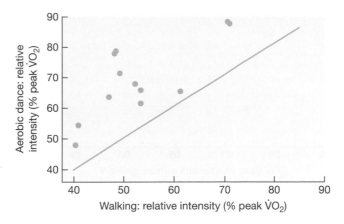

Figure 3.6 Scatter plot of Relative Intensity and Exercise Regime (with line of equality).

Analysis

Start by creating a scatter plot of subjects' Relative Intensity for the Aerobic Dance and Walking sessions, using the same scale for both axes (Figure 3.6). Add the line of equality (i.e. the line corresponding to all values where a subject's Relative Intensity is the same for both Exercise Regimes).

The sample range Relative Intensity for individuals for the Walking sessions was 40–70% of Peak $\dot{V}O_2$ while the sample range for the same individuals for Aerobic Dance was 47–87% of Peak $\dot{V}O_2$. All of the individuals in the study demonstrated a higher Relative Intensity for Aerobic Dance since all of the points lie above the line of equality in Figure 3.6.

Under certain circumstances (see General Comment following this illustration), the paired design of the study can be exploited and the analysis simplified by forming a new variable of the Difference in Relative Intensity – for example, by subtracting the Walking Relative Intensity from the Aerobic Dance Relative Intensity for each subject. This is the 'natural' direction since Aerobic Dance has higher values for every subject. This can be interpreted as a positive difference and indicates that a subject's Relative Intensity is higher for Aerobic Dance, while a negative difference indicates that a subject's Relative Intensity was higher for the Walking session.

A box plot of the Difference in Relative Intensity highlights once again that all individuals had a higher Relative Intensity for Aerobic Dance and suggests that the typical difference in Relative Intensity is approximately 15% favouring the Aerobic Dance session (Figure 3.7).

The summary statistics in Box 3.5 confirm that the sample mean Relative Intensity was higher for the Aerobic Dance session than the Walking session by 15% in the sample of data provided.

Box 3.5

```
Descriptive Statistics: Dance-Walk Relative Intensity

Variable     N    Mean   StDev   Minimum    Q1   Median     Q3   Maximum
Dance-Walk  12   15.29    7.91      3.42   8.48   15.02   19.94    29.02
```

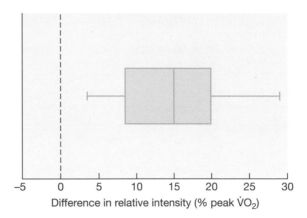

Figure 3.7 Box plot of Difference in Relative Intensity (Aerobic Dance minus Walking).

Conclusion

The typical Relative Intensity of the population of interest is likely to be higher by about 15% of Peak $\dot{V}O_2$ for the Aerobic Dance class compared to a Walking session. Note that the exercise intensity is sufficiently high in both modes of exercise to maintain or improve aerobic fitness in an elderly population (according to the American College of Sports Medicine aerobic fitness guidelines) if the sessions are carried out on a regular basis.

Reference: Grant, S., Corbett, K., Todd, K., Davies, C., Aitchison, T., Mutrie, N., Byrne, J., Henderson, E. and Dargie, H.J. (2002). 'A comparison of physiological responses and rating of perceived exertion in two modes of aerobic exercise in men and women over 50 years of age.' *British Journal of Sports Medicine*, **36**: 276–280.

General comment on the use of differences in paired data

An analysis based on the simple differences in a paired design is only justified if the observations in the relevant scatter plot are more or less 'parallel' to the line of equality across the full range x-axis. Such a scenario is common, for example, when the differences in a paired design (with levels Pre and Post) are not dependent on the Pre values. Figure 3.8 depicts such a pattern where the observations are more or less the same amount above the line of equality right across the horizontal scale.

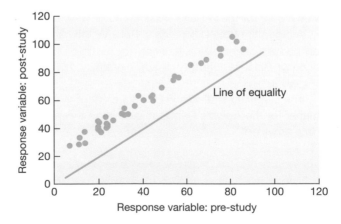

Figure 3.8 An example where analysing simple differences is appropriate.

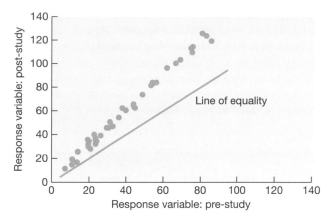

Figure 3.9 An example where analysing simple differences is not appropriate.

An analysis based on simple differences would not be appropriate, however, if the differences in any way depended on the magnitude of the response variable, i.e. there is a non-constant shift from the line of equality. One such scenario is depicted in Figure 3.9 where the change in the response variable is clearly dependent on the values of the variable Pre-Study. Methods for analysing such a situation for paired data are discussed in Chapter 7.

The simple case of paired data is now extended to that where the within-subject factor has three or more levels. The aim in general, as in the paired design, is to investigate differences, on average, across the three levels in the population of interest. A new plot, the **case profile plot**, is introduced. This plot highlights the *individual* pattern by connecting the data for each observation across the levels of the within-subject factor.

Illustration 3.6   **Deep water running**

Background

Deep water running (DWR) is performed by some athletes who wish to reduce the number of training sessions on land where the high impact of foot strikes may result in injury over time. Injured athletes who cannot sustain sessions on land due to pain or discomfort sometimes favour DWR. While DWR is not bio-mechanically the same as running on land, the movements are fairly similar. Despite the fact that lactate threshold (LT) is sometimes used to provide training intensity guidance, no comparison has been made between LT in DWR and during track and treadmill running. As some athletes use DWR, track and treadmill training, it would be useful to compare some physiological responses in the three settings. For example, comparing the heart rate at LT for DWR and track and treadmill running will help the athlete to adjust his/her training heart rate (if necessary) for a given exercise setting.

Study description

Eighteen well-trained male endurance runners were recruited to perform incremental tests using three-minute stages once for each of DWR, track running and treadmill running. The order in which the subjects carried out the three tests was determined using balanced 3×3 Latin squares (see Chapter 2) but unfortunately three runners withdrew from the study. Tests took place at the same time of day at least one week apart. The response variable was taken as Heart Rate at LT.

Aim

To compare typical Heart Rates at Lactate Threshold in deep water running, track running and treadmill running in well-trained male endurance runners.

Data

Name of data file: *Pool Running*
Response variable: Heart Rate (b.min^{-1})
Within-subject factor: Condition (3 levels: Track, Treadmill, DWR)

Analysis

Prepare a case profile plot of Heart Rate at LT connected by subject across the Conditions (see Figure 3.10).

The benefit of the case profile plot is immediately evident as such a plot highlights the *individual* pattern across the levels of the within-subject factor. There is no order inherent in the levels of the factor, however, so the patterns should not be interpreted in any longitudinal sense. The message is quite clear, though: individuals tend to have similar Heart Rates at LT while running on the Track and Treadmill, with a slight reduction in Heart Rate at LT when on the Treadmill compared with the Track. Heart Rate at LT in DWR is considerably lower than Heart Rate at LT in both Track and Treadmill running.

The 'typical' pattern exhibited in the case profile plot is not necessarily that experienced by every subject. Indeed, there are some patterns that are not consistent with the typical heart rate profile across the Conditions.

A (vertical) box plot of Heart Rate at LT for each Condition (Figure 3.11) gives a general indication of the changes across the three Conditions. Connecting the sample medians is a useful graphical procedure in such examples to visually highlight the typical pattern.

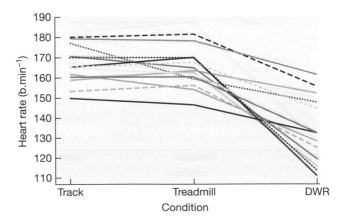

Figure 3.10 Case profile plot of Heart Rate at Lactate Threshold by Condition.

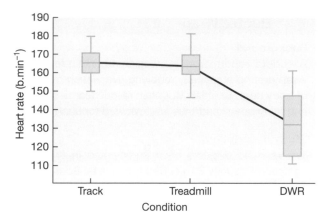

Figure 3.11 **Box plot of Heart Rate at Lactate Threshold for each Condition.**

Summary statistics (Box 3.6) are useful here to provide an impression of the typical changes across the Conditions.

Box 3.6

```
Descriptive Statistics: HR at Lact Thresh

Variable              Condition    N     Mean   StDev  Minimum        Q1  Median
HR at Lact Thresh     Track       15   165.99    8.96   149.80    160.04  165.50
                      Treadmill   15   164.57    9.02   146.56    159.48  163.60
                      DWR         15   132.24   16.73   110.71    115.16  132.00

Variable              Condition        Q3  Maximum
HR at Lact Thresh     Track        170.99   180.42
                      Treadmill    169.88   181.78
                      DWR          147.76   161.60
```

The sample mean Heart Rate at LT was highest for Track running (166 b.min^{-1}) followed by Treadmill running (165 b.min^{-1}), with the lowest sample mean for DWR (132 b.min^{-1}). The formal analysis for such designs is introduced in Chapter 9 and incorporates the important aspect that there are three responses for each subject.

Conclusion

This study suggests that mean Heart Rate at LT for well-trained male endurance runners is much lower in DWR than in track and treadmill running. It could therefore be concluded that the use of the same training heart rates for water and land running is inappropriate.

Reference: Coyle, J.R.L, Fairweather, S.C. (students), Grant, S., McCann, G. and MacIntyre P.D. (staff). (2002). 'A comparison of heart rate, rating of perceived exertion and stride frequency at lactate threshold during track, treadmill and deep water running.' University of Glasgow Sports Medicine student project.

The final example in this section involves two within-subject factors where a balanced design is used for only one factor while the second factor has a 'natural' ordering such as 'time' into study. Such a 'longitudinal' design is typical in sports and exercise research but this certainly does not apply to all two within-factor designs, however.

Illustration 3.7 **Bubble Wrap**

Background

Anecdotal reports from Norwegian mountain rescue teams suggest that a layer of Bubble Wrap around a casualty requiring evacuation from a mountain is useful in preventing loss of body heat. Scottish Mountain rescue teams currently use casualty bags which are bulky and fairly heavy and thus are awkward for such teams to transport to any accident.

Study description

Twelve male subjects each participated in two tests to compare a Bubble Wrap bag against a Casualty Bag currently in use by Scottish mountain rescue teams. Tests simulating weather conditions met in mountain rescue were carried out lying on a stretcher for 25 minutes in a cold ($-10°C$), windy (wind speed 2.7 m.s^{-1}) environment, separately for each bag. The design was such that half of the subjects were randomised to try out the Bubble Wrap first and the other half the Casualty Bag first. Reductions in Skin Temperature (averaged over four body sites) from the start of the study were recorded at 5-minute intervals throughout the test.

Aim

To investigate whether there is any difference in general in the Reduction in Skin Temperature between the two levels of Protection over the test duration under these simulated mountain weather conditions.

Data

Name of data file:	*Bubble Wrap*
Response variable:	Reduction in Skin Temperature (°C)
Within-subject factors:	Protection (2 levels: Bubble Wrap, Casualty Bag)
	Time (5 levels: 5, 10, 15, 20, 25 min)

Analysis

This design uses a single sample of 12 male subjects and incorporated two within-subject factors, namely Protection (with two levels) and Time (with five levels). Note that Protection is a within-factor as each individual had his skin temperature measured (across time) at *both* levels. If a different sample of males was used for each Protection, then Protection would then be a between-subject factor. Time itself is obviously a within-subject factor since each subject is measured at all five times with both Protections.

The response variable used is the Reduction in Skin Temperature, so the higher it becomes the colder the subject's skin is. It is essential to think clearly about the interpretation of any such response variable, e.g. if positive, what does this mean? A case profile plot of Reduction in Skin Temperature by Time separately for each Protection is given in Figure 3.12.

Each of the two sets of profiles is in general similar across subjects, although two subjects (i.e. numbers 5 and 9) tended to have a large initial decrease after 10 minutes when in the Casualty Bag but this disappears by 15 minutes, leaving the researcher wondering whether this was real or a mistake in the data recording. Clearly, the Bubble Wrap is much worse than the Casualty Bag as the subjects' skin temperature becomes much lower (and more quickly too) in the Bubble Wrap. The 'typical' overall pattern is perhaps clearer in box plots of Reduction in Skin Temperature with sample medians connected across time for each Protection (Figure 3.13).

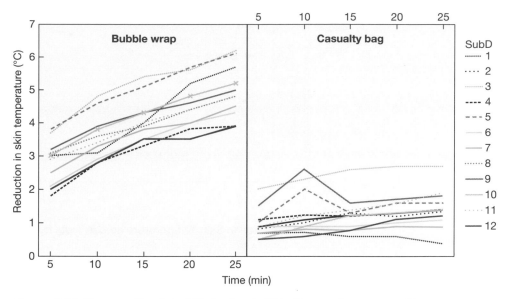

Figure 3.12 **Case profile plot of Reduction in Skin Temperature across Time.**

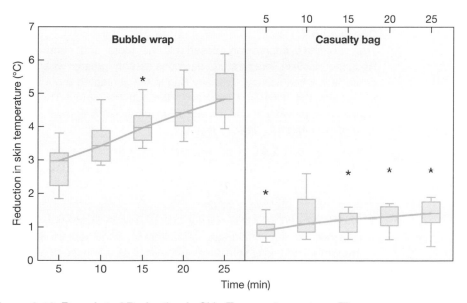

Figure 3.13 **Box plot of Reduction in Skin Temperature across Time.**

As the question of interest relates to determining the better overall protection, an additional graph that could be considered here is a plot of the sample mean Reduction in Skin Temperature connected across time for each bag superimposed on the one plot (Figure 3.14). The use of sample means is justified here as the box plots in Figure 3.13 all appear more or less symmetric and the assumption of Normality is relevant to the formal analysis introduced for such datasets in Chapter 10.

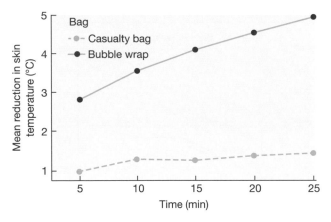

Figure 3.14 Mean Reduction in Skin Temperature across Time by Protection.

The effect of Time on Reduction in Skin Temperature, especially for Bubble Wrap, is apparent, but more importantly there is evidence that, in this sample, the Casualty Bag appears to outperform the Bubble Wrap by limiting the Reduction in Skin Temperature under such circumstances.

Conclusion

The subjective impression, based on the plots and summary statistics, is that the Reduction in Skin Temperature was considerably greater when using Bubble Wrap compared with when using a Casualty Bag in the simulated mountain rescue weather conditions, with the difference increasing through the study. The typical difference in skin temperature between the 'bags' after 5 minutes is 2°C in favour of the Casualty Bag, rising to approximately 4°C after 25 minutes.

Reference: Tsianos, G. (2004). 'Human responses to cold and hypoxia: implications for mountaineers.' PhD Thesis 13784, Glasgow University.

Additional comments on Illustration 3.7

1 The levels of (the within-subject factor) *Time* in Illustration 3.7 are strictly ordered (as opposed to the within-subject factor of Condition in Illustration 3.6–DWR/Track/Treadmill) and this is sometimes referred to as a 'longitudinal' factor.

2 One quick method to investigate whether there is an **Order effect** is to create a case profile plot for each Protection/Order (where Order indicates whether a specific Protection was used for the first or second test of a subject) combination and to see if there are any glaringly dissimilar profiles between the case profile plots of each Protection for each Order (Figure 3.15).

As Figure 3.15 shows, the case profile plots are quite similar for both Orders for each Protection, so it appears that the randomisation/balance worked out well. It is interesting to note that, of the two individuals who had a large initial decrease in skin temperature with the casualty bag, one used the casualty bag first and the other the casualty bag second, thus removing any suspicion that the protocol had in some way changed.

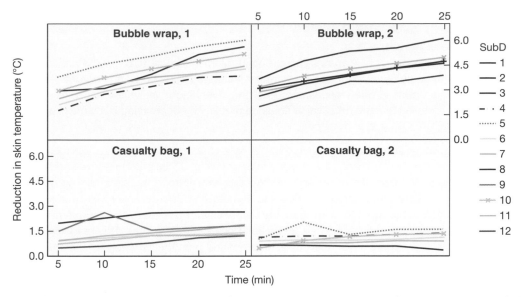

Figure 3.15 Case profile plot of Reduction in Skin Temperature across Time (with separate panels for each Protection/Order combination).

3.5 A sample of 18 full-time youth soccer players from a youth academy squad performed high-intensity aerobic interval training and neuromuscular strength training twice a week over a 10-week in-season period *in addition to* Normal soccer training and matches. Investigate whether this concurrent strength and endurance training intervention has improved the $\dot{V}O_2$ max of soccer players during the competitive in-season period by comparing the $\dot{V}O_2$ max from the start and the end of the season. The data are contained in the file *Training Intervention.*

3.6 Create a suitable case profile plot to investigate whether there is any evidence of a difference, on average, in Core Temperature Reductions between the methods of Protection under the simulated mountain weather conditions from the study described in Illustration 3.7. The data are contained in the file *Bubble Wrap.*

3.7 Designs with between-subject and within-subject factors

Probably the most commonly used design in sports and exercise science involves the use of one between-subject factor at two levels and one within-subject factor also at two levels (i.e. two independent samples of paired data) as described in Illustration 3.8. The approach needed in such designs often reduces to comparing the pairwise difference in the within-subject factor levels across the two levels of the between-subject factor (i.e. a two-sample comparison of the differences).

Illustration 3.8   Overweight women and exercise

Background

Being overweight is an ever-increasing problem in the western world. Problems associated with being overweight include a greater incidence of diabetes and coronary heart disease. One problem often encountered by the overweight is limited mobility. Exercise programmes have the potential to enhance mobility by decreasing body mass and by improving strength and endurance.

Study description

Twenty-six overweight (i.e. a body mass index of 25 or more) middle-aged females were randomly allocated as either an Exerciser or a Control. The Exercisers carried out a functional exercise programme (involving aerobic and strength exercises) for 12 weeks. One key variable used to investigate the usefulness of the exercise programme was the time taken for the women to walk 20 metres from a standing start. This response variable was one of a battery of variables measured pre and post the 12 weeks of the study.

Aim

To investigate the effect of a 12-week functional exercise programme for overweight women on 20 m Walking Time.

Data

Name of data file:	*20m Walk*
Response variable:	Walking Time (seconds)
Between-subject factor:	Regime (2 levels: Exercise, Control)
Within-subject factor:	Time (2 levels: Pre-Study, Post-Study)

Analysis

Start by creating a scatter plot of the Pre- and Post-Study Walking Times for each woman using a different label for the levels of Regime, i.e. the between-subject factor (Figure 3.16).

All of the Exercisers apart from one showed an improvement as their Pre-Study 20 m Walking Time is larger than their Post-Study 20 m Walking Time (i.e. points lie below the line of equality). Approximately half of the Controls did not improve in terms of 20 m Walking

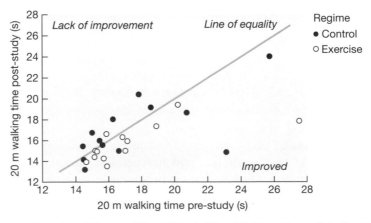

Figure 3.16 Scatter plot of Pre- and Post-Study 20 m Walking Times (labelled by Regime).

Time. There were two women, one on each treatment, who had considerably larger improvements than most. Both these subjects nearly halved their Walking Time over the study period.

As was seen in Illustration 3.5, it is in a sense 'natural' to use the differences between the Pre- and Post-Study 20 m Walking Times for each woman as long as any 'improvements' do not depend directly on the Pre-Study 20 m Walking Time. If the difference is calculated as 'Pre minus Post' Walking Times for each woman, then a positive difference represents an improvement (i.e. the time taken to walk 20 metres was less after, compared with before, the study). Summary statistics for the Differences in 20 m Walking Times, calculated in this manner, for the two samples are given in Box 3.7.

Box 3.7

```
Descriptive Statistics: Walk Difference (seconds)

Variable     Regime        N   Mean  StDev  Minimum      Q1  Median    Q3
Difference   Control      13  0.594  2.753   -2.540  -1.350  0.1301.720
             Exercise     13  1.666  2.558   -0.690   0.530  0.8501.810

Variable     Regime    Maximum
Difference   Control     8.320
             Exercise    9.750
```

These summary statistics provide reasonably convincing evidence that the exercise programme had a positive effect on most of the sample of women who undertook it. The typical improvement for the Exercisers, as evidence by the sample mean, is slightly over 1.6 seconds compared to around 0.5 second for the Controls. From the box plot of the differences (Figure 3.17) for each treatment, the majority of Exercisers demonstrate improvement. The typical improvement for the Controls was slightly above zero, with roughly equal proportions in the sample showing an improvement and a lack of improvement – a classical control performance.

When comparing the mean improvement for the two samples, an estimate of the likely exercise programme effect is given by the difference in the two sample mean improvements, i.e. $1.66 - 0.59 = 1.07$ seconds. What does a one-second improvement constitute to such women? As the Pre-Study walking times were typically 15 seconds, a one-second improvement represents a not insubstantial 6% improvement.

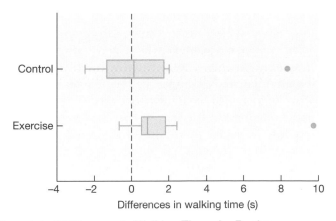

Figure 3.17 **Box plot of Difference in Walking Times by Regime.**

Conclusion

There is a strong suggestion that the exercise programme undertaken had a beneficial effect on the typical time taken to walk 20 metres in this sample of overweight middle-aged women. Those who undertook the exercise programme had a sample mean improvement of approximately 1 second *over* the Control sample. Such an improvement is of the order of magnitude of 6% given the typical 20 m Walking Times of such women.

Reference: Grant, S., Todd, K., Aitchison, T.C., Kelly, P. and Stoddart, D. (2004). 'The effects of a 12 week group exercise programme on physiological and psychological variables and function in elderly obese women.' *Journal of Public Health*, **118**, 31–42.

Additional comment on Illustration 3.8

The two women who made substantial improvements when compared to the others are highlighted as outliers in the box plots. In both cases the improvements recorded for these women will increase the sample mean improvement. The sample mean improvement when both women are excluded is −0.05 seconds for the Controls and 0.99 seconds for the Exercisers, a considerable drop of over half a second in each sample mean but leaving the difference of the difference in sample means between the treatments virtually unchanged (1.07 reduced to 1.04 seconds). As to whether these two women's results will have an overly important influence on the key question of interest, namely whether there is sufficient evidence in these samples to suggest a real improvement due to the exercise programme among overweight women, is an important question which will be returned to Chapters 4 and 5. Note further that not only do the outliers inflate the sample means but they also increase the sample standard deviations. The best approach if potential outliers appear in data is to analyse the data both with and without these outliers and compare the conclusions. In this case, the conclusions are likely to be very similar with and without these two subjects so there is no need to worry about whether to exclude these subjects or not.

Chapters 9, 10 and 11 describe and illustrate how to analyse designs incorporating both within-subject and between-subject factors. Suffice to say that the key graphs used there are the box plot and case profile plot.

3.8 Between-subject designs incorporating a covariate

In between-subject designs there can often be other continuous explanatory variables (called **covariates**) which are known or thought likely to influence the (response) variable of interest for each subject/observational unit. For example, in a longitudinal study comparing two different diets (the between-subject factor) in terms of increased basal metabolic rate (BMR), such a covariate could be an individual's body mass at the start of the study period. If the covariate does influence the response variable, then adjusting for this will improve the comparison of the between-subject factor (i.e. improve precision of estimates).

A suitable approach to summarising data from such a scenario is as follows:

1 Provide the usual summary statistics for the response variable (and for the covariate) such as the sample mean, median, minimum, maximum, standard deviation separately for each level of the between-subject factor.

2 Provide a **labelled scatter plot** of the response variable on the vertical (y) axis and the covariate on the horizontal (x) axis with a different symbol for each level of the between-subject factor.

Illustration 3.9   Grip strength

Background

In the sport of rock climbing the steeper the rock face is, generally, the more difficult the climb is graded. Climbs are graded from Moderate to Extreme (E), with E1 being the easiest climb on this E scale. A grading of Severe is between Moderate and Extreme and is not deemed to be a high climbing standard. It is reasonable to speculate that high levels of climbing-specific finger strength and perhaps grip strength are of great importance in elite climbing.

Study description

Independent samples of 10 Elite* (i.e. have successfully completed a climbing standard of E1 in the last 12 months), 10 Recreational (i.e. have successfully completed a climb no harder than Severe in the last 12 months) and 10 non-climbers (i.e. Controls) had the Grip Strength of their (dominant) right hand measured, as well as having their Body Mass recorded. All subjects were male.

*Termed elite in this study but the subjects are not at the highest level.

Aim

To compare average Grip Strength of the (dominant) right hand among the three populations of male climbers while adjusting for Body Mass if necessary.

Data

Name of data file:	*Grip Strength and Mass*
Response variable:	Grip Strength (newtons)
Between-subject factor:	Climber Type (3 levels: Control, Recreational, Elite)
Covariate:	Body Mass (kilograms)

Analysis

Start by providing box plots (Figure 3.18) and summary statistics (Box 3.8) of Grip Strength for each level of Climber Type.

There appears to be evidence of some moderate differences among the Climber Types with Elite climbers the strongest in terms of Grip Strength but even these are not clearly different from the Controls.

Box 3.8

```
Variable      Type           N    Mean   StDev  Minimum     Q1  Median      Q3
Strength(N)   Control       10   475.6    63.0    367.7   432.7   468.3   521.0
              Elite         10   555.1    96.5    387.4   454.8   605.6   623.9
              Recreational  10   490.3    85.1    353.0   410.7   519.8   563.9

Variable      Type        Maximum
Strength(N)   Control       588.4
              Elite         661.9
              Recreational  593.3
```

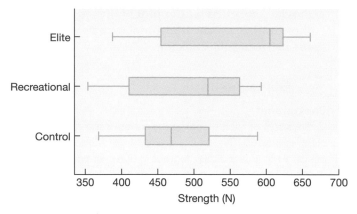

Figure 3.18 **Box plot of Grip Strength by Climber Type.**

The sample means and medians are quite similar within each Climber Type (although there is slight evidence of a lack of symmetry in the Grip Strength distribution in the Elite climber group). There are no outliers identified and therefore using the sample mean to summarise Grip Strength looks appropriate for the samples of Control and Recreational climbers. There is a noticeable skew in Grip Strength in the sample of Elite climbers, however. The subjective impression appears to be that Grip Strength, in general, is marginally highest for Elite climbers, but Grip Strength, in general, does not appear to be different for Recreational climbers and Controls.

However, it is important to consider the possibility that Grip Strength is dependent on Body Mass in order to improve the comparisons across Climber Types. To investigate this, provide a scatter plot of Grip Strength and Body Mass with separate labels for Climber Type (Figure 3.19).

From this plot a strong relationship between Grip Strength and Body Mass can clearly be seen and applies to all three Climbing Types. Further, it appears that, at almost all values of Body Mass from 55 to 90 kg, the Elite climbers have greater Grip Strength than either of the other two Types.

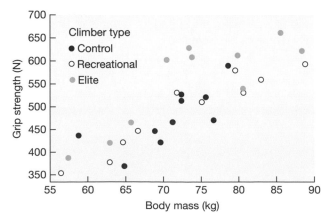

Figure 3.19 **Scatter plot of Grip Strength and Body Mass (labelled by Climber Type).**

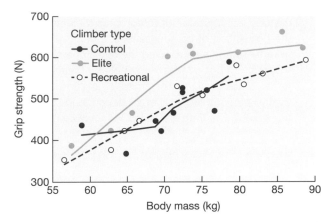

Figure 3.20 Scatter plot of Grip Strength and Body Mass (labelled by Climber Type with separate smoothers for each sample).

An indication of the dependency of the response variable on the covariate can be achieved by including a **smoother** to the plot for each level of the between-subject factor. A smoother provides an indication of the likely trend across 'bands' of the data moving from left to right across the horizontal axis. These 'bands' are then 'pasted' together in a mathematically smooth manner to give an indication of the overall trend (Figure 3.20).

The benefit of a smoother is that it allows the data to 'suggest' the likely dependence of the response on the covariate, which will aid in determining the likely relationship (e.g. a line, a quadratic curve etc.) to be used in modelling this relationship. There are similar relationships in Figure 3.20 for controls and Recreational climbers but the advantage of the Elite climbers over these others seems, if anything, to increase with increasing Body Mass.

Conclusion

Adjusting Grip Strength for Body Mass seems worthwhile and it appears, on adjustment, that Elite climbers do have considerably greater Grip Strength on average than either of the other two Climber Types who appear similar in Grip Strength profile. Any formal analysis to decide whether there is sufficient evidence to claim an actual difference in population mean Grip Strength would have to incorporate both Body Mass and Climber Type.

Formal methods for correcting or adjusting for potential covariates are introduced and illustrated in Chapter 7.

Reference: Grant, S., Hynes, V., Whittaker, A. and Aitchison, T. (1996). 'Anthropometric, strength, endurance and flexibility characteristics of elite and recreational climbers.' *Journal of Sports Sciences*, **14**: 301–309.

Exercises

3.7 Revisit the *BMR* data introduced in Exercise 3.4 and create a scatter plot of Body Mass on BMR with a separate label for each of the two diets. Does it appear that a woman's BMR is dependent upon her Body Mass? Is there any graphical evidence in the labelled scatter plot of a likely difference in BMR across the two diets when taking a woman's Body Mass into consideration?

3.8 A study was carried out to compare male and female physiological responses and the perception of breathlessness during Normoxic and Hypoxic exercise. The data from the study also allowed the researchers to investigate the dependence of (raw) $\dot{V}O_2$ max on Body Mass separately for Males and Females. Data for 10 males and 9 females are available for analysis. Is there any graphical evidence in the labelled scatter plot of a likely different dependence of (raw) $\dot{V}O_2$ max on Body Mass across the sexes? The data are called *VO_2 max by Sex*.

3.9 Modelling relationships (correlation and regression)

A common problem in sports and exercise science is to investigate whether two variables measured on the same subject are related in any way. Relationships between a pair of variables can involve two completely different interpretations. The first of these is where there is a *link* between the two variables but there is *no causal relationship*; a child's physical activity level midweek may be related to his/her weekend physical activity levels, but his/her midweek activity should, in general, have no influence on his/her weekend physical activity and vice versa. Neither variable has a specific 'role'. This is called a **correlation** problem.

In the second scenario there is a clear distinction between the specific roles played by the two variables; the key variable of interest (usually called the **response variable**) is assumed to be dependent upon the other (so-called) **explanatory variable**. For example, an oarsman's rowing time over 5000 m (the response variable) may be explained to a greater or lesser extent by his stroke length (the explanatory variable). It makes no sense to reverse the roles of these variables, i.e. to assume 5000 m rowing influences stroke length. The label 'response' variable has been used in many different contexts up to now as an identifier of the key variable of interest in a study. It is always used in this type of problem to refer to the variable (e.g. 5000 m rowing time) whose dependency on the explanatory variable is to be modelled. This scenario is referred to as a **regression** problem.

Regardless of which of these types of problem (i.e. correlation or regression) is pertinent to the example at hand, a single (hopefully random or representative) sample is obtained from a population of interest and the two continuous variables of interest measured for each subject. A new summary statistic is needed to describe the degree of relationship between these two variables.

The **population correlation coefficient** measures the linear dependence of two *continuous* variables. This can take values from −1 to +1, with the value zero corresponding to 'no linear relationship' between the two variables and +1 corresponding to the perfect (positive) linear relationship (i.e. if the value of one variable is high then the other variable will also be high). Naturally enough, the value −1 corresponds to the perfect negative relationship, with a high value of one variable always being associated with a low value of the other variable, and vice versa. In general, the closer to either −1 or +1 the population correlation coefficient, the stronger the relationship between the two variables.

A population correlation of above 0 but less than 0.5 could be considered a weak positive correlation, 0.5 to 0.8 a moderate positive correlation and above 0.8 a strong positive correlation. The same applies in the negative direction: a population correlation below 0 but above −0.5 signifies a weak negative relationship, −0.5 to −0.8 a moderate negative correlation and below −0.8 a strong negative correlation.

The corresponding summary statistic based on the data is called the **sample correlation coefficient** which naturally also takes values between −1 and +1 and, as may seem obvious, the sample correlation coefficient is used to estimate the (unknown) population correlation coefficient. At this stage all that is required is an appreciation that the sample correlation coefficient provides a measure of the *magnitude* and *direction* of the degree of *linear relationship* in the sample which can be used to provide an estimate of the likely magnitude of the linear relationship in the population of interest. The correlation coefficient is often misused in the interpretation of statistical analyses and will be considered in greater detail in Chapter 6 which deals exclusively with modelling the relationship between variables.

The following illustration involves summarising the relationship, if any, between physical activity levels in children measured (on a continuous scale) midweek and at the weekend. The scatter plot is the appropriate plot for such a scenario where there is no meaningful causal relationship.

Illustration 3.10   Physical activity in children

Background

Low levels of physical activity (PA) are considered to be a major factor in the obesity epidemic in young children at the present time. There is a need to measure PA in young children for a number of reasons including the assessment of interventions and the comparison of different populations. Accelerometers are now commonly used to measure PA. They can be used to monitor total PA. Accelerometers are small, lightweight and attached to the waist with a belt. In this study an Actigraph accelerometer was used which measures movement mainly in the vertical plane and the output is given in digital counts.

Study description

In a study of the PA of modern-day children under 5 years of age, each of a random sample of 76 pre-school children from the West of Scotland had his or her PA measured (using an accelerometer) on a Saturday and Wednesday within seven days of each other. Half of the children had their PA measured midweek and again on the following weekend while the remaining half were measured on a weekend and then the midweek following.

Aim

To examine the relationship, if any, between a child's PA, as measured by an accelerometer, midweek and at the weekend.

Data

    Name of data file: *Activity*
    Variables of interest: Midweek PA (counts per minute)
                           Weekend PA (counts per minute)

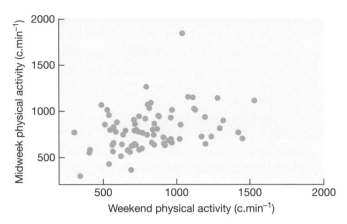

Figure 3.21 **Scatter plot of Midweek and Weekend Physical Activity in children.**

Analysis

Prepare a scatter plot (Figure 3.21) of the two variables; the choice of which variable to place on the either axis is completely arbitrary. In this particular example, it makes sense to use an identical scale on both axes as both variables are measuring the activity of the same child.

The plot suggests that the two variables have a weak positive relationship where Midweek PA tends to be high when the Weekend PA is also high. Those who were quite inactive midweek tend to be quite inactive at the weekend. There is considerable variability, however, in the overall pattern and so there is far from a perfect linear relationship between the two variables. There is one child (at the top of the plot) who was the extremely active midweek but only moderately active at the weekend.

The sample correlation coefficient (often known as the **Pearson correlation**) between the two PA measures is 0.34 for this sample, suggesting a positive linear relationship, albeit not very strong.

Conclusion

There appears to be, at best, a moderate positive relationship between midweek and weekend physical activity in children, when measured using an accelerometer.

Reference: Penpraze, V., Reilly, J.J., Montgomery, C., Kelly, L.A., Paton, J.Y., Aitchison, T. and Grant, S. (2006). 'Monitoring of physical activity by accelerometry in young children: how much is enough?' *Pediatric Exercise Science*, **18**: 483–491.

Additional comments on Illustration 3.10

1 There is no basis whatsoever to claim any causal relationship between the two variables in Illustration 3.10, particularly given that the order in which the data were recorded was not the same for all children – some were recorded first midweek then on the weekend while the reverse was true for the remainder.

2 It can be misleading to make an assessment on the strength of relationship between two variables of interest based on the sample correlation alone. The sample correlation is a function of the sample size and the range of values from which the data have been collected. Chapter 6 presents a method for 'translating' the sample correlation coefficient into a statement of the likely population correlation coefficient (the key parameter of interest) upon which a judgement as to the magnitude of the (linear) relationship can be made based on the guidelines given earlier in this chapter.

The next illustration shows a 'cause and effect' type relationship among middle-distance runners involving a response variable (i.e. 3 km Running Time) and a single explanatory variable (i.e. a derived variable based on blood lactate level of a runner).

Illustration 3.11   3 km Running times

Background
Laboratory tests have been used extensively to provide information about the relationship between physiological markers and distance running performance. Sub-maximal blood lactate variables are commonly used as such physiological markers, e.g. the running velocity required to raise the blood lactate to a predetermined concentration such as 4 mmol.L^{-1}.

Study description
Sixteen well-trained middle distance runners performed a 3 km time trial on an indoor 200 m track and an incremental running test on a treadmill from which the running velocity (km.h^{-1}) at a blood lactate concentration of 4 mmol.L^{-1} (v-4mM) was determined using interpolation.

Aim
To investigate the dependence, if any, of 3 km track running time on laboratory-measured running velocity (v-4mM) among well-trained middle distance runners.

Data
    Name of data file: *3 KRunning*
    Response variable: 3 km Running Time (minutes)
    Explanatory variable: v-4mM (km.h^{-1})

Analysis
Start by preparing a scatter plot with the response variable 3 km Time on the vertical (*y*) axis and the explanatory variable, v-4mM, on the horizontal (*x*) axis (see Figure 3.22).

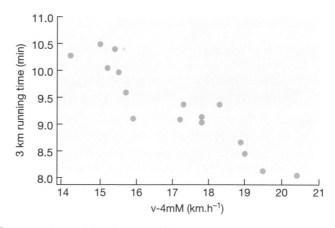

Figure 3.22 **Scatter plot of 3 km Running Time and v-4mM.**

The subjective impression from the scatter plot is that faster (i.e. lower) 3 km times are achieved by individuals with higher v-4mM scores. The general pattern, across the range of v-4mM in the sample, is plausibly linear. The sample correlation between the two variables is −0.926, suggesting a strong negative relationship between these two variables.

Conclusion

There is evidence of a strong negative linear dependence of 3 km time on blood lactate concentration of 4 mmol.L^{-1} in the sample of runners provided. Note that if this population relationship also applies at the individual level then it appears that improvements in an athlete's running velocity at a blood lactate concentration of 4 mmol.L^{-1} would result in lower (i.e. quicker) 3 km finishing times.

Reference: Grant, S., Craig, I., Wilson, J. and Aitchison, T. (1997). 'The relationship between 3 km running performance and selected physiological variables.' *Journal of Sports Sciences*, **15**: 403–410.

The next illustration highlights that care must be taken when using a correlation coefficient to summarise the relationship between two variables of interest (in both correlation and regression problems) when in fact the sample consists of data pooled from different populations.

Illustration 3.12 — Power and body mass

Background

Anaerobic power tests involve all-out effort and take place over relatively short periods of time, where power is defined as the rate of work per unit time. An assessment of anaerobic power can be made using a number of different procedures, one of which is the Wingate test. After a warm-up the subject pedals as fast as possible on a cycle ergometer against a predetermined resistance for 30 seconds. The Wingate test score used here is the maximum power attained in any of the six blocks of 5 seconds.

Study description

Fifteen female and 15 male subjects had a warm-up on a cycle ergometer followed by a Wingate test. The Peak Power output achieved by each subject was recorded, as was the Body Mass at the start of the test.

Aim

To investigate whether Anaerobic Power (as assessed by the Wingate test) is dependent upon the Body Mass of an individual.

Data

Name of data file: *Power*
Response variable: Anaerobic Power (watts)
Explanatory variable: Body Mass (kilograms)

Analysis

Create a scatter plot (Figure 3.23) with the response variable, Anaerobic Power, on the vertical (y) axis and the explanatory variable Body Mass on the horizontal (x) axis. Incorporate a smoother to visually assess the type of dependence of the response on the explanatory variable.

The sample correlation coefficient between Anaerobic Power and Body Mass is 0.851. This could be interpreted that a strong positive linear relationship exists between the two variables and that a person's Anaerobic Power has a strong positive dependence upon

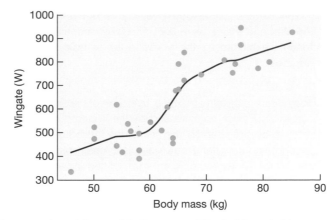

Figure 3.23 Scatter plot of Anaerobic Power and Body Mass (with a smoother).

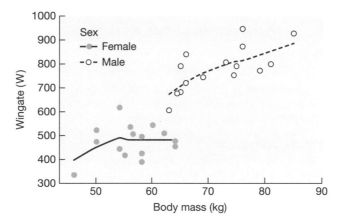

Figure 3.24 Scatter plot of Anaerobic Power and Body Mass (with a separate smoother for each Sex).

Body Mass. Care, however, must be taken as the correlation coefficient is only applicable in assessing the degree of *linear* relationship between two variables. There is evidence here based on the smoother that the relationship may not be linear as there appears to be a 'jump' for individuals with a Body Mass over 60 kg. A labelled scatter plot (Figure 3.24) of the Anaerobic Power and Body Mass data with separate symbols for Males and Females shows why this has occurred.

The 'jump' evident in the scatter plot of the sample as a whole is clearly due to sex. The dependence of Anaerobic Power on Body Mass appears much weaker for Females (who have lower Body Mass anyway) than for Males – at least in these subjects. Males tend to have higher Anaerobic Power (than Females), partly explained by their increased Body Mass. The dependency of Anaerobic Power on Body Mass appears moderately linear for Males. Females tend to show little relationship, if any, between Anaerobic Power and Body Mass although there is one female with a lower Anaerobic Power score for her Body Mass compared with the general pattern for Females, which makes the overall pattern for Females look non-constant at low Body Mass.

The sample correlation coefficients between Anaerobic Power and Body Mass for Females and Males were 0.21 and 0.69, respectively, highlighting the more positive relationship exhibited by the Males in the sample and the weak relationship, if any, for the Females.

Conclusion

Body Mass appears to be a useful explanatory variable in 'explaining' an individual's Anaerobic Power, as assessed by the Wingate test. Incorporating the additional valuable information provided by the sex of the individual is clearly necessary when exploring the dependence between Body Mass and Anaerobic Power, as measured by the Wingate test, with Males showing a different form of dependence from that shown by Females.

Reference: University of Glasgow Physiology and Sports Science Laboratory session.

The final example of this chapter involves a sample where data were collected to validate a 'historically reputed' relationship between two variables of interest in a regression context.

Illustration 3.13   Maximum heart rate and age

Background

Exercise guidelines suggest that carrying out aerobic exercise for 20 minutes at least three times a week at between 60% and 90% of an individual's maximum heart rate is likely to maintain or improve aerobic fitness. An individual's maximum heart rate is often estimated as '220 minus the age of the individual'.

Study description

A sample of 26 physically active males underwent an incremental treadmill exercise test to volitional exhaustion. The Maximum Heart Rate (max HR) of each subject during this test was recorded as was his Age.

Aim

To investigate whether the Maximum Heart Rate of individuals is indeed on average equal to 220 minus the Age of the individual.

Data

Name of data file:	*Max Heart Rate*
Response variable:	Maximum Heart Rate (b.min^{-1})
Explanatory variable:	Age (years)

Analysis

A scatter plot of Maximum Heart Rate against Age with the line representing Max HR = 220 − Age is given in Figure 3.25.

Maximum Heart Rate is the response variable of interest and Age is the explanatory variable here. The reverse makes little sense no matter how nice it would be if, by reducing a subject's Maximum Heart Rate, the subject's Age could also be decreased.

If the proposed relationship between Maximum Heart Rate and Age was indeed exact, all of the data points would fall on the 'reputed' line. This is clearly not the case. However, the variability in Maximum Heart Rate *about* the 'reputed' line is similar across the somewhat restricted range of ages (20–25-year-olds) and there is some suggestion that, *on average*, this relationship is plausible as, to an extent, the data follow a roughly symmetrical pattern above and below this 'reputed' line.

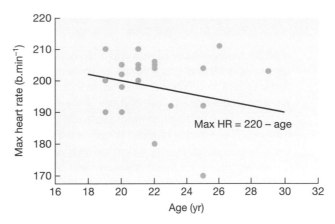

Figure 3.25 **Scatter plot of Maximum Heart Rate and Age.**

Conclusion

The 'reputed' relationship that Max HR = 220 – Age does not perfectly model Maximum Heart Rate on an individual level. There is a suggestion that the relationship may be true 'on average' but with a reasonably large level of variability of Maximum Heart Rate at any age.

Reference: Grant, S., Corbett, K., Amjad, A., Wilson, J. and Aitchison, T. (1995). 'A comparison of methods of predicting maximum oxygen uptake.' *British Journal of Sports Medicine,* 29: 147–152.

Additional comment on Illustration 3.13

Rather than imposing the (linear) '220 minus age' dependency of Maximum Heart Rate on Age, a smoother could be included on the scatter plot to see what dependence the data 'suggest' between the two variables of interest (Figure 3.26).

From the plot, it appears that, across the range of ages in this sample, there is little evidence of any dependence of Maximum Heart Rate on Age at all.

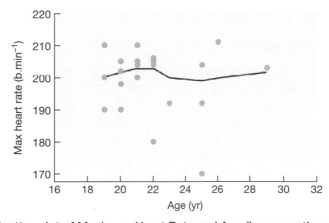

Figure 3.26 **Scatter plot of Maximum Heart Rate and Age (incorporating a smoother).**

Exercises

3.9 A direct measurement of maximum oxygen uptake ($\dot{V}O_2$ max) is commonly made using treadmill and gas analysis equipment. As this equipment is expensive and requires skilled personnel, alternative indirect methods for 'estimating' $\dot{V}O_2$ max have been developed. One of these is the Cooper walk/run test. In this test, subjects are asked to cover as much distance as possible in 12 minutes by walking or running. The distance covered is converted into a score for maximum oxygen uptake. Twenty-six physically active males took part in the study which involved both a Cooper test and a direct measurement of $\dot{V}O_2$ max where the subject ran on a treadmill until volitional exhaustion and his expired air was collected in a Douglas bag. Is there any suggestion of a substantial correlation between the Cooper test estimate of $\dot{V}O_2$ max and the direct measurement of this from the treadmill? The dataset is called *VO$_2$Test*.

3.10 Revisit the *3KRunning* data introduced in Illustration 3.11 and investigate whether $\dot{V}O_2$ max is, itself, a useful explanatory variable of 3 km Running Time among middle distance runners.

Summary

Spending time exploring the data available will always be worthwhile for the conscientious researcher. Suitable graphical techniques were presented in this chapter for exploring and summarising data arising from between- and within-subject designs (as well as combinations of these) and for contexts where the relationship between two variables is of primary concern.

All of the techniques presented in this chapter allow the researcher to provide a subjective impression regarding the key question(s) under consideration. However, formal techniques to establish an objective answer to the key question(s) are needed and will be the focus of the remaining chapters.

Technical appendix

Histogram

- One simple method to investigate the possible *shape* of a population distribution is to group the sample data into 'bins' (i.e. intervals) of equal width and then to count the number of observations in each bin. A **histogram** plots the frequency (count) of observations in a particular bin of the variable of interest against the central value of that bin. A histogram of the Haemoglobin Concentration for the sample of elite female athletes in Exercise 3.2 is given in Figure 3.27 with the bins as ≤11.5, 11.5 to 12.5, . . . , ≥14.5.

- If the variable of interest in the sample appears to be distributed in a symmetrical manner, it is plausible that the population distribution from which it arose was symmetrical. This appears to be the case in Figure 3.27. Why is symmetry so

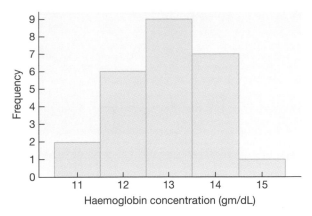

Figure 3.27 **Histogram of Haemoglobin Concentration (elite female athletes).**

important? The foundation of most statistical inference is based on an important symmetrical distribution, namely the Normal distribution – it was mentioned at the start of this chapter and it is about time it was formally introduced.

Normal distribution

- The Normal distribution (or Normal probability model) has a long history, dating to early work by de Moivre in 1733 and Gauss in 1794. Up to recently, a picture of Gauss and an illustration of the Normal distribution appeared on the German 10 Mark banknote. The distribution plays an important role in many applications in statistics as many samples follow this distribution. The distribution is fully described by two (population) parameters: a population mean and a population standard deviation. There is a family of Normal distributions characterised by all possible pairs of these two parameters. Indeed, the population mean and standard deviation alone provide sufficient information to completely specify a Normal distribution. As an illustration, the density curve for a Normal distribution with a population mean of 100 and a population standard deviation of 10 is given in Figure 3.28. The scale on the vertical axis has been hidden for convenience; suffice to say that it provides a measure of the proportion of the population contained in any interval on the *x*-axis.

- The shape of the Normal distribution is best described as bell shaped, symmetrical and having a single peak. The population mean is the middle of the distribution and it should therefore be no surprise that the population mean is equal to the population median for all Normal distributions.

- In the Normal distribution in Figure 3.28, the population proportion (i.e. the area under the curve) between 90 and 110 (i.e. the population mean ± one population standard deviation) appears to be larger than 50%. It is in fact closer to 68% regardless, in fact, of the actual population mean and population standard deviation. By moving out one additional standard deviation in either direction (i.e. another 10 units left and right and hence covering the range 80 to 120) it appears

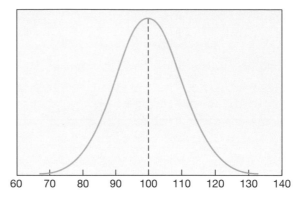

Figure 3.28 **An example of a Normal distribution.**

that the vast majority of the population are contained in this interval. The actual population proportion covered by this range is now in fact close to 95%.

● These are the general properties for any Normal distribution:
  ● Approximately 68% of the population are within 1 population standard deviation of the population mean.
  ● Approximately 95.5% of the population are within 2 population standard deviations of the population mean.
  ● Approximately 99.7% of the population are within 3 population standard deviations of the population mean.
  These properties apply only to Normal distributions.

● Figure 3.29 depicts two Normal distributions with the same population mean but different population standard deviations. Increasing the standard deviation corresponds to holding the two tails of the distribution and pulling them out symmetrically in both directions, decreasing the standard deviation corresponds to pushing the tails inwards and forcing the distribution closer to the mean.

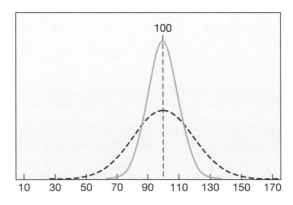

Figure 3.29 **Normal distributions (equal mean, different standard deviation).**

- If the data had really arisen from a Normal probability model then the sample is very likely to have similar properties to the population. For example, using the second property above, four times the sample standard deviation (i.e. two standard deviations on either side of the mean) should be roughly equivalent to the range of most (95%) of the data. This gives a simple arithmetical approximation that the sample standard deviation will be roughly one-quarter of the sample range. This result can be useful in estimating the sample standard deviation (needed for power calculations to guesstimate sample sizes for future studies) in published literature when only the sample median and range are provided. Of course, some evidence, typically graphical, of symmetry in the data should be present before applying this rough approximation. The approximation proves quite accurate using the Mont Blanc Ascent Time summary statistics (Illustration 3.1). The sample range was 3.83 hours and hence a quarter of this is 3.83/4 = 0.96 hours which is comparable to the actual sample standard deviation of 0.82 hours.

- A common misconception is to claim that 'the sample was Normally distributed' when in fact the correct statement is that the sample *arose* from a population which was Normally distributed. This is an important concept in statistics and often causes confusion. Listen out at the next conference for the amount of times that presenters claim that their samples are Normally distributed! In summary, if there is evidence of symmetry in the histogram and box plot as well as the sample mean and median being roughly equal, then the assumption that the sample arose from a Normal distribution will not be unreasonable. (Note the classic double negative statement often used by statisticians!)

- A natural question that might now arise is what patterns would be expected in a histogram or box plot that would cast doubt on the data having been generated by a Normal distribution. As an illustration, data were simulated from a Normal distribution in order to get a feel for the types of patterns that may arise. Following on from this, data simulated from non-symmetrical distributions were displayed and salient features in the accompanying histograms and box plots discussed.

- Four sets of data of increasing sample size have been generated from a population that was Normally distributed with mean 50 and standard deviation 5 (the shorthand for which is N(50, 5)). Note, from the histograms in Figure 3.30, that, as the sample size increases, the data appear more symmetrical. The histogram of the sample of size 60 ($n = 60$) is quite symmetrical and the sample mean is close to 50.

  There is some symmetry evident in the sample of size 30, but less so for the smallest sample of size 10. Box plots of the four samples are given in Figure 3.31 with the widths of the box plots proportional to the square root of sample size – a conventional way of 'adding' sample size to box plots of samples of different sizes.

  The sample median varies from sample to sample but all are quite close to the true median of 50. The interquartile range (IQR) is quite similar for the two larger samples and there is evidence of symmetry in each of these samples. Note that an observation has been flagged as an outlier in the sample of size 60 even though such an observation was generated from, and hence is an entirely plausible member of, this population.

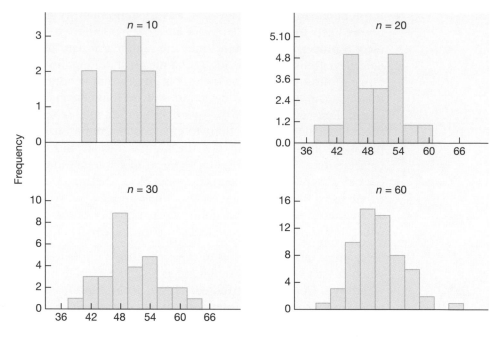

Figure 3.30 **Histograms of simulated data from a Normal distribution N(50, 5).**

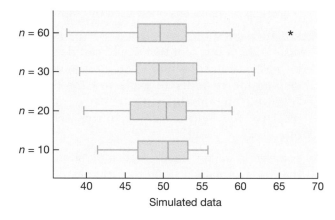

Figure 3.31 **Box plots of simulated data from a Normal distribution N(50, 5) (box width is proportional to sample size).**

- Be careful in judging the likely shape of the population distribution using a box plot alone, as the example in Figure 3.32 shows. Data were simulated from distributions that are symmetrical but clearly not Normally distributed, as the histograms show.

The distribution in the top left is an example of what is termed a **mixture distribution** (i.e. two separate populations such as Males and Females lumped together), while the data in the top right were generated from a distribution called a **uniform**

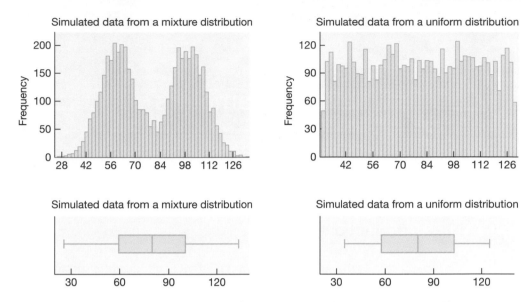

Figure 3.32 **Histograms and box plots of simulated data from mixture and uniform distributions.**

distribution (i.e. any value in the range of the variable is 'equally likely'). The interesting point is that looking at the box plot alone may well have resulted in an (incorrect) decision that the data arose from a Normal distribution. This example highlights the need to consider both a histogram and a box plot when assessing Normality or, better still, some more formal approach such as those featured in Chapter 5.

4 Estimating parameters

4.1 Introduction

Statistics is the subject of drawing inferences about some summary aspect of a population (i.e. a population parameter) based on a representative sample of the population. It is very unlikely that the researcher will ever have the time, enthusiasm or budget to carry out a census study (i.e. collect data on all members of a population) and he/she will instead have to rely on a (hopefully representative) sample of the population on which to base any inference.

The provision of a clear and useful subjective impression based on appropriate summary statistics and graphs is the first important step in handling any dataset. The previous chapter presented illustrations of how best to summarise a sample of data, both numerically and graphically, across a variety of common contexts in sports and exercise science. In each context, the most 'suitable' summary statistic was chosen and this depends crucially on the assumed probability model underlying the response variable of interest in the population. Throughout this chapter, and indeed much of this book, the assumption is made that each population can be adequately represented as a **Normal probability model** or **Normal distribution** and consequently interest will lie in **population means** as the relevant population parameters of interest. This assumption will, of course, have to be justified in all cases before any final conclusions can be drawn from any dataset.

Once this Normal model assumption has been justified, formal techniques are required that will allow (sample) estimates of the population means to be made that incorporate the natural variability produced from taking (random) samples. These involve mathematical ideas beyond the scope of this book and, in fact, are of little value in aiding understanding of the basic ideas of inference. What is important is that the assumed model can be used to quantify the likely variability in sample means (of the same sample size as that observed) across potentially different samples and hence the 'error' that will accrue from estimating a population mean from the actual observed sample of data from that underlying Normal population. This is the basis of the formal statistical model underlying this and subsequent chapters.

Interval estimation

Many of the questions considered in sports and exercise science research involve the estimation of population means. The sample mean is the best estimate of the population mean. If a different sample of the same size were taken, it is virtually certain that the corresponding estimate (sample mean) would be different for this and indeed any other sample (of the same size).

Every sample statistic involves some aspect of 'error' when used as an estimate of a population parameter. This 'error' is composed of two elements: sampling variability and poor sample design. The second of these can often be controlled and dramatically improved by implementing a sound study design as described in Chapter 2. There is, however, only limited control regarding sampling variability. Statistical theory provides a framework for combining a sample statistic and its sampling variability into a range of values likely to contain the population parameter (i.e. an **interval estimate**) rather than a single point estimate such as the sample mean. This often involves quantification of the so-called **estimated standard error** (*e.s.e.*) of the point estimate. *Interval estimation will be the most important tool in the researcher's statistical toolbox*. It is crucial that the researcher is able to interpret such interval estimates, understand exactly what information such intervals provide and appreciate the 'terms and conditions' that apply to such intervals.

For example, an estimate of the 'typical' Ascent Time for Mont Blanc was made using the sample mean from the data provided in Illustration 3.1. A different sample would have provided a different estimate/sample mean. So what is required is an (interval) estimate based on a range of values that takes into account this variability due to sampling. In Illustration 3.8, the 'benefit' of exercise for overweight women was estimated by the difference in the sample mean improvements in balance for the Exercisers over the Controls. A natural question to ask is whether the difference between the sample means is large enough to suggest an actual difference is present in the population of overweight women. Could it be that the numerical difference in sample means is due to natural variability in such samples and therefore not reflective of a 'real' difference in population means due to exercise? This chapter provides the methods needed to deal with these and many similar questions considered in sports and exercise science research. The end point in all such analyses is to provide a **range of values** for the parameter of interest (or difference of such) from which clear and suitable conclusions can be drawn.

Illustrations now follow on the basic and most common problems in sports and exercise science using data introduced in the previous chapter as well as some new datasets relevant to this chapter. In particular, the contexts covered involve the estimation of:

1 a single population mean;

2 the difference between two population means from separate samples (between-subject design involving a single factor at two levels);

3 the difference between two population means for paired data (within-subject design involving a single factor at two levels);

4 the difference between two population mean differences from separate samples (one between- and one within-subject factor each at two levels).

4.3 Interval estimation for a population mean

The sample mean is the best 'point' estimate available of the population mean of interest – it is, however, highly unlikely to equal the population mean exactly. An extension to a point estimate is an **interval estimate**, a range of values likely to contain the population parameter. Such an interval, often referred to as a **confidence interval**, is dictated by an arbitrary choice of 'confidence' which, by convention, is typically chosen to be 95% (see the technical appendix at the end of this chapter for more discussion on this). For example, a 95% confidence interval (CI) for a population mean is of the form:

Sample mean $\pm$ 2 * e.s.e. of the sample mean

where the e.s.e. (i.e. estimated standard error) of the sample mean is calculated by the sample standard deviation divided by the square root of the sample size. The e.s.e. provides an estimate as to the precision of the sample statistic: the larger the e.s.e. the less precise the statistic (in this case the sample mean) as an estimate of the corresponding parameter (in this case the population mean).

A 95% confidence interval ensures that, in repeated sampling, 95% of intervals produced by such a method will contain the true (but unknown) population parameter – almost always regardless of the value of this population parameter. Strictly speaking, nothing can be said about any actual, observed (95%) confidence interval, other than that such a method will often 'catch' the true value in the interval.

Statistical software, when possible, produces confidence intervals which are based not on the simple rule of 'twice the e.s.e.' but on the percentage point of the distributions known to describe the variability in the sample statistic under the assumed probability model (i.e. Student's t-distributions in the case of Normal models). For moderate and large sample sizes these are almost invariably very close to 2.

One important consideration that is typically required when a confidence interval for a population mean is calculated is that the variable of interest is Normally distributed in the population from which the sample arose. The graphical techniques for assessing Normality presented in the previous chapter will play an important role here to assess whether this assumption is reasonable or adequate.

When the key question of interest is to estimate a population mean from a single sample of data from a Normal distribution, the full analysis can be summarised as follows:

1 Provide summary statistics and a box plot of the variable of interest.

2 Investigate whether the variable of interest is likely to have arisen from a Normal distribution.

3 Provide an interval estimate of the likely values of the population mean.

4 Make an objective statement regarding the key question of interest given the interval estimate provided.

Illustration 4.1   5 m Sprint time in soccer players

Background

Soccer players are often involved in short-duration sprints during a game in order to make a tackle, intercept the ball or receive a pass. Thus, speed over 5 metres is deemed to be a very important attribute for soccer players. Regular measurement of 5 metre sprint speeds for soccer players will allow the assessment of the efficacy of training programmes and the impact of injuries.

Study description

As part of a fitness test battery in a professional soccer club, a sample of 43 elite soccer players performed a number of 5 metre sprints. After a warm-up, the players performed three sprints on an indoor track with a set recovery between each sprint. Times were recorded to one-hundredth of a second using electronic time gates. The fastest time from the three trials for each player was used in the analysis outlined below.

Aim

To estimate the mean 5 m Sprint Time for the population of professional soccer players.

Data

    Name of data file: *Soccer Fitness*
    Response variable: 5 m Sprint Time (seconds)

Analysis

Summary statistics for the 5 m Sprint Times are given in Box 4.1.

Box 4.1

```
Variable    N    Mean    StDev   Minimum      Q1   Median      Q3   Maximum
Sprint5    43  1.0691   0.0616    0.9100  1.0200   1.0600  1.1000    1.2100
```

The quickest time recorded among the 43 players was 0.91 seconds, whereas the slowest was 1.21 seconds. This range is quite wide considering that the distance was only 5 metres. The sample median is 1.06 seconds, which is nearly identical to the sample mean, suggesting the sample is roughly symmetrical. The symmetry (and lack of outliers) present in the box plot (Figure 4.1) suggest that 5 m Sprint Times may indeed follow a

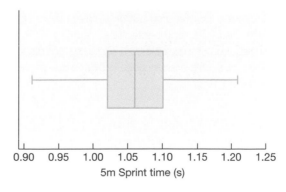

Figure 4.1 Box plot of 5 m Sprint Time.

81

Normal distribution in the population of comparable elite soccer players from which this is assumed to be a representative sample.

The sample mean is 1.07 seconds and is the 'best guess' of the true but unknown underlying population mean 5 m Sprint Time of elite soccer players but an interval estimate of the population mean must be produced by the researcher. The required one-sample 95% CI for the population mean 5 m Sprint Time is given in Box 4.2, and this interval (highlighted in bold) provides an estimate of the likely values of the population mean 5 m Sprint Time.

Box 4.2

```
One-Sample T: Sprint5

Variable      N       Mean      StDev     SE Mean          95% CI
Sprint5      43    1.06907    0.06160     0.00939   (1.05011, 1.08803)
```

Conclusion
On the basis of a 95% CI, it is likely that the population mean 5 m Sprint Time for elite soccer players is between 1.05 and 1.09 seconds.

Source: Sports Performance Unit, Scottish Premier League club.

Additional comment on Illustration 4.1

As the study is an observational study it is assumed (and hoped) that the sample provided is indeed representative of professional soccer players in general.

Illustration 4.2 **Mont Blanc ascent time (revisited)**

Background and study description
See Illustration 3.1 for details.

Aim
To provide an estimate of the typical Ascent Time for successful climbers of Mont Blanc (in good summer conditions).

Analysis
The sample mean Ascent Time is 4.26 hours (see Box 4.3). A box plot of the Ascent Times (Figure 3.2) exhibited a good deal of symmetry and suggested that Ascent Time may indeed follow a Normal distribution in the population of summer alpine climbers from which this is (hopefully) a representative sample.

The required one-sample 95% CI for the population mean Ascent Time is given in Box 4.3. This interval (highlighted in bold) provides an estimate of the likely values of the population mean Ascent Time.

Box 4.3

```
One-Sample T: Ascent Time

Variable        N       Mean      StDev     SE Mean          95% CI
Ascent Time   197     4.2589     0.8209      0.0585   (4.1436, 4.3743)
```

Conclusion

On the basis of a 95% CI it is likely that the population mean Ascent Time of climbers of Mont Blanc in summer is between 4 hours 10 minutes and 4 hours 20 minutes (i.e 4.14 to 4.37).

Additional comment on Illustration 4.2

Three climbers in the sample have Ascent Times that were previously flagged as atypically long compared with those of the rest of the sample (Figure 3.2). An interval estimate for the population mean *excluding* these climbers is 4.1 to 4.3 hours, which is very similar to the interval based on the complete sample (4.1 to 4.4 hours). In this example, therefore, the outliers are not all that 'influential' on the resulting interval estimate.

Exercises

4.1 Provide an interval estimate of the population mean Energy Expenditure for university students based on the Aerobic Dance/Popmobility data introduced in Exercise 3.1 Does it appear that the assumptions underlying the interval estimate are valid? The dataset is called *Popmobility*.

4.2 Provide an interval estimate of the mean Haemoglobin Concentration for female elite distance runners using the *Haemoglobin* data introduced in Exercise 3.2

4.4 Comparing two population means (the simplest between-subject design)

The need to compare two population means can arise from an observational study (two independent samples) or through a designed experiment (a single sample randomised into one of the two levels of a between-subject factor). Regardless of the context, the response variable of interest is recorded for each subject in both samples/levels and interest relates to the comparison of the population mean. The parameter of interest is the *difference* in population means and is estimated naturally by using the difference in the sample means. If the difference in the two population means is zero then the population means are identical. This simple fact is central in interpreting the results from two sample comparisons.

The formal analysis can be summarised as follows:

1 Provide summary statistics and a box plot of the response variable categorised by the levels of the between-subject factor.

2 Provide and comment on a suitable interval estimate of the likely difference in the population means.

3 If appropriate, make an objective statement as to whether zero is a plausible value for the difference in population means.

The assumptions on which this analysis is based are that the samples are independent and that the response variable of interest was sampled from underlying Normal distributions.

The first example in this section relates to data collected as part of an observational study. Following this, data arising from a simple between-subjects design with two levels are considered. In both examples the techniques needed are identical while the conclusions are, of course, dependent on the design employed. A clear inference cannot be drawn from an observational study but can be from a suitably designed experiment.

Illustration 4.3 Soccer fitness (revisited)

Background and study description
See Illustration 3.2 for details.

Aim
To compare the mean Counter Movement Jump (CMJ) Height in the populations of Senior and Youth soccer players.

Data
    Name of data file: *Soccer Fitness*
    Response variable: CMJ Height (centimetres)
    Between-subject factor*:   Squad (2 levels: Senior, Youth)

*Strictly speaking the term 'between-subject factor' is more appropriate for designed as opposed to observational studies.

Analysis
The sample of Senior players had a higher sample mean CMJ Height than the Youths by about 7 cm (Box 3.2). The box plot presented in Figure 4.2 is a slight variation of that in Figure 3.3, in that the width of the box is now proportional to the size of the sample to highlight the unequal sample sizes.

The assumption of Normality is questionable for population of Seniors as the median is not in the centre of the IQR. The CMJ Height distribution is plausibly Normal in the Youth population, however, based on the symmetry present in each box plot. The variability in the CMJ Height across both samples is reasonably similar.

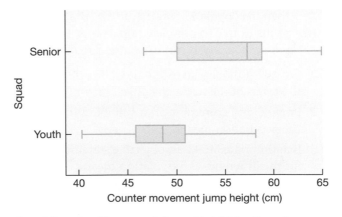

Figure 4.2 Box plot of Counter Movement Jump Height by Squad.

In order to make a formal comparison between the population of Senior and Youth elite players a 95% CI for the difference in population mean CMJ Height is required and is presented in Box 4.4.

Box 4.4

```
Two-sample T for CMJ(cm)

Squad         N        Mean       StDev      SE Mean
Senior       14       55.08        5.52         1.5
Youth        23       48.49        4.06        0.85

Difference = mu (Senior) - mu (Youth)
Estimate for difference: 6.59
95% CI for difference: (3.05, 10.13)
```

The output presents the sample sizes, means, standard deviations and estimated standard errors for each of the two samples. The estimate of the difference in the population means is given here as Senior Squad mean minus Youth Squad mean (i.e. $55.08 - 48.49 = 6.59$ cm). The difference in the sample means therefore is 6.59 cm favouring the Senior players. The 95% CI, a two-sample t-interval (highlighted in bold in Box 4.4), is for the difference in the population mean CMJ Height for the Senior Squad minus the population mean for the Youth Squad. This interval is interpreted in the same way as before; the interval provides a credible range for the likely value of the difference between the two population means.

The key point here is to realise that, **if zero does not lie in the interval, there is a significant difference between the two population means**. In this example, the 95% CI does not contain zero and therefore it is highly likely that there is *a difference* between the two population means. As the 95% CI for the difference in the population means is strictly positive there is evidence that CMJ Height, on average, is higher in the Senior players compared with the Youth players.

Conclusion

There is convincing evidence of a difference in the mean CMJ Height between the two populations of soccer players. The mean CMJ Height is likely to be higher in Senior players by between 3 and 10 cm *on average,* compared with Youth players.

Additional comments on Illustration 4.3

1 Be aware that this interval does not imply that the CMJ Height of *all* Senior players is higher by between 3 and 10 cm, but rather that the *average* difference in CMJ score across the squads is likely to be of this magnitude.

2 The Normality assumption relating to the CMJ Height distribution in Senior soccer players is questionable based on the (small) sample of Senior players available. This issue is returned to in Section 4.8 below.

The next example is of a classical experimental design where a single sample was chosen and then randomised to two levels of a between-subject grouping factor (e.g. intervention or control).

Illustration 4.4   Physiotherapy pain relief

Background
Ischaemic pain can be induced by applying a tourniquet to the arm just above the elbow to obstruct blood flow. The subject is asked to flex and relax the forearm muscles continuously for a short period of time (e.g. 1 minute). When the exercise is stopped, pain increases and typically becomes unbearable after about 8 minutes. This method is used in experimental studies of pain because it causes no permanent tissue damage.

Study description
A sample of 29 young healthy females was taken to investigate the effect of a mental distraction task on induced ischaemic pain. Subjects were randomly allocated to one of two methods of Pain Relief (i.e. Control and Distraction). A sub-maximal effort tourniquet technique (SETT) was used to induce ischaemic pain on a subject's non-dominant arm while she performed sets of 20 repetitions of hand gripping exercises at 75% of her maximal grip strength over a 100 second period. The distraction employed was a colour word Stroop test and this mental task consists of a pencil and paper Stroop task modified to cover 160 words typed in red, yellow, blue or green in a randomised order. Each word did not represent its colour meaning. While the distraction was being carried out, subjects recorded the time when they first felt pain, i.e. their perceived pain levels using a visual analogue scale (VAS) from the moment they acknowledged pain (i.e. their **pain threshold**) until they could not tolerate the pain any longer (i.e. their pain tolerance).

Aim
To investigate the effect of a mental distraction task on induced ischaemic pain by comparing the difference in population mean Pain Threshold between those on the intervention (i.e. Distraction) and Controls.

Data
Name of data file:	*Painrelief*
Response variable:	Pain Threshold (seconds)
Between-subject factor:	Pain Relief (2 levels: Control, Distraction)

Analysis
The summary statistics in Box 4.5 suggest a considerably higher Pain Threshold for those distracted, i.e. they tend to withstand the onset of pain longer than the Controls.

Box 4.5

```
Descriptive Statistics: Pain Threshold

Variable          Treatment      N   Mean  StDev  Minimum      Q1  Median      Q3
Pain Threshold    Control       14  35.29  21.71     3.00   17.25   31.50   52.50
                  Distraction   15   91.8   56.7      5.0    29.0   102.0   136.0

Variable          Treatment     Maximum
Pain Threshold    Control         78.00
                  Distraction     168.0
```

The box plots (Figure 4.3) highlight that Pain Threshold is more variable among those distracted than among the Controls. Each box plot appears reasonably symmetrical and consequently the Normality assumption for both Pain Threshold distributions appears reasonable.

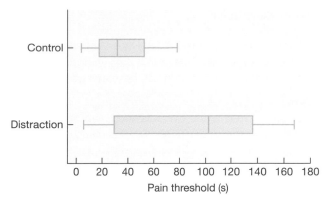

Figure 4.3 **Box plot of Pain Threshold.**

A 95% CI for the difference (for Distraction minus Control) in mean Pain Threshold (highlighted in bold in Box 4.6) is strictly positive and hence indicates that the Distraction has significantly increased the mean Pain Threshold time for this ischaemic pain procedure in young, healthy females.

Box 4.6

```
Two-Sample T-Test and CI: Pain Threshold, Treatment

Two-sample T for Pain Threshold

Treatment        N      Mean     StDev    SE Mean
Distraction     15      91.8      56.7        15
Control         14      35.3      21.7       5.8

Difference = mu (Distraction) - mu (Control)
Estimate for difference: 56.5
95% CI for difference: (23.4, 89.6)
```

Conclusion
In terms of the time to onset of the perception of ischaemic pain, a mental distraction Stroop task can significantly increase this by between 23 and 90 seconds on average.

The next example involves a designed experiment where the analysis is carried out to 'confirm' that the randomisation was effective in terms of the two samples being reasonably comparable at baseline (i.e. to check that the two randomised samples look to have arisen from the same population).

Illustration 4.5   Osteoporosis and exercise

Background
Osteoporosis is a fairly common condition in post-menopausal women. The porous bones in this population are susceptible to fracture. The consequences of a fracture can be very serious. For example, a fracture of the neck of the femur in elderly females is associated with a very poor prognosis and may include physical incapacity and death. Exercise programmes have the potential to increase the well-being of osteoporosis sufferers. For example, if the balance of these subjects could be improved, the subjects would be less likely to fall and therefore less likely to fracture.

Study description

A sample of 30 middle-aged osteoporotic women was randomised either to a twice-weekly physiotherapist-led exercise regime or to be a control. Physiological assessments, including a functional reach test measuring balance, were conducted on all women both before and after two months of the intervention (i.e. Exercise or Control).

Aim

To assess whether the Controls and Exercisers were comparable at baseline (i.e. immediately before the study) in terms of this measure of balance.

Data

Name of data file: *Osteoporosis*
Response variable: Balance (centimetres)
Between-subject factor: Regime (2 levels: Exerciser, Control)

Analysis

The sample mean Balance is nearly identical for the Controls and Exercisers at baseline, as can be seen in the summary statistics of Box 4.7.

Box 4.7

```
Descriptive Statistics: balance_Before

Variable          Regime     N    Mean   StDev   Minimum      Q1   Median      Q3
balance_Before    Control   14   27.00    7.14     15.24   22.86    27.05   33.02
                  Exercise  16   27.19    7.37     12.70   19.68    27.94   33.02

Variable          Regime   Maximum
balance_Before    Control    38.10
                  Exercise   39.37
```

The box plots (Figure 4.4) suggest that the Balance distributions are fairly similar. They both look quite symmetrical, and the underlying populations may therefore reasonably be assumed to have arisen from Normal distributions.

The sample variability (spread) is comparable in the two Regimes and none of the observations are flagged as possible outliers. In order to make a formal statement regarding

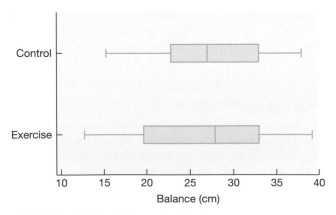

Figure 4.4 Box plot of Pre-Study Balance by Regime.

the difference in mean Balance between the two populations, a 95% CI for the difference in mean Balance is required and is given in Box 4.8.

Box 4.8

```
Two-Sample T-Test and CI: balance_Before, Regime

Two-sample T for balance_Before

Regime        N      Mean     StDev     SE Mean
Control      14     27.00      7.14         1.9
Exercise     16     27.19      7.37         1.8

Difference = mu (Control) - mu (Exercise)
Estimate for difference: -0.20
95% CI for difference: (-5.64, 5.25)
```

The 95% CI (highlighted in bold) is for the *difference* between the population means, i.e. it is the population mean Balance for Controls minus the population mean Balance for Exercisers. This 95% CI contains zero and therefore it is plausible that there is *no difference* between the two population means – especially since zero lies almost exactly in the middle of this interval estimate.

Conclusion

There is no evidence of a difference in mean Balance for Controls and Exercisers at baseline. The two samples may not have had identical Balance scores but there is evidence that the populations can be considered comparable at baseline *on average*. The difference in the two sample means can therefore be attributed to random sampling.

Reference: Mitchell, S., Aitchison, T. and Grant, S. (1998). 'Physiological effects of a structured 12 week exercise programme on post-menopausal osteoporotic women. Physical activity and health in the elderly.' *Physiotherapy*, **84**:157–163.

Additional comment on Illustration 4.5

It could be argued that, as randomisation was employed as part of the design, there is in fact no need to compare balance at baseline across the levels as the randomisation should 'ensure' comparability. This is really only a concern in small samples where randomisation may lead to sub-samples being different on certain characteristics.

Exercises

4.3 Compare the mean Haemoglobin Concentrations for the populations of Male and Female endurance runners using the *Haemoglobin* data (Exercise 3.1) and conclude whether or not there is a real and significant difference in these.

4.4 Investigate whether there is likely to be a difference in average Multi-Stage Shuttle Test Score between Youth and First team players using the *Soccer Fitness* data (Illustration 3.2). The response variable of interest here is called Bleep Test in the data file.

4.5 Provide evidence as to whether there is likely to be a difference in mean predicted $\dot{V}O_2$ max between Controls and Exercisers at baseline in the *Osteoporosis* data introduced in Illustration 4.5.

4.5 Interval estimation for paired data (the simplest within-subject design)

Recall that paired data arise in within-subject designs with a single factor at two levels. A pair of measurements is made on the same individual (e.g. $\dot{V}O_2$ max before and after a training intervention, isokinetic knee extensor strength of dominant and non-dominant leg) and are 'dependent' upon each other. If a particular individual's observation at the first level of the within-subject factor is high, it is not surprising that his/her observation at the second level will also be high, and vice versa. This dependence can often be exploited to reduce the problem to a single sample of differences and the resulting analysis is more similar to that of Section 4.3 (i.e. a single-sample problem) than the comparison of population means in Section 4.4 (i.e. a single between-subject design with two levels).

Assuming the use of simple differences is appropriate (see the General Comment in Section 3.6) and that the differences appear as if they arose from a single Normal population, then simply producing an *interval estimate for the population average difference* (between the levels) will allow quantification of the magnitude of the population average difference, if any, between the two levels of the factor. If the interval contains zero, then there is no significant difference in population means between the two levels of the factor.

Illustration 4.6 Training intervention

Background
Norwegian studies have shown that high-intensity aerobic interval training is effective in enhancing $\dot{V}O_2$ max in soccer players. This improvement in $\dot{V}O_2$ max has resulted in the players covering a greater distance during games. Strength training may improve running economy, sprinting and jumping performance.

Study description
A sample of 18 full-time youth soccer players from a youth academy performed high-Intensity aerobic interval training and neuromuscular strength training twice a week over a 10-week in-season period *in addition* to the usual regime of soccer training and matches.

Aim
To investigate whether a concurrent high-intensity interval training and neuromuscular strength improves on average the $\dot{V}O_2$ max of soccer players over a 10-week period.

Data
Name of data file:	*Training Intervention*
Response variable:	$\dot{V}O_2$ max (ml.kg^{-1}.min^{-1})
Within-subject factor:	Time (2 levels: Pre-Study, Post-Study)

Analysis
A scatter plot of the Pre-Study and Post-Study $\dot{V}O_2$ max values for each player is given in Figure 4.5.

All of the points on this plot lie above the line of equality, showing that the $\dot{V}O_2$ max readings are higher at the end of the 10-week period than at the start. As the Post $\dot{V}O_2$ max

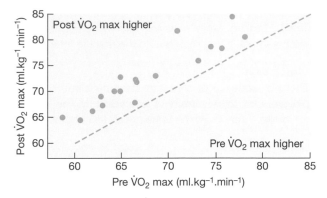

Figure 4.5 Scatter plot of Pre and Post $\dot{V}O_2$ max (with line of equality).

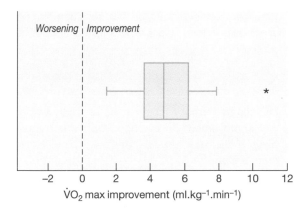

Figure 4.6 Box plot of improvement in $\dot{V}O_2$ max.

readings are more or less 'parallel' to the line of equality across the full range of Pre $\dot{V}O_2$ max readings, it is reasonable to assume that there is a systematic difference in the improvement between the start and end of the intervention and therefore the analysis can be based on these differences directly.

Create a new variable, of the difference in the two $\dot{V}O_2$ max readings (i.e. Post $\dot{V}O_2$ max minus Pre $\dot{V}O_2$ max) for each player. This new variable represents the improvement in $\dot{V}O_2$ max for each of the 18 players who underwent the training regime. A positive difference means that a player's $\dot{V}O_2$ max has improved, while a negative difference means that a player's $\dot{V}O_2$ max has worsened.

From a box plot (Figure 4.6) of the improvements in $\dot{V}O_2$ max it appears reasonable, from the symmetry present, to assume that the differences have arisen from a Normal population. There is one suggested outlier which may be worthy of further investigation.

An interval estimate for the *population average difference* of $\dot{V}O_2$ max across the ten-week period can now be calculated (Box 4.9) using a one-sample confidence interval as this is now no more than a single-sample problem.

Box 4.9

Variable	N	Mean	StDev	SE Mean	95% CI
VO2 Improvement	18	5.11111	2.25829	0.53228	(3.98809, 6.23413)

This interval suggests that the actual mean improvement is likely to be between 3.99 and 6.23 ml.kg^{-1}.min^{-1}. As this interval does not contain zero, there is evidence of a mean improvement in $\dot{V}O_2$ max due to the training intervention.

Conclusion

There is evidence of a real improvement in mean $\dot{V}O_2$ max among professional soccer players due to this training intervention. The mean improvement in the sample was 5.1 ml.kg^{-1}.min^{-1}, which is nearly an 8% improvement on the typical Pre-Study $\dot{V}O_2$ max of around 68 ml.kg^{-1}.min^{-1}.

Additional comment on Illustration 4.6

Note that in this design there was no 'natural' Control group. The soccer club officials decided that all of their players had to carry out the proposed intervention in addition to the usual training. Therefore it was not possible to find control subjects from within the club. The recruitment of controls from outside the club was considered to be inappropriate as random assignment would not be possible. This is an example of a 'poor but unavoidable' design.

Exercises

4.5 Investigate formally whether the strength and endurance training intervention had any improvement on average Squat Jump based on the sample of youth soccer players discussed in Illustration 4.6. The dataset is contained in the file *Training Intervention*.

4.6 Using the *WalkDance* data (Illustration 3.5), provide an interval estimate of the population mean difference in Relative Intensity between Aerobic Dance class and Walking sessions for elderly population of interest. Does there appear to be any significant difference between the two forms of exercise in terms of mean improvement in Relative Intensity?

4.6   One between-subject and one within-subject factor (each at two levels)

A design involving samples of paired data from two distinct and different populations is simply a design with one between-subject factor and one within-subject factor both at two levels. The methods needed to analyse such designs are in fact just those already presented in the previous sections of this chapter. The analysis required often reduces to nothing more than a comparison of the mean differences in the two samples.

The same assumptions as apply to two-sample comparisons apply here to the two samples of differences. The data are assumed to be random samples and the differences are assumed to have arisen from Normal populations. Of course, the assumption that the differences are not related to the initial values (see Section 3.6, General Comment) must be validated also.

Illustration 4.7   **Osteoporosis and exercise (revisited)**

Background and study description
See Illustration 4.5 for details.

Aim
To investigate whether or not such an exercise regime can significantly improve, on average, the balance of osteoporotic women over a two-month period of exercise over any 'natural' improvement of Controls.

Data
Name of data file:	*Osteoporosis*
Variable of interest:	Balance (centimetres)
Between-subject factor:	Regime (2 levels: Exerciser, Control)
Within-subject factor:	Time (2 levels: Before Study, After Study)

Analysis
First provide a plot (Figure 4.7) of Balance before the study against the Balance after completion of the study. Assess from this plot a sensible range of the variable being covered by both methods and then draw in the line of equality (i.e. the line of no change over the two months of the study).

Figure 4.7 shows clearly that most of the Exercisers improved their Balance over the study. It appears that there is, in general, a slight improvement for the Controls. Both regimes tend to show changes that are, in general, 'parallel' to the line of equality thus suggesting that there is a consistent and constant change not dependent, in any sense, on the magnitude of the subject's Balance. This ensures that the use of the simple 'improvements' (i.e. After Balance minus Before Balance) will give an adequate summary of the effect of the 'interventions'.

Figure 4.8 shows the box plots of these 'improvements' by Regime and further emphasises the substantial benefit that the Exercisers seem to enjoy in general.

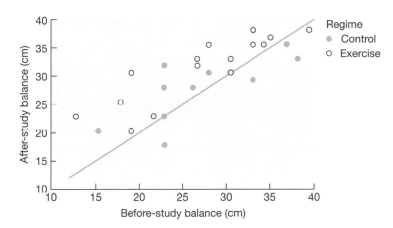

Figure 4.7 Scatter plot of Balance by Exercise Regime (with line of equality).

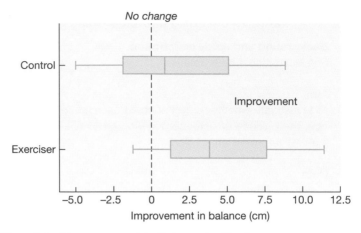

Figure 4.8 Box plot of Improvement in Balance by Regime.

Next, carry out a two-sample comparison of these improvements between the two Regimes to obtain the output in Box 4.10.

Box 4.10

```
Two-sample T for Imp Bal (After-Before)

Regime        N     Mean     StDev    SE Mean
Exercise     16     4.40      3.77       0.94
Control      14     1.31      4.26       1.1

Difference = mu (Exercise) - mu (Control)
Estimate for difference: 3.09
95% CI for difference: (0.05, 6.13)
```

Since the 95% CI is (just) strictly positive, there is evidence of an improvement in Balance, on average, of between 0.05 and 6.1 cm in favour of Exercisers, i.e. between a slight (0.05 cm) and a massive (6.1 cm) average increase in Balance.

Interval estimates for the average improvement in this measure of Balance for each Regime separately are shown in Box 4.11.

Box 4.11

```
One-Sample T: Imp Bal (A-B)_Control, Imp Bal (A-B)_Exerciser

Variable          N     Mean      StDev    SE Mean        95% CI
Imp Bal (A-B)_Co  14  1.30629   4.25823    1.13806  (-1.15234, 3.76492)
Imp Bal (A-B)_Ex  16  4.39738   3.76939    0.94235  ( 2.38881, 6.40594)
```

On the basis of these figures, it can be seen that, on average, Controls do not significantly improve over the study period (since the interval of −1 to 4 cm does include zero), whereas Exercisers do, in general, improve Balance by between 2 and 6 cm on average.

Conclusion

There is evidence that post-menopausal osteoporotic women can, on average, significantly improve their Balance (as measured by a functional reach test) with a two-month physiotherapist-led exercise regime.

A second illustration of this two-sample paired problem now follows, as such contexts are the most common in sports and exercise science and it is well worth looking at the different types of results that can arise.

Illustration 4.8   Exercise and the elderly (revisited)

Background and study description:
See Illustration 3.5 for details.

Aims

To compare the average difference in Relative Intensity during Aerobic Dance and Walking sessions for each sex separately and then to investigate whether the difference in Relative Intensity (if any) is, on average, similar for Males and Females.

Data

Name of data file:	*WalkDance*
Response variable:	Relative Intensity (% Peak $\dot{V}O_2$)
Between-subject factor:	Sex (2 levels: Males, Females)
Within-subject factor:	Exercise Regime (2 levels: Walking, Aerobic Dance)

Analysis

Once again start by creating a scatter plot of Relative Intensity for the two Exercise Regimes (Figure 4.9) with separate labels for Males and Females and include the line of equality on the plot.

All of the subjects had a higher Relative Intensity for Aerobic Dance than for Walking and there is a suggestion that this difference may be higher in Males than in Females as the symbols for the Males tend to lie further above the line of equality compared with those for the Females.

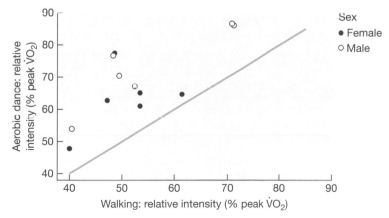

Figure 4.9 Scatter plot of Relative Intensity by Exercise Regime and Sex (with line of equality).

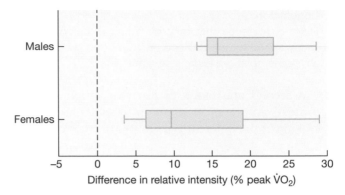

Figure 4.10 Box plot of Difference in Relative Intensity by Sex (Aerobic Dance minus Walking).

This difference is more clearly exhibited in a box plot of the Difference in Relative Intensity (i.e. Aerobic Dance minus Walking) by Sex (Figure 4.10).

When comparing the different Exercise Regimes, Males typically tend to have a higher Relative Intensity than Females – sample mean differences in favour of Aerobic Dance of 15% and 10%, respectively. Indeed, both samples, albeit small, provide evidence of significantly higher average differences in Relative Intensity for both Males and Females as the relevant interval estimates in Box 4.12 are both strictly positive. In particular, the likely mean difference in favour of Aerobic Dance is 12% to 24% for Males and 3% to 22% for Females.

Box 4.12

```
One-Sample T: Dance-Walk(M), Dance-Walk(F)

Variable          N       Mean     StDev    SE Mean       95% CI
Dance-Walk(M)     6      18.17      5.81       2.37    (12.07, 24.27)
Dance-Walk(F)     6      12.41      9.17       3.74    ( 2.79, 22.03)
```

The separate intervals provide evidence that, in the elderly population, both Males and Females tend to have a higher mean Relative Intensity when carrying out an Aerobic Dance session than when they take part in an individual Walking session.

The second aim of the study was to investigate whether this higher Relative Intensity in Aerobic Dance sessions is, on average, similar for Males and Females. A two-sample comparison of the differences in Relative Intensity between Males and Females is given in Box 4.13.

Box 4.13

```
Two-sample T for Dance-Walk(M) vs Dance-Walk(F)

                 N      Mean    StDev   SE Mean
Dance-Walk(M)    6     18.17     5.81      2.4
Dance-Walk(F)    6     12.41     9.17      3.7

Difference = mu (Dance-Walk(M)) - mu (Dance-Walk(F))
Estimate for difference: 5.76
95% CI for difference: (-4.46, 15.97)
```

Despite the fact that the sample mean difference was higher for Males, the 95% CI for 'Males minus Females' contains zero and, therefore, there is not sufficient evidence to claim that such an increase in Relative Intensity is higher in the population of elderly males compared with the population of elderly females.

Conclusion

The Relative Intensity was significantly higher on average for the Aerobic Dance session than the Walking session for both Males and Females in this elderly population. There was no evidence, however, that the typical difference between these types of session is different for the sexes.

Additional comment on Illustration 4.8

This result should be considered in conjunction with the fact that the sample sizes are very small. A larger sample may well have identified a difference between Males and Females and this study is likely to be lacking in power to have any chance of identifying a higher value for Males.

The preceding illustrations are examples of probably the most common study designs used in sports and exercise science. Indeed, such designs are revisited in Chapter 10 which deals specifically with within-subject designs of varying complexity.

Exercises

4.8 The Osteoporosis study used in Illustration 4.7 involved the measurement of other variables such as a measure of Flexibility, the sit-and-reach test. Investigate, using the methods above, whether the Exercisers improved on this measure of Flexibility significantly more on average than did the Controls. If so, how much more?

4.9 Ankylosing spondylitis (AS) is a debilitating condition which can have wide-ranging and varied effects, particularly in restriction of movement of the spinal and thoracic areas. An exercise programme may improve (i.e. increase) forced vital capacity (FVC) – the maximum volume of air that can be forcibly expired from the lungs measured in litres – in these patients. A sample of 42 AS sufferers were randomised to be either a Control or to undergo an Exercise Intervention for a period of 12 weeks. Is there evidence that the Exercise Intervention, on average, improved FVC significantly over Controls? If so, how much of a difference is there? The data are in the file *Ankylosing Spondylitis* on the accompanying website.

4.7 Prediction and tolerance intervals

One misconception in the interpretation of a confidence interval (CI) for a population mean is to consider it as providing an estimate of the likely value of a particular *individual* in the population. For example, the 95% CI calculated previously for the population mean Ascent Time of Mont Blanc was between 4 hours 10 minutes and 4 hours 20 minutes. This interval provides a likely range of values for the *population mean* and *not* a likely range for any future individual. Of course, the sample mean is still the best (point) estimate that could be used when predicting the actual Ascent Time of a future climber, but the corresponding interval estimate should naturally be wider to take into account the considerable variability in Ascent Time from climber to climber. The interval that is appropriate for a future (random) member of the population is called a **prediction interval (PI)**. This takes into account not only the uncertainty/error in the estimate of the population mean but also the population variability/standard deviation since the assumption throughout this section is still that the underlying population is Normally distributed.

Another form of interval encountered in sports and exercise science is the **tolerance interval (TI)**, or 'Normal' ranges as they are referred to particularly in medicine. These are ranges of values within which it is intended that a fixed proportion of the target population will lie. Such ranges are useful when generating 'reference ranges' for acceptable levels of particular substances in drug testing, as a benchmark to detect athletes who may be doping.

The difference between tolerance and prediction intervals is quite subtle and often causes confusion. The main point to consider is whether the researcher is trying to use the current sample to predict the actual value of a single future observation (i.e. a prediction interval) or to estimate the range of the variable covering the vast majority of the population (i.e. a tolerance interval).

4.7.1 Prediction intervals for a single future observation

A prediction interval provides a range of values within which an observation from a future individual in the population of interest would be likely to fall. It is important to appreciate the different type of interval estimate that is involved here. A confidence interval provides an estimated range for the population mean, whereas a prediction interval provides an estimated range for the likely value for a single member of the population.

The appropriate formula for a prediction interval (based on a Normal distribution assumption) is not given here. Suffice to say that it is similar to that for a confidence interval, with a correction applied to account for both the variability across individuals as well as the 'error' in estimating the mean.

Illustration 4.9   Avalanche survival

Background
Asphyxiation is a common cause of death in avalanche burial. This is often due to the accumulation of expired CO_2 in the immediate air supply, leading to the displacement of available oxygen. Recent studies have indicated that incorporation of a CO_2 scrubbing agent into a breathing apparatus may be a successful means of survival enhancement. Soda Lime is one of the most commonly used CO_2 removal agents used in anaesthetic practice.

Study description
A sample of 14 healthy subjects performed two blinded trials, one with a Soda Lime canister and one with a Placebo canister acting as a Control. Subjects breathed through a mouthpiece into a closed-circuit system attached to a Douglas bag containing 12 litres of 100% O_2. They were instructed to continue for as long as they could tolerate breathing from the system (i.e. their Tolerance Time). The design was balanced as seven of the subjects used the Soda Lime canister first while the other seven used the Placebo first.

Aim
To provide estimates of the likely Tolerance Time for a future person in a laboratory-simulated avalanche situation both with and without a Soda Lime canister.

Data

Name of data file: *Avalanche*
Response variable: Tolerance Time (minutes)
Within-subject factor: Canister (2 levels: Placebo, Soda Lime)

Analysis

Start by creating a scatter plot of subjects' Tolerance Times for the Placebo and Soda Lime canisters using the same scale for both axes (Figure 4.11) with the line of equality added.

The poorest Tolerance Time recorded was under 10 minutes and was for a subject who was not using the Soda Lime canister. The best Tolerance Time recorded was approximately 45 minutes for a subject using the Soda Lime canister. What is very clear is that *all* of the subjects in the study demonstrated increases in Tolerance Time when they used the Soda Lime canister since all of the points lie above the line of equality. The improvement in Tolerance Time does not appear to be dependent on the Tolerance Times in the Control condition, justifying the use of differences.

A box plot of the Difference in Tolerance Time (Soda Lime Tolerance Time minus Control Tolerance Time) suggests that the typical improvement in Tolerance Time is approximately 29 minutes, which is clearly considerable (Figure 4.12).

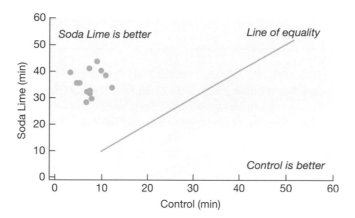

Figure 4.11 Scatter plot of Tolerance Times for Conditions.

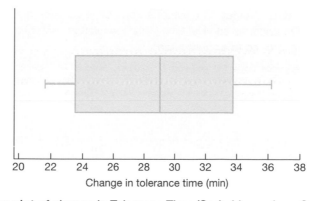

Figure 4.12 Box plot of change in Tolerance Time (Soda Lime minus Control).

99

A 95% CI for the population mean improvement provides definite evidence of an improvement, on average, in Tolerance Time in the population of climbers (Box 4.13) as the interval is wholly positive.

Box 4.13

```
One-Sample T: Soda Lime-Control

Variable                N      Mean    StDev     SE Mean      95% CI
Soda Lime-Control      14     28.38     5.17        1.38  (25.40, 31.37)
```

The results suggest that the Soda Lime canister may be of value in an avalanche situation. There is convincing evidence that the use of Soda Lime is likely to improve the average Tolerance Time by somewhere between 25 and 31 minutes when an individual is in such a simulated avalanche situation.

Although these results suggest an improvement on average, what is of more interest here is an estimate of the likely Tolerance Time for an *individual* with a Soda Lime canister in the simulated avalanche situation of this study. The required 95% PI is given in Box 4.14.

Box 4.14

```
95.0% Prediction interval is given by (25.18, 46.68).
```

This interval suggests that the likely Tolerance Time for an individual using a Soda Lime canister is between 25 and 47 minutes. The corresponding 95% PI for the likely Tolerance Time for an *individual* without a Soda Lime canister is between 2 and 13 minutes (Box 4.15). This suggests a considerably reduced Tolerance Time for individuals not using a Soda Lime canister.

Box 4.15

```
95.0% Prediction interval is given by (2.26, 12.82).
```

Conclusion

Based on the data provided, it is clear that, in the target population, using a Soda Lime canister is likely to improve the Tolerance Time for any particular individual by between 25 and 47 minutes. The use of a Soda Lime canister in a real avalanche situation may therefore enhance survival time. This speculation assumes that the laboratory findings can be transferred to a snow setting.

Reference: Doyle, P., MacGregor, N. (students), Grant, S., Aitchison, T. and Watt, I. (staff). 'The effectiveness of a soda lime canister in the enhancement of tolerance time, whilst breathing to and from a fixed volume of gas.' Physiology and Sports Science student project, University of Glasgow.

Additional comment on Illustration 4.9

There were two separate questions of interest: the likely Tolerance Time for an individual with and without the Soda Lime canister. Although the prediction intervals are massively different it is not strictly correct to claim an overall difference (on the individual level) on the basis that the prediction intervals do not overlap. This issue of 'multiple comparisons' will be revisited in detail in Chapter 7.

4.7.2 Tolerance intervals to cover a proportion of the population ('Normal' ranges)

A tolerance interval is used to investigate whether a particular observed individual is 'dissimilar' to the rest of the population. For example, what would be a range of values covering 95% of individual ascent times of Mont Blanc? If any particular climber's ascent time is not within this range, then he/she can be considered atypical (either fast or slow) of the target population. Such ranges are commonly used in medical literature and are intended as benchmarks for patient diagnosis where the term 'Normal range' is often applied – this usage of 'Normal' here has nothing whatsoever to do with the Normal distribution though.

When calculating a tolerance interval a choice of the *confidence* attached to the tolerance interval has to be made, in addition to the choice of the *proportion* of the population that this interval is intended to cover. The conventional choice for *both* of these is 95%.

Illustration 4.10 **Mont Blanc ascent time (revisited)**

Background and study description
See Illustration 4.2 for details.

Aim
To provide an interval estimate for the Ascent Time of 95% of the successful climbers of Mont Blanc in favourable summer conditions.

Analysis
This aim should be interpreted as requiring a tolerance interval with 95% coverage and 95% confidence (see Box 4.16). This interval provides an estimate of the Ascent Times that are likely for 95% of individuals in the population of successful climbers of Mont Blanc.

Box 4.16

```
   Tolerance (Confidence) Level:    95%
Proportion of Population Covered:    95%

     N            Mean            StDev           Tolerance Interval
    197         4.25892         0.820920          (2.49877, 6.01906)
```

Conclusion
It is likely that 95% of the actual Ascent Times in the population of successful climbers of Mont Blanc lie between 2.5 and 6 hours. A more practical interpretation is that it is unlikely that a climber making a successful ascent will be quicker than 2.5 hours or slower than 6 hours.

Additional comment

The assumptions made to generate prediction and tolerance intervals are the same as those needed for providing confidence intervals for a population mean, namely a random sample, independent observations and Normality.

4.10 According to some aerobic fitness guidelines, Relative Intensity (as measured by % Peak $\dot{V}O_2$) should be between 50% and 85% of Peak $\dot{V}O_2$ to maintain or improve aerobic fitness for most subjects. Using the *WalkDance* data (Illustration 3.5), calculate a 95% tolerance interval for Relative Intensity for 95% of the target population of elderly subjects who attend an Aerobic Dance class. Compare the result with the recommended guidelines.

4.11 The % Body Fat of a sample of elite soccer players was 'estimated' midway through a playing season using a variety of skinfold measurements. Calculate a Normal range that covers 95% of the % Body Fat readings for the target population of elite soccer players. A new player is on trial at the club and has a % Body Fat of 18%. What can be said about this player relative to the values already seen in the population? The dataset is called *Soccer Fitness*.

4.8 What if the Normality assumption is questionable?

4.8.1 Single-sample problems

A crucial assumption used in this chapter to calculate a Confidence interval for a population mean is that the data arose from a Normal distribution. The method of production of the CI is quite robust towards (i.e. not overly influenced by) departures from Normality if the sample is 'large' (typically 30 or more). However, the method does not work well in small samples that are not symmetrical (i.e. that have a degree of skewness) or which have outliers present.

If the Normality assumption is questionable, there are three possible approaches that can be considered:

1 Use a suitable transformation of the data.

2 Use a re-sampling technique that does not assume Normality.

3 Concentrate on the population median rather than mean.

A formal procedure for testing whether a sample was likely to have arisen from a Normal distribution will be presented in the next chapter. Rather than forcing an analysis based on an erroneous assumption of Normality on to data that appear non-Normal, there is no reason whatsoever not to transform the data to 'achieve' Normality on a different measurement scale. The standard Normal-distribution-based analysis can then be safely undertaken using this transformed variable.

Illustration 4.11 Walk In to Work Out

Background

Walking some or all of the way to work is one possible method of increasing physical activity, improving aerobic fitness and health and having a positive influence on the environment. As part of a study to encourage active commuting, a sample of 295 commuters who were interested in taking part in the study filled in a questionnaire about their recent history of walking habits as part of the baseline information for this study.

Study description

Subjects were randomised to receive the Intervention or to act as a Control. Those on the intervention received the 'Walk In to Work Out' pack, which contained written interactive material, local information about distances and routes, and safety information. The Controls did not receive the pack and continued with their usual lifestyle.

Aim

To estimate the typical time spent walking to work post-intervention for those who did not walk to work prior to the study.

Data

    Name of data file: *Walk to Work*
    Response variable: Walking Time (minutes)

Analysis

There were 14 commuters identified who did not walk to work prior to the study. As always, a sensible starting point for any continuous response variable is to generate useful summary statistics (Box 4.16).

Box 4.16

```
Descriptive Statistics: Walking Time

Variable        N    Mean   StDev   Minimum    Q1   Median      Q3   Maximum
Walking Time   14   125.1   126.5      25.0   34.5    85.0   165.0     450.0
```

The sample median Walking Time is 85 minutes whereas the 'middle half' of the sample (i.e. the IQR) walked between 35 and 165 minutes. One individual walked for over 7.5 hours that week. The sample mean Walking Time is considerably larger than the median (by nearly 40 minutes), suggesting that there may be some outliers or skewness to the right in the sample. Indeed, both these features are evident in the box plot (Figure 4.13) which has the data points included to specifically highlight the small sample size and possible outlier(s).

Based on the (possibly dubious) assumption that the underlying population of Walking Times follows a Normal distribution, a 95% CI for the population mean Walking Time is

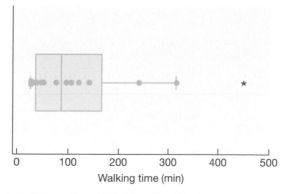

Figure 4.13 **Box plot of Time Spent Walking Pre-Study.**

given in Box 4.17 and suggests that the population average Walking Time is likely to be between 52 and 198 minutes per week.

Box 4.17

```
One-Sample T: Walking Time

Variable           N        Mean      StDev      SE Mean       95% CI
Walking Time      14       125.1      126.5        33.8    (52.0, 198.1)
```

The validity of this interval is questionable, however, due to the evidence of non-symmetry (and hence non-Normality) in the box plot. When it is unreasonable to assume that the sample has arisen from a Normal distribution, the first approach to consider is to **transform** the scale of measurement of the data, so that the transformed variable appears much more reasonably to be Normally distributed. The most common transformations applied when the data are *heavily skewed to the right* are to take the **logarithm** or the **square root** of the data. If the resulting transformed variable appears much more likely to be Normally distributed, an interval estimate for the population mean of the transformed variable can be calculated and the resulting interval 'back transformed' to the original scale of the variable of interest.

To illustrate this approach, a new variable – log(Walking Time) – was created by taking the (natural) logarithm of the Walking Times in the sample. The box plot (Figure 4.14) for the log-transformed variable suggests that the assumption regarding Normality is likely to be valid for this new transformed variable whose box plot looks reasonably symmetrical about the sample median.

A 95% CI estimate for the population mean using the log-transformed variable is given in Box 4.18.

Box 4.18

```
One-Sample T: log(Walking Time)

Log(Walking Time) 14 4.410 0.941  0.251 (3.867, 4.953)
```

The interval suggests that the mean log(Walking Time), for the population of interest, is likely to be somewhere between 3.87 and 4.95 (log minutes). Note that the interval reported is calculated on the log scale, while it would be much more informative to report the results

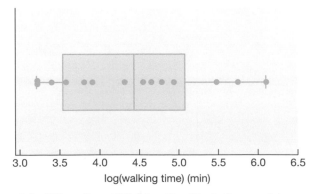

3.0   3.5   4.0   4.5   5.0   5.5   6.0   6.5

log(walking time) (min)

Figure 4.14 **Box plot of Time Spent Walking Pre-Study (log scale).**

in the original units. The simplest method of achieving this is to **back transform** each end of the interval. The appropriate inverse transformation for the log function is the antilog (i.e. the exponential function). Applying this to both ends of the interval gives exp(3.867) = 47.80 minutes and exp(4.953) = 141.603 minutes, yielding a 95% CI for the population mean Walking Time of 48 to 142 minutes. This method has shifted the estimate of the population mean to the left, having 'accounted' for the right skew in the data and substantially reduced the width of the interval estimate (i.e. from a range of $198.1 - 52 = 146.1$ minutes for the untransformed variable to $141.6 - 47.80 = 93.8$ minutes for this approach).

The second approach, if the Normality assumption appears untenable, has the quirky title of the **bootstrap**. It allows an estimate of a population mean to be made without requiring any assumptions about the underlying population distribution. As in all inferential methods, the bootstrap approach is heavily dependent on assuming that the sample collected is representative of the target population. The bootstrap can be applied to virtually any parameter that needs to be estimated in a population, and makes no formal assumptions regarding the population distribution. It was first put forward in the late 1970s but had to await the arrival of substantial computer power before it could be implemented. That time has now arrived and some claim that the bootstrap has revolutionised modern statistical inference.

The bootstrap procedure uses the following argument: if the data really are a random sample from the target population, then a 're-sample' from the actual data at hand can be considered a 'new' random sample which could have arisen from the population. The subtlety is that random samples from the original random sample tend to behave as random samples from the population. The re-samples are used to generate an estimate of the sampling variability in the sample mean (still the best estimate of the population mean) from which an interval estimate for the population mean can be calculated.

The results of generating a bootstrap confidence interval (using 2000 re-samples) for the population mean Walking Time are given in Box 4.19.

Box 4.19

```
95.0% Bootstrap interval for mean Walking Time (56.21, 181.6)
```

This bootstrap interval suggests that the population mean Walking Time is likely to be between 56 and 182 minutes, which is fairly similar to that produced from the raw data (dubiously) assuming Normality.

The final approach, if the Normality assumption appears untenable, is to *concentrate on the median* as a 'more appropriate' measure of the typical value of the population rather than the mean. Procedures for providing interval estimates for a population median are available, the most useful, perhaps, being the Wilcoxon procedure. Techniques that involve estimation of a population median do not require assumptions relating to the Normal distribution and are often termed 'non-parametric' procedures – a rather daft term since it is still a population parameter (i.e. the median) that is being estimated. These techniques use the 'order statistic' of the data (i.e. all the data 'written down' from smallest to largest) and obtain an interval estimate by moving in an appropriate number of observations from each end of the data. A natural question to ask is, why not therefore focus on such procedures in all scenarios? The reason against this is that the resulting intervals tend to be wider (i.e. less precise) than the corresponding interval estimate based on Normality, particularly in small samples. There are always statistical swings and roundabouts!

Returning to the Walking Time data, an interval estimate for the population median Walking Time is given (in bold) in Box 4.20.

Box 4.20

```
Wilcoxon Signed Rank CI: Walking Time

                                              Confidence
                     Estimated      Achieved    Interval
              N        Median     Confidence  Lower    Upper
Walking Time  14           93           94.8     50      195
```

This interval suggests that the population median Walking Time is likely to be somewhere between 50 and 195 minutes.

Conclusion

The interval estimates from the four approaches taken in this illustration are as follows:

Approach	95% CI (min)
Raw data	52 to 198
Log transformation	48 to 142
Bootstrap	56 to 182
Median (Wilcoxon)	50 to 195

Three of the approaches provided an estimate of the *population mean*, while the remaining approach concentrated on the *population median*. The original data were right skewed, suggesting that the mean may well not be a useful summary of the 'typical' Walking Time owing to the influence of those individuals who walked considerably more than the others. Indeed, this concern is highlighted in the table of results as the upper end of the interval estimates for the population mean (based on the raw data and using the bootstrap) are both 'shifted to the right' compared with the interval based on the log-transformed data (which looked plausibly symmetrical). The same can be said for the 95% CI for the population median. It should be noted also that all the interval estimates are based on quite a small sample of 14 observations but this is not an unusual sample size in sports and exercise science.

The overall conclusion is that the mean may not be the 'best' summary of the typical Walking Time in this population of interest. It could be argued that the 'best' estimate of the typical Walking Time is provided by the log transformation as the interval is shifted to the left and was the narrowest (i.e. most precise). A pragmatic conclusion is that, regardless of the approach taken, the typical amount of time spent walking in the week prior to the study is likely to be between just under 1 hour and up to around 3 hours.

Reference: Mutrie, N., Carney, C., Blamey, A., Crawford, F., Aitchison, T. and Whitelaw, A. (2002). 'Walk In to Work Out, a randomised controlled trial of a self help intervention to promote active commuting.' *Journal of Epidemiology and Community Health*, **56**: 407–412.

4.8.2 Comparing two population means

Normality assumptions also apply in a comparison of two sample means. The method of production of the confidence interval (based on the *t*-distribution) for the difference in the two population means is, however, quite robust to departures from Normality if each of the samples is 'large' (typically 30 or more). However, the method may not work well in small samples that are not symmetrical (i.e. that have a degree of skewness) or which have outliers present).

The same approaches introduced for one sample problems are appropriate here, namely:

1   Using a suitable transformation of the data.

2   Use a re-sampling technique that does not assume Normality.

3   Concentrate on the population medians rather than means.

This section presents two illustrations. In the first, a log transformation turns out to be useful; in the second the log transformation is inappropriate.

Illustration 4.12   Walk In to Work Out (revisited)

Background
See Illustration 4.11 for details.

Study description
Those individuals that did not walk to work at the start of the study but who now work walk were identified. In total there were 14 who received the Intervention and 12 Controls.

Aim
To compare the typical time spent walking to work Post-Study across the Treatments specifically for the cohort identified who now walk to work despite not walking to work prior to the study.

Data

Name of data file:	*Walk to Work*
Response-variable:	Walking Time (minutes)
Between-subject factor:	Treatment (2 levels: Control, Intervention)

Analysis
A box plot of Walking Time for the Controls and those who received the Intervention (Figure 4.15) reveals some interesting patterns. There is a slightly higher median Walking

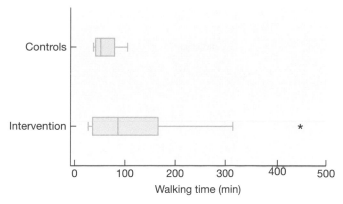

Figure 4.15 Box plot of Time Spent Walking by Treatment (six months post-intervention).

Time in the Intervention sample than in the Controls. There is a right skew in Walking Time present in both samples, with the variability considerably smaller among the Controls.

It is interesting to note that the sample of 12 Controls claim to spend slightly over an hour on average walking to work despite not walking to work prior to the study and not receiving the Intervention. This could be due to a change in mindset by virtue of being enrolled in such a study.

The 95% CI for the difference in mean Walking Time is given (in bold) in Box 4.21.

Box 4.21

```
Two-Sample T-Test and CI: Intervention, Controls

Two-sample T for Intervention vs Controls

                   N      Mean     StDev     SE Mean
Intervention      14       125       126          34
Controls          12      61.3      24.2         7.0

Difference = mu (Intervention) - mu (Controls)
Estimate for difference: 63.8
95% CI for difference: (-10.2, 137.9)
```

The difference in the sample mean Walking Time between the Treatments is 63.8 minutes; however, as the 95% CI of −10 to 138 minutes contains zero there is no evidence that the Intervention significantly improves Walking Time, on average, in the population of middle-class commuters.

The variability in Walking Time among the sample on the Intervention is more than double that for the Controls. A box plot with the individual data points highlighted (Figure 4.16) reveals that the two samples are in fact quite comparable but for three subjects who received the Intervention. This example highlights the importance of plotting *all* the data.

Given that the Normality assumption appears dubious for both Treatments as well as the existence of these three potential outliers, it is worth reanalysing the data to investigate whether these raise any major concerns with respect to the overall conclusion made.

As in Section 4.8.1, the first option considered is to use a log transformation. Note that a log transformation is appropriate as both samples exhibit a right skew. Log transformations

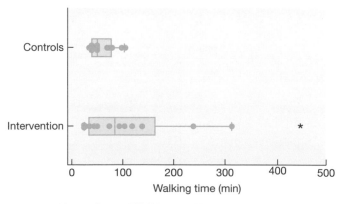

Figure 4.16 Box plot of Time Spent Walking by Treatment (six months post-intervention; individual data points shown).

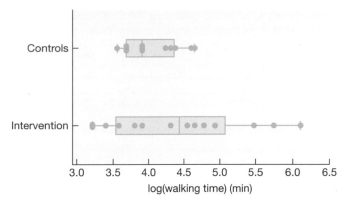

Figure 4.17 Box plot of Time Spent Walking by Treatment Post-Study (log scale).

are not appropriate for left-skewed data. A box plot of log(Walking Time) for both samples (with individual data points included) is given in Figure 4.17.

The log transformation has made the assumption of Normality much more credible for both Treatments than in the original scale of measurement. So, it is now reasonable to produce a 95% CI for the difference in population mean log(Walking Time) between the Treatments – this is given (in bold) in Box 4.22.

Box 4.22

```
Two-sample T for Log(Walking Time)

                  N       Mean      StDev      SE Mean
Intervention     14      4.410      0.941         0.25
Controls         12      4.047      0.380         0.11

Difference = mu (Intervention) - mu (Controls)
Estimate for difference: 0.363
95% CI for difference: (-0.216, 0.941)
```

Care must be taken when interpreting this interval, as it is represents an estimate of the *difference* in mean Walking Time between the Treatments on *the log scale*. However, when back transformed, this difference translates into an interval estimate for the *ratio* of population mean Walking Times in the original scale of measurement. Here, the interval estimate of the difference is –0.216 to 0.941 (in log minutes). Taking exponentials of each end of this interval results in an interval estimate for the ratio of means of 0.81 to 2.56. This allows the conclusion that those who received the Intervention are, on average, likely to spend between 0.81 and 2.56 *times* longer walking to work than Controls. The key deduction from this interval is that it contains the value 1 which corresponds to the two population mean Walking Times being equal, i.e. their ratio equals 1. Hence, *no significant difference* between the two Treatments has been identified.

The second approach is to use the bootstrap procedure to compare the two means in the original scale. An estimate of the sampling variability in the difference in the sample means (in the original units) is calculated by generating re-samples of the Intervention and Controls data and calculating the difference in the means from each pair of re-samples. A bootstrap confidence interval is then calculated using this estimated sampling variability. The 95% bootstrap CI for the Walking Time comparison is given in Box 4.23.

Box 4.23

```
95.0% Bootstrap interval for Difference in mean Walking Time (5.44, 139.19)
```

As the interval is strictly positive, there is evidence of a significant difference in mean Walking Times, with those on the Intervention likely to walk, on average, between 5 and 139 minutes *more* than Controls. As the interval is entirely positive there is evidence of a significant difference in mean Walking Time between the Treatments, favouring the Intervention. This is in contradiction to the previous two analyses of the same data.

The final approach is to compare the two medians (in the original scale) via a 95% CI for the difference in two population medians. The **Mann–Whitney** procedure is one such non-parametric approach and the required 95% CI is highlighted in Box 4.24.

Box 4.24

```
Mann-Whitney Test and CI: Intervention, Controls

                 N       Median
Intervention    14        85.0
Controls        12        50.0

Point estimate for ETA1-ETA2 is 20.0
95.2 Percent CI for ETA1-ETA2 is (-15.0, 80.0)
```

Note that the interval is listed as 95.2%. This is of no importance here and is merely a reflection that it is often not possible to attain the desired 95% confidence using the Mann–Whitney approach. The much more important result is that as the interval contains zero and consequently there is no evidence of a significant difference in the median Walking Time across the Treatments.

Conclusion

The (comparable) interval estimates from the different approaches taken in this illustration are as follows:

Approach	95% CI
Raw Data	−10 to 138
Bootstrap	5 to 139
Medians (Mann–Whitney)	−15 to 80

Only the Bootstrap approach identified a significant difference between the Treatments. This may well be due to the influence of the three possible outliers in the small sample. As the other approaches (including the log transformation) suggested no difference between the Treatments, then, even although the intervals are heavily 'loaded towards the Intervention', it is probably wise to claim that there is no conclusive evidence of a difference in mean Walking Time Post-Study among those receiving the Intervention compared with the Controls for those who did not walk to work at all before the study.

Additional comment on Illustration 4.12

It is worth noting that the study did have an overall positive effect on increasing the time spent walking to work by virtue of the results presented in Illustration 4.11. However, whether this increase was due to the Intervention is questionable as the improvement among the Controls is of a comparable magnitude.

The final example in this chapter involves a scenario where it is not appropriate to use a log transformation or indeed a comparison of medians.

Illustration 4.13 Soccer fitness (revisited)

Background and study description
See Illustrations 3.2 and 4.3 for details.

Aim
To compare the mean Counter Movement Jump (CMJ) Height in the populations of Senior and Youth soccer players.

Data

Name of data file:	*Soccer Fitness*
Response variable:	CMJ Height (centimetres)
Between-subject factor:	Squad (2 levels: Senior, Youth)

Analysis
As the assumption of Normality was questionable for the population of Senior players, given the left skew present in Figure 4.18, it is worth investigating whether this possible departure from Normality is having an influence on the final conclusion made.

The first thing to notice is that a log (or indeed a square root) transformation is not appropriate here as the median is skewed to the left in the box plot. The bootstrap procedure, however, is still appropriate and returned a 95% CI of the difference in mean CMJ Height of 3.31 cm to 9.81 cm favouring the Senior players.

The last option to consider is a comparison of population medians using the Mann–Whitney approach. A comparison of medians is slightly dubious here as one of the underlying assumptions of the Mann–Whitney approach is that the two distributions

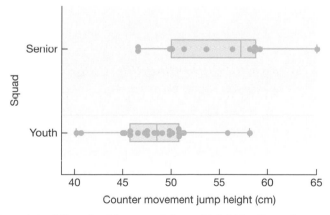

Figure 4.18 Box plot of Counter Movement Jump Height by Squad.

should be similar in shape but possibly different in median only. The departure, however, is clearly not dramatic and the results of the Mann–Whitney approach are given in Box 4.25.

Box 4.25

```
Mann-Whitney Test and CI: CMJump(cm)_Senior, CMJump(cm)_Youth

                          N      Median
CMJump(cm)_Senior        14      57.277
CMJump(cm)_Youth         23      48.514

Point estimate for ETA1-ETA2 is 7.620
95.3 Percent CI for ETA1-ETA2 is (2.537, 10.161)
```

Since the interval is entirely positive, the difference in CMJ Height medians is significant and is estimated to be between 2.5 cm and 10.2 cm favouring the Senior players.

Conclusion

The interval estimates from the different approaches taken in this illustration are as follows:

Approach	95% CI (cm)
Raw data	3.05 to 10.13
Bootstrap	3.31 to 9.81
Medians (Mann–Whitney)	2.54 to 10.16

All of the results provide the same conclusion and indeed similar estimates of the likely difference in the typical CMJ Height between Youth and Senior players. The overall conclusion therefore is that professional Senior soccer players tend to have a CMJ Height likely to be, on average, between 3 cm and 10 cm higher than professional Youth soccer players.

Exercises

4.12 There is a suggestion of a right skew in the % Body Fat distribution for Youth players in the *Soccer Fitness* data. Compare the typical % Body Fat between Youth and Senior soccer players using:

(a) a 95% CI for the difference in population means;

(b) a 95% CI for the difference in population means on the log scale;

(c) a 95% bootstrap CI the difference in population means;

(d) a 95% CI for the difference in population medians;

and make an overall conclusion.

Summary

The major aim when analysing data is usually to draw inferences (i.e. make conclusions) about the value of parameters in the population of interest, based upon the observed values of the summary statistics from the actual sample obtained. Interval estimation achieves this goal by providing a range of credible values for the population parameter of interest, be it a single parameter or a difference in two parameters. In particular, the sample mean and its estimated standard error can be used to make inferences about a population mean or differences in population means for data assumed to have arisen from Normal distributions.

Illustrations are presented in this chapter which introduce and demonstrate the use of interval estimation in two-sample and paired-sample problems in sports and exercise science where the response variable is continuous.

Prediction and tolerance interval estimation were introduced where interest lies in predicting at the individual level or for a range of the population, respectively. Several different procedures were introduced for handling situations where the Normal assumptions necessary for generating confidence intervals are dubious.

The next chapter introduces hypothesis testing as a different approach from interval estimation in data analysis. Several of the contexts analysed in this chapter will be re-analysed using hypothesis tests, and the benefits (or lack thereof) of hypothesis testing discussed.

Technical appendix

Interval estimation in general

- When an interval estimate is quoted, it is imperative that the population parameter being estimated is included in any statement. For example, it is not correct to say that '*the* 95% CI for 5 m Sprint Time is between 1.05 and 1.08 seconds', rather, '*a* 95% CI for the *population mean* Sprint Time of elite soccer players is between 1.05 and 1.08 seconds'. Methods to calculate interval estimates are available for a variety of parameters (e.g. mean, median, standard deviation). It must be made clear which population parameter is being estimated by the interval provided.

- The **confidence coefficient** is the percentage of occasions for which the *method* will, in the long run, capture the true population parameter. Typically, a confidence coefficient of 95% is chosen, an arbitrary but sensible and conventional choice. To be more conservative, a confidence coefficient of 99% could be used instead of 95%. However, the trade-off is that more conservative intervals are also much wider. For the 5 m Sprint Time example used in Illustration 4.1 the 95% CI was 1.050 to 1.088 seconds whereas the 99% CI is 1.043 to 1.094 seconds – a relatively large (roughly 35%) increase in the width of the interval for a relatively small gain (4%) in 'confidence'.

- It is always possible to make a CI narrower, i.e. more precise, while maintaining the desired degree of confidence by increasing the sample size. This may be easier said than done as time and monetary concerns will undoubtedly determine the maximum sample size available. Chapter 13 deals specifically with issues relating to interval width, sample size and the usefulness of small studies.

Two-sample *t*-interval

- The two-sample *t*-interval is quite robust to departures from Normality, if the samples are roughly similar in shape and size and are quite large (i.e. typically greater than 30 observations in each sample).

- The formula for calculating the estimated standard error (e.s.e.) for the difference in two sample means involves adding the separate errors for each sample mean. It is not quite that straightforward though as it is the squared e.s.e.'s that are added owing to the mathematics. The actual e.s.e. for the difference in means is defined as the square root of the sum of the e.s.e.'s of each of the two sample means. This result is highlighted here as it is an important component needed when determining the required sample size when comparing two means. It will come back to haunt you in Chapter 13.

Tolerance and prediction intervals

- Both tolerance and prediction intervals are quite sensitive to lack of symmetry (i.e. skewness) in the population. If the lack of Normality is a concern, it may be necessary to transform the data or to use re-sampling techniques.

- It is completely wrong to use a confidence interval for a population mean as a credible range for a future observation. An interval estimate for a population mean is a credible range for this parameter and not a yardstick to investigate whether an individual belongs to the population in question. One such misuse could be in the area of drug testing athletes where a confidence interval for a population mean is used (incorrectly!) as a range to detect the level of particular substances based on blood and urine concentration at the individual level. An athlete may have a value outside the confidence interval and be incorrectly identified as 'outside legal limits' where in fact a tolerance interval would have been a more appropriate method of comparison.

Using a transformation

- Care must be taken when intervals are interpreted, where an inverse transformation has been applied, as such intervals do not strictly represent the population mean on the original scale. Suggestions have been made to 'correct' these intervals by applying further 'correction adjustments' to each end of the interval, but they are generally not substantial in nature.

Bootstrap

- What is meant by a re-sample? Imagine the 14 Walking Times of Illustration 4.11 are written on pieces of paper and placed in a hat. Take a sample of size 14 from the 14 available, where an observation is chosen (at random) from the hat, recorded and then returned to the hat. This procedure continues until a new 're-sample' of size 14 (in this case) is taken and then the sample mean of this 're-sample' is calculated. This process is repeated many times (typically 1000, resulting in a large collection of 're-sample' sample means that behave very similarly to what might have happened had 1000 actual samples been taken from the population itself.

5 Testing hypotheses

5.1 Introduction

The previous chapter illustrated the use of interval estimation techniques to provide a range of plausible values for a population parameter based on the corresponding sample statistic and its estimated standard error. The resulting interval allowed statements to be made regarding the likely value of parameters (in particular the mean and median) in the population.

This chapter introduces hypothesis testing as a different option (and complement) to interval estimation. Several of the illustrations analysed in the previous chapter will be re-analysed using this different approach and the benefits (or lack thereof) of hypothesis testing discussed.

A **hypothesis test**, or **statistical test of significance**, is a procedure for making formal statements about whether a population parameter could conceivably take a particular predetermined value (often zero) based on a sample of data from the population.

5.2 Introduction to the null and alternative hypotheses

How could it be *proved* that all male basketball players are taller than 175 cm (5 feet 9 inches)? Even if the heights from a sample of thousands of male basketball players were recorded, and each one was taller than 175 cm, the hypothesis would still not be proven. If, on the other hand, a solitary basketball player smaller than 175 cm is found, the hypothesis has been disproved immediately. This example demonstrates that there is a simpler logical framework for disproving hypotheses than for proving them. For this reason, a hypothesis test typically begins by stating the *converse* of the key hypothesis of interest, called the **null hypothesis**, and attempts to disprove this.

A typical scenario involves the comparison of the mean of two distinct populations (e.g. a simple between-subject design with one factor at two levels). There are two possibilities under consideration: the population means are equal or the population means are different. Define the two competing hypotheses:

H_0: The difference in the population means is zero
H_1: The difference in the population means is not zero

where the first hypothesis H_0 is referred to as the **null hypothesis** and the second hypothesis H_1 is the **alternative hypothesis**. The alternative hypothesis is the hypothesis that must be true if the null hypothesis is false.

Both hypotheses are statements relating to population parameters and the object of the procedure is to decide whether the null hypothesis should be rejected. Rather than try to prove that the alternative hypothesis is true, the aim is to provide evidence against the null hypothesis, in favour of a more plausible alternative.

5.2.1 Measuring evidence against the null hypothesis: test statistics and *P*-values

What would constitute evidence against the null hypothesis in the comparison of the mean of two distinct populations? A natural choice for such a **test statistic** might be the difference in the two sample means. However, both sample means are *estimates* of their corresponding parameter. Recall from Chapter 4 that the estimated standard error (e.s.e.) provides an estimate as to the precision of the sample statistic, the larger the e.s.e. the less precise the statistic is as an estimate of the corresponding parameter. One proposed test statistic, used to provide evidence against the null hypothesis in a two-sample comparison of means, involves the ratio of the difference in the two sample means and the e.s.e of the difference in sample means. It is formally defined as:

$$t = \frac{\text{Difference in sample means}}{\text{e.s.e. of the difference in sample means}}$$

Numerical values of the *t*-test statistic distant (i.e. either negatively or positively) from zero suggest that the difference in sample means is large relative to the *combined* variability in their estimates; small values close to zero suggest that the sample means were quite close and that their difference is indistinguishable from the variability in their estimates.

A probability (of an event of interest) is always evaluated on a scale from 0 to 1 where the chances of the event of interest happening become more likely as the probability approaches 1 and less and less likely as it approaches 0. An equivalent way of looking at the test statistic above is to consider the probability of observing a more 'extreme' value than that actually observed from the data if the samples did arise from populations with the same population mean (i.e. if the null hypothesis was true). This probability is referred to as the ***P*-value** (P for probability) and is central in the decision-making process in hypothesis testing.

5.2.2 Statistical significance

The notion of statistical significance was introduced in Chapter 1 to represent an observed effect that was 'unlikely to have occurred by chance'. This is formalised in the hypothesis-testing paradigm by determining when a *P*-value is small enough to warrant rejecting the null hypothesis. The choice of such a 'small enough value' is known as the **significance level** and is traditionally set at 0.05, so that a *P*-value *less than or equal to 0.05* is thought to provide enough evidence to reject the null hypothesis. In such a case, the data are said to have produced a **statistically significant** conclusion and a decision is made to reject the null hypothesis.

The illustration on Soccer Fitness, introduced in Chapters 3 and 4, involved a comparison of two population means. A 95% Confidence Interval (CI) for the difference in population mean CMJ Height (Seniors minus Youths) ranged from 3.05 to 10.13 cm (Box 4.4), providing evidence of a higher mean CMJ Height in the population of Senior soccer players. It may be rightly claimed that that conclusion has been achieved by virtue of the 95% CI providing a credible range for the parameter of interest, namely the difference in the population means. This interval did not contain zero, implying that the population means are significantly different.

What is a hypothesis test adding to the evidence provided by the interval estimate? The answer is nothing! Historically, hypothesis testing was used before interval estimation ideas were 'developed' and, although it adds little, the approach is still used extensively in sports and exercise science – often pointlessly, as in this example. There are, however, a number of scenarios where it is useful – for example, in the ideas of model choice introduced in later chapters. Although hypothesis testing is, strictly speaking, unnecessary for the examples presented here, it is useful to introduce the basic idea here rather than in more complicated situations where interval estimation is much less effective or indeed even impossible.

5.3   Comparing two population means: the two-sample *t*-test

For completeness, and as an initial illustration for introducing the ideas of hypothesis testing in practice, an analysis of the *Soccer Fitness* data using hypothesis testing now follows.

Illustration 5.1   Soccer fitness (revisited)

Background and study description
See Illustrations 3.2 and 4.3 for details.

Aim
To compare the mean Counter Movement Jump (CMJ) Height in the populations of Senior and Youth soccer players.

Data

Name of data file:	*Soccer Fitness*
Response variable:	CMJ Height (centimetres)
Between-subject factor *:	Squad (2 levels: Senior, Youth)

*Strictly speaking the term 'between-subject factor' is more appropriate for designed as opposed to observational studies.

Analysis
The purpose of the analysis is to decide whether there is enough evidence in the sample data to suggest that the mean CMJ Height differs in the two populations. The box plots suggested that the CMJ Height distribution was plausibly Normal in both the populations

of Youth and Senior soccer players. The relevant null and alternative hypotheses for this example are:

H_0: The difference in *population* mean CMJ Height for Youth and Senior soccer players is zero

H_1: The difference in *population* mean CMJ Height for Youth and Senior soccer players is not zero

The output from the required two-Sample *t*-test is given in Box 5.1.

Box 5.1

```
Two-sample T for CMJ(cm)

Squad    N    Mean   StDev   SE Mean
Senior  14   55.08    5.52       1.5
Youth   23   48.49    4.06      0.85

T-Test of difference = 0 (vs not =): T-Value = 3.87
P-Value = 0.001 DF = 21
```

The value of the test statistic (referred to as **T-value** in the output) is 3.87 which is not directly interpretable. The more useful measure is the *P*-value (highlighted in bold in Box 5.1) which is reported as 0.001 and hence it can be claimed that, if the two populations had the same mean, the chances of observing a difference (at least as extreme) as in the actual two sample means is less than one in a thousand. Since this *P*-value is much less than the conventional significance level of 0.05, the null hypothesis can be rejected and hence the alternative hypothesis that the difference in the two population means is not zero, is assumed to be true.

Conclusion

There is convincing evidence of a significant difference in mean CMJ Height in the population of Senior and Youth soccer players ($P = 0.001$).*

*The convention of ($P = *.***$) is commonly used in journals as shorthand for reporting the result of a hypothesis test.

The basic ideas of hypothesis testing are further illustrated by revisiting the Osteoporosis study first introduced in Chapter 3 but from a slightly different slant. Recall that an initial aim of this study was to 'check' whether the typical Balance scores of Controls and Exercisers were 'similar' at baseline. Clearly, the desired outcome in such a scenario is not to reject the null hypothesis, and hence to 'justify' that the randomisation was effective in terms of comparability between the Treatments at baseline. This is, of course, not the standard approach in a hypothesis test, where the researcher usually hopes to reject the null hypothesis.

Illustration 5.2 **Osteoporosis and exercise (revisited)**

Background and study description
See Illustration 4.5 for details.

Aim
To assess whether the Controls and Exercisers were comparable at baseline in terms of this measure of Balance.

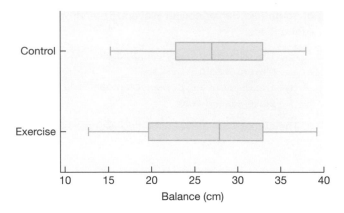

Figure 5.1 Box plot of Pre-Study Balance by Regime.

Data

Name of data file:	*Osteoposis*
Response variable:	Balance (centimetres)
Between-subject factor:	Regime (2 levels: Exerciser, Control)

Analysis

The sample median Balance is nearly identical for Controls and Exercisers at baseline (Figure 5.1). A Normality assumption for each population appears justified also thereby warranting the use of the two-sample test.

The null and alternative hypotheses for this example are:

H_0: The difference in *population* mean Balance for Exercisers and Controls (before the study) is zero

H_1: The difference in *population* mean Balance for Exercisers and Controls (before the study) is not zero

The corresponding two-Sample *t*-test output is given in Box 5.2.

Box 5.2

```
Two-sample T for Balance (cm) Before Study

Regime      N     Mean    StDev    SE Mean
Control    14    27.00    7.14       1.9
Exercise   16    27.19    7.37       1.8

Difference = mu (Control) - mu (Exercise)
Estimate for difference: -0.20
95% CI for difference:   (-5.64, 5.25)

T-Test of difference = 0 (vs not =): T-Value = -0.07
P-Value = 0.941 DF = 27
```

The *P*-value of 0.941 is (much) larger than 0.05 and hence there is no significant difference in mean Balance for the Exercise and Control Regimes. The *P*-value indicates that there is approximately a 94% chance of seeing at least as much a difference in sample means as observed *due to sampling variability alone* if the populations from which they were chosen had equal means. The data are thus 'very consistent' with the null hypothesis and there is no convincing evidence in the sample to suggest that the populations are different at baseline in terms of mean Balance.

Such a result tends to be reported as: 'there was no significant difference between the Regimes at baseline, in terms of mean Balance ($P = 0.94$)'. The difference in sample means is attributable to sampling variability and not to any systematic difference in the population means. *Notice that the same conclusion was available immediately by looking at the interval estimate of the difference in population means,* i.e. $(-5.64, 5.25)$. As the interval contains zero then it can be claimed that zero is a plausible value for the true difference in mean Balance (very much so since zero is in the middle of this interval), and hence there is no evidence against the population means being different.

Conclusion

There is no evidence of a significant difference in mean Balance between the Regimes at baseline ($P = 0.94$).

Additional comment on Illustration 5.2

The result for this analysis illustrates an important relationship between a 95% CI for a difference in population means and the two-sample *t*-test using a 5% significance level: *if the 95% CI does not contain zero, the corresponding P-value will be less than 0.05, and indeed vice versa.* The information provided by the *P*-value for the two-sample *t*-test (as to whether there is evidence of a significant difference) is also available by identifying whether zero lies in the 95% CI.

> However, the interval estimate is clearly more useful as it provides a range of credible values for the difference in population means.

Note that this comment applies only when the alternative hypothesis is 'population means are different'. There are other forms available for the alternative hypothesis (so-called one-sided tests), and the reader is referred to the technical appendix at the end of this chapter for more details.

Exercises

5.1 Use hypothesis testing to compare the mean Haemoglobin Concentration in the populations of Male and Female endurance runners (*Haemoglobin* data introduced in Exercise 3.2). Include suitable null and alternative hypotheses as well as an interpretation of the *P*-value. In addition, calculate an interval estimate for the difference in mean Haemoglobin Concentration between Male and Female endurance runners and confirm that the *P*-value and interval estimate provide the same conclusion.

5.2 Investigate whether there is likely to be a difference in average Multi-Stage Shuttle Test Score between Youth and Senior soccer players using the *Soccer Fitness* data (Illustration 3.2). The response variable of interest is called Bleep Test in the data file.

5.3 Provide evidence as to whether there is a likely to be a difference in mean 'Predicted' $\dot{V}O_2$ max between the Control and Exercise groups at baseline in the *Osteoporosis* data introduced in Illustration 4.5.

5.4 Data are available from a fitness test battery of youth soccer players in an academy at a professional soccer club *(YouthSoccer)*. Using these data, carry out a two-sample *t*-test to compare mean Squat Score for Under-17 and Under-19 players.

The chapter continues with examples of within-subject designs, once again starting with the simplest such design involving paired data.

5.4   Paired data (the simplest within-subject design)

The interval estimation strategy, employed in Chapter 4 for paired-sample problems, involved the creation of a new variable representing the difference (i.e. the change, improvement, reduction, as appropriate) in the response variable for each subject. An appropriate interval estimate for the *population mean difference* provides a range of credible values for the magnitude of the 'intervention effect', i.e. the difference in population means. In addition, it allows the researcher to determine if the difference can be deemed significant (i.e. whether the interval estimate excludes zero) but also allows the researcher to determine the direction of any change and its magnitude.

The corresponding hypothesis needed for analysing paired data is aptly called the **paired-sample *t*-test**. The null hypothesis in this case is that the population mean difference *is* zero, whereas the alternative hypothesis is that the population mean difference *is not* zero. Once again the hypothesis test offers little, if any, improvement on the information already provided by the corresponding confidence interval for a mean difference. This is demonstrated in the following illustration.

Illustration 5.3   Training intervention (revisited)

Background and study description
See Illustration 4.6 for details.

Aim
To investigate whether a concurrent strength and high-intensity interval training intervention has improved the $\dot{V}O_2$ max of the soccer players during the 10-week study period, by comparing the $\dot{V}O_2$ max at the start and the end of the intervention.

Data
Name of data file:	*Training Intervention.*
Response variable:	$\dot{V}O_2$ max (ml.kg^{-1}.min^{-1})
Within-subject factor:	Time (2 levels: Pre-Study, Post-Study)

Analysis
An interval estimate of the *average difference* of $\dot{V}O_2$ max across the intervention, in the population of such soccer players, provided a mean improvement between 3.98 and 6.23 ml.kg^{-1}.min^{-1}. This is included in the results from a paired *t*-test for the same comparison which are given in Box 5.3.

Box 5.3

```
Paired T for vo2 Max Post - vo2 Max Pre

                  N       Mean     StDev   SE Mean
vo2 Max Post     18    72.7667    5.9928    1.4125
vo2 Max Pre      18    67.6556    5.8426    1.3771
Difference       18    5.11111   2.25829   0.53228

95% CI for mean difference: (3.98809, 6.23413)
T-Test of mean difference = 0 (vs not = 0):
T-Value = 9.60 P-Value = 0.000
```

The *P*-value is given as 0.000. Be careful here as statistical software tends to round *P*-values off to three decimals. The actual *P*-value for this analysis is less than one in a billion. The convention is to round the value to the level of the last decimal provided by the software, i.e. < 0.001 here. The result provides convincing evidence of a significant mean difference in $\dot{V}O_2$ max over the 10-week study period since the *P*-value is (much) less than 0.05.

Conclusion

There was strong evidence of a significant improvement ($P < 0.001$) in mean $\dot{V}O_2$ max across the study, in the population of youth players of interest. This result alone is quite uninformative as it provides no indication of the likely magnitude of the improvement across the season. The 95% CI for the population mean improvement is once again much more informative as it quantifies the magnitude of such an improvement (i.e. around 4 to 6 ml.kg^{-1}.min^{-1} which corresponds roughly to a 6% to 10% improvement relative to a typical Pre-Study $\dot{V}O_2$ max of around 70 ml.kg^{-1}.min^{-1}.

Exercises

5.5 Carry out a paired *t*-test to investigate whether the Strength and Endurance Training Intervention had any significant improvement on Squat Jump for the sample of Youth soccer players discussed in Illustration 5.3. The dataset is contained in the file *Training Intervention*.

5.6 Use hypothesis testing to investigate whether the difference in mean Tolerance Time for the Control and Soda Lime canisters can be deemed significant, using the *Avalanche* data (Illustration 4.9). Explain why an interval estimate of the population mean difference in Tolerance Time is much more informative than the *P*-value reported in the paired-sample *t*-test.

5.5 One between-subject and one within-subject factor (each at two levels)

Interval estimation techniques for analysing designs with one between- and one within-subject factor were introduced in Chapter 4. For completeness, the two Illustrations from there are re-analysed using hypothesis tests as this is almost certainly the most common type of designed study in sports and exercise science.

Illustration 5.4   **Osteoporosis and exercise (revisited)**

Background and study description

See Illustrations 4.5 and 4.7 for details.

Aim

To investigate whether or not an exercise regime can significantly improve the Balance (as measured by functional reach test) of osteoporotic women over a two-month period of exercise over any 'natural' improvement of Controls.

Data

Name of data file:	*Osteoporosis*
Response variable:	Balance (centimetres)
Between-subject factor:	Regime (2 levels: Exerciser, Control)
Within-subject factor:	Time (2 levels: Before Study, After Study)

Analysis

The null and alternative hypotheses needed in a hypothesis test to compare the mean improvement (taken here as Balance 'After the Study' minus Balance 'Before the Study') over the study period are:

H_0: The difference in mean improvement in Balance for Exercisers and Controls in the *population* is zero

H_1: The difference in mean improvement in Balance for Exercisers and Controls in the *population* is not zero

The corresponding two-sample *t*-test output is given in Box 5.4.

Box 5.4

```
Two-sample T for Imp Bal (A-B)
Regime      N   Mean   StDev   SE Mean
Exercise   16   4.40   3.77    0.94
Control    14   1.31   4.26     1.1

Difference = mu (Exercise) - mu (Control)
Estimate for difference: 3.09
95% CI for difference: (0.05, 6.13)
T-Test of difference = 0 (vs not =): T-Value = 2.09
P-Value = 0.046 DF = 26
```

Since the *P*-value is (just) less than 0.05 the mean improvement is deemed significantly different. To make any meaningful comment from this statement it is necessary to look at the 95% CI for the population mean difference in improvement (as in Illustration 4.7 previously). The interval is strictly positive (i.e. a significant result has been identified), and both the direction and magnitude are available (i.e. the mean improvement is higher for the Exercisers).

In such scenarios, it is often thought interesting to investigate whether there was evidence of a significant mean improvement *separately* in each of the two Regimes, i.e. separately for Controls and Exercisers. The appropriate null and alternative hypotheses needed for such a hypothesis test involving the Controls would be:

H_0: The mean improvement in Balance for the Control *population* is zero

H_1: The mean improvement in Balance for the Control *population* is not zero

The *P*-value from the corresponding one-sample *t*-test (Box 5.5) is returned as 0.272 which is interpreted as insufficient evidence of a significant mean improvement in Balance in the Control population across the study.

Box 5.5

```
One-Sample T: Imp Bal (A-B)_Control,
Test of mu = 0 vs not = 0

Variable                N  Mean  StDev  SE Mean        95% CI      T      P
Imp Bal (A-B)Control   14  1.31   4.26     1.14  (-1.15, 3.76)  1.15  0.272
```

The equivalent hypothesis test for the Exercisers did return a significant result as the *P*-value is less than 0.001, as can be seen in Box 5.6.

Box 5.6

```
One-Sample T: Imp Bal (A-B)_Exercise
Test of mu = 0 vs not = 0

Variable                 N   Mean  StDev  SE Mean        95% CI      T      P
Imp Bal (A-B)_Exercise  16  4.397  3.769    0.942  (2.389, 6.406)  4.67  0.000
```

So, when considering Exercisers alone, there is evidence of a significant mean improvement in Balance across the intervention.

Conclusions

There was evidence of a significant difference in the mean improvement ($P = 0.046$) in Balance between Controls and Exercisers over the two-month intervention period. Furthermore, when considering the Controls and Exercisers separately, there was no evidence of a significant mean improvement for the Controls ($P = 0.272$) while there was convincing evidence for the Exercisers ($P < 0.001$).

Additional comment on Illustration 5.4

The results, while providing evidence of a significant intervention effect, give no indication as to likely magnitude of the typical improvement. Without this information it is impossible to decide whether the intervention is of any use in a practical setting, i.e. whether the typical improvement, although significant in a statistical sense, is 'large' enough to be worth investing in. An average improvement of 4.4 cm in the Exercisers is equivalent to a 16% improvement in Balance when expressed as a percentage of the sample mean Balance of the Exercisers at baseline of 27.2 cm. Thus, in addition to being significant, this is clearly a considerable improvement.

Illustration 5.5   **Exercise and the elderly (revisited)**

Background and study description
See Illustration 3.5 and 4.8 for details.

Aim
To compare Relative Intensity during the Aerobic Dance and Walking sessions overall and then separately for Males and Females.

Data

Name of data file:	*WalkDance*
Response variable:	Relative Intensity (% Peak V̇O₂)
Between-subject factor:	Sex 2 levels: Male, Female)
Within-subject factor:	Exercise Regime (2 levels: Walking, Aerobic Dance)

Analysis

The analysis required is identical to that presented in the previous illustration. The results of the separate hypothesis tests for Males and Females are given first (Box 5.7).

Box 5.7

```
One-Sample T: Dance-Walk(M), Dance-Walk(F)
Test of mu = 0 vs not = 0

Variable        N    Mean    StDev   SE Mean      95% CI         T      P
Dance-Walk(M)   6   18.17    5.81     2.37   (12.07, 24.27)   7.66   0.001
Dance-Walk(F)   6   12.41    9.17     3.74   ( 2.79, 22.03)   3.32   0.021
```

When reporting such analyses in a paper or a presentation it has become common practice to present the *P*-value without quoting the relevant null and alternative hypothesis. It is assumed that the hypotheses are obvious from the context! For example, the results given in Box 5.7 tend to be presented as: 'there was a significant difference in Relative Intensity when carrying out an Aerobic Dance class compared to a Walking session separately for both Males ($P = 0.001$) and Females ($P = 0.021$)'. Hypothesis testing has a language of its own which typically says very little in practical terms.

The output from a two-sample *t*-test needed to assess whether the higher Relative Intensity between Aerobic Dance and Walking sessions is the same, on average, between Males and Females is given in Box 5.8.

Box 5.8

```
Two-sample T for Dance-Walk(M) vs Dance-Walk(F)

                 N    Mean    StDev   SE Mean
Dance-Walk(M)    6   18.17    5.81      2.4
Dance-Walk(F)    6   12.41    9.17      3.7

Difference = mu (Dance-Walk(M)) − mu (Dance-Walk(F))
Estimate for difference: 5.76
95% CI for difference: (−4.46, 15.97)
T-Test of difference = 0 (vs not =): T-Value = 1.30
P-Value = 0.230 DF = 8
```

Similarly to the conclusion reached through the appropriate interval estimate (see Illustration 4.8), this hypothesis test confirms that there was no evidence of a significant difference in the average Aerobic Dance Relative Intensity over the Walking sessions between Males and Females ($P = 0.230$).

Conclusion

There was evidence that mean Relative Intensity was significantly higher when carrying out an Aerobic Dance session compared with a Walking session for both Males ($P = 0.001$) and Females ($P = 0.021$) in the elderly population targeted. There was no evidence, however, that the typical higher Relative Intensity was different across the sexes ($P = 0.230$).

5.7 The Osteoporosis study used in Illustration 4.7 involved the measurement of other variables such as a measure of Flexibility, the sit-and-reach test. Investigate, using the methods above, whether the Exercisers improved on this measure of Flexibility significantly more on average than did the Controls. If so, how much more?

5.8 Revisit the Ankylosing Spondylitis (AS) study (Exercise 4.9) and investigate whether there is evidence that the Exercise Intervention, on average, improved forced vital capacity (FVC) significantly over Controls.

The various interval estimation techniques and corresponding hypothesis tests presented so far all assume that either the response variable of interest in two-sample comparisons or the simple differences in paired studies arose from Normal distributions. Up to now the validity of this assumption has been investigated subjectively through box plots. Formal hypothesis tests exist, however, for precisely this purpose and are now introduced.

5.6 Testing for Normality

Several hypothesis tests exist for formally testing whether a variable of interest from a single sample is likely to have arisen from a Normal distribution. Examples here include the wonderfully named Shapiro–Wilks, Anderson–Darling, Kolmogorov–Smirnov and the D'Agostino–Pearson Omnibus tests. The null hypothesis is the same for each test, however, namely that the data arose from a Normal distribution, with the alternative hypothesis that the data originated from some other unspecified distribution. The hypothesis testing approach is useful here as there is really no 'interval estimate' available. Note also that, this time, *not rejecting* the null hypothesis is usually the desired result.

In addition, a **Normal probability plot** provides graphical evidence as to whether the Normality assumption is valid. The observed data, in ascending order, are compared to what values would be 'expected' if indeed the data were generated from a Normal distribution. This procedure is typically carried out by looking at a plot of the sample **percentiles** (the value of a variable below which a certain percentage of observations lie, e.g. there are 10% of observations in a sample less than the 10th percentile) against those 'expected'. The pattern of points in this plot of 'observed against expected from Normal distribution' should approximate a straight line if the Normal distribution is plausible for the variable of interest.

Box plots of data simulated from a Normal distribution were presented in Figure 3.31 in order to get a feel for the type of box plot that could arise for samples of data from Normal populations. Normal probability plots for the same data are given in Figure 5.2 to allow the reader to appreciate the 'real types of data' that can arise from a Normal distribution.

In general the points are randomly scattered in a linear manner about the 'reference' line representing where the data should appear if they were indeed a sample from a Normal population. The level of agreement, although not perfect, is quite

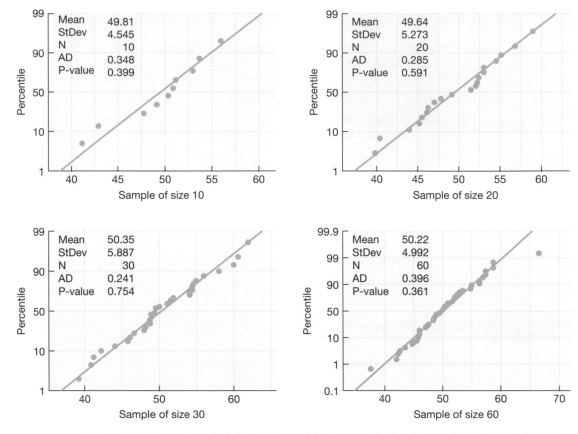

Figure 5.2 **Normal probability plots and Anderson–Darling Normality test (simulated data from a Normal distribution).**

good especially for the larger sample sizes. There are a few departures from a linear pattern evident in the plot for the smallest sample size, highlighting that such patterns are plausible under Normality.

In instances involving small samples it becomes more difficult to assess Normality from the plot alone and a hypothesis test can be useful here. The *P*-values from one such test, the Anderson–Darling Normality test (AD), are given in the legend in each plot in Figure 5.2. As all of the *P*-values here are greater than 0.05 there is no convincing evidence against Normality for any of the simulated samples under consideration.

Illustration 4.11 had as response variable the time an individual spent walking to work in a typical week. There was a suggestion based on the box plot of Walking Times that the data may not have arisen from a Normal population.

Illustration 5.6   Walk In to Work Out (revisited)

Background and study description
See Illustration 4.11 for details.

Aim
To formally investigate whether the response variable Walking Time could be assumed to have arisen from a Normal distribution.

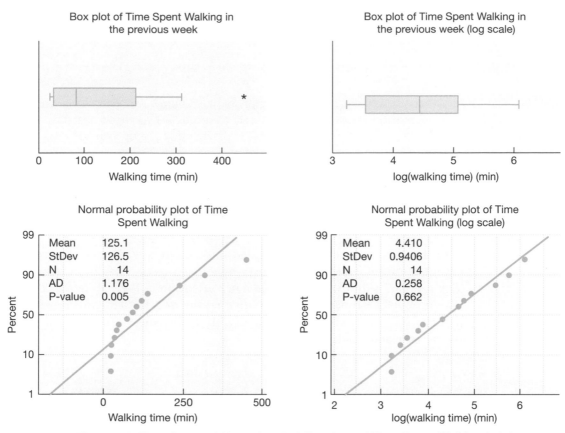

Figure 5.3 **Box plots and Normal probability plots of Time Spent Walking (original units and log scale).**

Data

Name of data file: *Walk to Work*
Response variable: Walking Time (minutes)

Analysis

Figure 5.3 presents box plots and Normal probability plots of Walking Time in the original units and on the logarithmic scale. The skew in the raw data is noticeable in the plots of Walking Time on the original scale where the median is positioned quite to the left in the IQR in the box plot and the 'smaller' Walking Times tend to fall below what would be expected under a Normal distribution. The log transformation appears successful as the box plot here appears reasonably symmetrical and the Normal probability plot of 'observed against expected values from a Normal distribution' follow more or less a straight line.

The P-value for the Anderson–Darling Normality test for the original data is given as being less than 0.005, and therefore the assumption of Normality can easily be rejected for the raw data. The P-value for the same test carried out using the log-transformed data is 0.662 and hence the null hypothesis is not rejected, suggesting that the Normality assumption may be valid in the log scale.

Conclusion

The box plots, Normal probability plots and P-values suggest that the Normality assumption is not justified for Walking Time on the original scale of measurement (i.e. minutes) but may well be justified on the log-transformed scale. Any analysis that has Normality as an assumption should therefore be carried out on the log-transformed data.

5.9 Prepare a Normal probability plot for the Energy Expenditure variable in the *Popmobility* data (Exercise 3.1) and carry out a hypothesis test for Normality. Comment on whether it is plausible to assume that Energy Expenditure is Normally distributed in the population of interest.

5.10 Prepare a Normal probability plot for Tolerance Time using the Control canister (*Avalanche* data, Illustration 4.9) and formally investigate whether this response variable may have arisen from a Normal distribution.

In the various illustrations presented throughout this chapter, the considerable advantage of interval estimation over hypothesis testing has been demonstrated. Many people (sadly) still give far too much attention to *P*-values (rather than focusing on interval estimates), and this often results in confused conclusions from hypothesis tests. This chapter concludes with a discussion regarding the misuse of significance and *P*-values in general.

5.7   The misuse of *P*-values: significance and importance

The term 'significant' literally means important, noticeable or having a special meaning. When the results of a hypothesis test are reported, the word 'significant' has acquired a new meaning to indicate that the resulting *P*-value was less than the chosen significance level (usually 0.05). There is a natural tendency to assume that a 'significant result' is therefore 'important' when this is not necessarily the case. Indeed, a study is often deemed to have been an immediate success if a significant result has been found!

A *P*-value may well be very small, say 0.00001, and the null hypothesis is therefore conclusively rejected. The hypothesis test has provided very convincing evidence of a significant difference, say, in the population means and everyone is excited. If, instead, a 95% CI for the true difference in population means is calculated and the results are returned as 0.5 to 1.0 seconds, would the level of excitement be as great? This depends on what is considered a meaningful or important difference given the aims of the study. If, for example, the interval represented an improvement in marathon finishing time (in seconds) the 'intervention' would be pointless; however, it would be very meaningful if it was a 100 m sprint time improvement.

Don't ignore the lack of significance, however! Failing to reject the null hypothesis may be due to the sample size being too small (i.e. a lack of power in the study), and a larger sample may well have detected a significant and important result. Always design the study carefully (Chapter 2), and use a sample size based on a power calculation (Chapter 13) to ensure that the study is worth carrying out at all.

Summary

Some people still use hypothesis testing in preference to interval estimation in analysing data. The take-home message from this book is to use interval estimation whenever possible, as hypothesis tests do not add anything useful to that already provided by the corresponding interval estimates, if they exist. A P-value is completely redundant once an interval estimate is available, but convention sadly still 'dictates' that P-values are quoted. *Never report a P-value and use words like 'statistically significant' without providing an interval estimate for the parameter of interest.*

P-values can be considered a 'Quasimodo' approach to statistical inference – ringing a bell to bring a result to people's notice. A significant P-value provides evidence of a significant effect but gives no impression of the magnitude of the likely effect size. Interval estimation does provide such an estimate from which a more practical conclusion can be drawn with regard to the main question of interest.

A natural question at this stage is to ask why it was considered worthwhile 'to confuse' the issue by introducing hypothesis testing when the use of interval estimates is clearer and not bogged down in (hypothesis testing) jargon. The answer is that a hypothesis testing approach can be useful in some scenarios, such as tests for Normality in this chapter and for statistical modelling techniques which are the focus of many of the remaining chapters.

Technical appendix

Two-sample tests

- The two-sample *t*-test (as well as the corresponding interval estimate) is based on several assumptions that must be checked before any final conclusions can be made. The samples are assumed to be **random** (i.e. random sampling was used or the subjects were randomly allocated to the two levels of the factor), and **independent** (i.e. no observation is in any way influenced by any other observation). The variable of interest is assumed to have a **Normal distribution** in each of the populations from which the samples arose. These assumptions, to differing extents, can be catered for by careful study design and checked by the use of box plots and Normal probability plots.

Pooled two-sample tests

- If the two samples arose from Normal distributions that had the *same* population standard deviation, a more powerful version of the two-sample *t*-test is available, the so-called **pooled two-sample *t*-test.** The estimated standard error (e.s.e.) of the difference in sample means uses separate estimates of the two sample standard deviations in the denominator in the two-sample *t*-test statistic (see the technical appendix in Chapter 4). In the pooled version of the test, the e.s.e. of the difference in sample means is replaced with a single pooled estimate calculated by combining the information from both sample standard deviations. Pooling the data may well provide a smaller estimated standard error, a larger test statistic and consequently a smaller *P*-value. In order to use a pooled two-sample *t*-test, evidence must be provided that the assumption of equality of the population standard deviations is valid. Several hypothesis tests exist (the *F*-test and Levene's test) to test this assumption but tend to be unreliable owing to extreme sensitivity to departures from Normality, especially when the two sample sizes are small or are considerably different.

● The advantage gained in using the pooled version is usually slight and more evident when the samples are smaller when it is, of course, more 'difficult' to test the equal variance assumption. For this reason, the two-sample *t*-test is recommended in general over the pooled version.

● The assumption of equal variances may be justified for the baseline comparison in the Osteoporosis and Exercise study (Illustration 5.2) as both Treatments are made up from random allocation of a sample that originated from a single population. The results from using the pooled *t*-test are given in Box 5.9.

Box 5.9

```
Two-Sample T-Test and CI: Balance (cm) Before Study, Regime
Two-sample T for Balance (cm) Before Study

Regime     N    Mean    StDev    SE Mean
Control    14   27.00   7.14      1.9
Exercise   16   27.19   7.37      1.8

Difference = mu (Control) - mu (Exercise)
Estimate for difference: -0.20
95% CI for difference: (-5.64, 5.25)
T-Test of difference = 0 (vs not =): T-Value = -0.07
P-Value = 0.941 DF = 28
Both use Pooled StDev = 7.2642
```

The pooled standard deviation is given (in bold) as 7.2642. The *P*-value and corresponding 95% CI are 0.941 and [−5.64, 5.25] which are in fact identical in this case to those reported for the 'un-pooled' two-sample *t*-test (Box 5.2).

One- and two-sided tests

● The alternative hypothesis in Illustration 5.1 (the CMJ Height comparison) was that there is a *difference in population mean* CMJ Height for Youth and Senior soccer players. The alternative hypothesis therefore represents two different 'directions' (mean CMJ Height could be higher in Senior players *or* mean CMJ Height could be higher in Youth players). This is termed a **two-sided** test as the alternative hypothesis is allowing for both 'directions'. A **one-sided** test involves only one 'direction' to be specified, as the test is interested only in detecting evidence in the 'direction' specified. For example, a one-sided alternative hypothesis could be:

H_1: The population mean CMJ Height is *higher* for Senior Soccer Players than for Youth Soccer Players.

The *P*-value from a one-sided test is adjusted to take into account the alternative hypothesis (it is actually half the *P*-value for the two-sided test) and it is therefore 'easier' to find a significant *P*-value in a one-sided test compared with a two-sided test. However, it is bad practice (if not in fact wrong) to decide whether to use this 'advantage' by deciding to specify a one-sided test having looked at the sample means as the data are now generating the hypothesis. There is no guarantee that another sample from the same population would have suggested the same alternative hypothesis. *Always specify an alternative hypothesis before analysing the data.* This issue is discussed in more detail in Chapter 7.

● One example of where a one-sided test may be appropriate is where a new training regime is being compared to one currently in use and there is interest in detecting that the mean of the response of interest (e.g. $\dot{V}O_2$ max) is 'better' for the new regime than for the one currently in use. The researcher is interested only in determining if convincing evidence exists that the new regime is superior.

Accepting a null hypothesis

● You can't! Accepting a null hypothesis is tantamount to making a factual statement about the value of a population parameter based on a sample estimate. A *P*-value greater than 0.05 is interpreted as lack of evidence in the sample to reject the null hypothesis of interest. This is not the same as saying that the null hypothesis 'can be accepted'. This may sound pedantic, but 'accepting' a null hypothesis is simply wrong. The logical conclusion is that there is insufficient evidence to reject the null hypothesis.

Interpreting a *P*-value

● A *P*-value is not the probability of the null hypothesis being true. The null hypothesis is assumed true and the evidence against it is quantified. The null hypothesis being true implies that any difference evident in, say, the sample means is purely a reflection of the natural sampling variation inherent in taking random samples from each of two identical populations. The *P*-value quantifies the chance of observing such a value of the test statistic (or one more extreme) if the null hypothesis was actually true. The lower the *P*-value, the more evidence against the null hypothesis.

● The *P*-value for the two-sample *t*-test for the CMJ Height comparison (Illustration 5.1) was less than one in a billion. If the researcher is happy to believe that he/she managed, simply by chance, to choose the two independent random samples from identical populations that appear approximately once in a billion then he/she should not reject the null hypothesis. On the other hand, the researcher may wish to claim that the evidence against the populations having the same mean is overwhelming. Surely the more sensible decision is that the population means are different from each other, i.e. there is convincing evidence that the difference observed in the sample means is large enough to rule out sampling variability as the likely cause.

Paired-sample *t*-test

- The assumptions of the paired *t*-test are that the subjects were randomly selected from the population of interest and are independent of one another as well as that the differences are Normally distributed. Clearly, the two observations for each subject are dependent but there should be no dependence between the actual subjects (e.g. athletes should produce their results individually rather than in competition against each other if considering, say, sprint times).

Tests of Normality

- The main concern with tests of Normality is their dependence on the size of the sample. It is often the case that sports and exercise science studies involve a relatively small number of subjects and many statisticians are wary of using tests of Normality to give a 'green light' to warrant the use of a hypothesis test (or interval estimate) that depends on the assumption of a Normal distribution in such scenarios. The decision to use a hypothesis test such as the two-sample or paired-sample *t*-test for small samples (less than 10 observations per level) based on the results of another hypothesis test (of Normality) is not an attractive prospect and should be avoided, if at all possible.

- It is quite likely that a Normality test will deliver a non-significant result when based on a small sample regardless of whether the population distribution was actually Normally distributed. The non-significant result is more a reflection of the lack of power of the test of Normality than a confirmation of Normality itself.

- Normality tests should not be used as a 'safety blanket', and a pragmatic approach should be taken when small samples are concerned, i.e. compare the final result to methods where Normality is not an issue such as the transformation, bootstrap or non-parametric approaches which were introduced in Chapter 4.

6 Modelling relationships: regression

6.1 Introduction

One challenge encountered in sports and exercise science is the investigation of whether one or more of a set of explanatory variables are related in any way to a particular *continuous* response variable.

In many instances, *predicting* the response variable for a future subject is the aim. For example, blood lactate endurance markers (of which there are many) are often used to predict an athlete's finishing time in a race. Prediction, however, may not be the primary aim in studies where the researcher is interested in identifying variables that *explain* significant proportions of the variability in the response in question. Examples here might involve identifying the variables that explain a person's percentage body fat (e.g. gender, age or exercise level) or studying to what extent physiological measures and recent altitude attained might explain the variability in successful ascent times on Mont Blanc.

The statistical technique required is called **regression** which allows the researcher to *model* the dependence of a response variable of interest on one or more explanatory variables. Recall that the response variable is the key variable of interest (the one the researcher wishes to predict or explain) while the explanatory variable is a variable used to model the variability in the response variable.

The first illustration presented is the simplest case where a *single* explanatory variable is available.

6.2 Simple linear regression

Simple linear regression is the name given to the statistical technique that is used to model the dependence of a response variable on a single explanatory variable – the word 'simple' refers to the fact that a *single* explanatory variable is available. Simple linear regression is appropriate if the average value of the response variable is a linear function of the explanatory, i.e. the underlying dependence of the response on the explanatory appears linear.

The simple linear regression model is of the form:

Response variable = Intercept + Slope * Explanatory variable
+ Random (natural) variability

where the intercept and slope are of key importance and must be estimated from a sample of data from the relevant population. Note that the model implies that the relationship between the response and the explanatory is linear (i.e. adequately represented by a line) with some random scatter about the line.

The **slope** represents the change in *average* response per unit increase in the explanatory. The **intercept** represents the average response when the explanatory is equal to zero (and is often only of limited importance).

6.2.1 Inference in regression: sample to population

If a different sample were chosen from the population, is it likely that the resulting estimated regression equation (line of best fit) will be exactly the same? By now the reader should realise that the intercept and slope are in fact nothing but estimates of the true parameters of interest, the *actual* intercept and slope relating to the population of interest. The estimated standard error (e.s.e.) for the sample intercept and slope are needed therefore in order that interval estimates can be provided for the true but unknown corresponding population parameters. This is the same logic as appears in virtually all chapters of this text – think sample statistic and subsequent confidence interval for the corresponding population parameter.

The estimated standard error of the slope has a secondary role as the basis of a test statistic to investigate whether there is evidence of a significant dependence of the response variable on the explanatory variable in the population.

Recall Illustration 3.11 where the primary aim was to investigate whether there was evidence of a dependence of a male athlete's subsequent 3 km Running Time on his blood lactate endurance marker (v-4mmol) measured in a laboratory. The analysis is taken a step further now using simple linear regression to provide a model of this dependence.

Illustration 6.1   3 km Running times (revisited)

Background
See Illustration 3.11 for details.

Study description
Sixteen male well-trained middle and long distance runners performed a 3 km time trial and a number of running tests in the laboratory, including an assessment of their running velocity $(km.h^{-1})$ at a blood lactate concentration of 4 $mmol.L^{-1}$(v-4mM) and at their lactate threshold (v-Tlac). All the laboratory testing took place on a motorised treadmill whereas distance running performance was determined by 3 km time trials on an indoor 200 m track.

Aims
To investigate whether there is sufficient evidence of a dependence of 3 km Running Time on v-4mM in the population of male runners of heterogeneous ability from which the samples arose.

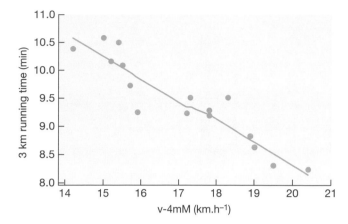

Figure 6.1 Scatter plot of 3 km Running Time and v-4mM (with a smoother).

Data

Name of data file: *3KRunning*
Response variable: 3 km Running Time (minutes)
Explanatory variable: v-4mM (km.h^{-1})

Analysis

Start by preparing a scatter plot (with a suitable smoother – see Chapter 3, Section 3.8) of 3 km Running Time on the vertical (*y*) axis and the explanatory variable, v-4mM, on the horizontal (*x*) axis (Figure 6.1).

The 'obvious' subjective impression is that faster 3 km Running Times are achieved by individuals with higher v-4mM scores. Further to this, the smoother suggests that the overall trend is plausibly linear.

A simple linear regression model was fitted and the resulting Minitab output containing the estimated intercept, slope and standard errors is presented in Box 6.1.

Box 6.1

```
The regression equation is
3km time = 15.8 - 0.373 v-4mM

Predictor       Coef   SE Coef       T       P
Constant     15.8223    0.6980   22.67   0.000
v-4mM        -0.37285   0.04067   -9.17   0.000

S = 0.291111   R-Sq = 85.7%   R-Sq(adj) = 84.7%
```

There is a significant dependence of 3 km Time on v-4mM by virtue of the *P*-value (highlighted in bold) for the null hypothesis that the population slope is zero. As the *P*-value is very small there is convincing evidence against the null hypothesis and a claim is made that the population slope is different from zero, i.e. there is a meaningful dependence of 3 km Running Time on v-4mM.

The intercept is estimated to be 15.8223 and the sample slope to be −0.37285 (both highlighted in bold in Box 6.1) and hence the regression equation (to two decimal places) is:

Average 3 km Running Time = 15.82 − 0.37 * v-4mM

This regression equation, superimposed on the original data, is given in Figure 6.2.

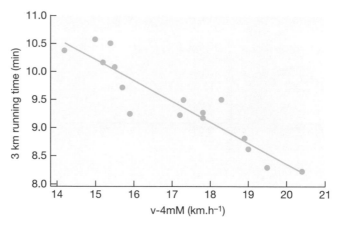

Figure 6.2 **Scatter plot of 3 km Running Time and v-4mM (with line of best fit).**

The information provided by the **sample slope** is that it is estimated that a 1 km.h^{-1} increase in v-4mM in a laboratory test will result in an improved 3 km Running Time of 0.37 minutes *on average*. Clearly, this is a meaningful improvement and indicates that distance runners should attempt to improve v-4mM by adopting an appropriate training regime.

The **sample intercept** states that an athlete with a v-4mM of zero will have an average 3 km Running Time of 15.8 minutes. This makes no sense and highlights an important feature of any regression line, namely that a *regression line is valid only for the range of data collected*. The minimum v-4mM recorded was 14.2 km.h^{-1} and the predicted 3 km Running Time for an athlete with this v-4mM value would be $15.82 - 0.37 * (14.2) = 10.56$ minutes, which is much more plausible. In general, never try to extrapolate the regression equation outside the range of the explanatory variable.

The estimated standard errors of the intercept and slope are given in Box 6.1 (under the column SE Coef) and are 0.6980 and 0.04067, respectively. When considering 95% confidence intervals for a population mean, the formula 'sample mean $\pm$ twice its estimated standard error' was used as a quick and robust method. The same approximation applies in simple linear regression where a 'rough' 95% CI estimate of population slope is calculated as 'sample slope $\pm$ twice its estimated standard error'. For example, using the output in Box 6.1, a rough 95% CI for the v-4mM regression coefficient is calculated as $-0.37285 \pm 2 * 0.04067 = (-0.45, -0.29)$. This interval is wholly negative providing evidence that the slope is significantly different from zero in the negative direction.

The approximation provided by the 'quick and robust method' is quite accurate and this is usually the case for moderate to large sample sizes. The same approach applies for the intercept but this, of course, is seldom of interest.

The estimated standard error of the intercept and slope can be used also to generate a form of 95% **confidence region** for the population regression equation (i.e. the underlying true line linking the average 3 km Running Time to v-4mM) (Figure 6.3).

The confidence region represents the 'band' where the true regression line could plausibly lie. If so desired, the graph can be used to approximate interval estimates of the mean 3 km Running Time in the population of well-trained middle and long distance runners. For example, a rough and ready approximation of the population mean 3 km Running Time for

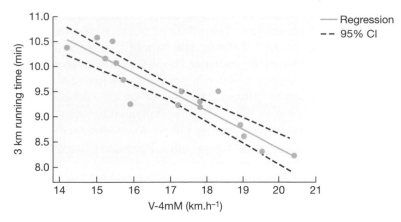

Figure 6.3 Scatter plot of 3 km Running Time and v-4mM (with 95% confidence region).

those runners with v-4mM equal to 18 appears to be somewhere between 9 and 9.5 minutes. The technically correct method is available from almost any statistical software (Box 6.2) and here leads to an estimate of the appropriate population mean as between 8.9 and 9.3 minutes.

Box 6.2

```
New
Obs     Fit   SE Fit       95% CI
  1   9.1109  0.0820  (8.9349, 9.2869)
```

Conclusion

There was evidence of a significant negative dependence ($P < 0.001$) of 3 km Time on v-4mM in the population of male runners. Further, it is estimated that 3 km Running Time decreases by between 0.29 and 0.46 minutes (on average) for every unit increase in v-4mM across a range of v-4mM from 14 to 20 km.h^{-1}.

Reference: Grant, S., Craig, I., Wilson, J. and Aitchison, T. (1997). 'The relationship between 3 km running performance and selected physiological variables.' *Journal of Sports Sciences*, 15: 403–410.

6.2.2 Assessing the adequacy of a simple linear regression

One of the key notions in regression is the concept of 'explained variability'. A useful regression model is one where the variability displayed in the response variable can be explained by its dependence on one or more explanatory variables. Indeed, this very notion is one basis for assessing the adequacy of regression models.

For example, in a simple linear regression the scatter about the regression line can be used to estimate the amount of variability in the response variable 'explained' by its dependence on the explanatory variable. If, for example, the data fall on a straight line then there is perfect dependence and all of the variability in the response is due to the explanatory variable. If, however, the data scatter considerably about the line of best fit then not all of the variability in the response is due to the explanatory variable. The 'amount' of explained variability is typically summarised by the R^2 **statistic**. The value of R^2 is always between 0 and 1 (or 0% and 100% when expressed as a percentage) where a value of 1 (100%) corresponds to perfect dependence of the response variable on the explanatory variable, i.e. all of the variation in the response is explained by the explanatory variable. At the other end of the scale, 0 corresponds to no dependence whatsoever of the response variable on the explanatory variable. The higher the value of R^2 the more 'useful' is the simple linear regression.

The reported value of the R^2 statistic in the regression output for the 3 km Running Time example (Box 6.1) is 85.7% and hence a considerable amount (i.e. 85.7%) of the variability in 3 km running performance is explained by its dependence on the v-4mM blood lactate endurance marker.

6.2.3 Assumptions for the simple linear regression model

There are important assumptions underlying a simple linear regression model, and these assumptions must be checked.

A simple linear regression has the following underlying assumptions:

1 The sample is representative of the population of interest and the subjects are independent (**independence** assumption).

2 The relationship between the mean response and the explanatory variable is linear in the population (**linearity** assumption).

3 The response exhibits variability about the population regression line in the shape of a Normal distribution (**Normality** assumption).

4 The standard deviation of the response is the same for any given value of the explanatory variable (**equal spreads** assumption).

The first assumption relates to the sample itself – if the sample is not representative of the population of interest all inference is extremely dubious. Independence is valid in the 3 km Running Times illustration as the response and explanatory variables were measured once only for each runner separately under standard conditions as individual time trials.

The assumption that relates to linearity can be checked by looking at the scatter plot. If the linearity assumption is valid, the overall pattern should resemble a linear pattern (a smoother is useful here).

The Normality and equal spreads assumptions relate to the distribution and spread of the response about the population regression line. To investigate whether these assumptions are plausible, based on the sample available, is best achieved using suitable **residual plots**.

A **residual** (in the regression context) is the difference between the observed value of the response and that predicted by the regression equation (the so-called **fitted value**) at the value of each subject's explanatory variable in turn. Two such residuals are highlighted in Figure 6.4 for runners 7 and 9, the former being a negative residual and the latter a positive residual.

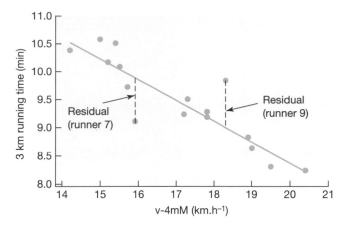

Figure 6.4 Scatter plot of 3 km Running Time and v-4mM (with line of best fit).

Residuals can be used to provide an indication of how well the model fits the data. One problem with using residuals, however, is that their values depend on the scale of the response variable. This makes it difficult to identify residuals that are 'too large' in a general sense. The conventional way of overcoming this is to **standardise** the residuals by dividing each one by an estimate of its standard error. Standardising the residuals makes their scale easier to interpret; values greater than 2 or less than −2, for example, are considered large and the validity/correctness of such observations would be worth rechecking. The value 2 is used since the vast majority (roughly 95%) of the standard Normal distribution lie between −2 and 2 and the assumptions in effect imply that the standardised residuals should roughly follow a standard Normal distribution.

The validity of the simple linear regression assumptions can be checked graphically using different plots of the standardised residuals. The two most useful residual plots are:

1 A plot of the standardised residuals (on the vertical axis) against the fitted values from the regression. If the *linearity* and *equal spreads* assumptions are valid, this plot should show a random scatter of points.

2 A Normal probability plot of the standardised residuals. This should be of a roughly linear shape if the *Normality* assumption is adequate.

A plot of the standardised residuals versus fitted values for the 3 km Running Times illustration is given in Figure 6.5. There is no evidence against the linearity or equal spreads assumption as the residuals appear to be scattered in a more or less random fashion at each value of v-4mM. Note also that one of the standardised residuals is (slightly) below −2 and it may be worth rechecking the data recorded for that individual (although, in fact, it would be expected that roughly 1 in 20 standardised residuals would be outside the range −2 to +2).

A Normal probability plot of the standardised residuals is given in Figure 6.6 and, since this is more or less linear, the Normality assumption appears justified.

In the technical appendix to this chapter, a selection of typical residual plots which make the simple linear regression assumptions doubtful are provided.

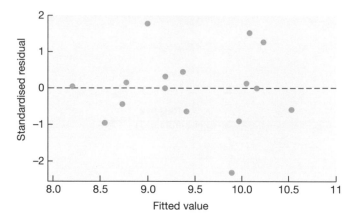

Figure 6.5 **Plot of standardised residuals versus fitted values.**

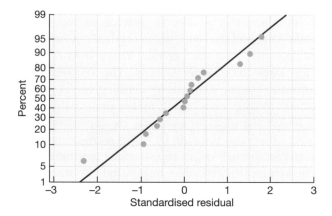

Figure 6.6 **Normal probability plot of standardised residuals.**

The next illustration highlights an area of sports and exercise science where there are conflicting opinions about how to handle the dependence of some response variables on the body mass of a subject. This particular illustration also shows a situation where the intercept is of interest.

Illustration 6.2 $\dot{V}O_2$ max and body mass

Background
$\dot{V}O_2$ max may depend on body mass. In sports and exercise science the dependence of such a variable on body mass is often removed by forming a new variable representing the ratio of the two variables, i.e. by dividing a subject's $\dot{V}O_2$ max (litres.min^{-1}) by body mass.

Study description
Twenty-three physically active males (sample mean age 30 years with a sample standard deviation of 4 years) took part in the study. Each performed an incremental treadmill test to volitional exhaustion to measure $\dot{V}O_2$ max. Gas collection was carried out using a metabolic cart. In addition their Body Mass was measured.

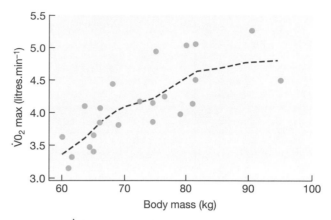

Figure 6.7 Scatter plot of V̇O₂ max and Body Mass (with a smoother).

Aim

To model the dependence of V̇O₂ max on Body Mass and to investigate whether a 'ratio-scaled variable' is appropriate to remove the dependence.

Data

Name of data file: *V̇O₂ max and Body Mass*
Response variable: V̇O₂ max (litres.min^{-1})
Explanatory variable: Body Mass (kilograms)

Analysis

The dependence of V̇O₂ max (litres.min^{-1}) on Body Mass is evident in Figure 6.7 and the dependence is plausibly a linear one based on the smoother. There is a suggestion, however, that the dependence may differ slightly for individuals with high Body Mass (>80 kg).

The main aim is to investigate whether forming a new 'ratio-scaled' variable, by dividing V̇O₂ max by Body Mass, in some sense removes the dependence of V̇O₂ max on Body Mass and therefore whether this ratio-adjusted variable encapsulates the dependence directly. If this approach is plausible it would imply that a simple linear regression model relating V̇O₂ max to Body Mass must have intercept zero, i.e. a person of zero Body Mass should have zero V̇O₂ max. This can be checked formally by fitting a simple linear regression model and either generating a 95% CI for the intercept and checking whether zero is a plausible value for the population intercept or carrying out a hypothesis test where the null hypothesis is that the population intercept is zero. Using the regression output given Box 6.3, there is evidence that the intercept is not significantly different from zero ($P = 0.25$) and hence there is some justification here to divide V̇O₂ max by Body Mass

Box 6.3

```
The regression equation is
Vo2max = 0.758 + 0.0463 Mass

Predictor       Coef    SE Coef      T        P
Constant      0.7582     0.6408   1.18    0.250
Mass        0.046305   0.008749   5.29    0.000

S = 0.388990    R-Sq = 57.2%    R-Sq(adj) = 55.1%
```

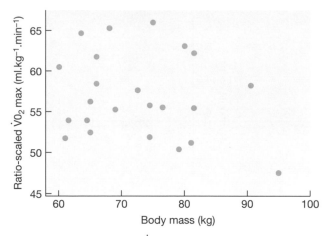

Figure 6.8 Scatter plot of Ratio-Scaled V̇O₂ max and Body Mass.

to remove its effect. (Notice that this is another atypical example where the desired result of a hypothesis test is not to reject the null hypothesis.)

The sample slope is positive and significant ($P < 0.001$), providing evidence of a dependence of V̇O₂ max on Body Mass regression equation where it is estimated that V̇O₂ max increases by 0.05 litres.min^{-1} per kilogram increase in Body Mass. The intercept is not significantly different from zero ($P = 0.25$) and hence a 'proportional model' could be appropriate here, in which case adjusting V̇O₂ max by simply dividing by Body Mass may be sufficient to remove its effect on V̇O₂ max.

A plot of the ratio-scaled V̇O₂ max (V̇O₂ max divided by Body Mass and multiplied by 1000 to provide values in ml.kg^{-1}.min^{-1}) is given in Figure 6.8.

The sample correlation between the ratio-scaled V̇O₂ max (now in units ml.kg^{-1}.min^{-1}) and Body Mass is -0.213 is given in Box 6.4.

Box 6.4

```
Correlations: Ratio Adjusted V̇O₂ Max, Body Mass

Pearson correlation of Ratio Adjusted V̇O₂ Max and Body Mass = -0.213
P-Value = 0.330
```

The P-value for the hypothesis test of zero correlation is not less than 0.05, providing evidence of no significant dependence of ratio-scaled V̇O₂ max on Body Mass.

Conclusion

The ratio-scaled V̇O₂ max/Body Mass appears to remove the dependence of V̇O₂ max (litres.min^{-1}) on Body Mass in the population of interest on the basis of a test for zero intercept in a simple linear regression model.

Reference: Grant, S., Aitchison, T, Henderson, E, Christie, E., Zare, S., McMurray, J. and Dargie, H. (1999). 'A comparison of the reproducibility and the sensitivity to change of visual analogue scales, Borg scales and Likert scales in Normal subjects during sub-maximal exercise.' *Chest*, **116**: 1208–1217.

6.3   Using simple linear regression to make predictions

The examples to date involved identifying whether there was evidence of a significant dependence of the response variable on the explanatory variable. Once a dependence has been established, the regression equation can be used for predictive purposes. The next illustration highlights such a scenario where data collected from a set of oarsmen are used to model the dependence of the time taken to complete a 5000 m race on a single explanatory variable, Peak Power, to allow prediction of 5000 m Rowing Time for any future oarsmen based on his Peak Power.

Illustration 6.3   Rowing performance

Background

Studies have reported that high levels of strength, power production, sound rowing technique and certain anthropometrical characteristics are all beneficial to rowing performance. The use of laboratory tests to determine the relationship between sporting performance and physiological variables is widespread. This information could be of value for training and testing of oarsmen.

Study description

Eighteen experienced male club and university rowers had their time recorded to complete a 5000 m standard course under simulated conditions on a rowing ergometer. In addition, each oarsman had his Peak Power measured on the ergometer.

Aim

To investigate the dependence of 5000 m rowing performance on Peak Power in order to predict likely 5000 m Rowing Time for a future oarsman with a specific value of Peak Power.

Data

    Name of data file: *Rowing5000m*
    Response variable: 5000 m Rowing Time (seconds)
    Explanatory variable: Peak Power (watts)

Analysis

The scatter plot (Figure 6.9) provides convincing evidence of a strong relationship (albeit not perfect) between the explanatory and response variables; the higher the Peak Power the lower (i.e. faster) the time taken to complete the 5000 m course. The smoother suggests that the relationship may be modelled adequately by a straight line, and consequently simple linear regression is an approach worth considering.

The output from fitting a simple linear regression model to the 18 observations (Box 6.5) provides formal evidence of a significant dependence of 5000 m Rowing Time on Peak Power as the P-value (for the hypothesis test of whether the slope is zero – highlighted in bold in the output) is considerably less than 0.05.

The estimated regression equation is:

$$\text{Average 5000 m Rowing Time} = 1518 - 0.593 * \text{Peak Power}$$

allowing a prediction of 5000 m Rowing Time to be made by multiplying Peak Power by 0.593 and subtracting this from 1518. For example, it is predicted that any oarsman of the

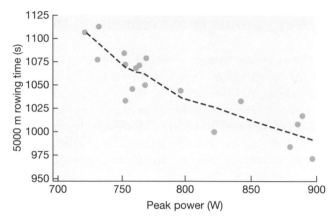

Figure 6.9 **Scatter plot of 5000 m Rowing Time and Peak Power.**

Box 6.5

```
Regression Analysis: 5000m time versus Peak Power (W)

The regression equation is
5000m time = 1518 - 0.593 Peak Power (W)

Predictor            Coef  SE Coef       T       P
Constant          1517.57    63.58   23.87   0.000
Peak Power (W)   -0.59288   0.07999   -7.41   0.000

S = 19.7508   R-Sq = 77.4%   R-Sq(adj) = 76.0%

Analysis of Variance

Source            DF      SS      MS      F       P
Regression         1   21429   21429   54.93   0.000
Residual Error    16    6242     390
Total             17   27670

Unusual Observations

         Peak
        Power
Obs      (W)   5000m time      Fit   SE Fit   Residual   St Resid
 14      753     1033.00   1071.13     5.63     -38.13      -2.01R
```

same standard as those in the sample with a Peak Power of 800 watts will have an average Rowing Time of $1518 - 0.593 * 800 = 1043.6$ seconds (i.e. 17.4 minutes).

The R^2 statistic of 77% suggests that the predictive power of the model is quite good. One oarsman was identified as having a (standardised) residual that may be worthy of attention. This standardised residual is negative, suggesting that this oarsman's Rowing Time is notably lower than those with an identical Peak Power.

The typical residual plots (Figure 6.10) needed for model assessment suggest that in general the residuals are consistent with the patterns needed to justify the assumptions for the simple linear regression model.

It is often of interest to make a prediction of the likely value of the response for a particular individual with a specific value of the explanatory variable. If this is the case a

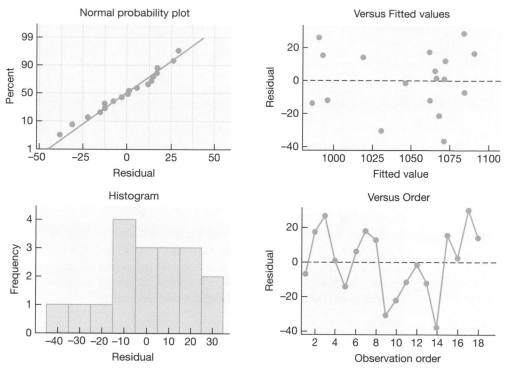

Figure 6.10 **Residual plots for 5000 m Rowing Time.**

prediction interval is appropriate as, in this illustration, it provides an estimate of the likely Rowing Time for a *single future* oarsmen with a particular Peak Power reading.

The plot of the fitted line with corresponding 95% prediction interval (PI) (Figure 6.11) suggests that the estimated 5000 m Rowing Time for a particular oarsman (with, say, a Peak Power of 800 watts) is between 1000 and 1100 seconds while the exact 95% PI (calculated by Minitab, Box 6.6) is given as 1000 to 1086 seconds.

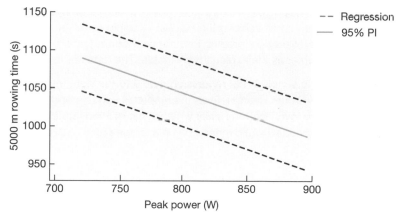

Figure 6.11 **Fitted regression of 5000 m Rowing Time and Peak Power (with corresponding 95% PI).**

Box 6.6

```
Predicted Values for New Observations

New
Obs      Fit   SE Fit        95% PI
  1  1043.26    4.69   (1000.23, 1086.30)
```

The width of the prediction interval is 86 seconds, which is quite wide given the sample range of Rowing Times recorded. Hence, even though the regression model is appropriate and the R^2 statistic is quite high, the model still lacks precision when predicting at the individual level.

Conclusion

There was convincing evidence that the dependence of 5000 m Rowing Time on Peak Power could be adequately modelled using a straight line. It is estimated that nearly 80% of the variability in 5000 m Rowing Time can be explained by its dependence on Peak Power. However, 95% PIs for future oarsmen of given Peak Power are quite wide (with respect to the range of 5000 m Rowing Times recorded).

Reference: Graham-Smith, P. and Ridler, A. (2006). 'The relationship between strength, power, flexibility, anthropometry and technique in predicting 2000 m and 5000 m rowing ergometer performance.' Paper presented at the 13th Commonwealth International Sports Conference, Melbourne.

Exercises

6.1 Revisit the *3KRunning* data introduced in Illustration 6.1 and use simple linear regression to model the dependence of 3 km Running Time on the velocity at Lactate Threshold (v-Tlac).

6.2 Twenty-four trained female cyclists completed an incremental test to volitional exhaustion on a cycle ergometer. Finger-tip capillary blood was sampled within 30 seconds of the end of each three-minute stage for calculation of Workrate corresponding to a blood lactate of 4 mM (P-4mM). Endurance Performance was assessed seven days later using a one-hour cycle test in which subjects were directed to achieve the highest possible average power output. Use simple linear regression to predict Endurance Performance using the P-4mM blood lactate marker as the explanatory variable. The data are in a file called *CyclingPower*.

6.3 Fit a simple linear regression model to the data introduced in Illustration 3.13, with Maximum Heart Rate as the response variable and Age as the explanatory variable and investigate formally whether the relationship between Maximum Heart Rate of individuals could indeed be on average equal to 220 minus the Age of an individual.

A simple linear regression model allows the researcher to model the dependence of a response variable on a single explanatory variable. It is often the case, however, that a response variable may be dependent on several explanatory variables and an extension to the simple linear regression model is needed.

6.4 Multiple regression

The **multiple (linear) regression** model is used in scenarios where the response variable is dependent on two or more explanatory variables. The first illustration revisits the data collected from the sample of oarsmen where an additional explanatory variable is available. A natural question to consider is whether a better model (in terms of predictive power) arises by including information contained in both these explanatory variables compared with the predictive power available by fitting a simple linear regression using either variable on its own.

The multiple linear regression model for two explanatory variables is of the form:

$$\text{Response variable} = \text{Intercept} + \text{Coeff1} * \text{Explanatory variable1}$$
$$+ \text{Coeff2} * \text{Explanatory variable2}$$
$$+ \text{random (natural) variability}$$

There is an important difference in the role of explanatory variables in multiple regression compared with simple linear regression. The regression coefficients for the two explanatory variables in the equation above (i.e. Coeff1 and Coeff2) represent the effect of one explanatory variable having *corrected* for the other.

Illustration 6.4 Rowing performance

Background
See Illustration 6.3 for details.

Study description
Eighteen experienced male club and university rowers had their finishing time recorded having completed a 5000 m race in addition to their Peak Power and Stroke Length (using video analysis).

Aim
To investigate whether 5000 m rowing performance depends on Peak Power and/or Stroke Length.

Data
    Name of the data file: *Rowing5000m*
    Variable of interest: 5000 m Rowing Time (seconds)
                           Peak Power (watts)
                           Stroke Length (metres)

Analysis
As in simple linear regression it is important to examine the relationships among all the variables involved by providing scatter plots and sample correlation coefficients for each pair of variables before any formal analysis is undertaken. Pairwise scatter plots are useful graphical summaries for multiple regression analyses as they provide a starting point for assessing the likely relationship between all variables (i.e. response and explanatory variables). The so-called **matrix scatter plot** for the three variables in question (with the

149

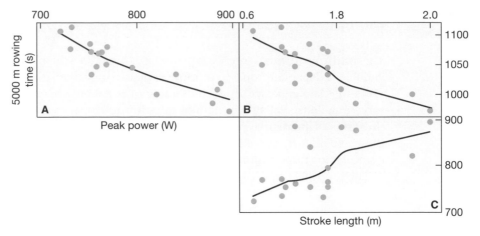

Figure 6.12 Matrix scatter plot of 5000 m Rowing Time, Peak Power and Stroke length (with smoothers superimposed).

response variable on the *y*-axis as always for appropriate plots, and smoothers superimposed) is presented in Figure 6.12.

The plot labelled A has Peak Power on the horizontal axis while in plot B Stroke Length is on the horizontal axis. These plots suggest a negative relationship between 5000 m Rowing Time and both Peak Power and Stroke Length where increasing values of Peak Power and Stroke Length are associated with better (i.e. lower) Rowing Times. The remaining plot (C) is a plot of the two explanatory variables, with Peak Power on the vertical axis and Stroke Length on the horizontal axis. This plot provides a visual impression as to whether the two explanatory variables are correlated, which indeed seems to be the case here.

The formal analysis starts by reporting the sample correlation coefficient (and *P*-value for the test of zero population correlation) for each pair of variables (Box 6.7).

Box 6.7

```
          5000m Rowing Time  Peak Power (W)
Peak Power (W)        -0.880
                      0.000

Stroke Length (m     -0.769          0.609
                      0.000          0.007

Cell Contents: Pearson correlation
               P-Value
```

There is evidence of a significant correlation between the response variable 5000 m Rowing Time and each of Peak Power ($r = -0.88$, $p < 0.001$) and Stroke Length ($r = -0.77$, $p < 0.001$). This suggests each explanatory variable may be a useful predictor of 5000 m Rowing Time in its own right in a regression model but the significant correlation between the two explanatory variables ($r = 0.61$, $p = 0.007$) suggests that either one of these variables may not be giving any information about 5000 m Rowing Time additional to that from the other variable. The next step is to use multiple regression to model the dependence of the response on both explanatory variables, and the results from fitting such a model are given in Box 6.8.

Box 6.8

```
The regression equation is
5000m Rowing Time = 1664 - 0.440 Peak Power (W) - 153 Stroke
                                                     Length (m)

Predictor                  Coef  SE Coef       T      P
Constant                1664.43    69.21   24.05  0.000
Peak Power (W)          -0.43992  0.08057   -5.46  0.000
Stroke Length (m)       -152.53     48.58   -3.14  0.007

S = 15.8455   R-Sq = 86.4%   R-Sq(adj) = 84.6%

Analysis of Variance

Source          DF     SS      MS      F      P
Regression       2  23904   11952  47.60  0.000
Residual Error  15   3766     251
Total           17  27670
```

The output is quite similar to that generated when fitting a simple linear regression except that the regression equation now has three terms: an intercept and regression coefficients for *each* of the two explanatory variables.

The estimated regression equation is given as:

Average 5000 m Rowing Time = 1664.43 − 0.44 * Peak Power − 152.5 * Stroke Length

Note that 'average' here denotes the population average for any individual with specific values of Peak Power and Stroke Length.

There is an important difference as to how the regression coefficients are interpreted compared with simple linear regression. The first term in the regression equation is an estimate of the intercept, i.e.1664 here. It represents the average 5000 m Rowing Time when both Peak Power and Stroke Length are equal to zero and, despite being of no practical interest, it is essential to the model, is significant and should be retained in the model. The regression coefficients for the two explanatory variables are of primary interest as they represent the change in the 'average' 5000 m Rowing Time per unit increase in the corresponding explanatory variable corrected for the other explanatory variable. The regression coefficient for Peak Power for example states that for every 1 watt increase in Peak Power, 5000 m Rowing Time decreases on average by 0.44 seconds, *if Stroke Length is held constant*. This 'effect' of Peak Power is *assumed* to be the same for every Stroke Length value. In a similar manner, the regression coefficient for Stroke Length is an estimate of the likely effect of Stroke Length on 5000 m Rowing Time in the population of oarsmen. The regression coefficient states that for every 1 m increase in Stroke Length, 5000 m Rowing Time decreases, on average, by 153 seconds if Peak Power is held constant. An increase of 1 m in Stroke Length is of course massive and a more sensible interpretation might be that for every 1 cm increase in Stroke Length 5000 m Rowing Time decreases, on average, by 1.53 seconds if Peak Power is held constant.

The next step in the analysis is to provide evidence as to whether the explanatory variables are significant in the population of oarsmen. In particular the null and alternative hypotheses for the *F*-test (revisited in Chapter 7) for providing evidence as to whether a multiple regression model contains at least one useful (i.e. significant) explanatory variable is as follows:

H$_0$: The *population regression coefficients* are zero for all explanatory variables
H$_1$: The *population regression coefficient* is different from zero for at least one explanatory variable

Clearly, if the null hypothesis is not rejected then it is plausible that the response variable has no dependence on any of the explanatory variables and the multiple regression model is a waste of time. The *P*-value for the *F*-test can be found in the section of the multiple regression output labelled 'Analysis of Variance'. In Box 6.8 the *P*-value (highlighted in bold) is <0.001 and a conclusion can be made that at least one of the explanatory variables is useful for predicting 5000 m Rowing Time. The remaining task is to identify which of the explanatory variables are responsible for this significant result and *separate tests* of the regression coefficients are available for precisely this purpose.

The *P*-value for testing whether the regression coefficient for Peak Power is zero (see Box 6.8) is less than 0.001 so there is convincing evidence that Peak Power has a significant effect on 5000 m Rowing Time, *after allowing for the effect of Stroke Length*. The *P*-value for testing the regression coefficient for Stroke Length is 0.007, providing convincing evidence that Stroke Length has a significant effect on 5000 m Rowing Time, *after allowing for the effect of Peak Power*. Hence both explanatory variables are separately useful and significant explanatory variables of 5000 m Rowing Time.

Note that it might seem unnecessary at this stage to consider the result of the *F*-test and instead go straight to the separate tests for the regression coefficients and pick off those that are significant. There are several problems with this approach, however, as will be seen in a later illustration.

Assessing the adequacy of a multiple linear regression

Recall that the predictive power of a simple linear regression model, as estimated by the R^2 statistic, is related not only to the precision in the estimates of the regression coefficients but also to the scatter about the line of best fit. The smaller the scatter, then the better the fit of the model to the data and consequently the larger the value of R^2 will be. The same principle applies in multiple regression but a slight adjustment must be made to the R^2 statistic as it *will always increase* whenever an additional variable is included in the model *regardless of whether it is significant or not*. The adjustment takes into account the number of explanatory variables in the model and the appropriately named R^2-**adjusted** statistic should be reported. The interpretation of the adjusted statistic is the same however, providing an indication of the predictive power of the model. The R^2-adjusted for the two-explanatory model in question (Box 6.8) is 84.6% (a slight reduction on the corresponding R^2 of 86.4%), suggesting that a considerable amount of the variability in 5000 m Rowing Time is explained by an oarsman's Peak Power and Stroke Length. The remaining 15.4% is attributed to random variation not explained by this multiple regression model.

Using multiple regression to make predictions

Predictions can be made using the regression equation for any further subject from the same population whose Peak Power and Stroke Length are known. For example, the predicted 5000 m Rowing Time for an individual oarsman with Peak Power of 800 watts and a stroke length of 1.8 metres is 1038.7 seconds (Box 6.9) with an accompanying 95% PI (prediction interval) for one such oarsman.

The likely 5000 m Rowing Time for such an oarsmen is between 1003 and 1074 seconds. This estimate, based on using two explanatory variables, is only marginally narrower

Box 6.9

```
Predicted Values for New Observations
New
Obs     Fit  SE Fit       95% PI
  1  1038.71    4.09  (1003.43, 1073.98)
```

than the corresponding prediction interval from a simple linear regression with Peak Power alone. Despite the significant increase in R^2-adjusted, the improvement in actual precision is still negligible in any practical terms.

Conclusions

There is evidence that both Peak Power and Stroke Length are useful explanatory variables of 5000 m Rowing Time ($P < 0.001$ for both explanatory variables). It is estimated that for every 1 cm increase in Stroke Length, 5000 m Rowing Time decreases on average by 1.53 seconds if Peak Power is held constant. Similarly, for each 1 watt increase in Power Output, 5000 m Rowing Time decreases on average by 0.44 seconds if Stroke Length is held constant. The R^2-adjusted for the model is 84.6%, further suggesting that both Power Output and Stroke Length are important characteristics of rowing performance. Despite this, the width of 95% PIs are not reduced much from those based on Peak Power alone.

Reference: Graham-Smith, P. and Ridler, A. (2006). 'The relationship between strength, power, flexibility, anthropometry and technique in predicting 2000 m and 5000 m rowing ergometer performance.' Paper presented at the 13th *Commonwealth International Sports Conference*, Melbourne.

6.4.1 Assumptions for the multiple linear regression model

A multiple linear regression model has the following underlying assumptions:

1 The sample is representative of the population of interest and the observations are independent (**independence** assumption).

2 The relationship between the average response and each of the explanatory variables is linear in the population (**linearity** assumption).

3 The response exhibits variability about the population linear regression model in the shape of a Normal distribution (**Normality** assumption).

4 The standard deviation of the response is the same for any given value of the explanatory variables (**equal spreads** assumption).

Residual plots are again the key (graphical) diagnostics for checking the validity of these assumptions. As in simple linear regression, plots of the standardised residuals against the fitted values and against each explanatory variable in turn can be used to assess the linearity and equal spreads assumptions. If these assumptions are reasonable, plots of the residual plots against the fitted values (and against each explanatory) should exhibit a random pattern. The Normality assumption can be checked via a Normal probability plot of the standardised residuals. If so required, plotting the standardised residuals in the order the data were recorded to investigate for a 'time order' effect can check the independence assumption.

These residual plots are shown in Figure 6.13 for the 5000 m Rowing Time illustration.

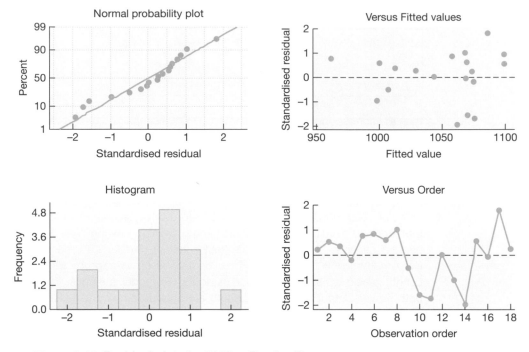

Figure 6.13 **Residual plots for 5000 m Rowing Time.**

The independence assumption appears justified as there is no reason to believe that any oarsman's 5000 m Rowing Time should be influenced by any other oarsman as the oarsmen were recorded on separate trials. There does not appear to be any striking pattern in the Order plot.

The Normal probability plot of the standardised residuals resembles a (plausibly) linear pattern and so the Normality assumption looks plausible. Although none of the standardised residuals were reported as atypically large or small (as all fall within −2 and +2), there is a suggestion of increasing variability with increasing 5000 m Rowing Time.

The next illustration involves a multiple linear regression example with three potential explanatory variables.

Illustration 6.5   Body fat and anthropometry

Background
Densitometry is a standard approach used to 'measure' (percentage) body fat and involves the use of underwater weighing. It is of interest to determine if other variables, body mass, height and age are of some use in the 'measurement' of (percentage) body fat.

Study description
As part of a PhD study at Glasgow University, a student obtained a representative sample of 78 West of Scotland males, aged between 18 and 30 years, and 'measured' their % Body Fat (by densitometry), Body Mass, Height and Age.

Aim
To model the dependence, if any, of % Body Fat on Body Mass, Height and Age in males.

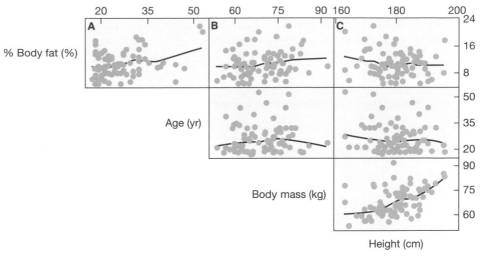

Figure 6.14 Matrix scatter plot of % Body Fat by Age, Body Mass and Height (with smoothers superimposed).

Data

Name of data file:	*%Body Fat Male*
Response variable:	%Body Fat (%)
Explanatory variables:	Height (centimetres)
	Weight (kilograms)
	Age (years)

Analysis

The matrix scatter plot of the % Body Fat and the three explanatory variables (with smoothers included) is given in Figure 6.14.

The main plots of interest are labelled A, B and C, representing the scatter plots of the response variable (on the vertical axis) against the three explanatory variables. It appears that there is a slight positive dependence of % Body Fat on Body Mass and Age and a possible negative dependence of % Body Fat on Height. An (anticipated) positive relationship is noticed between Height and Body Mass with little or no relationship between Age and Body Mass or between Age and Height.

These subjective impressions are backed up by fitting a multiple linear regression (Box 6.10) where the P-value for the F-test is significant ($P = 0.004$), suggesting that at least one of the three potential explanatory variables is a useful predictor. The separate tests identify Age and Body Mass ($P = 0.02$ in both cases) as significant explanatory variables while there is not quite enough evidence that Height ($P = 0.07$) is making a significant contribution to a model already containing Age and Body Mass.

The P-value from the F-test provided evidence that at least one of the explanatory variables is significant and, on examining the appropriate P-values, Age and Body Mass are identified as the only significant explanatory variables responsible. It appears that knowing a person's height does not provide any additional information, in terms of explaining the variability in % Body Fat as measured by densitometry among males in the West of Scotland, once information on a person's Age and Body Mass is available.

Conclusion

In the West of Scotland at least, a male's Age and Body Mass were identified as being significant explanatory variables ($P < 0.05$ in both cases) of a male's % Body Fat. Despite

Box 6.10

```
The regression equation is
%Body Fat = 20.0 + 0.120 Age +0.131 BodyMass -0.119 Height

Predictor        Coef   SE Coef      T       P
Constant        19.96     10.64   1.88   0.065
Age           0.11959   0.05182   2.31   0.024
Body Mass     0.13130   0.05740   2.29   0.025
Height       -0.11935   0.06496  -1.84   0.070

S = 3.58239    R-Sq = 16.2%    R-Sq(adj) = 12.8%

Analysis of Variance

Source             DF       SS      MS      F       P
Regression          3   183.40   61.13   4.76   0.004
Residual Error     74   949.68   12.83
Total              77  1133.08
```

identifying two useful explanatory variables the R^2-adjusted for this two variable model is only 13%, suggesting that these variables alone explain a very small amount of variability in % Body Fat.

Reference: Maria T. Espinosa-Zepeda (1995). 'Metabolic rate related to body composition in lean muscular humans.' PhD thesis University of Glasgow.

Additional comment on Illustration 6.5

The required residual plots (Figure 6.15) did not demonstrate any concerns regarding the assumptions underlying the multiple regression model fitted.

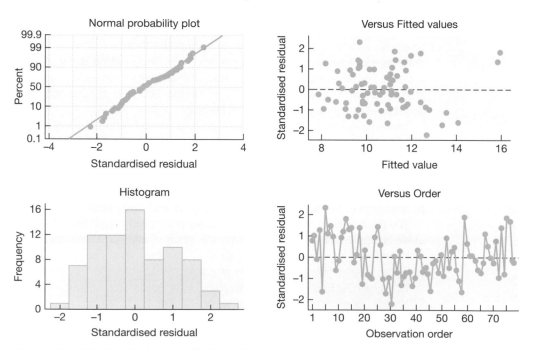

Figure 6.15 Residual plots for % Body Fat.

Exercises

6.4 Using the *3KRunning* data introduced in Illustration 6.1 fit a multiple linear regression model with 3 km Running Time as the response variable and investigate whether an athlete's V̇O₂ max is an additionally useful explanatory variable in a model already containing v-Tlac.

6.5 Data are available also for the 2000 m Rowing Times for the same sample of oarsmen introduced in Illustration 6.3. Use multiple regression to investigate whether Peak Power and Stroke Length are useful explanatory variables over this distance also and based on the final model make a prediction as to the likely 2000 m Rowing Time for an oarsman with a Peak Power of 793 watts and a Stroke Length of 176 cm.

6.5 Variable selection techniques

The multiple regression illustrations to date have all adopted the same approach for the identification of useful and significant explanatory variables: check if the *F*-test is significant and then use the separate tests of the regression coefficients for each possible explanatory variable to identify which explanatory variables are responsible for the significant *F*-test. The importance of following this approach is now highlighted and, in particular, it is shown why it is dangerous to consider the separate tests alone.

Illustration 6.6   3 km Running times (revisited)

Background and study description
See Illustration 3.11 and 6.1 for details.

Aim
To examine if an individual's running velocity at Lactate Threshold (v-Tlac) is a useful predictor in addition to v-4mM when predicting 3 km Running Time.

Data
Name of data file:	*3KRunning*
Response variable:	3 km Running Time (minutes)
Explanatory variables:	v-4mM (km.h^{-1})
	v-Tlac (km.h^{-1})

Analysis
A matrix scatter plot (Figure 6.16) highlights the negative dependence of 3 km Running Time on the two explanatory variables and that two explanatory variables are highly correlated (plot A). The sample correlation between the two explanatory variables is 0.99 and they provide essentially the same information about 3 km Running Time.

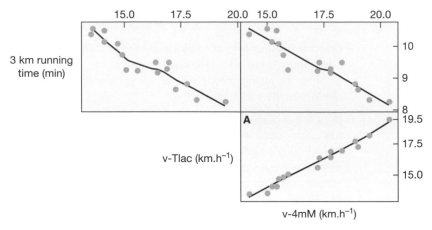

Figure 6.16 Matrix scatter plot of 3 km Running Time, v-Tlac and v-4mM (with smoothers).

A multiple linear regression with v-Tlac and v-4mM as the two explanatory variables gave the results in Box 6.11.

Box 6.11

```
The regression equation is
3ktim = 15.8 - 0.273 v-Tlac - 0.114 v-4mM
Predictor      Coef  SE Coef       T       P
Constant    15.7596   0.6974   22.60   0.000
v-Tlac      -0.2733   0.2576   -1.06   0.308
v-4mM       -0.1138   0.2476   -0.46   0.653

S = 0.289815   R-Sq = 86.9%   R-Sq(adj) = 84.8%


Analysis of Variance

Source           DF       SS      MS       F       P
Regression        2   7.2171  3.6086   42.96   0.000
Residual Error   13   1.0919  0.0840
Total            15   8.3090
```

In the F-test (Analysis of Variance output in Box 6.11), the null hypothesis that both population regression coefficients are zero is rejected with a P-value <0.001 providing evidence that at least one of the explanatory variables is significant and useful. However, when examining the separate tests for the regression coefficients, neither that for v-Tlac ($P = 0.308$) nor that for v-4mM ($P = 0.653$) is significant. In addition, the R^2-adjusted value is 84.8%, so that the overall regression model appears to be worthwhile while the separate tests have failed to identify any significant predictor. How can this be?

The usefulness of an explanatory variable in a multiple regression model may be 'masked' or hidden by the inclusion of another explanatory variable highly correlated to it. If there is no correlation between any pair of explanatory variables, the estimated regression coefficient for any possible explanatory variable will not depend on those for the other explanatory variables in the model. If some of the explanatory variables are correlated with each other, the estimated regression coefficients may depend on which other explanatory variables are included in the model.

Problems of this type involving highly correlated explanatory variables are common in human studies. It is relatively easy to spot this problem when there are only two explanatory variables. In the case where there are more than two:

1 Examine the correlation coefficients and identify pairs of explanatory variables that are highly correlated (i.e. a sample correlation greater than 0.8 or less than -0.8).

2 Check if the F-test is significant while the separate tests are not.

A useful statistic to consider here is the variance inflation (VIF); if the VIF is bigger than 10 this indicates that correlation among the explanatory variables exists. The VIF for v-Tlac and $\dot{V}O_2$ max are both 37.4 which gives a strong indication of correlated explanatory variables.

The solution to this problem is simple in the two explanatory variable scenario: just include the more useful explanatory variable. Which of the two candidate explanatory variables is more useful can be decided by fitting simple linear regressions separately for each explanatory variable and then choosing the one which gives the higher R^2 value.

The R^2 value for the simple linear regression with v-Tlac as the single predictor was 87% whereas including v-4mM as the solitary predictor the resulting model had an R^2 value of 86%. There is clearly little to choose between these possible explanatory variables.

Conclusion

The v-4mM and v-Tlac lactate endurance markers are highly correlated ($r = 0.99$). Indeed, there is little to choose between the two explanatory variables in terms of which is the more useful explanatory variable when predicting 3 km Running Time based on the data available. The R^2 value for the simple linear regression model containing v-Tlac as the explanatory variable was marginally larger (87%) than that for the model containing v-4mM (86%). The choice of best model can therefore be made on pragmatic reasons such as which of these two explanatory variables is the 'easier' to measure.

The problem is slightly more complicated when there are three or more possible explanatory variables to consider. Two different strategies have been developed over the past 30 years for choosing the 'best' set of explanatory variables.

6.5.1 Best subsets and stepwise regression

The first strategy is called **best subsets** and avails of modern computing power by actually fitting all the regression models possible with the set of available explanatory variables. The number of possible models depends on the number of possible explanatory variables, e.g. for 2 explanatory variables, there are three possible models, but for 4 explanatory variables there are 16 possible models and with 10 explanatory variables there are over 1000 possible models. The R^2-adjusted statistic and a criterion known as Mallows' Cp are used to identify the 'best' model.

The second strategy, **stepwise regression**, fits models in a sequential manner by including or removing explanatory variables one at a time at each step if deemed significantly useful. The forward stepwise procedure starts by first identifying the explanatory variable that is most useful (i.e. has the lowest P-value or highest R^2 when fitted alone). At each subsequent step, every variable not at present in the model is tested to see whether including it makes a significant contribution to the model. In addition, the explanatory variables already in the model at this step are now tested to see whether any of them should be excluded by virtue of including the new variable at this step, if any of course. The process ends when no further explanatory variable is deemed worthy of inclusion or exclusion.

Best subsets and stepwise regression techniques are now illustrated on data where a collection of five possible explanatory variables is suggested as being useful in predicting the endurance time of a track cyclist.

Illustration 6.7   Power output prediction in cycling

Background

Blood lactate endurance markers are often used for predicting endurance performance, typically using performance data obtained in a time trial. The identification of any significant markers for a given population will help coaches and athletes decide which markers might be used to evaluate changes in performance.

Study description

Twenty-four trained female cyclists completed an incremental exercise test on a cycle ergometer. Finger-tip capillary blood was sampled within 30 seconds of the end of each three-minute stage for analysis of plasma lactate. The following plasma lactate endurance markers were calculated: Lactate Threshold (P-Tlac), DMax (DMax), LT-log-log (P-Tlac.ll), P-4 mmol.L^{-1} (P-4mM) and work rate corresponding to a 1 mM rise from baseline (Rise.1.PB). Endurance performance was assessed 7 days later using a one-hour cycle test in which subjects were directed to achieve the highest possible average power output (AV Power).

Aim

To use stepwise regression and best subsets to identify the essential subset of these plasma lactate markers needed to predict AV Power.

Data

Name of data file:	*CyclingPower*
Response variable:	AV Power (watts)
Explanatory variables:	P-4mM (watts)
	P-Tlac (watts)
	P-Tlac.ll (watts)
	DMax (watts)
	Rise.1.PB (watts)

Analysis

The matrix scatter plot of the response variable and the five possible explanatory variables is given in Figure 6.17.

The top row of plots consists of the scatter plots of the response variable (on the *y*-axis) against each of the Plasma Lactate Marker explanatory variables in turn. All of the Plasma Lactate Markers look as if they may indeed be (singly) useful predictors of Power Output. However, a closer look at the plots of the explanatory variables against each other highlights the fact that many of them are strongly correlated with each other. For example, the scatter plot labelled A is a plot of the P-4mM and Rise.1.PB markers, with the sample correlation between these two variables being 0.96. All the markers are clearly highly correlated

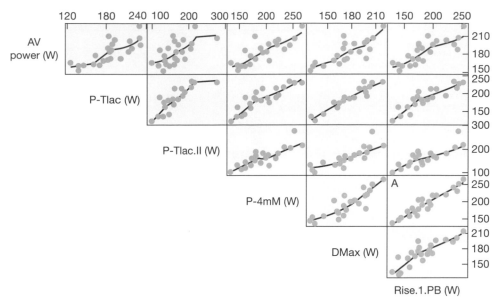

Figure 6.17 **Matrix scatter plot of AV Power and various Lactate Markers.**

as, when fitting a multiple regression model with all five explanatory variables (i) none of the separate tests identifies any useful predictor despite a significant *F-test* statistic, and (ii) the VIF values are larger than 10 for most of the explanatory variables (Box 6.12).

Box 6.12

```
The regression equation is
AV Power = 76.3 - 0.102 P-Tlac - 0.200 P-Tlac.ll +
           0.155 P-4mM + 0.411 DMax + 0.304 Rise.1.PB

Predictor    Coef   SE Coef      T      P     VIF
Constant    76.29     18.52   4.12  0.001
P-Tlac     -0.1017   0.2812  -0.36  0.722  13.734
P-Tlac.ll  -0.1995   0.1195  -1.67  0.112   4.077
P-4mM       0.1553   0.2380   0.65  0.522  13.631
DMax        0.4112   0.3132   1.31  0.206  11.186
Rise.1.PB   0.3043   0.2662   1.14  0.268  16.392

S = 11.0160   R-Sq = 73.3%   R-Sq(adj) = 65.9%

Analysis of Variance

Source          DF      SS      MS     F      P
Regression       5  6010.2  1202.0  9.91  0.000
Residual Error  18  2184.3   121.4
Total           23  8194.5
```

The first approach considered is best subsets regression analysis, and the results from this are given in Box 6.13. All possible regression models are fitted and the best (typically two) models for each subset size are displayed.

Box 6.13

```
Response is AV Power
                                                  P       R
                                                  -       i
                                                  T       s
                                              P   l       e
                                              -   a   P   .
                                              T   c   -   D   1
                                              1   .   4   M   .
                              Mallows         a   l   m   a   P
Vars   R-Sq   R-Sq(adj)         Cp        S   c   l   M   x   B
   1   67.0        65.5        2.3   11.088                   X
   1   64.5        62.9        4.0   11.495        X
   2   68.7        65.7        3.1   11.050    X               X
   2   68.7        65.7        3.2   11.057            X   X
   3   72.5        68.4        2.5   10.609    X       X   X
   3   71.4        67.1        3.3   10.826    X   X   X
   4   73.2        67.5        4.1   10.761    X   X   X   X
   4   72.7        67.0        4.4   10.848  X X       X   X
   5   73.3        65.9        6.0   11.016  X X   X   X   X
```

The first column, entitled Vars, indicates the number of explanatory variables in the model where the variables are listed vertically. For brevity, only the best (as determined by the R^2-adjusted value) two models for each subset size are displayed. Summary statistics for that model are given in the corresponding line, where an X is used to indicate those explanatory variables included in the (best two) models. For example, the first line represents output from the simple linear regression model which contained Rise.1.PB as the single best explanatory variable which had an R^2-adjusted of 65.5%. The second best simple linear regression model identified had P-4mM as the explanatory variable with a slightly lower R^2-adjusted of 62.9%.

An additional statistic is available to help guide the researcher and this is called the **Mallows' Cp** statistic. This statistic is useful for identifying the number of explanatory variables needed in the 'best' model – the best model is the one in which the number of parameters (i.e. the intercept and explanatory variables) is close to the Cp statistic value. According to the output in Box 6.13, the model with the highest R^2-adjusted and a Cp statistic value close to the number of parameters in the model is the three (explanatory) variable model with an R^2-adjusted of 68.4 and a Cp of 2.5. The three explanatory variables in this model are identified as P-Tlac.II, DMax and Rise.1.PB. However, as the increase in R^2-adjusted value is marginal when compared with the much simpler one-variable model (based on Rise.1.PB only), there is little justification for recommending this three variable model. The extra effort required to collect and include data on these additional two explanatory variables is not worthwhile given the minimal improvement in terms of model performance.

Stepwise regression is the other strategy to consider. The procedure (Box 6.14) stopped after the first step, claiming that the only variable needed is Rise.1.PB as no other variable was identified as making any further meaningful or significant contribution in addition to Rise.1.PB.

Box 6.14

```
 Alpha-to-Enter: 0.15   Alpha-to-Remove: 0.15

Response is AV Power (W) on 5 predictors, with N = 24

Step              1
Constant       101.2

Rise.1.PB      0.442
T-Value         6.68
P-Value        0.000

S               11.1
R-Sq           66.99
R-Sq(adj)      65.49
Mallows Cp      2.3
```

Conclusion

There is evidence that Power Output in female cyclists is dependent on several Plasma Lactate endurance markers. There is also evidence that several of these explanatory variables are strongly correlated with each other and are in essence providing the same 'information' as each other. On the basis of the results when using best subsets and stepwise regression techniques, the most useful regression model involved a single explanatory variable, namely the work rate corresponding to a 1 mM rise from baseline ($P < 0.001$) which explained 67% of the variability in the Power Output.

Reference: adapted from Bishop, D., Jenkins, D.G. and Mackinnon, L.T. (1998). 'The relationship between plasma lactate parameters, Wpeak and endurance cycling performance.' *Medicine and Science in Sports and Exercise*, **30**: 1270–1275.

Exercises

6.6 Revisit the *Rowing Performance* data introduced in Illustration 6.4 and use both best subsets and stepwise regression to identify the 'best' model for predicting 2000 m Rowing Time considering all available explanatory variables.

6.7 Several other sub-maximal and maximal tests were performed in addition to the v-4mM and v-Tlac blood lactate endurance markers used in Illustration 6.1. These included sub-maximal running tests at two velocities – 14.5 km.h^{-1} (Rel. 14.5) and 16.1 km.h^{-1}(Rel. 16.1) – to determine the athletes' running economy (the amount of oxygen used for a given running speed) and predicted velocity at VO$_2$ max, (v-V̇O$_2$ max). Use both best subsets and stepwise regression to identify which, if any, of the potential explanatory variables available for analysis are essential for prediction of 3 km Running Time.

All of the Illustrations in this chapter to date have involved only continuous explanatory variables. In the next section, methods are discussed and illustrations presented of regression problems that involve categorical explanatory variables (which can be thought of as between-subject factors) in addition to continuous explanatory variables.

6.6   Incorporating categorical explanatory variables into a multiple regression model

As a first example, data are presented from an observational study to investigate whether an individual's body mass is a useful predictor of anaerobic power. In particular, does it appear that sex, in addition to body mass, may be a useful explanatory variable?

Illustration 6.8   Power and body mass (revisited)

Background and study description
See Illustration 3.12 for details.

Aim

To investigate whether Anaerobic Power (as assessed by the Wingate test) is dependent upon the Body Mass and Sex of an individual.

Data

Name of data file:	*Power*
Response variable:	AP Wingate (watts)
Explanatory variables:	Body Mass (kilograms)
	Sex (2 levels: Male, Female)

Analysis

Start by preparing a scatter plot of AP Wingate and Body Mass using a separate label (and smoother) for each Sex (Figure 6.18).

The suggestion from this plot is that there is a reasonable dependency of AP Wingate on Body Mass in Males but really not so in Females. The formal analysis should start by fitting a multiple regression model including both Body Mass and Sex as explanatory variables (a so-called additive model for Body Mass and Sex). Care must be taken with regard to the categorical variable in order to create an explanatory variable to represent a person's Sex. This can be achieved quite easily by use of an **indicator** variable – a variable that takes the value 0 or 1. Here we use 1 to represent a Male and 0 to represent a Female. (You could, of

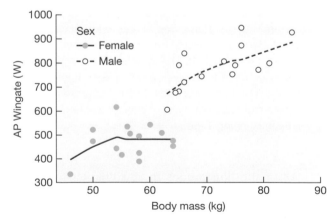

Figure 6.18 Scatter plot of AP Wingate and Body Mass (with separate smoothers by Sex).

course, use 1 for Females and 0 for Males, although it is strongly recommended that the baseline level (corresponding to 0) is that with the lower sample mean of the Response, in this case as chosen.) This indicator variable can be incorporated directly into a regression model as an additional explanatory variable. The results from fitting such a model with Body Mass as a continuous explanatory and the indicator variable Sex(M = 1/ F = 0) are shown in Box 6.15.

Box 6.15

```
The regression equation is
Wingate = 85 + 6.93 Body Mass + 200 Sex(M=1/F=0)

Predictor       Coef   SE Coef     T      P
Constant        85.0    126.5   0.67   0.507
Body Mass       6.926   2.219   3.12   0.004
Sex(M=1/F=0)199.55      43.16   4.62   0.000

S = 71.3831    R-Sq = 84.6%   R-Sq(adj) = 83.5%

Analysis of Variance

Source          DF     SS      MS      F      P
Regression       2   756025  378012  74.18  0.000
Residual Error  27   137580   5096
Total           29   893604
```

The F-test in the analysis of variance table provides evidence that at least one of the explanatory variables is significant, and indeed the separate tests suggest that Sex and Body Mass are both significant. The Body Mass regression coefficient estimates that AP Wingate increases by 6.93 watts on average per kilogram increase in Body Mass, while the Sex regression coefficient estimates that Males have an AP Wingate that is, on average, 200 watts greater than that of Females for any given value of Body Mass.

The regression equation for Females is:

$$\text{Wingate} = 85 + (6.93 * \text{Body Mass}) + (200 * 0)$$

$$= 85 + (6.93 * \text{Body Mass})$$

as Females correspond to the indicator variable being equal to zero. This model suggests that for every unit increase in Body Mass, AP Wingate increases by 6.93 watts on average in Females.

What is the regression equation for Males? Males correspond to the indicator variable taking the value 1, and applying this to the regression equation yields:

$$\text{Wingate} = 85 + (6.93 * \text{Body Mass}) + (200 * 1)$$

$$= 285 + (6.93 * \text{Body Mass})$$

so that for every kilogram increase in Body Mass, AP Wingate increases by 6.93 watts on average in Males.

Note that the model assumes that the effect (i.e. regression coefficient) of Body Mass on AP Wingate is the same for both Males and Females (i.e. a **parallel lines** model) and that the only difference is in the intercept, which estimates the difference in mean AP Wingate between Males and Females, assumed constant over the full range of Body Mass in this dataset. A plot of these two regression equations (Figure 6.19) highlights this point;

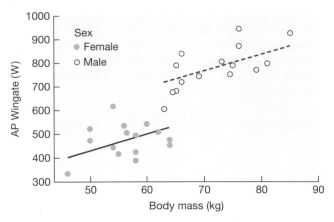

Figure 6.19 **Scatter plot of AP Wingate and Body Mass (parallel lines model).**

the slopes of the two regression lines are the same (i.e. the lines are assumed to be parallel) and differ only in intercepts.

Do the data support this assumption? The smoothers in Figure 6.19 suggest that the dependence of AP Wingate on Body Mass may differ for Males and Females and there may be a need for *separate slopes*. One simple way to test this is to extend the regression model to allow for separate slopes, thereby allowing the dependence of AP Wingate on Body Mass to differ for Males and Females.

To fit a separate slopes multiple regression model, a separate slopes term is needed which is formed by creating a new variable to represent the interaction by simply multiplying the two explanatory variables in question, in this instance Body Mass and the indicator variable Sex (M = 1/F = 0). The output from fitting the model with the two explanatory variables and the new interaction term 'Sex (M/F) * BodyMass' is given in Box 6.16.

Box 6.16

```
The regression equation is
Wingate = 315 + 2.85 Body Mass - 195 Sex(M/F) +
          6.36 Sex(M/F)*BodyMass

Predictor              Coef  SE Coef       T       P
Constant              315.0    206.0    1.53   0.138
Body Mass             2.845    3.641    0.78   0.442
Sex(M/F)             -194.6    284.8   -0.68   0.500
Sex(M/F)*BodyMass     6.365    4.547    1.40   0.173

S = 70.1476   R-Sq = 85.7%   R-Sq(adj) = 84.0%
Unusual Observations

        Body
Obs    Mass  Wingate    Fit  SE Fit  Residual  St Resid
  1    54.0    616.3  468.6    20.1     147.7      2.20R
```

The regression coefficient for the interaction term is not significant ($P = 0.173$), suggesting that separate slopes are not necessary after all. The simpler parallel slopes model is justified, i.e. the effect of Sex is additive. Note that neither of the explanatory variables (i.e. Body Mass and Sex) in Box 6.16 now appears significant even though they both were in the simpler parallel lines model (i.e. the effect of Sex is simply added to the linear effect of Body Mass). This is an example of **model over-fitting**: too many explanatory variables have been included causing real significant effects to be submerged. A simpler model without the interaction term (Box 6.15) is more appropriate. The model must now be refitted without the interaction term and the appropriate final model is that given in Box 6.15.

Conclusion

There is evidence that Anaerobic Power, as measured by the Wingate test, is significantly related to both Body Mass ($P = 0.004$) and Sex ($P < 0.001$) where the effect of Sex is additive. The R^2-adjusted for the parallel lines model is 83.5% suggesting that a considerable amount of the variation in Anaerobic Power is explained by its dependence on Body Mass and Sex.

If a similar analysis is performed, this time using Anaerobic Power (as measured by the Margaria test) as the response, there is evidence of a significant interaction between Body Mass and Sex, i.e. a **separate slopes model** is justified.

Illustration 6.9 **Power and body mass (revisited)**

Background and study description
See Illustration 3.12 for details.

Aim
To investigate whether Anaerobic Power (as assessed by the Margaria test) is dependent upon the Body Mass and Sex of an individual.

Data
Name of data file:	*Power*
Response variable:	AP Margaria (watts)
Explanatory variables:	Body Mass (kilograms)
	Sex (2 levels: Male, Female)

Analysis
A scatter plot of AP Margaria and Body Mass (Figure 6.20) suggests a stronger dependence of AP Margaria on Body Mass in Males than in Females.

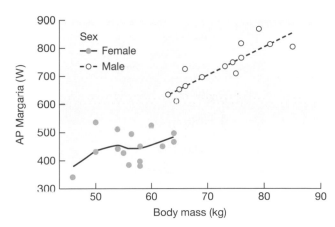

Figure 6.20 Scatter plot of AP Margaria and Body Mass (with separate smoothers by sex).

A separate slopes multiple regression model provided evidence that this is indeed the case as there is a significant interaction between Body Mass and Sex ($P = 0.045$ in Box 6.17). None of the other separate tests for Body Mass and Sex is significant, but these tests are now wholly irrelevant as the interaction term is significant and hence the model is more complex than just a simple additive model.

Box 6.17

```
The regression equation is
Margaria = 265 + 3.26 Body Mass - 245 Sex(M/F) +
                            6.58 Sex(M/F)*BodyMass
Predictor              Coef   SE Coef      T       P
Constant              265.0    141.9    1.87   0.073
Body Mass             3.264    2.507    1.30   0.204
Sex(M/F)             -245.5    196.1   -1.25   0.222
Sex(M/F)*BodyMass     6.583    3.131    2.10   0.045

S = 48.3067   R-Sq = 91.4%   R-Sq(adj) = 90.5%
```

Estimates of the separate regression equations for Males and Females can be calculated by substituting in the relevant values for indicator variable as before. For example, the regression equation for Females is:

$$\text{AP Margaria} = 265 + (3.26 * \text{Body Mass}) - (245 * 0) + (6.58 * 0 * \text{Body Mass})$$
$$= 265 + (3.26 * \text{Body Mass})$$

and hence, in Females, AP Margaria rises by 3.26 watts on average per kilogram increase in Body Mass. The estimated regression equation for Males is calculated by inserting a 1 for the value of Sex(M/F) in the regression equation:

$$\text{AP Margaria} = 265 + (3.26 * \text{Body Mass}) - (245 * 1) + (6.58 * 1 * \text{Body Mass})$$
$$= (265 - 245) + (3.26 + 6.58) \text{Body Mass}$$
$$= 20 + (6.84 * \text{Body Mass})$$

and hence AP Margaria in Males rises by 6.84 watts on average per kilogram increase in Body Mass.

A scatter plot with separate fitted regressions (each with a different slope) for Males and Females is presented in Figure 6.21.

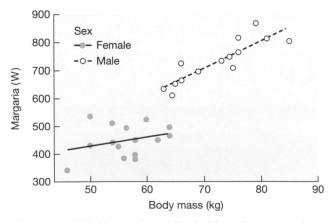

Figure 6.21 Scatter plot of AP Margaria and Body Mass (separate slopes model).

Conclusion

The dependence of Anaerobic Power, as measured by the Margaria test, on Body Mass differs for Males and Females. It is estimated that AP Margaria increase by 6.84 watts, on average, per unit increase in Body Mass in Males whereas in Females this average increase is estimated to be 3.26 watts.

Exercises

6.8 Use multiple regression modelling to model the dependence of Anaerobic Power (determined this time using the Lewis nomogram) on Body Mass and Sex using the *Power* dataset introduced in Illustration 6.8. Fit the parallel slopes and the separate slopes models and decide whether an interaction term is needed to reflect the possible different dependence of AP Lewis on Body Mass for Males and Females.

When there are a large number of explanatory variables (both continuous and categorical) it can be quite cumbersome to fit models with all the relevant terms involving different intercepts and slopes across the categorical explanatory variables. A different approach is available, called regression trees, which offers some nice features, as the next section highlights.

6.7 Regression trees

The regression tree technique is similar to regression in that categorical and continuous explanatory variables that are useful predictors of the response variable can be identified. The technique needed to grow a regression tree is beyond the scope of this book, but suffice to say that the approach differs in that the 'model' that arises from fitting the tree is very intuitive and easy to interpret, unlike a regression model with a large number of explanatory variables. It is basically an empirical approach rather than a formal analysis (unlike most of the techniques dealt with in this book), but is at least free of assumptions and may well give good insight into the structure of the data, if carefully and conservatively carried out. It is best illustrated through an example.

Illustration 6.10 Mont Blanc ascent time (revisited)

Background
See Illustration 3.1 for details.

Study description
In August 2002, 285 climbers passing through the Gouter Hut as they prepared to climb Mont Blanc completed a questionnaire which included questions on subject characteristics and the maximum altitude reached over the past 14 days (maxL14).

Aim

To determine what are the best predictors of Mont Blanc summer Ascent Time for 194 successful climbers on whom all these variables were recorded.

Data

Name of data file:	*Mont Blanc Ascent*
Response variable:	Ascent Time (hours)
Explanatory variable:	Age (years)
Between-subject factors:	Maximum Altitude Climbed (3 levels: <3000 m, 3000 − 4000 m, >4000 m)
	Sex (2 levels: Male, Female)

Analysis

Using the physiological and climbing history information taken from the subjects at the Gouter Hut on the ascent phase of the climb, a regression tree was derived in an attempt to find a simple structure for those explanatory variables (and their 'splits') which were useful in predicting Ascent Time (Figure 6.22).

The tree involves a series of simple two-level rules (i.e. splitting rules) for the explanatory variables that ultimately lead to a predicted value for the response. At each decision point (i.e. node) the most useful explanatory variable – for predicting Ascent Time – and its corresponding 'split (for continuous explanatory variables) or level (for categorical explanatory variables) is given. An individual 'drops' down the tree to the left at any node

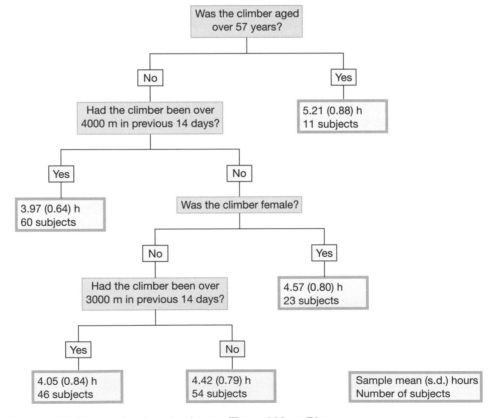

Figure 6.22 Regression tree for Ascent Time of Mont Blanc.

where the split condition is true, or to the right where the split condition is not true. For example, the most useful split among all the explanatory variables was Age, with a split of Age at 57 years. Those climbers aged 57 years or younger 'drop' down the left hand side of the tree, where the next useful predictor identified for this particular subset is whether they have climbed over 4000 m in the past fortnight. Those 60 climbers who have made such a climb drop left and meet a 'terminal' node (i.e. no other variable was found to be a useful predictor for this subset). The predicted mean Ascent Time for climbers aged 57 years or younger and who have climbed over 4000 m in the past fortnight is estimated to be 3.97 hours which is simply the sample mean of the 60 subjects in this subset. In addition, it is useful to note that these 60 subjects have a sample standard deviation of 0.64 hours.

The remaining climbers (who are over 57 or who are younger but have not climbed over 4000 m in the past fortnight) are next split by Sex, where the Female climbers had a predicted mean Ascent Time of 4.57 hours. Additional information is needed for the Males before a prediction can be made. Maximum Altitude re-enters the tree for this specific subset of Male climbers but only for those that had climbed between 3000 and 4000 m in the past fortnight with a predicted mean Ascent Time of 4.05 hours and for those who climbed less than 3000 m with a predicted Ascent Time of 4.42 hours.

Notice also that the tree has been drawn with increasing average Ascent Time from left to right in order to suggest the 'pecking order' of climbing ability subsets. Those climbers aged 57 and over had the highest predicted Ascent Time where no other explanatory variable but Age was deemed useful for this subset.

Reference: Tsianos, G., Woolrich, L., Watt, M., Peacock, A., Aitchison, T., Montgomery, H., Watt, I. and Grant, S. (2005). 'Prediction of performance on the ascent of Mont Blanc.' *European Journal of Applied Physiology*, **96**: 32–36.

Regression trees provide a fairly simple representation of the data with a clear message that may not be available from any formal analysis. The skills needed to grow and prune one of these trees are complex, however, and it is advised that an expert be consulted before gardening commences.

Summary

Techniques for assessing and modelling the relationship between a continuous response variable and one or more explanatory variables were introduced. In some instances, predicting the response variable was the main aim of the analysis, whereas in other studies the sole interest was to identify what contribution, if any, potential explanatory variables make to the overall variability in the response variable.

Simple linear regression involves models with a single explanatory variable, whereas multiple linear regression includes several explanatory variables in the model. However, both assume that the average response depends on the explanatory variable(s) in a linear fashion. Examples were given illustrating how to interpret the regression coefficients and how to test the significance of these in the populations of interest.

In summary, when fitting a multiple regression model to data:

- Statistical software will provide estimates of the regression parameters and accompanying estimated standard errors.
- The *F*-test is used to assess whether one (if not more) of the explanatory variables in the model is significantly related to the response variable.

- Separate tests applied to each explanatory variable separately indicate whether the variable has a significant effect on the response variable, in the presence of the other variables in the specific model.

The assumptions underlying simple and multiple regression were discussed and the use of residual plots to check the validity of these assumptions presented. Prediction through interval estimation was demonstrated. Variable selection techniques to deal with correlated explanatory variables, and the problems this correlation can pose when fitting multiple regression models, were introduced.

Tree-based procedures provide an alternative approach to identifying more complicated relationships between a response variable and a collection of explanatory variables.

One extension to regression models not considered in this chapter is where the dependence of a response on an explanatory variable may be better modelled by a curve. The statistical techniques necessary for modelling polynomial as well as non-linear relationships (of which there are many) are beyond the scope of this book, but the reader should be aware that they exist.

Technical appendix

Simple linear regression

- A smoother should not be confused with a fitted regression line. Recall that a smoother provides an indication of the likely trend across 'bands' of the data moving from left to right across the horizontal axis where the 'amount' of smoothing is up to the user. The smoother gives a general indication of the likely relationship between the variables and is useful in determining what the underlying relationship to represent the dependency of the response variable on the explanatory.

- An estimate of the standard deviation of the population variability about the regression line(s) (i.e. the natural scatter about the linear relationship in the population) is typically labelled S in regression output (see Box 6.1 where S is 0.291111).

Residual plots

- Examples of patterns which would make the simple linear regression assumptions relating to linearity and constant variance doubtful are given in Figure 6.23.

    In the first plot the residuals have a distinct curvilinear pattern, indicating that the linearity assumption is dubious. This can often be seen directly from the scatter plot where the data points may appear to follow a curved rather than linear shape.

    The second plot depicts a scenario where the variability (scatter) increases as the magnitude of the response variable increases, i.e. as the response variable becomes larger the greater the variability there. One approach to consider in such circumstances is to apply a **variance stabilising transformation** to the response variable such as a log, square root or reciprocal. Fitting a simple linear regression of the *transformed* response variable on the explanatory variable (the appropriate transformation determined by investigating subsequent residual plots in order to find a transformed response variable where this phenomenon has in effect disappeared) often removes problems relating to non-constant variance in a relatively easy

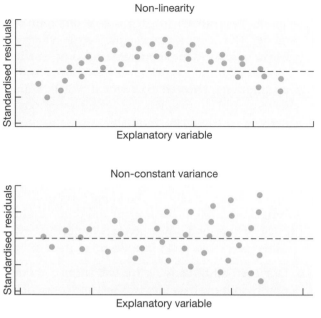

Figure 6.23 Residual plots indicating non-linearity and non-constant variance.

manner. If a transformation of the response variable does not remedy the problem of non-constant variance, the researcher should seek advice from a statistician.

The R^2 statistic

- The formal term for the R^2 statistic is the **coefficient of determination** (the sample correlation coefficient squared).

- If all the points fell on the line (i.e. a perfect linear relationship exists), the sample correlation coefficient would equal 1 and the R^2 statistic would equal 100%. The smaller the R^2, the more the scatter about the line.

- Most statistical software packages automatically identify data points which may have a large influence on the position of the regression line, or which lie a long way away from the regression line. The researcher can check how influential a particular observation is on the model in question by refitting the same model without this observation. If there is a considerable change in the regression coefficient estimates and/or the R^2-adjusted statistic and hence the overall conclusion, this influential observation should be investigated further. Excluding observations just to improve the R^2-adjusted is not acceptable!

Variable selection techniques

- With a larger number of potential explanatory variables the problem becomes more difficult as the number of possible models to choose from can be enormous. If there are k explanatory variables available for analysis, the number of possible regression models is $2^k - 1$. For example, if 20 explanatory variables are available there are 2^{20} (roughly 1 million) possible models that the researcher could investigate. A daunting task.

- The best subsets and stepwise regression procedures may occasionally suggest different final models as each uses a different criterion for deciding on the best model. How does the researcher decide which of these models is the best one to use in practice? One approach is to consider the 'simplest' model from the multiple different models, which have similar R^2-adjusted values, while satisfying the assumptions (checked via residual plots). 'Simplest' may be the model with the fewest number of explanatory variables or may be judged on how difficult or expensive an explanatory variable will be to measure, provided of course that the reduction in R^2-adjusted was not too great.

- Variable selection approaches are often not driven by a particular research hypothesis and are instead data driven. As such, there is no guarantee that the final model will generalise to the population of interest. This may not be such a concern if *predicting the response* is the primary aim of the study, as future performance of the model will give an indication of whether those variables deemed useful predictors do in fact live up to their billing.

- One method to consider for validating a model in a prediction study is to randomly split the data into two sets and to use stepwise or best subsets regression to identify the best model(s) on one half of the data and apply the models to the other half of the data. Choose the model which performs best when applied to the second half of the data. This approach will give some indication of the likely predictive ability of the model in a future sample but requires the dataset to be sufficiently large.

- A word of caution is needed when variable selection tools are used in studies where prediction is not the primary goal but rather the identification of significant explanatory variables. A good scientist *starts* with a hypothesis, collects data on variables believed at the outset to be potentially important explanatory variables (from previous studies for example), and then investigates whether the data are consistent with the hypothesis. By first collecting data and then using the analysis to suggest a hypothesis is poor practice and runs the risk of identifying models that are a feature of the sample only and will not generalise to the population of interest.

- Be aware that stepwise regression uses only complete cases, i.e. no missing values for any variable, which often results in a lot of data being excluded from the analyses.

Power and sample size determination in regression problems

- One major problem to be aware of in multiple regression is that with a large number of explanatory variables and a small sample size it is often possible to find a model which apparently fits the data remarkably well. Such models are often extremely unreliable and tend not to generalise to the population of interest. As a rule of thumb, some statisticians suggest that:

  1 the sample size should be at least 10 times the number of explanatory variables considered; and
  2 the maximum number of explanatory variables to include in the final model should be no more than the square root of the sample size.

7 Investigating between-subject factors: independent observations

7.1 ## 7.1 Introduction

The analyses presented to date involving between-subject factors have all been simple two-sample comparisons from observational studies (e.g. Youth and Elite soccer players) or designed experiments where the between-subject factor had two levels (e.g. Intervention and Controls). In this chapter the **general linear model (GLM)** is presented as a method for comparing the mean of a continuous response variable across one or more between-subject factors, each with an arbitrary number of levels, and if necessary while adjusting for one or more continuous explanatory variables.

Illustrations were given in Chapters 4 and 5 where the main aim was to compare means of samples from two distinct populations in an observational study or the means of two levels for a between-subject factor in a designed study. In both cases interval estimation was used to quantify the likely difference between the population means or the two-sample *t*-test was used if a hypothesis-testing approach was preferred. Of course, many studies will involve comparisons of three or more means, be it from observational or designed experiments. Therefore an extension to the two-sample comparison is needed. The standard method used has the somewhat strange title of **analysis of variance (ANOVA)** as it turns out that the variability in the observations can be split up into components some of which reflect differences in population means among the levels of between-subject factors. Although *t*-tests (two-sample and paired-sample) were the key hypothesis tests for Chapter 5, the **F-test**, named after the (in)famous English statistician Sir Ronald Fisher (1890–1962), is the basic hypothesis test for ANOVAs. Despite a recurring theme in this book to avoid hypothesis tests if at all possible, ANOVA does require hypothesis tests at least at the preliminary stage of the analysis. Once evidence is provided that there are significant differences among the levels of one or more between-subject factors, interval estimation is used to estimate which levels have different population means.

The simplest ANOVA involves a single between-subject factor (with three or more levels) and is known as a one-way ANOVA. The ANOVA procedure, however, is very flexible and can incorporate as many between-subject factors (each with an arbitrary number of levels) as needed. Indeed, it can be extended to allow for the adjustment of continuous explanatory variables (often referred to as **covariates**) which may influence the response variable.

ANOVA is based on the general linear model, which involves a general modelling framework for the comparison of means while allowing for the inclusion of as many between-subject factors and covariates as required, for any imbalance in the design (i.e. unequal sample/sub-sample sizes) and for any dependency within the observations such as multiple measurements on the same subject under different conditions or at different times into the study (see Chapters 9 to 11).

Despite apparent differences in study designs across the scenarios covered in this chapter, *all* of the analyses presented can be performed using a GLM routine available in any statistical software package. This avoids any confusion that may arise when trying to identify the appropriate ANOVA routine when analysing data – go straight for the GLM!

The steps involved in fitting a general linear model with between-subject factors are as follows:

1 Clearly identify the hypotheses of interest and the appropriate underlying population (or populations).

2 Plot the data by means of box plots for each of the samples involved and provide a subjective answer as to which, if any, of the corresponding population means appear to differ.

3 If the assumptions underlying the GLM appear justified, formally investigate whether it is possible to reject the null hypothesis that all the population means are equal.

4 If there is evidence to reject the null hypothesis, carry out a suitable **multiple comparison procedure** (a detailed examination of the differences between the sample means) to investigate where the differences among the population means are likely to occur.

5 Summarise and report the conclusions using appropriate results and graphs.

The GLM is first demonstrated in a study involving a single between-subject factor with three levels. Following this, more complicated illustrations are introduced involving two or more between-subject factors as well as studies with between-subject factors and covariates.

7.2	**One-way ANOVA: a general linear model with one between-subject factor**

The simplest application of a GLM involves testing for significant differences among population means across three or more levels of a between-subject factor, a so-called **one-way ANOVA**. A more accurate description would be 'one-factor' ANOVA as the 'one' refers to the fact that there is a *single between-subject factor* of interest.

Such data may arise from observational studies where samples are taken from three or more different populations. For example, a sports scientist is interested in comparing the climbing-specific finger strength of three different grades of climber. She takes a random sample from each grade and records the Grip Strength and grade for each climber in each sample. Do the data provide evidence of a significant difference in the mean Grip Strength in the three populations of climbers?

Methods for comparing between-subject factors with three or more levels are also needed in designed experiments where a sample from a single population has been randomised to one of three or more levels of a between-subject factor. Recall Illustration 3.3 where each of a sample of 30 middle distance club-standard runners was randomly allocated to one of three Treatments. The first sub-sample received no treatment (i.e. were Controls), the second carried out twice daily Progressive Muscle Relaxation while the third adopted Meditation techniques on a daily basis. After two weeks the Exercise Heart Rate at the end of an exercise regime was measured for every runner from each of the three Treatments. The question of interest is whether or not there were any significant differences among the average changes in Exercise Heart Rates for these three Treatments (i.e. if applied to the whole population of middle distance club-standard runners).

Appropriate analyses including one-way ANOVAs for the data from these two studies (one observational and one designed) are now provided.

Illustration 7.1   Grip strength (Illustration 3.9 revisited)

Background

In the sport of rock climbing the steeper the rock face is, generally, the more difficult the climb is graded. Climbs are graded from Moderate to Extreme (E), with E1 being the easiest climb on this E scale. A grading of Severe is between Moderate and Extreme and is not deemed to be a high climbing standard. It is reasonable to speculate that high levels of climbing-specific finger strength and perhaps grip strength are of great importance in elite climbing.

Study description

Independent samples of 10 Elite (i.e. have successfully completed a climbing standard of E1 in the last 12 months), 10 Recreational (i.e. have successfully completed a climb no harder than Severe in the last 12 months) and 10 non-climbers (i.e. Controls) had the Grip Strength of their (dominant) right hand measured, as well as having their Body Mass recorded. All subjects were male.

Aim

To compare average Grip Strength of the (dominant) right hand among the three populations of male climbers.

Data

Name of data file:	*Grip Strength and Mass*
Response variable:	Grip Strength (newtons)
Between-subject factor:	Climber Type (3 levels: Control, Recreational, Elite)

Analysis

Summary statistics (Box 7.1) and a box plot (Figure 7.1) are presented in order to provide a subjective impression of the differences (if any) in the mean Grip Strength across the Climber Types. A box plot of Grip Strength for the three Types suggests that Grip Strength tends to be higher for Elite climbers than for the other two populations, Recreational climbers and Controls.

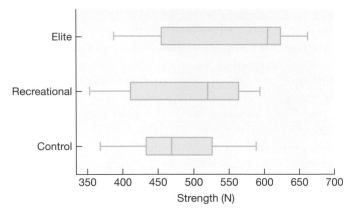

Figure 7.1 **Box plot of Grip Strength by Climber Type.**

Box 7.1

```
Descriptive Statistics: Strength(N)

Variable      Type          N   N*    Mean   SE Mean   StDev   Minimum      Q1
Strength(N)   Control      10   0    475.6     19.9    63.0     367.7   432.7
              Elite        10   0    555.1     30.5    96.5     387.4   454.8
              Recreational 10   0    490.3     26.9    85.1     353.0   410.7

Variable      Level       Median     Q3    Maximum
Strength(N)   Control      468.3   521.0    588.4
              Elite        605.6   623.9    661.9
              Recreational 519.8   563.9    593.3
```

Remember that a box plot displays (among other things) the sample median. However, if each sample did arise from a Normal distribution (a necessary assumption for a one-way ANOVA which is considered later in this section), then the sample mean and median should be quite similar. This appears to be the case except perhaps for the sample of Elite climbers (see Box 7.1).

The relevant null and alternative hypotheses for this example are:

H_0: The *population* mean Grip Strengths are the same for the three Climber Types

H_1: The *population* mean Grip Strengths are not all the same for the three Climber Types

The task is to use the data available to determine whether there is sufficient evidence to reject the null hypothesis. This can be achieved by fitting a GLM with Grip Strength as the response and Climber Type as the single between-subject factor. The output from fitting this GLM is displayed in Box 7.2.

The output from the model is quite forbidding at first glance. However, the key piece of information is the *P*-value (highlighted in bold). Since the *P*-value here (0.092) is greater than 0.05, the null hypothesis of equal population mean Grip Strengths cannot be rejected. It must therefore be concluded that there are no significant differences among the population mean Grip Strengths of the three Climber Types.

Box 7.2

```
General Linear Model: Strength(N) versus Level

Factor    Type    Levels    Values
Type      fixed        3    Control, Elite, Recreational

Analysis of Variance for Strength(N), using Adjusted SS for Tests

Source   DF      Seq SS   Adj SS   Adj MS     F      P
Type      2       35718    35718    17859   2.61   0.092
Error    27      184734   184734     6842
Total    29      220451

S = 82.7163    R-Sq = 16.20%    R-Sq(adj) = 9.99%

Unusual Observations for Strength(N)

Obs   Strength(N)       Fit   SE Fit   Residual   St Resid
  9       387.363   555.056   26.157   -167.694      -2.14 R
```

Conclusion

There was no convincing evidence ($P = 0.092$) of any significant difference in mean Grip Strength between the populations of Elite, Recreational and non-climbers.

Reference: Grant, S., Hynes, V, Whittaker, A. and Aitchison, T. (1996). 'Anthropometric, strength, endurance and flexibility characteristics of elite and recreational climbers.' *Journal of Sports Sciences,* **14**: 301–309.

The second illustration in this section involves data arising from a completely randomised design with one between-subject factor with three levels.

Illustration 7.2   **Relaxation and running performance (revisited)**

Background and study description
See Illustration 3.3.

Aim

To determine which, if either, of the relaxation methods (Meditation or Progressive Muscular Relaxation (PMR)) significantly reduces exercise heart rate on average compared with Controls over a two-week period.

Data

    Name of data file: *Relaxation*
    Response variable: Reduction in Heart Rate (b.min^{-1})
    Between-subject factor: Treatment (3 levels: Control, Meditation, PMR)

Analysis

There is a single between-subject factor of interest called Treatment with three levels: Control, Meditation and PMR. The question of interest is whether the differences in the sample means are large enough to be declared significant and the 'best' Treatment identified? It is important to realise that the response variable considered here (i.e. the Reduction in Heart Rate) is in fact the difference between the heart rate before the study and the heart rate at the end of the study. It is clear from the box plot (Figure 7.2) that Meditation produces, in general, larger Reductions in Heart Rate than either of the other

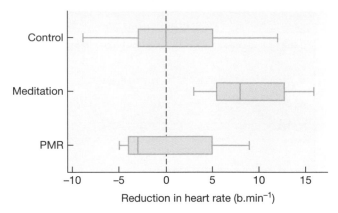

Figure 7.2 Box plot of Reduction in Heart Rate by Treatment (with vertical line representing 'no change').

two Treatments and that the sample mean Reductions for the Control and PMR Treatments are both almost zero on average, suggesting no improvement for either.

The summary statistics (Box 7.3) confirm that the variability within each Treatment is quite similar and there is no concern here regarding the equal variances assumption.

Box 7.3

```
Variable    Group         N     Mean   StDev   Minimum        Q1      Median     Q3
Reduction   Control      13    0.846    5.55     -9.00     -3.00        0.00    5.00
            Meditation    8    8.75     4.33      3.00      5.50        8.00   12.75
            PMR           7    0.429    5.47     -5.00     -4.00        3.00    5.00

Variable    Group       Maximum
Reduction   Control       12.00
            Meditation    16.00
            PMR            9.00
```

A GLM was fitted (Box 7.4) to assess whether the population mean responses are the same for the three Treatments.

Box 7.4

```
Factor       Type    Levels   Values
Treatment    fixed        3   Control, Meditation, PMR

Analysis of Variance for Reduction, using Adjusted SS for Tests

Source        DF    Seq SS   Adj SS   Adj MS      F        P
Treatment      2    371.09   371.09   185.55   6.81    0.004
Error         25    680.91   680.91    27.24
Total         27   1052.00

S = 5.21884    R-Sq = 35.28%    R-Sq(adj) = 30.10%

Unusual Observations for Reduction

Obs   Reduction      Fit   SE Fit   Residual   St Resid
  7     12.0000   0.8462   1.4474    11.1538       2.22 R
```

Conclusion (part 1)

Since the *P*-value from the one-way ANOVA ($P = 0.004$) is much smaller than 0.05, the null hypothesis of all three population mean Reductions in Heart Rate being equal can be rejected and therefore it can be concluded that there are some differences in the population mean responses to the different Treatments.

Having established the presence of some differences among the Treatments it is necessary to identify which Treatments are significantly different and to *quantify* the likely difference in mean Reduction in Heart Rate between the Treatments. This is achieved by using a **multiple comparison** procedure to generate a set of simultaneous interval estimates for all the pairwise comparisons (i.e. for the differences in population mean Reduction in Heart Rate between *each pair* of Treatments).

7.2.1 Multiple comparison procedures

A multiple comparison procedure can be carried out using either hypothesis tests or interval estimates but the preferred approach in this book is, as always, the latter. Any pairwise comparison that returns an interval estimate which does not contain zero provides evidence that the pair of population means are significantly different.

Remember that there is a 5% probability of any 95% CI not containing the true population value that it is intended to contain. So, if many 95% CIs for pairwise comparisons are considered at one time, then there will be a much greater than 5% probability that at least one of these intervals will not contain the true difference in the appropriate population means. One consequence of this is that there are likely to be too many spuriously declared differences among the population means and hence no agreement with the one-way ANOVA. An adjustment is needed therefore to the intervals from each pairwise comparison to ensure that the conclusions about pairwise differences agree with the conclusion from the one-way ANOVA. This adjustment basically ensures that, when all the pairwise comparisons are looked at together, there is at least a 95% probability that all the relevant intervals contain their true population mean differences or, equivalently, that there is at most a 5% chance of a spuriously declared difference in any paired comparison when in fact there are no differences among any of the population means (and hence will be compatible with the conclusion to a one-way ANOVA with a 5% significance level).

The merits of two of the more popular procedures, namely the Bonferroni and Tukey procedures, are now discussed. Both methods provide a set of interval estimates of the difference, which are, in both cases, of the form:

Difference in sample means $\pm$ A multiple of the e.s.e. of the difference

where e.s.e. is the estimated standard error.

The only difference between the Bonferroni and Tukey procedures is the choice of multiple used in the calculation.

The Bonferroni procedure (after Carlo Bonferroni (1892–1960)) is quite simple: instead of generating a separate 95% CI for each pairwise comparison, each interval is made wider so that the set of intervals has a 'collective' confidence of 95%. The phrase 'simultaneous confidence interval' is often used to describe such a set of pairwise intervals.

In general, the adjustment needed is to provide confidence intervals with individual confidence of

$$100 \times \left[1 - \frac{0.05}{\text{No. of comparisons}} \right]$$

For example, if four pairwise comparisons are required and a simultaneous confidence of 95% is required, the Bonferroni method adjusts each comparison/interval estimate's confidence coefficient by calculating $100 * (1 - 0.05/4) = 98.75\%$, i.e. calculate separate 98.75% confidence intervals for each pairwise comparison.

The Tukey procedure (after John Tukey (1915–2000)) works on a slightly different (but more complicated) method for determining the multiple for each confidence interval while controlling for the number of intervals required. The Tukey approach is considered a less conservative approach than the Bonferroni method, especially when a small number of intervals are needed. For this reason, the Tukey method is generally preferred. The Bonferroni method, however, is easier to calculate in practice (as later illustrations will highlight).

A GLM, when fitted to the Relaxation data of Illustration 7.2, provides evidence that mean Reduction in Heart Rate was not equal in the three Treatments. There are three pairwise comparisons of interest here, namely Control versus Meditation, Control versus PMR, and Meditation versus PMR. The results from applying the Tukey multiple comparisons procedure to these data are given in Box 7.5.

Box 7.5

```
Tukey 95.0% Simultaneous Confidence Intervals
Response Variable Reduction
All Pairwise Comparisons among Levels of Treatment

Treatment = Control   subtracted from:

Group          Lower   Center   Upper
Meditation     2.067   7.9038   13.741
PMR           -6.507  -0.4176    5.672

Treatment = Meditation   subtracted from:

Group    Lower   Center   Upper
PMR     -15.04   -8.321   -1.599
```

Notice that the confidence intervals are given the label 'Simultaneous Confidence Intervals' to highlight the fact that the confidence associated with the *set* of all three intervals is (at least) 95%.

The first interval in Box 7.5 is for Meditation minus Control and is 2.1 to 13.7 b.min^{-1} which is entirely positive. Therefore, it can be concluded that the mean Reduction in Heart Rate is significantly greater for Meditation compared with Controls (i.e. Meditation results in a larger reduction in mean Heart Rate compared with 'no treatment' of at least 2.1 b.min^{-1} and at most 13.7 b.min^{-1}). As the second interval does contain zero, there is no strong evidence that the PMR is any more or any less effective than 'no treatment' in terms of mean Reduction in Heart Rate. The fact that the third interval is entirely negative provides evidence that Meditation also does significantly better than PMR in terms of average Reduction in Heart Rate (i.e. the mean Reduction in Heart Rate for Meditation *subtracted from* the mean Reduction in Heart Rate for PMR is *negative,* hence the mean Reduction for Meditation must be larger than for PMR).

More importantly, these intervals give some idea of the magnitude of the 'benefit' of Meditation in that it is likely to reduce mean Heart Rate by between 2 and 14 beats.min^{-1} more than 'no treatment' and by between 2 and 15 b.min^{-1} more than PMR.

The conclusion to the analysis of Illustration 7.2 can now be completed as follows.

Illustration 7.2 **(continued)**

Conclusion (part 2)

This study provides evidence of a significant difference in mean Reduction in Heart Rate across the three Treatments of interest ($P = 0.004$). In particular, Meditation is significantly better at reducing Heart Rate by between 2 and 13 b.min^{-1} on average, when compared with Controls and by between 2 and 15 b.min^{-1} on average, when compared with those using PMR. There was no evidence of a significant difference between the Controls and those using PMR.

As a suitable summary of the conclusion it is worth writing down the names or letters pertaining to each Treatment in order of increasing sample mean Reduction in Heart Rate and underlining pairs of variables that are not significantly different.

Treatment	PMR	C	M
Sample mean	0.43	0.85	
Reduction in Heart Rate (b.min^{-1})			8.75

Such a summary provides both an estimate of the response for each Treatment (through the sample mean) and a graphical method to identify which of the Treatments were/were not significantly different.

Additional comment on Illustration 7.2

The response variable used in the analysis was the simple difference in heart rate over the two-week period. Strictly speaking, this is an example of repeated measures data where Time is a within-subject factor with two levels. The two levels have been 'collapsed' by virtue of taking the difference. Often the requirements of analysing such simple differences are met, however. If there are any concerns relating to analysing the simple differences, methods for analysing combinations of between- and within-subject factors are given in Chapter 10.

7.2.2 Assessing the adequacy of a one-way ANOVA

The assumptions for a one-way ANOVA are as follows:

1   The samples obtained are random.

2   All observations are independent of each other.

3a In an *observational study* the underlying populations are Normally distributed with equal standard deviations but possibly different means.

3b In a *designed experiment* the underlying population is Normally distributed with equal standard deviations but possibly different means for each between-subject factor level.

In the previous chapter, hypothesis tests of equality of population standard deviations (or variances) were not recommended as such tests tend not to be particularly powerful when used on small samples. Thankfully, the GLM is robust to non-equal standard deviations when there are equal numbers in each sample (or sub-sample); it is not so robust if the sample sizes are unequal.

A practical rule of thumb to consider is that differences in sample standard deviations are a concern only if the largest of the sample standard deviations is larger than twice the smallest standard deviation.

In the Grip Strength illustration (Illustration 7.1), the largest standard deviation (96.5) is less than twice the smallest ($2 \times 63 = 126$) and the assumption of equality of population standard deviations is deemed reasonable. The same applied in the Relaxation and Running Performance illustration (Illustration 7.2), as the sample standard deviations were similar in each of the three Treatments.

The Normal distribution assumption can be checked informally using box plots by looking for symmetry in each sample separately. A better approach, however, is to use **residual plots** in a similar manner to that presented for regression models in Chapter 5. A residual in a GLM is the difference between observed and expected values for each observation, e.g. each individual Grip Strength measurement minus the respective sample mean. The same plots as introduced in Chapter 6 are needed here, namely a Normal probability plot of the residuals and a plot of the residuals against the fitted values (Figure 7.3).

There is nothing in the plots in Figure 7.3 to raise any concerns regarding the underlying model assumptions.

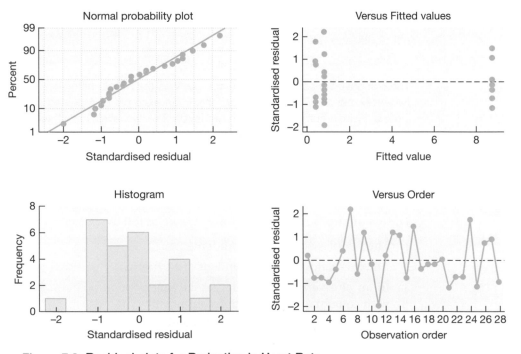

Figure 7.3 **Residual plots for Reduction in Heart Rate.**

7.1 Climbing Specific Finger Strength was recorded in addition to Grip Strength for the sample of male climbers introduced in Illustration 7.1. Fit a GLM to investigate whether there are any significant differences in Climbing Specific Finger Strength on average among the three Climbing Types.

7.2 In August 2002, 285 climbers passed through the Gouter Hut as they prepared to climb Mont Blanc. Each was questioned about the maximum altitude reached over the past 14 days, which was coded into three levels: <3000 m, 3000–4000 m and >4000 m. Fit a GLM to investigate whether mean Ascent Time is significantly different between any of the levels of maximum altitude reached for the successful climbers. The data are called *Mont Blanc Successful*.

In many experiments, researchers often wish to compare several populations on more than one between-subject factor of interest or to examine a number of between-subject factors and, in particular, combinations of these and their resulting effect on the response variable of interest (e.g. whether dieting or exercise or a combination of both will reduce a person's body mass). The next section concentrates on such studies where two between-subject factors – each consisting of at least two levels – are considered and the response variable is measured on (usually) an equal number of subjects for each of the levels of the factors. The one-way ANOVA is extended to account for the fact that two factors are of interest and its name should therefore come as no surprise.

7.3 Two-way ANOVA: a general linear model with two between-subject factors

A **two-way ANOVA** is an extension of one-way ANOVA allowing the researcher to quantify the effect of two between-subject factors. Once again the model can be fitted using a GLM, but now including a second between-subject factor. It has the added advantage of determining whether the combined effect is greater than the sum of the two separate effects, i.e. whether an **interaction** is present.

In Illustration 3.4, an observational study was introduced where data on 145 Males and 140 Females were recorded to investigate whether participating in Regular Exercise would increase a person's Well-being (as measured on a subjective visual analogue scale). There are three key questions to be answered in the analysis:

1 Does Well-being differ, on average, between those who are Regular Exercisers and those who are not?

2 Does Well-being differ, on average, between the Sexes?

3 Is the average difference in Well-being between those who are Regular Exercisers and those who are not different for Males and Females?

Or, the equivalent question:

3* Is the average difference in Well-being between Males and Females different for those who are Regular Exercisers and those who are not?

The first two questions relate to comparing the difference between levels of the between-subject factor whereas both forms of the third question relate to comparing the difference of differences, i.e. is the difference between the levels of one of the between-subject factors comparable across the levels of the other.

These three questions are often referred to in statistical jargon as:

1 Is there a **significant main effect** of Regular Exercise?

2 Is there a **significant main effect** of Sex?

3 or 3* Is there a **significant interaction** between Regular Exercise and Sex?

A two-way ANOVA offers an improvement over a one-way ANOVA as the two between-subject factors are studied simultaneously. The procedure is similar to a one-way ANOVA in that P-values are used to provide evidence of whether differences in the sample means are significant. Once again, multiple comparisons (where appropriate) are used to provide interval estimates of the significant factor level differences in the population.

The following steps are needed to carry out a two-way ANOVA:

1 Prepare box plots and summary statistics of the response variable across the levels of the two factors.

2 Fit the *full model*, i.e. the model containing the two main effects and the interaction term.

3 If there is a significant interaction, use a suitable multiple comparisons procedure on all the pairwise level combinations of both Factors *or* a subset of clear interest.

4 If there is no significant interaction, but there is a significant main effect for either or both the factors, use a suitable multiple comparisons procedure on each significant factor separately.

5 Prepare suitable residual plots to check the assumptions underlying the model.

The first illustration presented is an observational study followed by an illustration relating to a designed experiment.

Illustration 7.3 Sprint speed in rugby

Background

Speed is important in rugby for attack (in an attempt to score a try) and defence (to prevent a try). It is of interest to determine if one of the characteristics that distinguishes professional and amateur rugby players is sprint speed. In addition, it is considered worthwhile to determine if there is a consistency between forwards and backs, i.e. are professional forwards as well as backs faster than their amateur counterparts?

Study description

A sample of 12 backs and 12 forwards were selected at random from an amateur and a professional rugby team. The players were asked to sprint over a distance of 20 metres from a standing start. There are two factors of interest: Status (Amateur and Professional) and Position (Backs and Forwards).

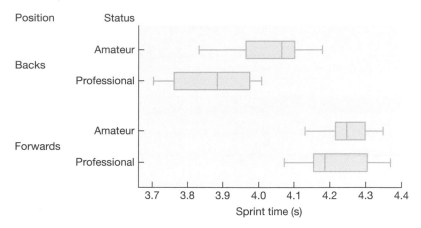

Figure 7.4 **Box plot of Sprint Time by Status and Position.**

Aim

The researcher has specified that she is only interested in comparing the *squads* to each other (i.e. Amateur Backs to Amateur Forwards and Professional Backs to Professional Forwards) and the *positions* to each other (i.e. Amateur Backs to Professional Backs and Amateur Forwards to Professional Forwards).

Data

Name of data file:	*Rugby Sprint Time*
Response variable:	Sprint Time (seconds)
Between-subject factors:	Status (2 levels: Professional, Amateur)
	Position (2 levels: Back, Forward)

Analysis

There are two between-subject factors of interest, Status and Position, each with two levels, and interest lies in investigating whether the sample mean Sprint Times are significantly different due to the factors in question.

The samples are random from the population of interest. It appears plausible that the response variable is Normally distributed in the populations of interest (Figure 7.4), and that the standard deviations are similar enough not to warrant special attention (Box 7.6). Furthermore, the box plot suggests a difference in median Sprint Time between Amateurs and Professionals for Forwards and Backs, where the difference is more noticeable among the Backs. Note that in this example low values represent faster players as the response variable is measured in units of time.

Box 7.6

```
Results for Status = Amateur
Variable  Position   N    Mean    StDev
Sprint    Backs      12   4.0459  0.1003
          Forwards   12   4.2512  0.0658

Results for Status = Professional
Variable  Position   N    Mean    StDev
Sprint    Backs      12   3.8622  0.1095
          Forwards   12   4.2239  0.0955
```

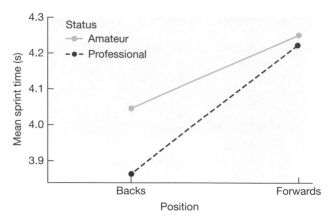

Figure 7.5 **Plot of mean Sprint Time by Squad and Position.**

The sample of Professional Backs was 0.18 seconds faster on average when compared with the Amateur Backs whereas the difference in the corresponding Forwards was considerably less at 0.03 seconds. These differences suggest the presence of an interaction, as the difference in the mean response within position is not the same for the Amateurs when compared with the Professionals. This is highlighted in the plot of the mean Sprint Time for each factor level (Figure 7.5), where a difference is evident between the Forwards and Backs and that Professional Backs differ from Amateur Backs.

Notice from the plot that the difference between the mean Sprint Time is much smaller for the Forwards than for the Backs. Hence it makes little sense to discuss the difference in (mean) Sprint Time without taking both factors into consideration simultaneously.

These subjective impressions suggest that there may be main effects due to Status (Professional players appear to be quicker on average compared with Amateurs) and Position (Backs tend to be faster than Forwards) and an interaction between Status and Position (i.e. the difference between the Backs appears to be greater than between the Forwards).

A formal analysis to test these impressions is obtained by fitting a GLM with Status and Position as main effects and specifying the inclusion of the Status/Position interaction term (Box 7.7). *Always start by investigating the hypothesis test for the interaction term.* A significant interaction in a two-way ANOVA implies that there is a 'combined' effect of the two factors, and therefore *both* main effects are important, *regardless* of whether their individual P-values are significant or not.

There is evidence of a significant interaction between the two factors ($P = 0.006$). As the interaction term is significant, the remaining task is to identify which Status/Position combinations are responsible for the significant interaction term. There is one observation deemed 'unusual', namely an Amateur Back who is faster, when compared with the average speed of the other Backs, than the Professionals.

There are six possible comparisons available if all pairwise comparisons are of interest. As the researcher specified before the study that she was interested only in comparing the Positions across Status to each other, only four comparisons are needed.

Predetermined comparisons are examples of **contrasts** and the four relevant comparisons can be obtained by calculating 98.75% Bonferroni adjusted confidence intervals for each comparison required (Box 7.8).

Box 7.7

```
General Linear Model: Sprint versus Status, Position

Factor    Type    Levels  Values
Status    fixed      2    Amateur, Professional
Position  fixed      2    Backs, Forwards

Analysis of Variance for Sprint, using Adjusted SS for Tests

Source           DF   Seq SS   Adj SS   Adj MS       F      P
Status            1  0.13344  0.13344  0.13344   15.03  0.000
Position          1  0.96447  0.96447  0.96447  108.64  0.000
Status*Position   1  0.07340  0.07340  0.07340    8.27  0.006
Error            44  0.39060  0.39060  0.00888
Total            47  1.56191
S = 0.0942199   R-Sq = 74.99%   R-Sq(adj) = 73.29%

Unusual Observations for Sprint

Obs   Sprint      Fit   SE Fit  Residual  St Resid
  4  3.83014  4.04586  0.02720  -0.21572     -2.39 R
```

Box 7.8

```
         (Backs - Forwards)                 P-value
Amateurs       (-0.30, -0.11)               <0.001
Professionals  (-0.48, -0.25)               <0.001

         (Amateurs - Professionals)
Backs          ( 0.07, 0.30)                <0.001
Forwards       (-0.06, 0.12)                 0.43
```

The first interval is strictly negative, providing evidence that the mean Sprint Time is higher (i.e. slower) for Forwards than for Backs in the population of Amateur players.

There is a significant difference in Sprint Time when Position is compared in the Professionals as the interval does not contain zero.

A difference in mean speed is *only noticeable*, however, when comparing Amateur and Professional Backs, where the Professional Backs tend to be faster on average. There was no significant difference between Professional and Amateur Forwards. This interval reflects the fact that any suggestion of Professional rugby players being significantly quicker, on average, compared with Amateur rugby players is evident only among the Backs.

Conclusion

This study provides evidence of a significant difference in mean Sprint Time between Amateur and Professional rugby players where Backs were significantly faster than Forwards in both Amateur and Professional players ($P < 0.001$ for both) and Professional Backs are significantly faster than Amateur Backs ($P < 0.001$). There was no significant difference between Amateur and Professional Forwards ($P = 0.43$), however. In particular, the Professional backs are likely to be between 0.25 and 0.48 seconds quicker on average compared with Professional Forwards and between 0.07 and 0.30 seconds faster, on average, when compared with Amateur Backs. The fact that the Professional Backs are faster than their counterparts is highly suggestive that differences in sprint speed are a distinguishing factor between elite and non-elite players in the Backs. Similarly, Backs (Professional and Amateur) will generally have a sprint speed advantage when they encounter Forwards.

To summarise these results, the sample means of the Status/Position combinations are written in ascending order of Sprint Time and those pairs, of the combinations *of interest*, which are not significantly different (i.e. those pairs above whose interval estimates do not contain zero), are underlined.

Combination	Professional Backs	Amateur Backs	Professional Forwards	Amateur Forwards
Sample mean Sprint Time (seconds)	3.86	4.04	4.22	4.25

Reference: Reid, S., Fleming, E. (students), McLean, D. and Grant, S. (supervisors) (2004). 'A comparison of sprint performance using three different sprint tests in rugby players.' Physiology and Sports Science student project, University of Glasgow.

Assessing the adequacy of a two-way ANOVA

A two-way ANOVA assumes the following:

1 All the observations are **independent** of each other.

2 The underlying distribution of the response variable of interest for any combination of the two factors is **Normal**.

3 All the population **standard deviations** (for the different combinations) are the same but the population means may be different.

The model is quite robust to departures from Normality while the equality of the standard deviations (spreads) rule of thumb applies again; this assumption is of concern only if the largest of the sample standard deviations is no more than twice the smallest.

As in a one-way ANOVA, the simplest way of checking the Normality and equal spreads assumptions is by means of box plots – simply ensure that each sample median is roughly in the middle of each box (Normality) and that the lengths of the boxes are about the same (equal spreads). The summary statistics and box plots presented for the Sprint Time comparison suggest that the Normality and equal spreads assumptions are adequate.

The residual plots for the data in Illustration 7.3 confirm the assumption of Normality by virtue of the strong linear pattern noticeable in the Normal probability plot and the near perfect symmetry present in the histogram of the residuals (Figure 7.6). Finally, the plot of the (standardised) residuals versus the fitted values does not suggest the presence of outliers nor is there any systematic component noticeable in the residuals order plot.

Additional comments on Illustration 7.3

1 It may be tempting to generate the complete set of Status/Position pairwise comparisons and then to pick off the ones of interest. Be careful! There is a trade-off in the width of each interval given the number of intervals requested; the more requested the wider (and hence less precise and less likely to be significant) each subsequent interval will be. Box 7.9 displays the full set of Status/Position pairwise confidence intervals where the four intervals of primary interest are highlighted in bold.

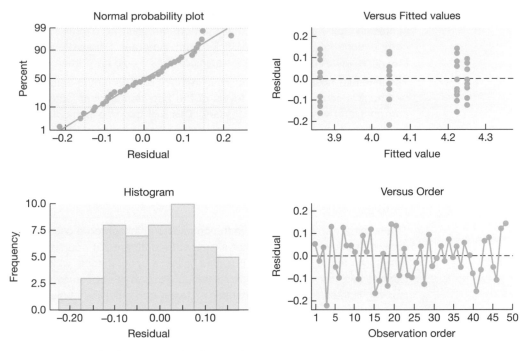

Figure 7.6 **Residual plots for Sprint Time.**

Box 7.9

```
Bonferroni 95.0% Simultaneous Confidence Intervals
Response Variable Sprint
All Pairwise Comparisons among Levels of Status*Position

Status = Amateur
Position = Forwards   subtracted from:

Status          Position   Lower    Center    Upper
Amateur         Backs      -0.3116  -0.2053   -0.0990
Professional    Forwards   -0.1335  -0.0272    0.0790
Professional    Backs      -0.4952  -0.3890   -0.2827

Status = Amateur
Position = Backs    subtracted from:

Status          Position   Lower    Center    Upper
Professional    Forwards   0.0718   0.1781    0.28432
Professional    Backs      -0.2899  -0.1837   -0.07739

Status = Professional
Position = Forwards   subtracted from:

Status          Position   Lower    Center    Upper
Professional    Backs      -0.4680  -0.3617   -0.2554
```

Notice that each interval is (marginally) wider than the corresponding interval presented in Box 7.8. Note also that the two intervals not deemed 'interesting' (i.e. the comparisons of Professional Backs with Amateur Forwards and of Professional Forwards with Amateur Backs) are significant as would have been expected.

2 These results raise an interesting issue in that it is important to determine before the experiment is carried out which levels of the between-subject factors are of interest to compare and which are unnecessary. This will become particularly important when each of the between-subject factors have a large number of levels. Generating a lot of uninteresting comparisons will make those intervals of primary concern less precise and a significant comparison may be missed. This is not to say that cherry picking a subset of intervals purely to achieve significance is valid. This is termed **data-snooping** and should be avoided. A fuller discussion of this topic is given in the technical appendix to this chapter.

3 The summary table presented in the conclusion highlighted those comparisons, of the subset of interest, that were not significantly different. Of course, the table could be misinterpreted to represent all possible pairwise comparisons, which was not the case. Despite this, the results from Box 7.9 indicate that, had all been performed, the comparison highlighted in the summary table as being non-significant would in fact be the only non-significant among all the pairwise comparisons.

The two-way ANOVA example presented above relates to an observational study. However, ANOVA is also appropriate when analysing data generated from experimental studies such as a completely randomised design.

Illustration 7.4   Electrical muscle stimulation

Background
Electrical muscle stimulation (EMS) has been used in the training of athletes and to help with the rehabilitation of some patient groups. Bio-Medical Research Ltd has produced a device which can apply electrical stimulation to the abdominal muscles.

Study description
Twenty-eight physically inactive female and male subjects were recruited. A double blind study was used where equal numbers of male and female subjects were randomly assigned to receive an intervention or to act as a control. All subjects carried out training sessions 5 days per week for 30 minutes each session, over a 6-week period. The device provided electrical stimulation to those on the intervention whereas the apparatus used by the Controls provided electrical stimulation that was of no benefit (known as sham treatment). This allowed the Controls to believe that the device was functioning (i.e. blinding); however, the amount of electrical stimulation administered was of no benefit (known as a sham treatment). Tests were conducted at Baseline and 6 weeks later. The isometric abdominal strength of the abdominal muscles was measured while the subjects carried out five contractions on a Biodex dynamometer where the mean of the two highest torque scores was recorded.

Aim
To determine the effects of a 6-week training programme with the device on the isometric strength of the abdominal muscles.

Data

Name of data file:	*Biodex*
Response variable:	Isometric Abdominal Strength (newton metres)
Between-subject factors:	Device (2 levels: Control, Treatment)
	Sex (2 levels: Male, Female)

Analysis

Summary statistics (Box 7.10) for the response variable, categorised by the two between-subject factors, suggest a considerable improvement for Males and Females receiving the Treatment. Note the response variable is the improvement in Isometric Abdominal Strength (IAS) from baseline so the analysis involves simple differences.

Box 7.10

```
Results for Sex = Female

Variable          Device        N    Mean   StDev  Minimum      Q1   Median      Q3
IAS Improvement   Treatment    13   17.31   16.82    -1.00    5.25    12.00   22.50
                  Control      14    1.04    5.90   -15.50   -1.25     3.25    5.50

Variable          Device      Maximum
IAS Improvement   Treatment     62.00
                  Control        6.00

Results for Sex = Male

Variable          Device        N    Mean   StDev  Minimum      Q1   Median      Q3
IAS Improvement   Treatment    13   22.62   17.74     1.00    9.00    22.00   28.25
                  Control      12    3.29    5.12    -8.50   -0.75     4.50    7.38

Variable          Device      Maximum
IAS Improvement   Treatment     72.00
                  Control       10.00
```

The sample mean improvement is similar in Males and Females; however, the standard deviation is considerably larger among those receiving the Treatment than among the Controls (Figure 7.7).

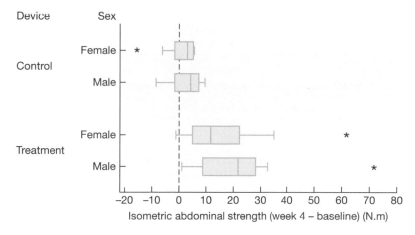

Figure 7.7 **Box plot of Isometric Abdominal Strength Improvement by Device and Sex.**

193

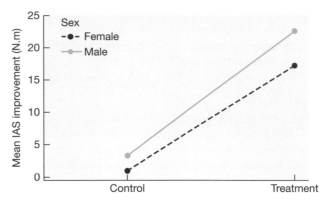

Figure 7.8 Plot of mean Isometric Abdominal Strength Improvement by Device and Sex.

The plot of the mean IAS for each factor level (Figure 7.8) highlights that Males experienced a slightly larger mean improvement than did Females for both Devices (i.e. a possible main effect due to Sex). The similarity in mean improvement for both Males and Females on Treatment suggests that an interaction may not be present.

The two-way ANOVA (Box 7.11) identifies a non-significant interaction (P = 0.671) but does identify a significant main effect of Device (P < 0.001). Despite the higher mean improvement for Males there is no evidence of a significant main effect due to Sex (P = 0.294).

Box 7.11

```
General Linear Model: IAS Improvement versus Device, Sex

Factor   Type    Levels   Values
Device   fixed        2   Treatment, Control
Sex      fixed        2   Female, Male

Analysis of Variance for IAS Improvement, using Adjusted SS for Tests

Source       DF    Seq SS   Adj SS   Adj MS      F      P
Device        1    4158.2   4105.7   4105.7   24.90  0.000
Sex           1     185.8    185.4    185.4    1.12  0.294
Device*Sex    1      30.2     30.2     30.2    0.18  0.671
Error        48    7914.3   7914.3    164.9
Total        51   12288.5

S = 12.8406    R-Sq = 35.60%    R-Sq(adj) = 31.57%
```

The next step is to fit a reduced model by dropping the interaction term from the model to investigate properly whether either one or other or both main effects exist (Box 7.12).

Once again, only the Device main effect is deemed significant with a minimal change in the P-value for the main effect of Sex compared with that from the full model. A multiple comparison procedure is not needed here to identify which levels of the between-subject factor Device are different from each other since there are only two levels. However, as the

Box 7.12

```
General Linear Model: IAS Improvement versus Device, Sex

Factor   Type   Levels  Values
Device   fixed      2   Treatment, Control
Sex      fixed      2   Female, Male

Analysis of Variance for IAS Improvement, using Adjusted SS for Tests

Source  DF   Seq SS  Adj SS  Adj MS      F      P
Device   1   4158.2  4084.7  4084.7  25.19  0.000
Sex      1    185.8   185.8   185.8   1.15  0.290
Error   49   7944.5  7944.5   162.1
Total   51  12288.5

S = 12.7331   R-Sq = 35.35%   R-Sq(adj) = 32.71%
```

sample standard deviation among those on Treatment is considerably more than twice that among Controls (Box 7.13) the results of the Tukey procedure are somewhat dubious as this procedure assumes equal standard deviations.

Box 7.13

```
Descriptive Statistics: IAS Improvement

Variable          Device      N   Mean  StDev Minimum     Q1  Median     Q3
IAS Improvement   Treatment  26  19.96  17.15   -1.00   7.25   19.25  24.13
                  Control    26   2.08   5.57  -15.50  -1.00    3.50   5.50

Variable          Device    Maximum
IAS Improvement   Treatment   72.00
                  Control     10.00
```

A simple solution here is to recognise that the problem has now reduced to no more than a simple two-sample comparison of improvements (see Chapters 4 and 5), and as this does not assume equal standard deviations the resulting confidence interval is appropriate. This is presented in Box 7.14 and is entirely positive, providing convincing evidence of a Device effect.

Box 7.14

```
Two-Sample T-Test and CI: IAS Improvement, Device

Two-sample T for IAS Improvement

Device      N  Mean  StDev  SE Mean
Treatment  26  20.0   17.2      3.4
Control    26  2.08   5.57      1.1

Difference = mu (Treatment) - mu (Control)
Estimate for difference: 17.88
95% CI for difference: (10.66, 25.11)
T Test of difference = 0 (vs not =): T-Value = 5.06
P-Value = 0.000  DF = 30
```

Interval estimates of the mean Isometric Abdominal Strength improvement (Box 7.15) highlight a significant Treatment effect as the confidence interval is strictly positive. Although there is a small sample mean improvement in Controls, it is not significant.

Box 7.15

```
One-Sample T: IAS Improvement_Control, IAS Improvement_Treatment

Variable                       N    Mean   StDev  SE Mean       95% CI
IAS Improvement_Control       26    2.08    5.57     1.09  (-0.17,   4.33)
IAS Improvement_Treatment     26   19.96   17.15     3.36  (13.03,  26.89)
```

Note that a Bonferroni adjustment could be made to both of the intervals in Box 7.15 if so desired (i.e. changes from 95% to 97.5% CIs).

Conclusion

There is convincing evidence that the use of the device for 5 days per week for 30 minutes each session, over a 6-week period, results in a significant increase in mean Isometric Abdominal Strength (IAS) among inactive people. As Sex did not have a significant effect it is sufficient to summarise the improvement due to Treatment alone. Those on the Treatment demonstrated a significant mean improvement of between 13 and 27 $N \cdot m$ while no significant improvement was evident in Controls. An estimate of the magnitude of the difference in mean improvement (over Controls) is 18 $N \cdot m$ in favour of those on the Treatment with a corresponding 95% CI of 10.66 to $25 \cdot 11 \cdot N \cdot m$.

Once again, a useful summary of these results is available by writing down the sample averages of all four Device/Sex combinations, in ascending order of sample mean IAS underlining those pairs of combinations which are not significantly different.

Combination	Control Female	Control Male	Treatment Female	Treatment Male
Sample mean IAS ($N \cdot m$)	1.0	3.3	17.3	22.6

The non-significant difference in improvement (between the Sexes) in the Controls is relatively clear from these sample means as is the significant (and similar) improvements for Males and Females on the Treatment.

Exercises

7.3 The background and study description for the *Wellbeing* data are given in Illustration 3.4. Use two-way ANOVA to investigate whether there is evidence that being a Regular Exerciser had a positive effect on a person's Well-being and whether any such effect differs between Males and Females.

7.4 Use a two-way ANOVA to investigate the improvement in Abdominal Endurance (as assessed using the American College of Sports Medicine paced curl-up test) due to Device and/or Sex, in the *Biodex* data introduced in Illustration 7.4.

All of the examples to date involve a continuous response variable and one or two between-subject factors. It is quite common, however, to record additional information on potential explanatory variables that may help to explain the variability evident in the response and therefore improve the precision of the comparison of the response variable across the levels of the between-subject factors, suitably adjusted for any significant continuous explanatory variables (or covariates as they are often known).

7.4 ANCOVA: correcting for a covariate in ANOVA

In many studies involving between-subject factors, there are often continuous explanatory variables, known as **covariates**, which are thought likely to influence the response variable. For example, the first Illustration presented in this chapter was an analysis of Grip Strength across different Climber Types where the results suggested no significant difference in mean Grip Strength. Given that a climber's Body Mass is likely to be related to his/her Grip Strength, an analysis incorporating this covariate (i.e. Body Mass) may well improve the comparison across Climber Types.

Before a fair comparison of the levels of any between-subject factor can be achieved, the effect of any significant covariates must be corrected for by means of an **analysis of covariance** (ANCOVA for short). ANCOVA combines features of regression and ANOVA and applies to either observational or designed studies. The basic idea is to extend the ANOVA model to include covariates in addition to the between-subject factors already under consideration. Including information provided by one or more covariates may well improve the precision of between-subject factor comparisons and adjust such comparisons for imbalances in important subject characteristics.

The model assumed is that the response variable depends linearly on the covariate for each treatment and that the slopes of all those linear regressions (i.e. for each level of the between-subject factor) are equal.

Illustration 7.5 Grip strength (revisited)

Background and study description
See Illustration 7.1.

Aim
To compare average Grip Strength of the (dominant) right hand among three populations of male climbers (i.e. Elite, Recreational and non climbers' Controls) while adjusting for Body Mass if necessary.

Data
Name of data file:	*Grip Strength and Mass*
Response variable:	Grip Strength (newtons)
Between-subject factor:	Climber Type (3 levels: Control, Recreational, Elite)
Covariate:	Body Mass (kilograms)

Analysis
The numerical and graphical summaries presented previously suggested that there is evidence of some moderate differences in Grip Strength among the Climber Types. A scatter plot of Grip Strength against Body Mass, with separate labels and smoothers for Climber Type (Figure 7.9), demonstrates a strong positive relationship between Grip Strength and Body Mass as well as demonstrating how, at the same Body Mass, there appears to be a clear advantage in Grip Strength of the Elite climbers.

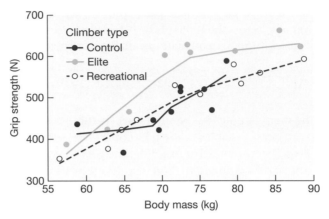

Figure 7.9 **Scatter plot of Grip Strength and Body Mass (labelled by Type of Climber with separate smoothers for each sample).**

There is one between-subject factor of interest, namely Climbing Type (with three levels) and one covariate, namely Body Mass. As Grip Strength clearly depends upon Body Mass, any comparison of Grip Strength will undoubtedly be improved by incorporating Body Mass into the model.

The output from fitting an ANCOVA to the Grip Strength data is displayed in Box 7.16.

Box 7.16

```
General Linear Model: Strength(N) versus Climber Type

Factor         Type   Levels  Values
Climber Type   fixed       3  Control, Elite, Recreational

Analysis of Variance for Strength(N), using Adjusted SS for Tests

Source         DF  Seq SS  Adj SS  Adj MS      F      P
Body Mass       1  151206  137016  137016  74.66  0.000
Climber Type    2   21528   21528   10764   5.86  0.008
Error          26   47718   47718    1835
Total          29  220451

S = 42.8405   R-Sq = 78.35%   R-Sq(adj) = 75.86%

Term          Coef  SE Coef      T      P
Constant    -70.74    67.32  -1.05  0.303
Body Mass   7.9660   0.9220   8.64  0.000
```

From the *P*-value reported for Body Mass it is clear that not only does Body Mass significantly affect Grip Strength (*P* < 0.001) but also, having corrected for Body Mass, Climber Type is now highly significant (*P* = 0.008). The last line of the output gives an estimate of the change in Grip Strength per kilogram increase in Body Mass (i.e. the common slope) of 7.96 N.

Note that there are now significant differences among the three Climber Types when correcting for Body Mass whereas the one-way ANOVA fitted to the same data but ignoring Body Mass (Illustration 7.1) showed (wrongly) no evidence of a Climber Type effect on Grip Strength.

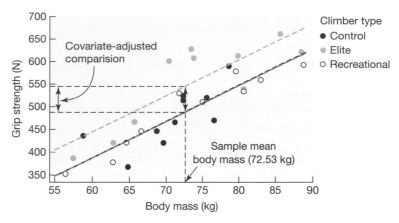

Figure 7.10 **Scatter plot of Grip Strength by Body Mass and Climber Type (parallel lines model).**

To assess which Climber Types are different, an appropriate multiple comparison procedure, while adjusting for Body Mass, is needed. Based on the parallel line model, the average Grip Strength at the overall average Body Mass of the thirty subjects is estimated for each Climber Type separately. For example, the adjusted mean Grip Strength for Elite Climbers and for Non-climbers at a Body Mass of 72.5 kg (the sample mean Body Mass) is highlighted in Figure 7.10 and is 545.1 and 488.7 N for the two types, respectively.

The estimated adjusted difference in mean Grip Strength for Elite climbers compared with the Controls is therefore $545.1 - 488.7 = 56.4$ N in favour of the Elite climbers. A multiple comparison procedure can now be used to determine whether this Body Mass adjusted difference (and those involving the other Climber Type comparisons) is significant (Box 7.17).

Box 7.17

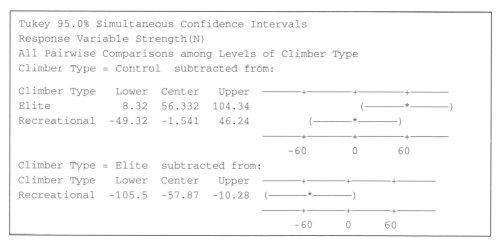

Since the first of these intervals is wholly positive it can be concluded that Elite climbers have, on average, a significantly greater Grip Strength than Control climbers of the same Body Mass. As the second interval has zero lying almost in the centre of the interval there

199

is little evidence to suggest any difference between Recreational climbers and Controls in terms of Grip Strength even adjusting for Body Mass. Finally, as the third interval is strictly negative it can be concluded that Elite climbers have, on average, a significantly greater Grip Strength than Recreational climbers, once again while adjusting for Body Mass.

Conclusion

There is convincing evidence that, when adjusting for Body Mass, Elite climbers have a higher mean Grip Strength than Recreational climbers and non-climbers (Controls) by between 10 and 106 N and by 8 and 104 N, respectively. There was no evidence of a significant difference in mean Body Mass adjusted Grip Strength between Recreational climbers and Controls.

A useful summary in an ANCOVA with one between-subject factor is to write down the adjusted means, in ascending order of the response, underlining those means that are not significantly different.

Climber Type	Control	Recreational	Elite
Sample mean adjusted* Grip Strength (N)	<u>487.2</u>	<u>488.7</u>	545.1

*adjustment made at sample mean Body Mass of 72.5 kg

Reference: Grant, S., Hynes, V, Whittaker, A. and Aitchison, T. (1996). 'Anthropometric, strength, endurance and flexibility characteristics of elite and recreational climbers.' *Journal of Sports Sciences*, **14**: 301–309.

Model checking for an ANCOVA model with one covariate

The key assumption in the ANCOVA model with one covariate is that of 'parallel lines', which in Illustration 7.5 implies a common slope for all three Climbing Type's regression of Grip Strength on Body Mass. This can be checked subjectively by fitting separate regressions of Grip Strength on Body Mass for each Climber Type separately and assessing whether the resulting lines of best fit look parallel (Figure 7.11).

In this instance, the fitted separate regressions model of Figure 7.11 looks virtually identical to the fitted parallel lines model in Figure 7.10 and there appears to be no

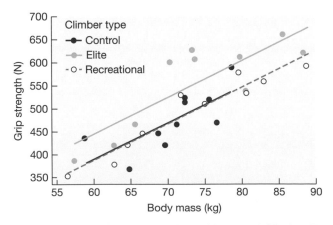

Figure 7.11 Scatter plot of Grip Strength by Body Mass and Climber Type (separate slopes model).

concern with this assumption. A formal assessment of the 'parallel lines' assumption can be made by including an interaction term in the GLM to produce the output in Box 7.18.

Box 7.18

```
General Linear Model: Strength(N) versus Climber Type

Factor        Type    Levels  Values
Climber Type  fixed       3   Control, Elite, Recreational

Analysis of Variance for Strength(N), using Adjusted SS for Tests

Source                 DF  Seq SS  Adj SS  Adj MS      F      P
Body Mass               1  151206  105392  105392  53.01  0.000
Climber Type            2   21528     248     124   0.06  0.940
Climber Type*Body Mass  2       5       5       2   0.00  0.999
Error                  24   47713   47713    1988
Total                  29  220451

S = 44.5877   R-Sq = 78.36%   R-Sq(adj) = 73.85%
```

Since the *P*-value for the test of 'no differences in slopes of the three regressions of Grip Strength on Body Mass' is 0.999, there is clearly no reason to question the assumption of parallel lines in the ANCOVA model. The usual residual plots showed no problems with the other assumptions of Normality and equal spreads about the regressions on Body Mass.

Exercise

7.5 The basal metabolic rate (BMR) measures the energy expenditure of an individual in a standardised resting situation. Twenty-four 20–30-year-old women were randomised to either a 'Normal' controlled diet or a Protein-Reduced diet. Each woman had her BMR measured after three months on the specific diet (see Exercise 3.4 for more details). Compare the two diets in terms of their effect of protein intake on the BMR in the population of women of interest while adjusting (if necessary) for Body Mass. The name of the data file is *BMR*.

7.5 Allometric scaling

ANCOVA is a general approach for adjusting a treatment comparison for a covariate. Scaling is an alternative approach to ANCOVA for adjusting between-subject comparisons for a response variable; however, the key difference is that the covariate is invariably Body Mass. The simplest scaling approach is that of ratio scaling, where the response variable is simply divided by Body Mass. The ratio-scaled variable is then used as the new 'Body Mass corrected' response. This simple approach is only relevant under certain circumstances. An example of this was given in Illustration 6.2, where the dependence of $\dot{V}O_2$ max on Body Mass was 'removed' by forming the ratio-scaled variable $\dot{V}O_2$ max/Body Mass. Indeed, $\dot{V}O_2$ max has appeared as a response variable in several illustrations in this book and the units employed, namely $ml.kg^{-1}.min^{-1}$, indicate that the response is in fact a Body Mass scaled variable.

A second approach, which has gained acceptance in sports and exercise science, is that of **allometric scaling**. The word 'allometry' refers to the study of the change in proportion of a body as a consequence of growth. Allometric scaling equations are available that purport to describe the relationship between Body Mass and many body process (e.g. $\dot{V}O_2$ max). The idea is to re-express the response variable as a Body Mass scaled variable using the appropriate scaling equation and then to use this scaled response variable for any future analyses.

The most popular form of scaling involves a simple power law equation:

$$\text{Response variable} = a * \text{Body Mass}^b$$

where the constant term a and exponent term b must be estimated from the data. Such equations are very common in biology to model the dependence of species size on land mass. Indeed, power laws arise in a surprisingly large number of naturally occurring phenomena, such as the size of cities, stock market returns and even the length of time football managers last in a post before being fired.

The coefficients of the allometric scaling model (i.e. a and b) can be estimated easily using regression. The reason for doing this is that the allometric scaling equation, using the laws of logarithms, becomes

$$\log(\text{response}) = \log a + [b * \log(\text{Body Mass})]$$

which re-expresses the original non-linear power equation as a linear equation. A simple linear regression model, with log(response) as the response variable and log(Body Mass) as the explanatory variable, can now be fitted to the transformed data. The antilog of the estimated intercept provides an estimate of a while the estimated slope estimates b.

The next illustration involves allometric scaling incorporating a between-subject factor comparison.

Illustration 7.6　Grip strength (revisited)

Background and study description
See Illustrations 7.1 and 7.5.

Aim
To compare Grip Strength across the Climber Types, while adjusting for Body Mass, using the allometric scaling model.

Data

Name of data file:	*Grip Strength and Mass*
Response variable:	Grip Strength (newtons)
Between-subject factor:	Climber Type (3 levels: Control, Recreational, Elite)
Covariate:	Body Mass (kilograms)

Analysis

Start by creating the log-transformed Grip Strength and Body Mass variables. As Climber Type is a between-subject factor with three levels (Control, Recreational and Elite), replacing it with a set of indicator variables will facilitate the analysis. Create an indicator variable called Recreational and code climbers 1 if a Recreational climber and 0 otherwise, and a second indicator variable called Elite and code climbers 1 if an Elite climber and 0 otherwise.

The analysis then simply becomes a multiple regression model with log(Grip Strength) as the response variable and log(Body Mass) and the indicator variables representing Elite and Recreational climbers as explanatory variables (Box 7.20).

Box 7.20

```
Regression Analysis: log(Grip Strength) versus log(Body Mass), Elite, ...

The regression equation is
log(Grip Strength N) = 1.11 + 1.18 log(Body Mass) + 0.106 Elite
                     - 0.0027 Recreational

Predictor           Coef   SE Coef      T      P
Constant          1.1140    0.5555   2.01  0.055
log(Body Mass)    1.1843    0.1303   9.09  0.000
Elite             0.10611   0.03820  2.78  0.010
Recreational     -0.00272   0.03804 -0.07  0.944

S = 0.0848133   R-Sq = 79.4%   R-Sq(adj) = 77.0%
```

The power law equations can now be calculated for each Climber Type. The estimated exponent term is 1.18 (highlighted in bold) and applies to *each* Climber Type as the parallel lines (common slope) model was assumed appropriate (see Illustration 7.5). The constant term (*a*) for the allometric scaling equation for the Control climbers, is simply the antilog of the intercept term in Box 7.20, as both indicator variables are set to zero, namely exp(1.14) which is equal to 3.05. The constant term for the allometric scaling equation for the Recreational climbers is calculated by adding the intercept and the regression coefficient for the Recreational indicator variable, i.e. exp(1.114 − 0.00272), which is equal to 3.04. Finally, the constant term for the allometric scaling equation for the Elite climbers is calculated as exp(1.114 + 0.10611) which equals 3.39.

The estimated allometric scaling equations for the dependence of Grip Strength (GS) on Body Mass for the three Climber Types are as follows:

Controls: Grip Strength = 3.04 * Body Mass$^{1.18}$
Recreational: Grip Strength = 3.04 * Body Mass$^{1.18}$
Elite: Grip Strength = 3.39 * Body Mass$^{1.18}$

What is of more importance is the comparison of Grip Strength across Climber Type while adjusting for Body Mass. This can be carried out by calculating an **allometric-scaled response variable** for each subject as

$$\text{Allometric-scaled Grip Strength} = (\text{Body Mass}^b)/\text{Grip Strength}$$

Note that the slope of the log-log regression (i.e. the *b* term in model above) is common to all Climber Types as there was evidence (Illustration 7.5) that a parallel lines model was plausible. A box plot of allometric-scaled Grip Strength (Figure 7.12) suggests that it is typically higher in Elite climbers than in either of the other Climber Types, which themselves are quite similar.

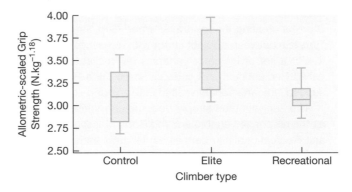

Figure 7.12 Box plot of allometric-scaled Grip Strength by Climber Type.

On the basis of fitting a one-way ANOVA to the allometric-scaled Grip Strengths (Box 7.21) the significant P-value for the Climber Type ($P = 0.009$) provides evidence of a difference in mean allometric-scaled Grip Strength across Climber Type.

Box 7.21

```
General Linear Model: Allo Ratio Scaled versus Climber Type

Factor        Type    Levels  Values
Climber Type  fixed        3  Control, Elite, Recreational

Analysis of Variance for Allo Ratio Scaled, using Adjusted SS for Tests

Source        DF   Seq SS   Adj SS   Adj MS     F     P
Climber Type   2  0.85861  0.85861  0.42931  5.70  0.009
Error         27  2.03232  2.03232  0.07527
Total         29  2.89093

S = 0.274356   R-Sq = 29.70%   R-Sq(adj) = 24.49%
```

A Tukey multiple comparison procedure (Box 7.22) identifies Elite climbers as having significantly larger allometric-scaled Grip Strength, on average, compared with

Box 7.22

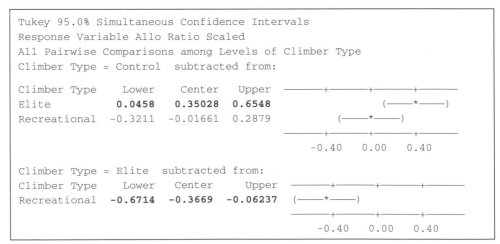

Recreational and Control climbers, with no significant difference between these latter two Climber Types.

The analysis based on the allometric-scaled response variable has identified a significant Climber Type effect. However, the result, in terms of the magnitude of the difference between the Climber Types, is hard to interpret. The response variable is now in units of newtons.kg$^{-1.18}$.

An alternative approach to creating this allometric-scaled response variable is to use an ANCOVA to compare mean Grip Strength across Climber Type, adjusting for Body Mass as a covariate (Box 7.23). Then, having confirmed significant differences among the Climber Types, provide Tukey-based pairwise multiple comparisons among the Climber Types and finally take the antilogs of each pairwise confidence interval.

Box 7.23

```
Factor        Type   Levels  Values
Climber Type  fixed     3    Control, Elite, Recreational

Analysis of Variance for log(Grip Strength N), using Adjusted SS for Tests

Source          DF   Seq SS   Adj SS   Adj MS      F      P
log(Body Mass)   1  0.64278  0.59416  0.59416  82.60  0.000
Climber Type     2  0.07640  0.07640  0.03820   5.31  0.012
Error           26  0.18703  0.18703  0.00719
Total           29  0.90620

S = 0.0848133   R-Sq = 79.36%   R-Sq(adj) = 76.98%

Term            Coef   SE Coef     T      P
Constant      1.1484   0.5575   2.06  0.050
log(Body Mass) 1.1843  0.1303   9.09  0.000

Tukey 95.0% Simultaneous Confidence Intervals
Response Variable log(Grip Strength N)
All Pairwise Comparisons among Levels of Climber Type
Climber Type = Control  subtracted from:

Climber Type    Lower      Center    Upper
Elite         0.01130    0.106113   0.20092
Recreational -0.09714   -0.002719   0.09170

Climber Type  ————+————+————+————
Elite                         (——*——)
Recreational          (——*——)
              ————+————+————+————
                 -0.12    0.00    0.12

Climber Type = Elite  subtracted from:

Climber Type    Lower    Center    Upper   ————+————+————+————
Recreational  -0.2031   -0.1088  -0.01461   (——*——)
                                           ————+————+————+————
                                            -0.12    0.00    0.12
```

The ANCOVA has identified significant Body Mass and Climber Type effects (as expected). The (Tukey) pairwise multiple comparisons identify a significant difference between Elite and both Recreational and Control climbers (again as expected). As the response variable is being analysed on the log scale, the antilog of the intervals provide an estimate of the *ratio* of mean Grip Strength between the Climber Type populations. For example, Elite Climbers are estimated to have Body Mass adjusted mean Grip Strength of between 1.01 and 1.22 times that of Control climbers (i.e. exp(0.01130) to exp(0.2092)), while Recreational climbers have Body Mass adjusted mean Grip Strength of between 0.72 and 0.98 times that of Elite climbers (i.e. exp(−0.2031) to exp(−0.01461)). In order to keep the Climber Type comparisons consistent, an alternative summary is that Elite climbers are estimated to have Body Mass adjusted mean Grip Strength of between 1.01 and 1.39 times that of Recreational climbers (i.e. 1/0.98 and 1/0.72, respectively).

Conclusion

A comparison of mean allometric-scaled Grip Strength identified a significant Climber Type effect ($P = 0.009$) where Elite climbers had higher allometric-scaled adjusted mean Grip Strength of between 0.05 and 0.65 N.kg$^{-1.18}$ compared with Control climbers, and of between 0.06 and 0.67 N.kg$^{-1.18}$ compared with Recreational climbers.

As in previous illustrations, a useful summary table which highlights those levels of the between-subject factor that did and did not differ significantly is available by presenting the allometric-scaled means in ascending order and underlining those means that are not significantly different.

Climber Type	Control	Recreational	Elite
Sample mean allometric-scaled* Grip Strength	3.1	3.1	3.5

*Grip Strength/Body Mass$^{1.18}$

An alternative comparison of mean log(Grip Strength) across Climber Type (while adjusting for Body Mass, also on the log scale) allows a more useful comparison of Grip Strength across Climber Type as the units involved are more 'meaningful'. Elite climbers are estimated to have Body Mass adjusted mean Grip Strength of between 1.01 and 1.22 times that of non-climbers and of between 1.01 and 1.39 times that of Recreational climbers.

Reference: Grant, S., Hynes, V., Whittaker, A. and Aitchison, T. (1996). 'Anthropometric, strength, endurance and flexibility characteristics of elite and recreational climbers.' *Journal of Sports Sciences*, **14**: 301–309.

Additional comments on Illustration 7.6

1 A scatter plot of the allometric-scaled Grip Strength against Body Mass suggests that the dependence on Body Mass has been removed, and this is confirmed with the correlation nowhere near significantly different from zero (Figure 7.13).

2 A rough 95% CI for the slope (i.e. exponent term in the allometric scaling model) is $1.1843 \pm 2 * 0.1303 = (0.9, 1.4)$. As this interval contains 1, there is a case to make that an analysis involving the simple Body Mass scaled response variable (i.e. Grip Strength divided by Body Mass) is justified rather than one based on the allometric Body Mass scaled response (i.e. Grip Strength divided by Body Mass to the power 1.18).

3 Note that the use of indicator variables to represent a categorical explanatory variable with three levels needed only two indicator variables in the model. This is because the third level corresponds to setting two of the indicator variables included in the model to zero. The choice as to which level of the categorical explanatory variable to exclude is important and the advice here is always to exclude the level that has the smallest sample mean response, i.e. the non-climbers (Controls) in Illustration 7.6.

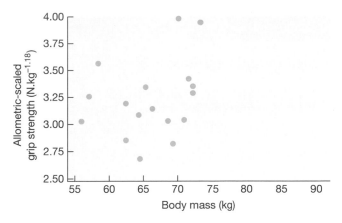

Figure 7.13 Scatter plot of allometric-scaled Grip Strength and Body Mass.

Exercises

7.6 For each subject in Illustration 7.6 calculate the simple ratio-scaled variable by dividing Grip Strength by Body Mass. Compare the three Climber Types using this new proposed Body Mass adjusted variable by means of a one-way ANOVA.

7.7 A study was carried out to compare male and female physiological responses and the perception of breathlessness during Normoxic and Hypoxic exercise (see Exercise 3.8). The data from the study ($\dot{V}O_2$ *max by Sex*) also allowed the researchers to investigate the dependence of (raw) $\dot{V}O_2$ max on Body Mass separately for Males and Females. Data for 10 males and 9 females are available for analysis. Calculate the allometric equations for Males and Females and compare the mean Body Mass adjusted $\dot{V}O_2$ max in Males and Females using a suitably scaled response variable.

Summary

The reader should now be comfortable with the use of the general linear model to compare population means of a continuous response variable in observational studies involving three or more samples or in designed studies with one or two between-subject factors.

Analysis of covariance was introduced as an extension to ANOVA for including continuous explanatory variables (covariates) which might influence the response variable. Allometric scaling is an alternative approach for adjusting a response variable for a covariate in such cases.

Although this chapter has considered only two between-subject factor examples, it is hoped that an understanding of the approaches needed to analyse studies involving three or more between-subject factors will make other statistics textbooks dedicated to ANOVA and ANCOVA more easily digestible and analysing such designed studies less of an ordeal.

Technical appendix

ANOVA and the *F*-test

- The test statistic employed in an ANOVA, the so-called *F*-statistic (after Sir Ronald Fisher) is defined as:

$$F = \frac{\text{Between-sample variability}}{\text{Within-sample variability}}$$

For example, in the Grip Strength example (Illustration 7.1) the within-sample variability is the variability in Grip Strength in one Climber Type compared with another of the *same* Climber Type, whereas the between-sample variability is the variability in Grip Strength in one Climber Type compared with that of *another* climber Type.

- It is intuitive that if the between-sample variability is large relative to the within-sample variability, the population means are likely to differ. On the other hand, if this ratio is small then it is unlikely that the population means differ. This is best understood by examining a picture of each of these two scenarios in turn (Figure 7.14) using two different datasets. In the upper plot in Figure 7.14 the difference in the means (depicted using black triangles) is not very large *compared* with the variability within the samples. The opposite is the case in the lower plot where the means are considerably distinct compared with the variability within each sample.

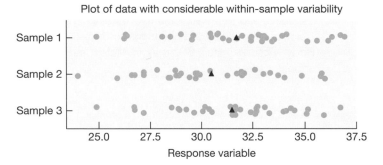

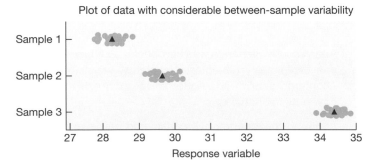

Figure 7.14 **Inferring differences in population means from the degree of within- and between-sample variability.**

The data depicted in Figure 7.14 provide 'evidence' of differences in the population means by virtue of a larger between-sample variability compared with the within-sample variability.

- The F-statistic is tedious to calculate and there is nothing of interest to be gained by learning to calculate it by hand. Typically these calculations are displayed for convenience in an ANOVA table. For historical reasons, the ANOVA table is reproduced as part of the ANOVA output, when all that is really necessary is the value of F-statistic and, more importantly, the corresponding P-value.

Equal variance assumption

- ANOVA procedures are reasonably robust when the population standard deviations are not equal and, in particular, when there are equal numbers in each sample, but not so robust if the sample sizes are unequal.

- As mentioned previously, a rule of thumb often used to validate the equal variances assumption is that the largest of the sample standard deviations is no larger than twice the smallest standard deviation. This is a highly conservative rule and, indeed, in relatively small samples (e.g. 10 observations per factor level), the difference in smallest to largest sample standard deviation can be as large as four times before the equal variance assumption becomes a concern. Recall from Chapter 4 that the use of hypothesis tests of equality of population standard deviations (or variances) was discouraged as such tests tend not to be particularly powerful when used on small samples. The same advice is given here.

Two-sample t-test and one-way ANOVA

- If two population means are compared, then a one-way ANOVA will give the same results as the *pooled* two-sample t-test for independent samples (i.e. comparing the means of two independent samples while assuming equality of the two population variances). The results will differ when performing a two-sample t-test where the variances are not assumed equal. Although the GLM can be used for two-sample comparisons the advice is to use the specific two-sample routines given in Chapters 4 and 5 and not to consider the GLM in this case.

Multiple comparisons

- Multiple comparison procedures are appropriate only when an ANOVA returns a significant P-value.

- There are currently nearly 20 multiple comparison procedures available in the statistical literature, with much debate as to which is the best   multiple indeed!

- A multiple comparison procedure aims to identify which population means are responsible for a significant F-test. These methods are all appropriate when the equal variance assumption is valid and the sample size is similar in each group. Balanced designs, where equal sample sizes are used, are always to be preferred to unbalanced designs and one of the (several) reasons for this is that multiple comparison procedures work better (i.e. have more power) if the sample sizes are equal.

Subsets of pairwise comparisons

- The key requirement is that the comparisons of interest must be specified as part of the study hypothesis and *before* the data are collected. To look at the data and let the sample means suggest 'interesting' comparisons is likely to generate spurious conclusions unlikely to be confirmed in further studies. Sample means from samples of different populations that are apparently different in one study may well not be so different in random samples obtained in a separate but otherwise identical study. Letting random variation govern inference is bad science and basically wrong. This is a difficult concept to grasp and raises several questions. What is the difference in deciding now rather than earlier that these comparisons are of interest? Wouldn't the same results be found in either case? Surely the data are suggesting something about the factor levels that may not have been thought about before the study? One reason for this is that it may simply be random variability that has produced these differences; for example, in three separate samples, one of them has to have the largest mean and another the smallest – all quite natural, so the researcher must take this into account.

- The correct approach is to take note of such differences and design a new experiment to test this specific new hypothesis. Reusing the data to test hypotheses that the data were not intended to pre-study, is akin to claiming a significant result that was due to nothing more than natural sampling variation.

- Consider the following two scenarios: an amateur golfer takes a shot from distance and the ball bounces over the bunker and lands in the hole. He then claims that this was his intention. Is he likely to be believed? What if he predicted what would happen before he took the shot? Which outcome would be more impressive? The same applies with selecting pairwise comparisons. If the researcher declares beforehand which comparisons he/she thinks may be significant and the analysis backs up the hypothesis, the results are impressive. It is inappropriate to allow your results to depend on sampling variation alone.

Assumptions for the one-way ANOVA

- If the assumptions underlying a one-way ANOVA appear dubious, there are simple remedies that can often be applied. A discussion of each assumption is given in turn here, and remedies (where appropriate) suggested.

  - *Sample(s) chosen are random and represent the population(s) of interest.* If the samples collected in an observational study are not representative of the target population of interest, or if randomisation procedures were not employed in an experimental study, it will be difficult to justify any inference to the populations of interest.
  - *The observations are independent.* If the data are not independent – for example, multiple measurements on the same subject – none of the ANOVA models presented in this chapter are valid. Depending on exactly how the multiple measurements were collected, the methods presented in Chapters 9 to 11 may cover such scenarios.

- *Populations are Normally distributed with equal standard deviations (i.e. variances) but possibly different means.* If a transformation does not achieve what appears to resemble Normal distributions then a so-called non-parametric hypothesis test called the **Kruskal–Wallis test** is available. This test uses the sample medians rather than means with appropriate multiple comparison procedures based on the Mann–Whitney interval estimation method described in Chapter 3. However, this approach should be used only if the assumption of Normality is really dubious for at least one sample, and in this situation it would be prudent to consult a statistician. The *F*-test underpinning the ANOVA model is quite robust to departures from Normality in a similar manner to the two-sample *t*-test.

- Departures from the assumption of equal spreads are more serious, as discussed earlier when considering multiple comparison procedures. In some cases, transforming the response variable may simultaneously make both the Normality and equal spreads assumption more plausible. If a transformation does not remedy the problem, some approximation-based procedures are available to 'adapt' ANOVA to deal with unequal variances to some extent.

- If the Normality assumption is valid but the standard deviations are unequal it is advisable to abandon ANOVA completely and to calculate separate confidence intervals for each pairwise comparison using the two-sample methods presented in Chapter 3 where the equal variance assumption was not required. A multiple comparison adjustment (e.g. Bonferroni) is needed for the confidence coefficient to correct for the number of comparisons required.

- Finally, if all else fails and the Normality and the equal spreads assumptions are both unreasonable then it is not possible to use the Kruskal–Wallis test, since it also assumes equal spreads. All is not lost, as recent advances in re-sampling techniques and, in particular, the bootstrap are available as alternatives. If the above situation arises, consult a statistician!

Interactions

- If an ANOVA identifies a significant interaction between two factors, then both main effects of both factors must be included in the model, *regardless* of whether they are declared significant or not in the full ANOVA table. The significant interaction, by itself, implies that the main effects are important. However, the relationship between the factors is not additive.

Analysis of covariance

- A GLM model that incorporates covariates is called an analysis of covariance (ANCOVA) model. It is no more than an extension of the multiple regression model. The reason for using ANCOVA rather than fitting a multiple regression is that there is a subtle difference between the two approaches. In a multiple regression, interest lies in modelling the dependence of the response on the explanatory variables whereas in an ANCOVA the key element is to compare the mean response across the levels of the between-subject factor(s) of interest while *adjusting* for the effect (if any) of the covariate(s).

Allometric scaling

- As there was no interaction between Climber Type and Body Mass in Illustration 7.5, a simple parallel lines regression model (on the log-log scale) was all that was required to estimate the constant term and exponent in the allometric scaling equations. If, however, a significant interaction had been identified, then a separate slopes model would have been required. This can be fitted quite easily using multiple regression with indicator variables or, more simply, by fitting a separate simple linear regression for each level of the between-subject factor.

8 Modelling categorical data

8.1 Introduction

Categorical variables are used to represent data where the observations represent an outcome involving one of a number of possible levels of category (e.g. Win or Lose a game of squash, use the Stair or an Escalator in an Underground station, shoulder pain caused by Impingement, Instability or Neither) and not an outcome able to be measured on a continuous scale (e.g. VO_2 max, Resting Heart Rate, Exercise Tolerance Time). A categorical variable where there are two levels (e.g. Male or Female, Pain or No pain, Successful or Not successful) is termed a **binary** or **binomial** variable while a categorical variable with more than two levels is termed a **multinomial** variable (e.g. No, Partial or Full response to treatment, Hamstrings or Calf or Other leg injury). Note also that categorical variables can be either **nominal**, i.e. have no order (e.g. Agree or Disagree with referee's decision), or **ordinal**, i.e. have an inherent order (e.g. Slight, Moderate or Severe depression). There are some techniques which are suitable for modelling ordinal variables but these are beyond the scope of the current text. All forms of handling categorical variables in this text assume only that the variables are nominal and thus categories can be interchanged or pooled without changing the results of the analysis.

While Chapter 3 introduced ideas for summarising and graphing continuous variables and Chapters 4 to 7 introduced formal statistical techniques for handling continuous response variables, this chapter pulls together ideas from all these chapters and adapts and applies them for categorical response variables. All the techniques and procedures introduced in this chapter are quite similar to the equivalent procedures for continuous variables based on the ideas introduced in Chapters 4 to 6 for interval estimation, hypothesis testing and modelling relationships (regression). In essence, the major difference is that, for categorical data analysis the Normal distribution plays virtually no role at all. All categorical data are assumed to have arisen from a multinomial (or, in the case of two levels, a binomial) distribution, and this distribution, unlike the Normal, requires only one key assumption that all observations on different subjects are independent of one another.

8.1.1 Summaries for categorical variables

A different set of sample statistics is needed to summarise data where the response variable is categorical, compared with that used for continuous response variables. It is nonsensical to use sample means, medians, quartiles, etc., as summaries of a categorical variable, especially a nominal one. Hence the box plot is ruled out. Given the nature of the variable, it is more natural to consider a count of the number of observations in the sample for each level and, more importantly, express these as percentages/ proportions (e.g. the total number and percentage of climbers to reach the summit of Mont Blanc from a specified sample and the corresponding number and percentage who failed to reach the summit). Pie charts or bar charts are introduced here as the most useful graphical displays for categorical data.

When there are data involving a single categorical variable of interest (with several levels) from one or more samples of different and distinct populations, then the procedure is as follows:

1 Provide sample counts and percentages for each level of each sample.

2 Create a pie and/or bar chart of these for each sample.

8.1.2 Formal analyses for categorical data

Most of the ideas of interval estimation and hypothesis testing introduced in Chapters 4 to 7 are applicable here too. The key difference, however, is that the main interest for categorical variables lies in **population proportions** whereas for continuous variables it is almost always in population means. Note that the sample percentage/proportion of any level of a categorical variable will be the obvious estimator of the population percentage/proportion of that level. Just think of proportion and percentage as identical. Be aware also that sample fraction (i.e. on a scale of 0 to 1) can be used rather than sample percentage (i.e. on a scale of 0 to 100), but these are in effect the same thing.

8.2 Interval estimation for categorical variables

Interval estimation is to be preferred to hypothesis testing for categorical as well as for continuous variables where possible. However, as has been seen in Chapters 6 and 7 on modelling relationships and comparing three or more population means, respectively, hypothesis tests can play an important role in model selection and hence be an essential tool in choosing the final model suitable to describe a dataset on which conclusions can be based.

This section considers the use of interval estimation of population proportions for binary and multinomial categorical response variables in single samples and for comparing these across samples from two different and distinct populations. The general approach, as always, is to provide a simple summary, preferably graphical, followed by a formal analysis, and to bring these together for the appropriate conclusions.

The sample proportion is the best **estimate of the population proportion** and can be used to construct interval estimates for population proportions by using the 'standard large sample theory' form introduced in Chapter 4 for population means – as long as the sample size is reasonably large. For categorical data, think of samples in the hundreds as large, unlike continuous data where samples of twenty or more are sufficient to allow 'large sample theory' to apply. The standard interval estimate here (a so-called approximate 95% confidence interval (CI)) will be of the form:

Estimate of population proportion $\pm$ 2 * e.s.e. of the estimate

where e.s.e. is the estimated standard error.

The e.s.e. in such circumstances is a function of only the sample proportion itself and, more importantly, the sample size, with the e.s.e. being inversely proportional to the square root of sample size (see the technical appendix at the end of this chapter for details). There is little need to worry about the use of the phrase 'approximate 95%' as this is really just a technical aspect of the construction of such credible intervals.

The interval estimation of a population proportion for a single sample of a binary or binomial categorical variable is considered in Illustration 8.1.

Illustration 8.1   Mont Blanc ascent

Background
Many people aspire to climb Mont Blanc (4807 m), the highest mountain in western Europe. Anecdotal evidence from Alpine guides suggests that only 70% of those who attempt to climb Mont Blanc actually do so, failure being due mainly to the adverse effects of altitude. See Illustration 3.1 for more details.

Study description
The most popular route to the summit of Mont Blanc is via the Gouter Hut, which is situated at 3817 m on the western flank of the mountain. Over a period of six days, 210 climbers who spent the night at the Gouter Hut prior to their attempt on the summit had a selection of physiological and demographic variables recorded both before and after their attempt.

Aim
To provide a summary of these data and to estimate the population proportion of such individuals who achieve a successful climb of Mont Blanc from the Gouter Hut (under similar conditions to the six days when sampling occurred).

Data
Name of data file: *Mont Blanc Ascent*
Response variable: Ascent Success (Yes/No)

Analysis
First, the frequency (and percentage) of each category should be reported (Box 8.1) followed by either a pie chart or bar chart of the variable of interest using the frequency (i.e. count) or percentage of successful ascents as the category label summary (Figure 8.1). Note that the variable of interest here is binary as there are just two levels (i.e. No and Yes).

Box 8.1

```
Tally for Discrete Variables: Ascent Success

 Ascent
Success  Count   Percent
     No     12      5.71
    Yes    198     94.29
     N=    210
```

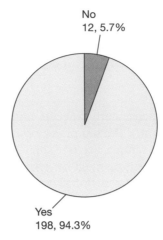

No
12, 5.7%

Yes
198, 94.3%

Figure 8.1 **Pie chart of Ascent Success.**

The appropriate interval estimate (strictly speaking for the population fraction rather than the population percentage/proportion, but this can be easily converted by multiplying by 100) is given in Box 8.2.

Box 8.2

```
Test and CI for One Proportion: Ascent Success

Event = Yes

Variable              X    N  Sample p          95% CI
Ascent Success      198  210  0.942857  (0.902311, 0.970128)
```

Conclusion

The interval estimate suggests that between 90% and 97% of climbers who leave the Gouter Hut manage to climb Mont Blanc, with around 94% being the most plausible estimate of this. Note that this is considerably higher than the anecdotal value of around 70% quoted by guides which may be relevant from a lower level than the Gouter Hut or may be due to self-sampling of subjects at the Gouter Hut itself.

Reference: Tsianos, G., Woolrich, L., Watt, M., Peacock, A., Aitchison, T., Montgomery, H., Watt, I. and Grant, S. (2005). 'Prediction of performance on the ascent of Mont Blanc.' *European Journal of Applied Physiology*, **96**: 32–36.

Interval estimation of population proportions in a single sample of a multinomial categorical variable is considered in Illustration 8.2 where, while the main interest may be in the population proportions of each category separately, there may also be interest in comparing the population proportions of two different levels of the *same* categorical variable.

Illustration 8.2 Gaelic football injuries

Background

Gaelic football is a field game which could be described (by the non-Irish) as similar to rugby and soccer and is run by the Cumann Lúthchleas Gael (Gaelic Athletic Association, GAA). Although Gaelic football is popular in Ireland, there have been few prospective studies that have made a detailed investigation of injuries in elite players.

Study description

The injuries encountered by a sample of 323 male elite Gaelic footballers were recorded for the duration of a playing season (January to September 2004).

Aim

To provide a summary of the injuries sustained and to estimate the proportion of Hamstrings Injuries at this elite standard of Gaelic football. Further, to compare the proportions of Hamstrings and Quadriceps Injuries in this population in order to determine if one of these is more prevalent.

Data

Name of data file: *GAA Injuries*

Response variable: Injury (Ankle/Groin/Hamstrings/Knee/Quadriceps/Shoulder)

Analysis

First, the frequency/count (and percentage) of each type of injury should be reported (Box 8.3). This must be followed by either a pie chart (Figure 8.2) or bar chart (Figure 8.3) of the location of the injury using the frequency (i.e. count) or percentage of total injuries as the category label summary.

Box 8.3

```
   Injury       Count      Percent

    Ankle        50        15.48
    Groin        38        11.76
Hamstrings       91        28.17
     Knee        62        19.20
Quadriceps       49        15.17
 Shoulder        33        10.22
```

The pie chart (Figure 8.2) shows that Hamstring Injuries are the most common type in this sample, followed by Knee Injuries; Shoulder Injuries are the least prevalent. The bar chart (Figure 8.3) displays the same information as the pie chart but in a slightly different

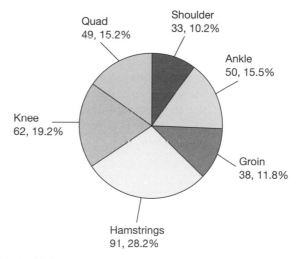

Figure 8.2 Pie chart of Injury.

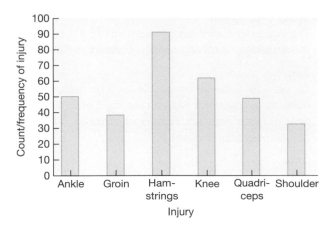

Figure 8.3 **Bar chart of recorded Injuries over a season in Gaelic football (elite Gaelic footballers – 323 Injuries).**

format. There is a choice whether the frequency or percentage should be used as the scale for the vertical (*y*) axis. A good practice to consider is the use of the raw count for the axis scale but to report the percentage also. A percentage alone could be very misleading if the sample size is small (<100 for categorical variables).

The sample proportion of Hamstrings Injuries was 28% but, based on a sample of 323 injuries of which 91 were Hamstrings, what can really be said about the proportion of Hamstrings Injuries in Gaelic football in general? The answer is based on a 95% CI for the (population) proportion from this sample (Box 8.4). From this it can be concluded that between 23% and 33% of Gaelic football injuries are to the Hamstrings.

Box 8.4

```
Test and CI for One Proportion

Sample       X    N   Sample p          95% CI
Hamstrings   91   323   0.281734   (0.233329, 0.334193)
```

The sample proportion of Hamstrings Injuries was 28% and that of Quadriceps Injuries was 15% in this sample of 323 injuries. What can be said in general about the difference of proportions of Hamstrings and Quadriceps Injuries in Gaelic football? The separate (approximate) 95% CIs for the population proportions of Quadriceps and Hamstrings Injuries among Gaelic Footballers are given in Box 8.5 and there is clearly no overlap between these intervals so it is therefore fair to conclude that Hamstrings Injuries are more prevalent than Quadriceps Injuries here.

Box 8.5

```
Test and CI for One Proportion

Sample       X    N   Sample p          95% CI
Hamstrings   91   323   0.281734   (0.233329, 0.334193)
Quadriceps   49   323   0.151703   (0.114386, 0.195552)
```

However, it is a more efficient use of the data, and indeed more informative, to produce an (approximate) 95% CI for the difference in these population proportions. With respect to any difference in population proportions of Hamstrings and Quadriceps Injuries, the sample proportions are 28% (91/323) and 15% (49/323), respectively, giving an estimated difference in population proportions of 28 − 15 = 13%. The e.s.e. of this difference in population proportions can be evaluated as 3.6% (see technical appendix for details) and the resulting interval estimate would therefore be:

$$13\% \pm 2 * 3.6\%, \quad \text{i.e. } +6\% \text{ to } +20\%$$

As this interval is entirely positive, it can be confirmed that Hamstrings Injuries are significantly more prevalent in Gaelic football than Quadriceps Injuries. Further, it can be added that this difference is at least 6% and at most 20% 'in favour' of Hamstrings.

Conclusion

Between 23% and 33% of Gaelic football injuries involve the Hamstrings, assuming that this sample, taken over a full season at elite level, is indicative of other seasons. It would be unfair, however, to claim that this was also true of other grades of Gaelic football. Further, Hamstrings Injuries are significantly (by between 6% and 20%) more common than Quadriceps Injuries at the elite level of Gaelic football.

Reference: Newell, M., Newell, J., Henry, A. and Grant, S. (2006). 'Incidence of injury in elite Gaelic footballers.' *Irish Medical Journal*, 9: 269–271.

The comparison in Illustration 8.2 involved two levels within the same sample but interest often lies in the difference in population proportions of a categorical variable between two distinct and different populations based on independent samples from these populations and this is covered in Illustration 8.3.

Illustration 8.3   **Hamstrings injuries in Gaelic football**

Background

Each injury in the sample of 323 male elite Gaelic footballers described in Illustration 8.2 also had the source of the injury (i.e. in Training or in a Game) recorded.

Aim

To provide a summary of these data and to investigate whether the proportion of Gaelic football injuries which are Hamstrings related differs between Training and competitive Games.

Data

Name of data file:	*GAA Injuries*
Response variable:	Injury (Ankle/Groin/Hamstrings/Knee/Quadriceps/Shoulder)
Between-subject factor:	Source of Injury (2 levels: Training and Game)

Analysis

First report the frequency (and percentage) of each category of injury by source (Box 8.6) followed by pie charts of category of injury for each source (Figure 8.4).

It appears that the number of injuries was slightly less in Training than in Games but, in terms of Hamstrings Injuries, there is a sizable difference in the sample proportions: 37% of Training injuries are Hamstrings as opposed to only 22% during Games.

219

Box 8.6

Tabulated statistics: Injury, Source				Tabulated statistics: Injury, Source			
	GAME	TRAINING	All		GAME	TRAINING	All
Ankle	38	12	50	Ankle	20.32	8.82	15.48
Groin	20	18	38	Groin	10.70	13.24	11.76
Hamstrings	**41**	**50**	91	Hamstrings	**21.93**	**36.76**	28.17
Knee	41	21	62	Knee	21.93	15.44	19.20
Quadriceps	27	22	49	Quadriceps	14.44	16.18	15.17
Shoulder	20	13	33	Shoulder	10.70	9.56	10.22
All	**187**	**136**	323	All	100.00	100.00	100.00
Cell Contents:		Count		Cell Contents:		% of Column	

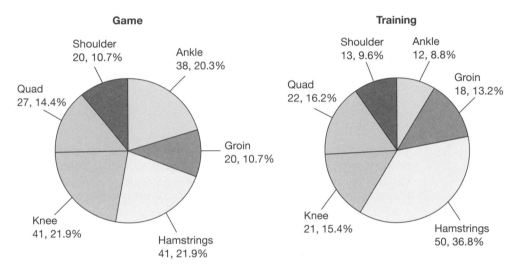

Figure 8.4 Pie chart of Injury by source.

To ascertain whether this is a 'real/true' difference, produce a 95% CI for the difference in population proportions of Hamstrings Injuries between Training and Games (Box 8.7).

Box 8.7

```
Test and CI for Two Proportions

Sample       X    N   Sample p
Training    50  136   0.367647
Game        41  187   0.219251

Difference = p (Training) - p (Game)
Estimate for difference:  0.148396
95% CI for difference:  (0.0479806, 0.248811)
```

This interval is based on the usual form involving the point estimate which is the difference of sample proportions, 37% − 22% = 15% (here in the form 'Training minus Game' in terms of proportion of injuries which are Hamstrings related), and its corresponding e.s.e. of 5% (see technical appendix for details). Hence the interval estimate for the difference in population proportions, i.e. 'Training minus Game', is:

5% to 25%

How should this interval estimate be interpreted? Taking account of the sampling variability, the true difference in the proportions of Hamstrings injuries at Training as opposed to in Games is likely to be somewhere between 5% and 25%. Since this interval does not contain zero and is entirely positive, then the (population) proportion of Hamstrings Injuries during Training is significantly greater than that during competitive Games.

Conclusion

Between 5% and 25% more Hamstrings Injuries in Gaelic football occur in Training than in competitive Games.

Additional comment on Illustration 8.3

The significantly higher proportion of Hamstrings Injuries in Training is worthy of investigation. One area that could be considered is the content of the training sessions. Some teams carry out repeat sprints near the end the sessions when the players are tired. This practice may promote hamstring injury.

Exercises

8.1 All members of a sample of Glasgow University (GU) students were questioned regarding whether they were 'regular' exercisers, defined as a subject who takes part regularly in a minimum of three sessions per week of at least 20 minutes aerobic activity at, or above, 65% of maximum heart rate. The dataset *Wellbeing* contains this information as well as the sex of the students. Provide and comment on an interval estimate for the GU student population proportion who 'regularly' exercise. Is there a significant difference between the GU male and female population proportions who 'regularly' exercise?

8.2 For the *GAA Injuries* data introduced in Illustration 8.2, provide and comment on an interval estimate for the population proportion of Ankle Injuries in Gaelic football. Do the population proportions of Ankle Injuries differ significantly between injuries sustained in Training and in competitive Games?

8.3 A randomised controlled trial was carried out in Glasgow and aimed to establish if a self-help intervention, delivered via written interactive materials, could increase active commuting behaviour in workplaces. The data in this exercise refer to the Alteration (after 3 months) in Journey Stage of Change (SOC). This categorical variable refers to the change (over the 3 months of the study) in a subject's intention to 'actively commute'. (More details of the study are given in Illustration 8.9.) For the Intervention, what is the likely population proportion that will report such an Alteration to be Positive? Is the difference between the Positives and the Negatives significantly greater than zero (for the Intervention)? Is there a significant difference in Positives between the Intervention and Control?

	Alteration in Journey SOC			
	Negative	None	Positive	Total
Intervention	19	45	56	120
Control	23	60	34	117

8.3   Hypothesis tests and categorical variables

In general, interval estimation is a more informative procedure in data analysis than hypothesis testing. However, the latter has a considerable role to play in at least the first stages of comparing multinomial variables across different populations, particularly through the so-called chi-squared test. The first step in comparing two or more populations through samples of a categorical variable with two or more levels is to be able to reject the null hypothesis that the underlying sets of population proportions for the categorical variable are the same for both populations. If and when this is achieved, the next step would be to ascertain for which levels of the variable the population proportions were different. This approach is similar to that covered in Chapter 7 for one-way Analysis of Variance (ANOVA) of continuous variables where the ANOVA is used to reject a simple null hypothesis and only then is a follow-up (multiple comparisons) procedure used to investigate where these significant differences are.

The basic hypothesis test for categorical variables is the **chi-squared test**, usually denoted by χ^2 and defined as:

$$\chi^2 = \sum \left(\frac{(\text{Observed} - \text{Expected})^2}{\text{Expected}} \right)$$

This test statistic is appropriate because, for every level of every sample, it considers the differences between the observed count/frequency and the corresponding expected count/frequency if the null hypothesis is true (i.e. that the population proportions of each level of the categorical variable are the same for all populations being investigated). These are then summed over all levels of all samples to create the observed value of the test statistic. Only when this statistic is 'too large' will the null hypothesis (of all populations following the same multinomial distribution) be rejected.

This test statistic is well approximated when the null hypothesis is true by one of the family of so-called chi-squared distributions. The relevant member of this family is determined by the degrees of freedom – this is discussed briefly in the technical appendix. As a rough guide, assume that the relevant chi-squared distribution is appropriate as long as none of the expected counts are less than two.

When there are (independent) data from two or more populations for a multinomial variable, then the chi-squared test is known as a **comparison of multinomials** and uses a null hypothesis that all the populations have the same multinomial distribution. This is now illustrated for the cases of a binary variable compared across three populations (Illustration 8.4) and of a multinomial variable with three levels compared across two populations (Illustration 8.5).

Illustration 8.4   Health promotion poster campaign

Background

Basic changes in lifestyles and life choices are thought by some to be a simple way of improving health profiles. One approach to this is through the use of motivational posters encouraging commuters or shoppers to use stairs rather than escalators when both of these are available, for example in Underground stations. Researchers in Glasgow devised a set of motivational posters emphasising the benefits of stair use on cardiovascular health.

Study description

Observers recorded the number of commuters using the escalator and stairs respectively at St Enoch Underground station in Glasgow on Wednesdays, between 9 and 10 a.m. This was carried out one week before a set of such motivational posters were put up. It was repeated during the second of three weeks when the posters were on constant display. Two weeks after the removal of the motivational posters, the use of stairs and escalator were remeasured. In total, 895 female commuters were observed over these three occasions.

Aim

To investigate what impact, if any, the Poster Campaign had on the proportion/percentage of Female commuter stair users in St Enoch Underground station.

Data

The resulting counts of Stair and Escalator Use for Female commuters were recorded as follows:

Females who used	Escalators	Stairs
Before	266	14
During	272	32
After	284	27

Response variable: Stair Use (Escalator/Stair)
Between-subject factor: Time (3 Levels: Before, During, After study)

Analysis of Female Stair Use

First plot the data using a pie chart of the sample proportions of Stair Use by Time (Figure 8.5).

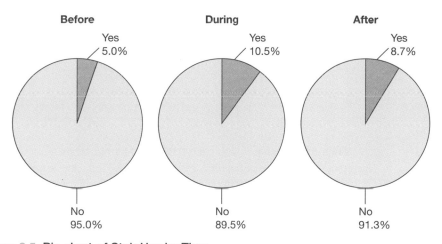

Figure 8.5 Pie chart of Stair Use by Time.

Table 8.1

Time	Sample size	Stair Users	% Stair Use
Before	280	14	5.0
During	304	32	10.5
After	311	27	8.7

The relevant summary statistics are just the sample proportions in Table 8.1.

It appears that there is a slight improvement in Stair Use During the campaign, but is this real and does it fall back After the campaign?

The formal analysis involves the test of the null hypothesis that the population proportion of Stair Use has remained constant over the three times and takes as the null (H_0) and alternative (H_1) hypotheses:

H_0: The population proportions of Stair Use are the *same* for the three Times
H_1: The population proportions of Stair Use are *not the same* for the three Times

The test used to compare population proportions from two (or more) independent samples is the chi-squared test. When carried out on the sample data (Box 8.8), the test yields an observed value of the test statistic of 6.12 which is just significant when compared to a chi-squared distribution with two degrees of freedom (i.e. $P = 0.047$).

Box 8.8

```
Chi-Square Test: Stair, Escalator

Expected counts are printed below observed counts
Chi-Square contributions are printed below expected counts

         Stair   Escalator   Total
Before      14         266     280
         22.84      257.16
         3.420       0.304

During      32         272     304
         24.80      279.20
         2.093       0.186

After       27         284     311
         25.37      285.63
         0.105       0.009

Total       73         822     895

Chi-Sq = 6.118, DF = 2, P-value = 0.047
```

Since this P-value is less than 0.05, the null hypothesis can be rejected and it can be concluded that the population proportions of Stair Use are not the same for the three Times. However, the test does *not* indicate at which of the three Times there are significant differences in the proportion of Stair Use.

To discover this, it is necessary to carry out pairwise comparisons of all three Times in terms of population proportions using the interval estimation procedures introduced in Section 8.2. However, allowance has to be made for the fact that there are three comparisons being made (Before/During, Before/After, and During/After), as was the case for pairwise multiple comparisons after a (significant) ANOVA (see Section 7.2). In this instance, with three comparisons to be made, the intervals will be calculated as (approximate) 98.3% CIs so that collectively the confidence to be attached to all three intervals together will be at least 95%. These Bonferroni-based intervals are therefore of the form:

Difference in sample proportions $\pm$ 2.387 * e.s.e. of the difference

where e.s.e. is the estimated standard error of the Difference in Sample Proportions of Stair Use and 2.387 is the relevant multiple for the Bonferroni correction. These intervals are presented in Box 8.9 and Table 8.2.

Box 8.9

```
Test and CI for Two Proportions

Sample   X    N    Sample p
Before   14   280  0.050000
During   32   304  0.105263

Difference = p (Before) - p (During)
Estimate for difference:  -0.0552632
98.3% CI for difference: (-0.107524, -0.00300272) Before-During

And so on to include
98.3% CI for difference: (-0.0859945, 0.0123611)  Before-After

98.3% CI for difference: (-0.0382714, 0.0751643)  During-After
```

Table 8.2

Comparison	Point estimate	Interval estimate
Before–During	−5.5%	−10.8% to −0.3%
Before–After	−3.7%	−8.6% to +1.2%
During–After	1.8%	−3.8% to +7.5%

The only one of these three intervals not containing zero is that for Before–During (i.e. −10.8% to −0.3%) and hence the population proportion of Stair Use increased by at least 0.3% and at most 10.8% during the campaign.

Conclusion

The only significant difference is that the Female commuter population proportion Stair Use Before the campaign is less than that During the campaign. The proportion using the Stairs After the campaign is not significantly different from that either Before or During the campaign. Perhaps a rather unsatisfactory conclusion, but it still can be claimed that the poster campaign did raise the population proportion Stair Use among Females at least during the campaign and possibly retained some of this increase in Stair Use after the end of the campaign.

Reference: Blamey, A. Mutrie, N. and Aitchison, T. (1995). 'Health promotion by encouraged use of stairs.' *British Medical Journal*, **311**: 289–290.

Illustration 8.5   **Back pain at work**

Background

Back pain is a common health problem in western society. While the proportion of the population involved in manual work has decreased dramatically since the Second World War, it is still of interest to determine if the incidence of back pain is greater in those involved in manual work compared with non-manual workers. If differences between manual and non-manual workers were found, it may be possible to target the vulnerable workers to identify the possible causes of the greater incidence of back pain.

Study description

A recent study of lower back pain in Scottish industry looked at the effect of the type of work (i.e. Manual or Non-Manual) on the severity of back pain over the previous six months. Samples of each of these two populations (1215 Manual and 1283 Non-Manual workers) were taken from a carpet factory in the north-east of Scotland assumed to be representative of all adult males in the Scottish manufacturing industry.

Aim

To compare the distribution of the Severity of Back Pain for Manual and Non-Manual workers in the Scottish manufacturing industry.

Data

The summary data from the samples are:

Severity of Back Pain	Type of Worker	
	Non-Manual	Manual
None	508	224
Modest	583	407
Severe	192	584
Total	1283	1215

Response variable: Severity of Back Pain (None/Slight/Severe)
Between-subject factor: Type of Worker (2 levels: Non-Manual, Manual)

Analysis

This is an example of a multinomial variable, Severity of Back Pain, with three levels (None/Modest/Severe) being compared across two populations (Non-manual and Manual workers). As always, provide a graphical display via a pie chart, which should contain the sample proportions for each sample separately (Figure 8.6).

It appears from the pie charts that there is a much greater proportion of Severe Back Pain among Manual than Non-Manual workers. This can be investigated formally through a chi-squared test using as null (H_0) and alternative (H_1) hypotheses:

H_0: The population proportions of Severity of Back Pain
     are the *same* for Manual and Non-Manual workers
H_1: The population proportions of Severity of Back Pain
     are the *not the same* for Manual and Non-Manual workers

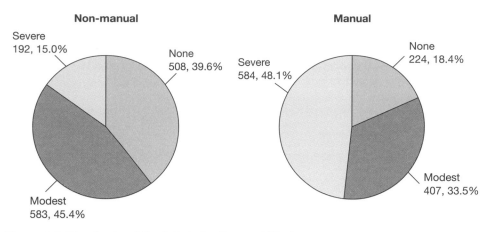

Figure 8.6 Pie charts of Back Pain for Types of Worker.

The resulting output is given in Box 8.10 and it is clear that the null hypothesis can be rejected ($P < 0.001$).

Box 8.10

```
Chi-Square Test: Non-Manual, Manual
Expected counts are printed below observed counts
Chi-Square contributions are printed below expected counts

         Non-Manual   Manual   Total
  None          508      224     732
             375.96   356.04
             46.371   48.966

Slight          583      407     990
             508.47   481.53
             10.923   11.534

Severe          192      584     776
             398.56   377.44
            107.055  113.046

Total          1283     1215    2498

Chi-Sq = 337.895, DF = 2, P-value = 0.000
```

Note that, in Box 8.10, the observed frequency, expected frequency under the null hypothesis and contribution to the chi-squared statistic are given for each cell in the contingency table. For example, for Non-Manual Workers with No Back Pain there were 508 such workers in the sample while 375.96 would have been expected if the null hypothesis were true, resulting in a contribution of 46.371 to the final chi-squared statistic of 337.895. As can also be seen from Box 8.10, it is the Severe category of Back Pain that gives rise to the 'biggest contributions' to the chi-squared test statistic and hence these are where the most important deviations from the null hypothesis of no difference in distribution of back pain between Non-Manual and Manual workers occur.

The next step is to formally ascertain which levels of Severity of Back Pain are different in terms of population proportions between Manual and Non-Manual workers, and this is achieved through a set of Bonferroni multiple comparisons of Non-Manual versus Manual population proportions for each of the levels of Severity of Back Pain displayed in Box 8.11.

Box 8.11

```
Set of Bonferroni 95% CIs for differences between
                              Population proportions in each level

 Level      Estimated proportions      Difference       Interval Estimate
          Non-Manual    Manual        (NonMan - Man)       of difference

 None        0.396       0.184            0.212          ( 0.169 , 0.254)
 Slight      0.454       0.335            0.119          ( 0.073 , 0.166)
 Severe      0.150       0.481           -0.331          (-0.373 ,-0.289)
```

Since the first two intervals are entirely positive, it can be concluded that the population proportions of None or Slight Back Pain are significantly higher for Non-Manual than for Manual workers, and by large amounts, e.g. the population proportion of those with No Back Pain in Non-Manual workers is between 17% and 25% higher than that for Manual workers. Further, the third interval in Box 8.11 is entirely negative, confirming that the population proportion of Non-Manual workers with Severe Back Pain is significantly smaller than that for Manual workers. Once again this is a substantial difference of between 29% and 37%.

Conclusion

The distribution of Severity of Back Pain is significantly different for Non-Manual and Manual workers in the Scottish manufacturing industry, with a significantly greater proportion of Severe Back Pain sufferers among Manual workers.

Source: Data were taken from a PhD project, Glasgow University.

Exercises

8.4 The results for Male commuters in the health promotion poster campaign described in Illustration 8.4 are given below.

Males who used	Escalators	Stairs
Before	215	25
During	176	41
After	239	28

Investigate what impact, if any, the poster campaign had on the proportion/percentage of Male commuter Stair Users.

8.5 For the data in Exercise 8.3, investigate whether the distribution of the Alteration (after 3 months) in Journey Stage of Change (SOC) is significantly different between the Intervention and Control.

8.4 Association and categorical variables

All the illustrations in the previous section are examples of hypothesis tests involving the comparison of a categorical variable (either binary or multinomial) across two or more populations. However, the same procedure with a different choice of null and alternative hypotheses allows the investigation of whether two categorical variables measured on the same subjects are dependent upon one another (the categorical equivalent of correlation). This is usually referred to as a **test of association** with the words 'association' and 'dependence' interchangeable and in effect meaning that, if a subject belongs to a specific level of one categorical variable, then this will influence which level of the other categorical variable this subject will belong to, e.g. if a subject is right-handed, then will he/she be likely to be right-footed as well (and vice versa), and correspondingly for left-footed and handedness? Note that the roles of the two categorical variables are completely interchangeable here (similar to 'correlation') and this is in essence a 'bivariate' problem with the cross-tabulation of the two categorical variables being carried out with either variable on the rows and the other on the columns of the so-called **contingency table**.

The null and alternative hypotheses here are:

H_0: The two categorical variables are *independent* of each other
H_1: The categorical variables are to some extent *dependent* on each other.

If the null hypothesis can be rejected (by effectively the same chi-squared test as in the previous section comparing the observed and expected frequencies (under the null Hypothesis being true) of all the combinations of the two categorical variables), then it can be concluded that there is some form of (unspecified) dependence between these categorical variables.

Illustration 8.6 Higher PE and sex

Background
Physical education (PE) in Scottish schools not only delivers the teaching of games and skills to pupils but also provides the opportunity for some pupils to make an in-depth study of PE and the possibility of gaining a qualification, namely Higher PE. It has been suggested by egalitarians that the sex of the head of PE in a school has a bearing on the provision of Higher PE in that school, or indeed vice versa, that the provision or not of Higher PE at the school might influence whether it was a male or female who was promoted to the post of head of department. Female head PE teachers are likely to be younger and may have been trained at a different institution from their male counterparts. These factors could have a bearing on the Higher PE provision in schools.

Study description
As part of a PhD thesis at Glasgow University, a survey was carried out in 151 Scottish secondary schools. Information obtained from this survey included the sex of the head of PE in the school and whether the school currently offered a Scottish Higher in physical education.

Aim
To investigate any interdependence between the provision or not of Higher PE in Scottish secondary schools and the Sex of the head PE teacher.

Data

The table of results was as follows:

School teaches Higher PE	Sex of Head of PE	
	Male	Female
Yes	69	18
No	52	12

Response variables: Sex of Head PE (Male/Female)
Higher PE Taught (Yes/No)

Analysis

The two binary response variables are interchangeable in the sense that it could be argued that each may influence the other rather than one constituting a 'cause' and the other an 'effect'. Accordingly, while pie charts are useful to look for an association between the variables, it could be either variable that was used to generate pie charts of one variable for each level of the other. Figure 8.7 presents both possible sets of pie charts from either of which it can be seen that the sample proportions in one of the variables (e.g. School teaches Higher PE) are more or less the same for each value of the other variable (e.g. Male and Female Head of PE, respectively). Therefore, it looks very unlikely that there is any association between these two binary variables.

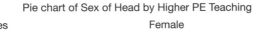

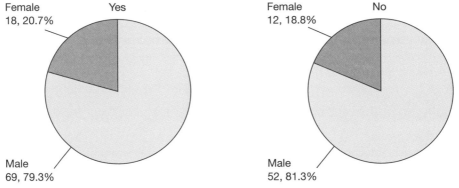

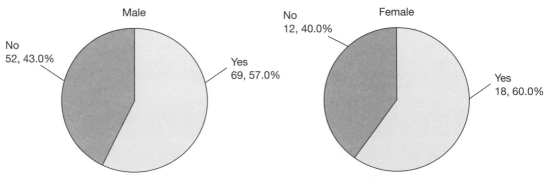

Figure 8.7 Pie charts of Sex of Head of PE and Higher PE Teaching.

The formal analysis requires a test of association of the binary variables denoting the Sex of the Head of PE at the school and whether the school offers Higher PE. The null and alternative hypotheses here are:

H_0: Teaching of Higher PE and Sex of Head of PE are *independent* of each other
H_1: These variables are to some extent *dependent* on each other

The output from a chi-squared test of association is given in Box 8.12 and, since the *P*-value is 0.768, the null hypothesis cannot be rejected.

Box 8.12

```
Chi-Square Test: Sex of Head by Higher PE Teaching

Expected counts are printed below observed counts
Chi-Square contributions are printed below expected counts

         Male  Female  Total
  Yes      69      18     87
         69.72   17.28
         0.007   0.030

   No      52      12     64
         51.28   12.72
         0.010   0.040

Total     121      30    151

Chi-Sq = 0.087, DF = 1, P-value = 0.768
```

Conclusion

There is no evidence of any dependence or association between whether a Scottish secondary school offers Higher PE and the Sex of the Head of PE at that school.

Reference: MacPhail, A. (2001). 'The social construction of higher grade physical education: teacher curriculum decision making and pupil subject choice.' PhD thesis 12416, Glasgow University.

Although the previous illustration did not show any interdependence, many examples do, and this is true of the next illustration. However, as with correlation between continuous variables, it is useful to have a measure of **association** between two categorical variables and this is achieved through the sample statistic known as Cramer's V. However, the range of possible values for the chi-squared test statistic depends on both the sample size and the number of rows and columns in the table. Cramer took account of this in producing a measure of association that must always lie between 0 and 1, with 0 denoting no association and 1 signifying perfect association. His measure, **Cramer's V**, is defined as:

$$\sqrt{\left(\frac{\text{Chi-squared statistic}}{\text{Sample Size} * (m-1)} \right)}$$

with *m* the smaller of the number of rows and the number of columns.

There are no generally agreed guidelines as to how to interpret Cramer's V across its full range from 0 to 1, but, clearly, the closer to 1 the better the association.

Illustration 8.7   Satisfaction with variety and length of exercise classes

Background

Customer satisfaction is now a key requirement of university sports facilities and must be serviced by regular consumer surveys. Most institutions offer taught exercise classes, often at lunchtime, but the length and variety of these can be considerably different from university to university.

Study description

A recent survey sampled from the thousands of members of Glasgow University's Sports and Recreation Service (SRS) included questions on whether members were satisfied with the Length of the taught exercise classes (mainly held at lunchtime) and the Variety of the classes (e.g. circuits, aerobic dance). Four hundred and twenty-four members of the SRS answered both these questions in the survey held in 2007.

Aim

To investigate any interdependence between member satisfaction with the Length of classes and member satisfaction with the Variety of classes at the SRS.

Data

The survey provided the following frequencies of satisfaction for these two variables:

	Variety of classes	
Length of classes	No	Yes
No	11	18
Yes	76	319

Response variables: Satisfied with Variety (Yes/No)
Satisfied with Length (Yes/No)

Analysis

Although most members (319 out of 424) are satisfied with both of these aspects of classes, there is clearly more dissatisfaction with the Variety than with the Length of classes (11 + 18 = 29 dissatisfied with the Length but 11 + 76 = 87 dissatisfied with the Variety). From one (Figure 8.8) of the two possible pie charts, it can be seen that the sample proportions of those dissatisfied with Length of classes is slightly greater for those also dissatisfied with the Variety (i.e. 12.6%) than for those satisfied with the Variety (i.e. 5.3%). Thus there is a suggestion of a link or association of the form that those dissatisfied with one aspect of the classes are more likely to be dissatisfied with the other too.

This is confirmed by the output from a chi-squared test of association of the satisfaction of these two aspects of classes at SRS (Box 8.13). Here the null hypothesis of 'no association' can be rejected with a P-value of 0.025. Further, from consideration of the contributions to the chi-squared test statistic, it can be seen that the major departure from 'no association' is among those dissatisfied with both Length and Variety (11 members in the sample were dissatisfied with both whereas only 5.95 would be expected to be such if there was no association).

Here, Cramer's V is equal to 0.12, i.e. $\sqrt{\{5.787/[424 * (2 - 1)]\}}$ and so is not particularly large although the association is significantly different from zero (from the chi-squared test). This conclusion of a small degree of association can be corroborated from the

Box 8.13

```
Tabulated statistics: Length_of_Classes, Variety_of_Classes

Rows: Length_of_Classes    Columns: Variety_of_Classes

            No      Yes      All

No          11       18       29
           5.95    23.05    29.00
         4.2850   1.1062        *

Yes         76      319      395
          81.05   313.95   395.00
         0.3146   0.0812        *

All         87      337      424
          87.00   337.00   424.00
              *        *        *


Cell Contents:        Count
                      Expected count
                      Contribution to Chi-square

Pearson Chi-Square = 5.787, DF = 1, P-value = 0.016
Likelihood Ratio Chi-Square = 5.018, DF = 1, P-value = 0.025
```

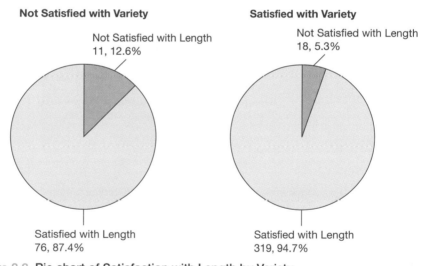

Not Satisfied with Variety

Not Satisfied with Length
11, 12.6%

Satisfied with Length
76, 87.4%

Satisfied with Variety

Not Satisfied with Length
18, 5.3%

Satisfied with Length
319, 94.7%

Figure 8.8 **Pie chart of Satisfaction with Length by Variety.**

sample proportions seen in Figure 8.8 as the change in dissatisfaction moves only a relatively small amount, i.e. from 12.6% to 5.3%.

Conclusion

There is a rather mild but significant dependence between whether members of the SRS at Glasgow University are satisfied with the Length and with the Variety of the taught classes, with those dissatisfied with one of these aspects likely also to be dissatisfied with the other.

Reference: Member Survey of Sports and Recreation Service, Glasgow University, 2007.

The previous two illustrations dealing with association in contingency tables (i.e. in the cross-tabulation of two categorical variables) have involved only binary variables. The following illustration deals with an example where both variables have three levels.

Illustration 8.8   GAA injuries – footwear by pitch condition

Background

See Illustration 8.2 for details. There may be certain factors associated with injury in Gaelic football. One possible factor is the footwear worn by the players and another would be the condition of the pitch, but these are likely to be related since choice of footwear may be dependent upon the state of the pitch.

Study description

The injuries sustained by a sample of 323 male elite Gaelic footballers were recorded for the duration of a playing season (January to September 2004) as well as the ground conditions when the injury occurred and the type of footwear being worn by the player at that time. As can often happen with such surveys, only 267 injuries had the footwear and pitch condition recorded.

Aim

To investigate whether there is an association between the type of Footwear and the Condition of the pitch (dry, hard or wet) for GAA injuries.

Data

The contingency table for the 267 injuries with both these variables recorded is as follows:

	Footwear		
Pitch Conditions	Blade	Moulded	Studs
Dry	39	51	74
Hard	3	8	4
Wet	14	5	69

Response variables: Pitch Conditions (Dry/Hard/Wet)
Footwear (Blade/Moulded/Studs)

Analysis

These two categorical variables (each with three levels) do appear to be associated as can be seen from Figure 8.9, with Studs being preferred more for Wet conditions than for Hard, etc. However, be aware that the sample sizes for Hard conditions are substantially smaller than for the other conditions.

The formal test of association is displayed in Box 8.14 (page 236) and gives a clearly significant result with $P < 0.001$, so it can be concluded that there is an association between Footwear and Pitch Conditions in the population of Gaelic football injuries. Consideration of the contributions to the chi-squared test statistic in Box 8.14 reveals, among other things, that there are a substantially greater number of players wearing Studs in Wet conditions than would be expected if there were no link between Footwear and Pitch Conditions. For this example, Cramer's V is equal to 0.26, suggesting overall a moderate degree of association.

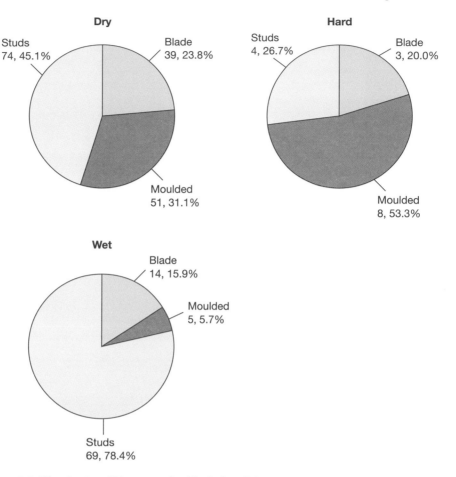

Figure 8.9 **Pie charts of Footwear by Pitch Conditions.**

Conclusion

There is a significant and moderate association between the type of Footwear used and the Pitch Conditions among the population of Gaelic football Injuries with the wearing of Studs in Wet conditions giving rise to an unexpectedly large proportion of injuries.

Reference: Newell, M., Newell, J., Henry, A. and Grant, S. (2006). 'Incidence of injury in elite Gaelic footballers.' *Irish Medical Journal*, 9: 269–271.

Additional comment on Illustration 8.8

The last line of the output in Box 8.14 notes that two cells of the table (corresponding to the Hard/Blades and Hard/Moulded combinations) have 'expected counts' less than 5 (i.e. expected counts or frequencies if the null hypothesis of 'no association' were true). The reason that this is mentioned in the output is that the *P*-value is evaluated based on the approximation that this 'Pearson chi-squared test statistic' follows a so-called chi-squared probability distribution and this approximation will not be adequate if some of the 'expected counts' are too small! As a practical rule of thumb, only be concerned if some of the 'expected counts' are less than two and, if this is the case, then the simple solution is to pool categories with small counts together.

Box 8.14

```
Tabulated statistics: Conditions, Footwear

Rows: Conditions   Columns: Footwear

        BLADES   MOULDED    STUDS     All
DRY         39        51       74     164
         34.40     39.31    90.29  164.00
         0.616     3.476    2.940       *

HARD         3         8        4      15
          3.15      3.60     8.26   15.00
         0.007     5.396    2.196       *

WET         14         5       69      88
         18.46     21.09    48.45   88.00
         1.076    12.279    8.717       *

All         56        64      147     267
         56.00     64.00   147.00  267.00
             *         *        *       *

Cell Contents:      Count
                    Expected count
                    Contribution to Chi-square

Pearson Chi-Square = 36.702, DF = 4, P-value = 0.000
Likelihood Ratio Chi-Square = 40.272, DF = 4, P-value = 0.000

* NOTE * 2 cells with expected counts less than 5
```

Exercises

8.6 In the survey described in Illustration 8.6, each Head of PE in the schools sampled had his/her length of service recorded as well as his/her sex. From these data, presented below for schools which did teach Higher PE, is there evidence of any interdependence between the Sex of a Head PE Teacher in Scottish schools and their Years in Teaching in such schools?

	Sex of Head of PE	
Years in Teaching	Male	Female
<10y	36	7
>10y	33	11

8.7 In a recent survey of members of the Sports and Recreation Service (SRS) at Glasgow University, each person was asked about his/her weekly level of usage (≤1, 2–4, ≥5 times) of the SRS central facility both in Term time and during the

Vacations. From these data, is there evidence of any association between the Level of Usage of the SRS in Term and Vacation?

Term usage of SRS	Vacation usage of SRS		
	Seldom	Moderate	Often
Seldom	87	14	4
Moderate	54	92	30
Often	252	205	972

8.5   Paired data and categorical variables

There is a context in categorical data which is the equivalent of the paired-sample problem for continuous variables (see Sections 4.5 and 4.6). On some occasions, a categorical variable may be observed on the same subjects at two different times or under different conditions. There is likely therefore to be a clear and significant association between these two values of the same categorical variable and interest will centre on whether the population proportions of this categorical variable are the same at these two times or under these two conditions. Such a situation is handled by another test based on the chi-squared distribution called a **test of marginal symmetry** (or sometimes **marginal homogeneity**) where the null hypothesis this time is that the distribution of the categorical variable is the *same* at both times or under both conditions. When there are only two levels of the categorical variable being considered, this procedure is often known as McNemar's test.

Illustration 8.9   Walk In to Work Out

Background
Active commuting (walking or cycling some or all of the way to work) is one possible avenue for increasing physical activity, improving aerobic fitness and health and having a positive influence on the environment. Psychologists have defined five Stages of Change for active commuting which can be described as Pre-Contemplation, Contemplation, Preparation, Action, and Maintenance (with these stages being coded 1 to 5 in the analysis). There is a standard questionnaire for evaluating the Stage of Change of any individual.

Study description
A randomised controlled trial was carried out in Glasgow aiming to establish if a self-help intervention, delivered via written interactive materials, could increase active commuting behaviour in workplaces. One hundred and ninety-two members of local educational and health establishments entered into the study, of whom 93 were randomised to be Controls and 99 received the Intervention. Each subject filled in a questionnaire, both pre and 3 months into the study, from which his/her Stage of Change was evaluated.

Aim
To investigate whether, for Controls, there was any difference in the population proportions of the five Stages of Change (SOC) from Before the study to 3 months into the study.

Data

The summary contingency table for all 93 Control subjects is as follows:

SOC Before	SOC 3 months				
	1	2	3	4	5
1	3	0	0	1	0
2	11	24	11	6	1
3	2	3	6	6	1
4	1	0	1	3	2
5	0	1	0	2	8

Response variables: SOC Before Study (1/2/3/4/5)
SOC at 3 months (1/2/3/4/5)

Analysis

It is obvious from the data that there is a substantial association between a subject's SOC Before and 3 months into the study since most of the data lie in the diagonal terms of the table. To investigate whether there are any changes in the population proportions of SOC at these times, attention must focus on the margins of the data table (i.e. the so-called marginal sample proportions). These are given in Table 8.3 which contains the marginal totals and, in brackets, the marginal percentages.

The sample (marginal) percentages are nearly the same as the frequencies since the sample size is almost 100. So the obvious shifts are increases in the sample proportions of SOC categories 1 and 4 and a corresponding decrease in SOC category 2 from before the study to 3 months into it. This is confirmed by the pie chart (Figure 8.10).

The formal test of the null hypothesis that there is no difference in the (marginal) population proportions uses the full data table and not just the marginal frequencies in Table 8.3 and correspondingly would be more powerful* than a simple comparison of the two sets of marginal proportions using the appropriate two-sample comparison of multinomial distributions introduced in Section 8.3 and used in Illustration 8.5.

*In the sense that this test of marginal symmetry will have a greater chance of identifying a true difference in SOC population proportions than the corresponding two-sample comparison of multinomial distributions.

The result of the test of marginal symmetry is:

Chi-squared test statistic = 25.6 compared to a chi-squared(4) distribution with $P = 0.0002$

Since the P-value is (much) less than 0.05, the null hypothesis that the population multinomial distributions of SOC Before and 3 months into the study are the same must be rejected.

Table 8.3

SOC	Before	3 months
1	4 (4%)	17 (18%)
2	53 (57%)	28 (30%)
3	18 (19%)	18 (19%)
4	7 (8%)	18 (19%)
5	11 (12%)	12 (13%)

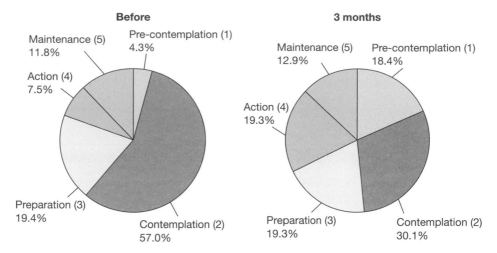

Figure 8.10 **Pie chart of Stage of Change by Time into Study.**

Having ascertained that at least some of the SOC levels have different population pro-portions at 3 months compared with before the study, the question is which levels? This can be achieved yet again by carrying out a pairwise multiple comparisons procedure (see Section 7.2) using the Bonferroni method. Here the set of interval estimates is given in Table 8.4 and interest lies in which intervals, if any, do not contain zero and hence confirm a significant difference. These intervals show that there is a clear decrease in the popula-tion proportion at SOC level 2 (i.e. Contemplation) corresponding to increases in popu-lation proportions at levels 1 (Pre-Contemplation) and 4 (Action) which might well be interpreted as some form of 'random change' in either direction but at least change!

Table 8.4

	Difference in population proportions (3 months minus Before)	
SOC level	Point estimate	Bonferroni Intervals
1	14%	(3%, 24%)
2	−27%	(−38%, −16%)
3	0%	(−14%, +14%)
4	12%	(0%, 24%)
5	1%	(−6%, +9%)

Conclusion

There is evidence of a significant change in the population proportions of SOC levels from Before the study to 3 months into the study among Controls, with significant shifts from level 2 to levels 1 and 4 (i.e. from Contemplation to Pre-contemplation and Action, respectively).

Reference: Mutrie, N., Carney, C., Blamey, A., Crawford, F., Aitchison, T. and Whitelaw, A. (2002). 'Walk In to Work Out: a randomised controlled trial of a self help intervention to promote active commuting.' *Journal of Epidemiology and Community Health*, **56**: 407–412.

Additional comment on Illustration 8.9

The raw frequencies off the diagonal in this dataset are quite small, with six cells having zero counts. As the individual cells do not play any great role in the analysis this is much less of a problem than in tests of association. Indeed, if the researcher felt inclined to pool cells here by, say, combining levels 1 and 2 (i.e. Pre-Contemplation and Contemplation) as well as 4 and 5 (i.e. Active and Maintenance), then the resulting data would be as follows:

SOC Before	SOC 3 months		
	1, 2	3	4, 5
1, 2	38	11	8
3	5	6	7
4, 5	2	1	15

Giving the corresponding marginal totals (percentages) as:

SOC	Before	3 months
1, 2	57 (61%)	45 (48%)
3	18 (19%)	18 (19%)
4, 5	18 (19%)	30 (32%)

Again, the test of marginal symmetry would prove highly significant ($P < 0.0001$) and hence it would appear that there would be significant shifts in SOC levels but this time they would comprise a decrease from pooled levels 1 and 2 into pooled levels 4 and 5 which is not what the full data actually show. The moral, then, is not to pool any levels of categorical variables without considerable care and justification.

Exercises

8.8 For the Walk In to Work Out study described in Illustration 8.9, investigate using the data below whether, for the Intervention, there was any difference in the population proportions of the five Stages of Change (SOC) from Before the study to 3 months into the study.

SOC Before	SOC 3 months				
	1	2	3	4	5
1	0	0	0	1	2
2	14	13	7	20	7
3	2	2	8	5	5
4	0	0	1	3	2
5	1	1	0	0	5

Marginal totals (percentages) are:

SOC	Before	3 months
1	3 (3%)	17 (17%)
2	61 (62%)	16 (16%)
3	22 (2%)	16 (16%)
4	6 (6%)	29 (29%)
5	7 (7%)	21 (21%)

8.9 Anecdotal reports from Norwegian mountain rescue teams suggest that one layer of Bubble Wrap (BW) around a casualty requiring evacuation is useful in preventing loss of body heat (see Illustration 3.7). The aim of this particular part of the study was to compare BW against a casualty bag (CB) currently in use by Scottish mountain rescue teams. Twelve male subjects each participated in two tests (one for each bag). Tests were carried out lying on a stretcher in a cold ($-10°C$), windy (wind speed 2.7 m.s^{-1}) environment. The response variable considered here is the Shivering Status of the subject after 60 minutes and is categorised as None, Slight or Severe. Is there evidence that the population proportions of Shivering Status are significantly different for BW and CB?

Shivering		Casualty Bag		
		None	Slight	Severe
Bubble	None	3	0	0
Wrap	Slight	4	2	0
	Severe	2	0	1

8.6 Modelling relationships with a categorical response variable

8.6.1 Introduction to logistic regression

So far, this section has concerned itself with handling the analysis of a categorical response variable by itself as well as being compared across a between-subject factor. However, it is entirely possible to extend the ideas of Chapter 6 on modelling relationships to the case where the response variable is categorical (although only the case of a binary response is considered here in detail) and the explanatory variables are either continuous, categorical or a mixture of both. The formal name of the technique is **logistic regression**, or more accurately when the response is binary, binary logistic regression.

First, however, be aware that the idea of a population proportion is in effect synonymous with the idea of probability. For example, assume that for the binary variable of 'would like/not like a personal fitness trainer', the population proportion who would like a personal trainer was 20% (and hence 80% would not like a personal trainer). Then a randomly sampled individual from the target population will have a probability equal to 0.20 that he/she 'would like a personal trainer' and correspondingly 0.80 of not wanting a personal trainer. Further, in betting terms, this is equivalent to stating that the **odds** of a randomly sampled individual 'liking a personal trainer' are 1 to 4 (i.e. 0.20 to 0.80, a ratio of 1 to 4) and usually quoted therefore as 4 to 1 against.

In general, therefore, for any binary variable the odds are defined as the ratio of the two population proportions, and it is 'odds' or strictly speaking the **logarithm of the odds** which is used as the basis or link between the binary response variable and possible explanatory variables. In fact, if there is a binary response variable with two levels (*A* and not *A*) and corresponding population proportions *PA* and $100 - PA$, respectively, then the **logistic regression model** assumes that the logarithm of the odds on *A*, which is $\log_e[PA/(100 - PA)]$ will be a *linear* function of the explanatory variables. For example, with a single explanatory variable (and taking logarithms to the base e), this would be a model of the form:

$$\log_e\{PA/(100 - PA)\} = \text{Intercept} + \text{Slope} * \text{Explanatory variable}$$

where the intercept and slope are unknown but can be estimated from a sample of data from the relevant population.

Although this appears similar to the linear regression model introduced in Chapter 6, they are not at all the same. Here, there is no suggestion of any variability about the linear function at all, and the log odds being linear is merely a mathematically convenient way of modelling population proportions for a binary response variable in terms of possible explanatory variables. Hopefully this will become clearer through the following illustration.

Illustration 8.10   Post-natal depression, coping and exercise

Background

Pregnancy can often result in major psychological trauma for the mother. A midwife in a West of Scotland hospital believed that regular exercise would benefit expectant (and recent) mothers not only physically but also mentally. Subsequently, she devised a simple questionnaire to 'measure' various aspects of a mother's mental health with respect to how she coped with the pregnancy. This Coping Assets score ranged from 0 to 50, with high values denoting subjects who were having only a few problems coping with the pregnancy and indeed life in general.

Study description

A sample of 39 pregnant women had their Coping Ability assessed and scored by the questionnaire early in pregnancy (around 12 weeks). All the women in the sample considered here undertook a twice-weekly exercise programme devised and taught by a midwife. These women were also assessed for Post-Natal Depression three months after delivering a singleton healthy baby and this was categorised as one of two possible outcomes (i.e. Moderate or Low Post-Natal Depression). See Illustration 10.2 for more details, including a (randomised) comparison with Controls.

Aim

To investigate whether the Early Pregnancy Coping Assets score can be used to model the proportion of regularly exercising pregnant women who develop Moderate, as opposed to Low, Post-Natal Depression.

Data

Name of data file: *PN Depression and Exercise*
Response variable: Post-Natal Depression (Slight/Moderate)
Explanatory variable: Early Pregnancy Coping Assets (score from 0 to 50)

Analysis

Here the explanatory variable is the continuous variable of the Coping Assets score obtained around 12 weeks into the pregnancy, with the response variable being the binary variable consisting of whether the woman is suffering Moderate or Low Post-Natal Depression 3 months after the baby was born (all babies in this sample were born healthy at term, i.e. around 40 weeks).

The first step in any analysis is to plot the data using a box plot (Figure 8.11) of the possible explanatory variable (Early Pregnancy Coping Assets) for each of the two possible levels of the response variable (Moderate or Low). In such box plots it is conventional to put the (binary) response variable on the vertical axis and the explanatory on the horizontal axis as would be done in simple linear regression (see Chapter 6). The inclusion of the actual data points on box plots in such contexts enables the researcher to compare the relative frequency of, in this case, Low to Moderate Post-Natal Depression for different 'slices' of the possible explanatory variable. Here it appears that those with Moderate Depression tended to be those subjects who had a poor (i.e. <35) Coping Assets score early in the pregnancy.

The formal analysis would involve a linear logistic regression with Post-Natal (PN) Depression (categorised as Moderate or Low) as the response variable and Coping Assets score (in Early Pregnancy) as the possible explanatory variable.

The output from such a (linear) logistic regression model is contained in Box 8.15 and the first item to consider is the *P*-value for the test of the null hypothesis that 'Coping Assets score in Early Pregnancy has no effect on Post-Natal Depression'. Since this *P*-value is 0.031, this hypothesis can be rejected and hence PN Depression level (i.e. Low or Moderate) does depend significantly on Coping Assets Score in Early Pregnancy.

Further from Box 8.15, the fitted (linear) logistic regression model would be of the form:

$$\log_e\{P(Moderate)/P(Low)\} = 2.642 - 0.1101 * CA$$

where *P(Moderate)* is the proportion of the pregnant women who exercise and have a Coping Assets score of *CA* early in pregnancy but still develop Moderate PN Depression.

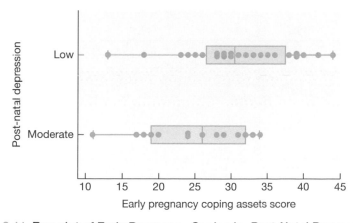

Figure 8.11 **Box plot of Early Pregnancy Coping by Post-Natal Depression.**

Box 8.15

```
Binary Logistic Regression: PN Depression by Coping Assets score (in Early
Pregnancy)
Link Function: Logit
Response Information

Variable                    Value      Count
PN Dep Level_Exercise       Moderate      15   (Event)
                            Low           24
                            Total         39

Logistic Regression Table
                                                           Odds       95% CI
Predictor                  Coef    SE Coef      Z       P  Ratio  Lower Upper
Constant                2.64238    1.46996   1.80   0.072
Coping Assets Score   -0.110108  0.0511742  -2.15   0.031   0.90   0.81  0.99

Log-Likelihood = -23.204
Test that all slopes are zero: G = 5.561, DF = 1, P-value = 0.018
```

Correspondingly, P(Low), the proportion who develop Low PN Depression, is $1 - P(Moderate)$. The interpretation of this is mainly through the 'Coef' (see Box 8.15) of the Coping Assets score, which is estimated here as -0.1101 but is better interpreted through its equivalent odds ratio of 0.90 (see Box 8.15). This means that, for every increase of one unit on the Coping Assets score, the odds on a woman having Moderate PN Depression decrease by a factor of 0.90. Consequently, a reduction of 5 units, say, on the Coping Assets score will reduce the odds on Moderate PN Depression by a factor of 0.90^5 (i.e. a factor of 0.59). Not perhaps the easiest concept or result to understand, but a plot of the fitted model, together with 95% confidence bands for the true underlying (linear) logistic regression, is presented in Figure 8.12 and gives, perhaps, a more informative view of the results of a logistic regression.

From the fitted model plot in Figure 8.12, it can be seen that low values of Coping Assets scores, such as 10 to 15, correspond to high probabilities (population proportions)

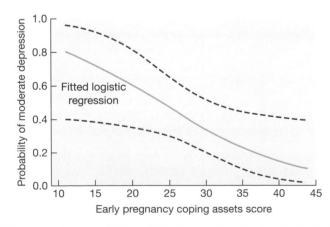

Figure 8.12 Fitted logistic regression of PN Depression on Coping in Early Pregnancy (and 95% (I)).

of Moderate PN Depression (around 0.8 or 80%) whereas high values of Coping Assets correspond to low probabilities of Moderate PN Depression (e.g. for women with a Coping Assets score over 40, less than 20% – probability of 0.20 – are likely to develop Moderate PN Depression).

Conclusion

For women who exercise throughout their pregnancy, the proportion of those who develop Moderate Post-Natal Depression decreases significantly with their assessed ability to cope early in the pregnancy. Such women with an early pregnancy Coping Assets score of less than 25 (see Figure 8.12) will be more likely than not (i.e. probability greater than 0.5) to develop Moderate Post-Natal Depression (i.e. if a woman has a score of less than 25 then she will be 'odds on' to develop Moderate Post-Natal Depression).

Reference: Jeanie Blakely Rankin (1999). 'Primigravid women and the effects of exercise on psychological well-being, pregnancy and birth outcome.' PhD thesis, University of Glasgow.

Additional comments on Illustration 8.10

1 The assumption of a linear logistic regression model can be assessed using a hypothesis test known as the Hosmer–Lemeshow test taking as its null hypothesis that the linear logistic regression model is appropriate for this dataset. The results of this test for the Post-Natal Depression data are presented in Box 8.16. The P-value of 0.499 ensures that the null hypothesis cannot be rejected and hence the linear logistic regression model is adequate to describe the relationship of PN Depression on the Coping Assets score in early pregnancy.

Box 8.16

```
Goodness-of-Fit Tests

Method            Chi-Square   DF       P
Hosmer-Lemeshow      1.3888     2     0.499

Table of Observed and Expected Frequencies:
                Group

Value        1     2     3     4    Total
Moderate
   Obs       1     4     5     5     15
   Exp      1.8   2.7   5.1   5.3
Low
   Obs       9     5     7     3     24
   Exp      8.2   6.3   6.9   2.7
Total       10    9     12    8      39
```

2 The study actually involved a randomised controlled trial of the effect of regular exercise for pregnant women and the overall results of this on PN Depression are shown in Box 8.17. These clearly show that Exercisers had significantly reduced population proportion of Moderate or Severe PN Depression compared with Controls (chi-squared test with $P < 0.001$). The analysis contained in Illustration 8.10 shows that, even among Exercisers, PN Depression will be generally 'less' but will still depend on a woman's ability to cope early in pregnancy.

Box 8.17

```
Tabulated statistics: Exercise Regime, PN Depression

Rows: Exercise Regime   Columns: PN Depression

            Low   Moderate   Severe    All

Control      2       22        10       34
Exercise    24       13         2       39

All         26       35        12       73

Cell Contents:        Count
```

<table>
<tr><td>8.7</td><td>Logistic regression in more complex problems</td></tr>
</table>

The ideas of multiple linear regression and analysis of variance in Chapters 6 and 7, respectively, dealt with modelling the dependence of continuous response variables on (usually continuous) explanatory variables and/or (categorical) between-subject factors. Similar ideas can be extended to the basic logistic regression model introduced in the previous section to allow the modelling of categorical response variables on continuous or categorical explanatory variables, again through the idea of odds rather than population proportions. Once more the illustrations here are restricted to a binary response variable, but the ideas can be extended to cover categorical response variables with three or more levels. The first illustration (on personal trainers) is the binary categorical equivalent of a two-way ANOVA (see Section 7.3) and the second (on active commuting) has three potential explanatory variables (one continuous, one ordinal and the third a between-subject factor) so is really the extension of a one-way ANCOVA (see Section 7.4) with two possible covariates. Both of these illustrations and almost all such examples in practice will have the problem of model selection from a number of potential covariates/factors and their main effects and interactions. The approach to model selection will be similar to that discussed in Section 6.5 on variable selection but suitably adapted to allow for a categorical response variable.

Illustration 8.11 Personal trainer

Background
There has been a considerable increase in the number and use of personal trainers not only in the USA but also in the United Kingdom. This vogue activity can be expensive but the costs could be mitigated by corporate use of such trainers.

Study description
The Sports and Recreation Service (SRS) at Glasgow University carried out an online survey in 2007 of their members' current opinions. Over 1600 members responded. One of the questions in the survey asked whether the respondent would be interested in a Personal Trainer Service through the SRS. Various demographic information on the sample respondents was also collected, such as the Sex and the Membership Status of the individual (i.e. Academic Staff or Student or Other – the last of these comprised technical and administrative staff etc.).

Aim

To investigate whether the population proportion of Glasgow University Sports and Recreation Service members interested in the use of a Personal Trainer Service depends upon the Sex and/or Membership Status of an individual.

Data

Name of data file:	*Personal Trainer*
Response variable:	Personal Trainer? (Yes/No)
Between-subject factors:	Membership Status (3 Levels: Other, Staff, Student)
	Sex (2 Levels: Male, Female)

Analysis

The response variable is whether or not the individual would like a Personal Trainer Service, while the possible explanatory variables (between-subject factors) are Sex and Membership Status. Pie charts of the two outcomes (i.e. support or not for a Personal Trainer Service) by these possible between-subject factors are presented in Figure 8.13.

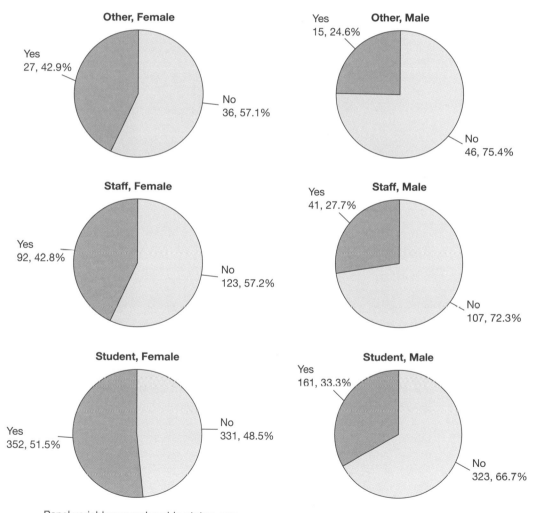

Panel variables: membership status, sex

Figure 8.13 Pie charts of interest in a Personal Trainer Service.

247

These suggest that Females are more likely than Males to want a Personal Trainer Service as well as Students being more likely to want this than Staff or Others. These subjective impressions are perhaps more clearly seen from the sample proportions for all the six sub-categories of Sex and Membership Status (given in Box 8.18) with 52% of Female Students in the sample welcoming the idea of a Personal Trainer Service as opposed to only 25% of Male 'Others' in the sample welcoming this.

Box 8.18

```
Tabulated statistics: Membership, Sex, Personal_Trainer

Rows: Membership /  Sex     Columns: Personal_Trainer
                        No      Yes      All

Other
          Female        36      27       63
                     57.14   42.86   100.00
          Male          46      15       61
                     75.41   24.59   100.00

Staff
          Female       123      92      215
                     57.21   42.79   100.00
          Male         107      41      148
                     72.30   27.70   100.00

Student
          Female       331     352      683
                     48.46   51.54   100.00
          Male         323     161      484
                     66.74   33.26   100.00

All
          All          966     688     1654
                     58.40   41.60   100.00

Cell Contents:      Count and % of Row
```

The formal analysis will consist of a logistic regression model with Sex and Membership Status as potential explanatory variables (i.e. between-subject factors), which assumes only that the logarithm of the odds on an individual wanting a Personal Trainer Service may depend on a main effect of Sex, a main effect of Membership Status and an interaction between these (see Section 7.3 for discussion of these terms and their application for a continuous response variable). The output from such a logistic regression with the 'full model' for Sex and Membership Status is presented in Box 8.19.

The key result here is the P-value of 0.918 for the interaction between Sex and Membership Status. This is clearly non-significant so it is safe to assume that any effects of Sex and Membership are additive, i.e. any difference in the log odds of wanting a Personal Trainer Service between Males and Females is the same for all three Membership Status categories. Therefore the next step is to fit an additive model (see Box 8.20) and investigate the significance separately of Sex and Membership Status.

The relevant P-values of <0.001 for Sex and 0.012 for Membership Status indicate that both Sex and Membership Status significantly and separately affect the logarithm of the

Box 8.19

```
Full Model
Binary Logistic Regression: Personal_Trainer versus Sex, Membership

Link Function: Logit

Response Information

Variable          Value   Count
Personal_Trainer  Yes       688   (Event)
                  No        966
                  Total    1654

Factor Information
Factor                   Levels  Values
Sex                           2  Female, Male
Membership                    3  Other, Staff, Student

Logistic Regression Table                                         Odds
Predictor                  Coef    SE Coef      Z      P   Ratio
Constant              -0.287682   0.254588  -1.13  0.258
Sex
 Male                 -0.832909   0.391434  -2.13  0.033    0.43
Membership
 Staff               -0.0027137   0.289507  -0.01  0.993    1.00
 Student              0.349195    0.265851   1.31  0.189    1.42
Sex*Membership
 Male*Staff           0.164048    0.453824   0.36  0.718    1.18
 Male*Student         0.0751484   0.410353   0.18  0.855    1.08

Tests for terms with more than 1 degree of freedom

Term                 Chi-Square  DF       P
Membership Status       6.00392   2   0.050
Membership Status*Sex   0.17109   2   0.918
```

odds on wanting a Personal Trainer Service in a simple additive fashion. The resulting final model is that the logarithm of the odds on 'would like a Personal Trainer Service' is obtained from the Coef column in Box 8.20 and is:

$=-0.325$	for Female Others (the baseline combination)
$=-0.325 - 0.745$	for Male Others
$=-0.325 + 0.062$	for Female Staff
$=-0.325 - 0.745 + 0.062$	for Male Staff
$=-0.325 + 0.382$	for Female Students
$=-0.325 - 0.745 + 0.382$	for Male Students

These translate (see Additional Comment 5 below) into the estimates of the corresponding population proportions in Table 8.5, from which the Sex effect (Females more likely to want Personal Trainer Service) and Membership Status effect (Students more likely to want Personal Trainer Service than either Others or Staff) can be seen.

Box 8.20

```
Additive Model
Logistic Regression Table
                                             Odds      95% CI
Predictor          Coef    SE Coef     Z      P  Ratio  Lower  Upper
Constant       -0.325274  0.197859  -1.64  0.100
Sex
 Male          -0.744832  0.104623  -7.12  0.000   0.47   0.39   0.58
Membership
 Staff          0.0620229 0.222271   0.28  0.780   1.06   0.69   1.64
 Student        0.381786  0.201822   1.89  0.059   1.46   0.99   2.18

Tests for terms with more than 1 degree of freedom
Term              Chi-Square  DF      P
Membership          8.86014    2    0.012

Log-Likelihood = -1092.194
Test that all slopes are zero: G = 61.595, DF = 3, P-value = 0.000

Goodness-of-Fit Test
Method            Chi-Square  DF       P
Hosmer-Lemeshow     0.039618    2    0.980

Table of Observed and Expected Frequencies:
(See Hosmer-Lemeshow Test for the Pearson Chi-Square Statistic)
                   Group
Value      1      2       3       4   Total
Yes
  Obs      56    161     119     352    688
  Exp    55.1  161.9   119.9   351.1
No
  Obs     153    323     159     331    966
  Exp   153.9  322.1   158.1   331.9
Total    209    484     278     683   1654
```

Table 8.5

Estimated proportions	Male	Female
Other	0.26	0.42
Staff	0.27	0.43
Student	0.33	0.51

Conclusions

For members of this Scottish University's Sports and Recreation Service, the population proportion of those wanting a Personal Trainer Service depends on the Sex and Membership Status of individuals. Females are significantly more likely than Males to want this service as are Students over Staff and Other members.

Reference: Member Survey of Sports and Recreation Service, Glasgow University, 2007.

Additional comments on Illustration 8.11

1 The output in Boxes 8.19 and 8.20 gives estimated coefficients of the effects on the log odds of the levels of each between-subject factor relative to a baseline level chosen, in

this instance by Minitab, using the alphabetical order of the levels (e.g. Female in Sex from Male/Female and Other in Membership Status from Other/Staff/Student). The exponentials (antilogs) of the estimated coefficients are therefore the ratio of the odds of each other level to this baseline level. For example, the odds on Males wanting a Personal Trainer Service (PTS) are exp(−0.745) = 0.47 times the odds on Females wanting a PTS, and hence Males, in terms of odds, are roughly half as likely to want a PTS as Females. This is referred to in the output as the **odds ratio** for Sex.

2   For Membership Status, the baseline level is 'Others', with estimated odds ratios of 1.06 for Staff and 1.46 for Students. This means that Others and Staff have more or less the same odds on wanting a PTS whereas the odds on a Student wanting a PTS are roughly one and a half times that of Others (and consequently of Staff).

3   The additive logistic regression model for these two between-subject factors (i.e. Sex and Membership Status) adequately describes these data as the Hosmer–Lemeshow test statistic has a *P*-value of 0.98 (see Box 8.20) and hence the null hypothesis that this model is true for the population cannot be rejected. In fact, this test uses the chi-squared test statistic and compares observed frequencies of each of the six possible combinations of Sex and Membership Status to those expected frequencies under this additive logistic regression model. These are displayed at the end of the output in Box 8.20 and it can be seen there that the observed and expected frequencies are close for all six cells.

4   There is no need for any 'linear' assumption in this model since neither of the possible explanatory variables is continuous in nature. The assumption of linearity of the log odds is only required for continuous explanatory variables.

5   The 'transformation' or 'translation' from the logarithm of the odds to the corresponding population proportion first uses the exponential function (this is the antilog, or inverse or opposite, of the logarithmic function to the base e) to produce the odds. Then obtain the population proportion from the odds using the fact that since:

$$\text{Odds} = \frac{\text{Population proportion}}{(1 - \text{Population proportion})}$$

then:

$$\text{Population proportion} = \frac{\text{Odds}}{(1 + \text{Odds})}$$

For example, from the Coef in Illustration 8.11, the log odds of 'would like a PTS' among Male Other SRS Members would be −0.325 − 0.745 = −1.07, whose exponential is 0.343. Hence the estimated population proportion of Male Others who 'would like a PTS' is 0.343/(1 + 0.343) = 0.26.

Illustration 8.12   Active commuting

Background

Active commuting (walking or cycling some or all of the way to work) is one possible way of increasing physical activity, improving aerobic fitness and health and having a positive influence on the environment. There are five Stages of Change for active commuting which can be described as follows: Pre-Contemplation, Contemplation, Preparation, Action, and

Maintenance. Self-efficacy for exercise and physical activity can be described as a person's confidence that they can overcome typical barriers to exercise. See Illustration 8.9 for more details.

Study description

A randomised controlled trial was carried out in Glasgow and aimed to establish if a self-help intervention, delivered via written interactive materials, could increase active commuting behaviour in workplaces. One hundred and ninety-two members of local educational and health establishments entered into the study, of whom 93 were randomised to be Controls and 99 received the Intervention. Each subject filled in a questionnaire, both pre and 3 months into the study, from which his/her Stage of Change and Self Effficacy scores were calculated.

Aim

To investigate whether the Intervention significantly increased the population proportion of those who improved their Stage of Change (SOC) over the 3-month period of the study and whether this also depended on the pre-study Self-Efficacy and Stage of Change of a subject.

Data

Name of data file:	*Active Commuting*
Response variable:	SOC Change (Improved SOC/Not Improved)
Explanatory variables:	Self Efficacy score (pre-study)
	Stage of Change (pre-study)
Between-subject factor:	Regime (2 levels: Intervention, Control)

Analysis

The possible explanatory variables are the continuous pre-study Self Efficacy score, the ordinal pre-study Stage of Change (coded as 1 to 5 from Pre-contemplation to Maintenance), the between-subject factor of Regime (two levels: Intervention and Control), with the response variable being the binary variable consisting of whether or not a subject's SOC changed for the better (i.e. increased on this scale of 1 to 5). Sample proportions of 'Improvers' by Regime and SOC pre-study are given in Box 8.21 and a box plot of Self Efficacy by SOC Change is given in Figure 8.14. These allow a subjective impression that the Intervention is having a positive effect on SOC Change proportions especially for a pre-study SOC of 2 (i.e. among Contemplators) and for those with high Self Efficacy scores pre-study.

A formal analysis would involve a logistic regression with a binary response variable of SOC Change with Improved SOC as the event modelled (i.e. that for which odds are evaluated). The model for the log odds on Improving SOC is assumed to depend upon a linear effect of Self Efficacy and SOC pre-study, a main effect of Regime and interactions (i.e. different slopes) of Regime with each of Self Efficacy and SOC pre-study. The results of fitting this 'full model' are displayed in Box 8.22.

The results show that neither of the 'interactions' is significant (*P*-values of 0.137 and 0.160, respectively). Indeed, if either was removed from the model, then the other would still prove non-significant. So, both terms can be removed from the model and a simple additive model fitted (see Box 8.23).

Box 8.21

```
Tabulated statistics: SOC pre-study, Regime, SOC Change

Rows: SOC pre-study / Regime   Columns: SOC Change

                      Improved         Not
                      SOC        Improved   All
1
    Control           1                3     4
    Intervention      3                0     3
2
    Control           18              35    53
    Intervention      34              27    61
3
    Control           7               11    18
    Intervention      10              12    22
4
    Control           2                5     7
    Intervention      2                4     6
5
    Control           0               11    11
    Intervention      0                7     7
All
    All               77             115   192

Cell Contents:        Count
```

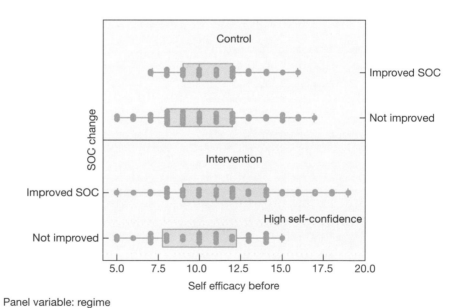

Panel variable: regime

Figure 8.14 Box plot of Self-Efficacy pre-study by SOC Change and Regime.

Box 8.22

```
Binary Logistic Regression: SOC Change versus Self Efficacy, SOC pre-study,
...
Link Function: Logit
Response Information

Variable      Value            Count
SOC Change    Improved SOC       77    (Event)
              Not Improved      115
              Total             192

Logistic Regression Table

                                                             Odds
Predictor                   Coef      SE Coef      Z      P  Ratio
Constant                -0.399857    1.01300   -0.39  0.693
Self Efficacy pre-study  0.0709405  0.0884541   0.80  0.423  1.07
SOC pre-study           -0.465062   0.255530   -1.82  0.069  0.63
Regime
 Intervention            0.491155   1.40251     0.35  0.726  1.63
Regime*SOC pre-study
 Intervention           -0.624088   0.419768   -1.49  0.137  0.54
Regime*Self Efficacy pre-study
 Intervention            0.169743   0.120937    1.40  0.160  1.19
```

Box 8.23

```
Binary Logistic Regression: SOC Change versus Self Efficacy, SOC pre-study,
...
Link Function: Logit
Response Information

Variable      Value            Count
SOC Change    Improved SOC       77    (Event)
              Not Improved      115
              Total             192

Logistic Regression Table

                                                     Odds      95% CI
Predictor              Coef     SE Coef      Z      P  Ratio  Lower  Upper
Constant           -0.711784  0.708742   -1.00  0.315
Self Efficacy pre-  0.164585  0.0581233   2.83  0.005   1.18   1.05   1.32
SOC pre-study      -0.748720  0.203361   -3.68  0.000   0.47   0.32   0.70
Regime
 Intervention       0.789623  0.320022    2.47  0.014   2.20   1.18   4.12

Log-Likelihood = -114.543
Test that all slopes are zero: G = 29.512, DF = 3, P-Value = 0.000
```

Now, all three terms in this additive model prove significant with *p*-values of 0.005, <0.001 and 0.014, respectively. Therefore the resulting final fitted model is that the logarithm of the Odds on 'improving SOC' is equal to:

$$-0.712 + 0.165 * \text{Self Efficacy} - 0.749 * \text{SOC pre-study}$$

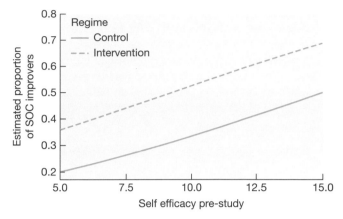

Figure 8.15 **Fitted logistic regressions for SOC pre-study = 2 (Contemplation).**

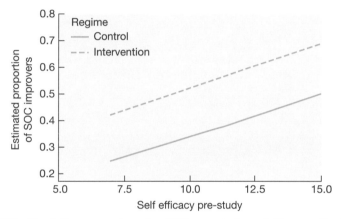

Figure 8.16 **Fitted logistic regressions for SOC pre-study = 3 (Preparation).**

for Controls and

$$-0.712 + 0.165 * \text{Self Efficacy} - 0.749 * \text{SOC pre-study} + 0.790$$

for the Intervention. Since the odds ratio for Intervention is estimated as 2.20 (i.e. exp (−0.790)), this means that, having corrected for pre-study Self Efficacy and SOC, the Intervention will increase the odds on a subject improving his/her SOC by a multiple of around 2 (i.e. a substantial increase in odds).

Since the intervention is really only particularly relevant for levels 2 and 3 (i.e. Contemplators and Preparers) of the SOC pre-study, the final fitted model is displayed for these levels in Figures 8.15 and 8.16, respectively. The figures show clearly not only the effect of the Intervention but also the effect of increasing Self Efficacy on the odds and hence population proportion of SOC Improvers.

These final fitted model plots allow relatively simple interpretation in that, for both pre-study SOC levels, the population proportion of SOC Improvers will increase with increasing pre-study Self Efficacy score regardless of Regime, and that the effect of the Intervention is to raise the population proportion by around 15% over Controls across both pre-study SOC levels and all values of Self Efficacy.

Conclusion

For health and education staff in Scotland, a self-help intervention can significantly increase the population proportion who improved their Stage of Change for active commuting over a 3-month period. The odds on improving Stage of Change increase by a multiple of around 2 (95% CI of 1.2 to 4.1). This finding is true even when correcting for the significant effects of the pre-Intervention Self Efficacy and Stage of Change of subjects.

Reference: Mutrie, N., Carney, C., Blamey, A., Crawford, F., Aitchison, T. and Whitelaw, A. (2002). 'Walk In to Work Out: a randomised controlled trial of a self help intervention to promote active commuting.' *Journal of Epidemiology and Community Health*, **56**: 407–412.

Additional comments on Illustration 8.12

1   This time the Hosmer–Lemeshow *P*-value turns out to be 0.048 and therefore the model is rejected. However, this is really an artefact of the fact that SOC pre-study is not linear and is in fact not really relevant unless the SOC is 2 or 3 (i.e. Contemplator or Preparer) since there are so few Pre-Contemplators and this intervention is not aimed at those in the Action or Maintenance Stages (i.e. 4 or 5).

Box 8.24

```
Binary Logistic Regression: SOC Change vs. Regime, Self Efficacy ...
Link Function: Logit
Response Information
Variable     Value          Count
SOC Change   Improved SOC      69   (Event)
             Not Improved      85
             Total            154

Logistic Regression Table
                                                     Odds      95% CI
Predictor                Coef    SE Coef      Z     P  Ratio Lower Upper
Constant             -2.21228   0.682520  -3.24  0.001
Regime
 Intervention         0.703546  0.339269    2.07  0.038  2.02  1.04  3.93
Self Efficacy Before  0.153383  0.0598740   2.56  0.010  1.17  1.04  1.31

Log-Likelihood = -99.956
Test that all slopes are zero: G = 11.912, DF = 2, P-value = 0.003

Goodness-of-Fit Tests
Method           Chi-Square  DF       P
Hosmer-Lemeshow      7.5729   7   0.372

Table of Observed and Expected Frequencies:
(See Hosmer-Lemeshow Test for the Pearson Chi-Square Statistic)
                                Group
Value          1     2     3     4     5     6      7     8     9   Total
Improved SOC
  Obs          5     5     8     9     9     6     14     7     6      69
  Exp        4.7   4.9   7.5   8.6   7.9   9.2   11.9   9.7   4.5
Not Improved
  Obs         14    11    13    12     8    12      7     8     0      85
  Exp       14.3  11.1  13.5  12.4   9.1   8.8    9.1   5.3   1.5
Total         19    16    21    21    17    18     21    15     6     154
```

2   If a logistic regression is carried out only for this specific target population (i.e. Contemplators and Preparers) and using Self Efficacy pre-study and Regime as the potential explanatory variables, the output contained in Box 8.24 is obtained.

From this output, the Hosmer–Lemeshow P-value is 0.372 so there is no reason to reject the model with a main effect of Regime and a linear effect of Self Efficacy. In fact, the estimated Intervention odds ratio of 2.02 is not really any different from that based on the full sample (i.e. 2.20) nor indeed the estimated odds ratio for the effect of Self Efficacy which only changes from 1.18 to 1.17.

Exercises

8.10   Elderly women who have suffered a femur fracture are given a course of physiotherapy before discharge in either a day hospital or in a geriatric unit. Such women are then still at risk of a serious fall at home and have major health and mobility problems. Each of a sample of 105 such women in the East End of Glasgow had an Elderly Mobility Score (EMS) measured on discharge and were then followed up for 3 months where the response variable measured was whether such a woman did or did not have a serious fall in this 3-month period. Do either the EMS on discharge and/or the Location (i.e. Day Hospital or Geriatric Unit) of physiotherapy treatment for elderly women recovering from a fractured femur significantly affect the 'likelihood' of a serious fall in the three months after discharge? The data are in the file *Elderly Mobility*.

8.11   In the survey described in Illustration 8.7, members of the Sports and Recreation Service (SRS) were asked whether they were satisfied with the Variety of lunchtime classes. Investigate whether the population proportion of SRS members satisfied with the Variety of lunchtime classes depends upon the Sex and/or Membership Status of an individual. The data are in the file *Variety in Classes*.

8.8   Classification trees

When there are many possible explanatory variables, both continuous and categorical in nature, and there is any doubt about the assumptions underlying a linear logistic regression model, there is always the option of applying the technique of classification trees to the data (a close relative of the technique of regression trees briefly discussed in Section 6.7). This is a slightly more empirical approach than most formal models dealt with in this book but is, at least, effectively free of assumptions and may well give good insight into the structure of the data if carefully and conservatively carried out. Basically, the technique involves a series of subdivisions of the data to find a simple split of the data at each step which best separates out the levels of the categorical response variable. If the reader likes impressive-sounding jargon, this is sometimes referred to in academic circles as binary recursive partitioning. The approach is very flexible and often throws up interesting results but should not be approached in a cavalier or mindless fashion. Most 'Trees' software will initially throw out an excessive full split of the data which

257

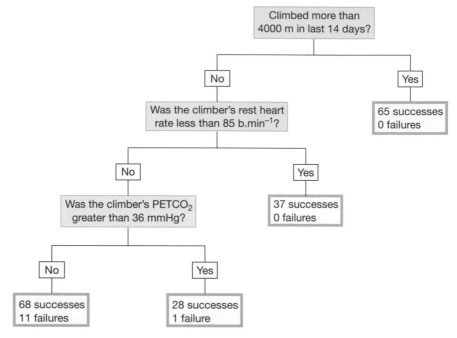

Figure 8.17 **Tree diagram for *Mont Blanc* data.**

must, in the current jargon, be severely 'pruned' back for *any reasonable predictive performance in future* for data from the same target population. The sensible approach to implementing the results of a classification tree analysis is to be highly conservative and consider only splits which can be well substantiated with sufficient data. It is advisable also to assess the future predictive use of such trees by applying the procedure to a further sample of data which was not used in the construction of the tree itself.

Illustration 8.1 looked at the population proportion of climbers who succeeded in reaching the summit of Mont Blanc from the Gouter Hut. Using the physiological and climbing history information taken from the subjects at the Gouter Hut on the ascent phase of the climb, a classification tree was derived with the simple binary response of Ascent Outcome (i.e. Success/Failure) and is displayed in Figure 8.17. Here it is obvious that a specific sub-population of climbers will have a substantially reduced population proportion/probability of Ascent Success, with 68 successes and 11 failures in this sub-sample. These are climbers who:

1 had not climbed above 4000 m in the previous 14 days;

2 had a resting heart rate at the Gouter on ascent of greater than 85 b.min^{-1};

3 had an end tidal CO_2 (PETCO$_2$) less than 36 mmHg at the Gouter Hut.

This is a fairly simple representation of the data with a clear message that may not be available from any formal analysis and, as such, illustrates well the potential of classification trees. Be careful, however, in the use of trees and always consult an expert when any attempt is made to grow and prune one of these trees!

Summary

This chapter covers a wide range of procedures used to model categorical variables assumed to have arisen from a multinomial distribution/population. Such variables will have a relatively small number of levels/categories (e.g. <6) and often are just binary variables (i.e. with two levels) assumed to have arisen from a binomial distribution/population.

The following procedures for categorical variables were illustrated in this chapter:

- Interval Estimation for a population proportion (i.e. a specific level of the categorical variable).
- Interval estimation comparing these across two or more distinct populations.
- Interval estimation comparing levels within a categorical variable.
- Hypothesis tests comparing a categorical variable across two or more distinct populations (comparison of multinomials).
- Hypothesis tests investigating association between two different categorical variables in the same sample (test of association).
- Hypothesis tests for paired categorical data (test of marginal symmetry).
- Modelling the dependence of a binary categorical variable on potential explanatory variables (logistic regression).
- Model selection in logistic regression and the use of classification trees.

All of these are really quite similar to the equivalent procedures for continuous variables based on the ideas introduced in Chapters 4, 5 and 6 for interval estimation, hypothesis testing and modelling relationships (regression). The key difference is that, for categorical variables, the Normal distribution plays no part at all. It is from a multinomial (or in the case of two levels, a binomial) distribution that the sample is assumed to have been generated, and this distribution, unlike the Normal, requires only the one key assumption that all observations on different subjects are independent of one another. Thus, there are few requirements for model checking – except in the case of logistic regression.

Technical appendix

Section 8.2

- The e.s.e. of the sample proportion (sp) is:

$$\sqrt{\left(\frac{sp * (1 - sp)}{\text{Sample size}}\right)}$$

- The e.s.e. of the difference in sample proportions (sp_1 and sp_2) *from the same sample* is:

$$\sqrt{\left(\frac{[sp_1 * (1 - sp_1)] + [sp_2 * (1 - sp_2)] + [2 * sp_1 * sp_2]}{\text{Sample size}}\right)}$$

- The e.s.e. of the difference of sample proportions (sp_A and sp_B) *from separate samples* (of sample sizes s_A and s_B, respectively) from two distinct populations is given by:

$$\sqrt{\left(\frac{sp_A * (1 - sp_A)}{s_A} + \frac{sp_B * (1 - sp_B)}{s_B} \right)}$$

Section 8.3

- In order to determine which particular chi-squared distribution is appropriate for a particular example, an integer, usually referred to as the 'degrees of freedom,' is required. The degrees of freedom (usually abbreviated to DF) depends on the number of levels of the categorical variable and the number of populations being compared. In fact, for any example comparing a multinomial variable with $L \geq 2$ levels across samples from $K \geq 1$ populations then the degrees of freedom will be $(L - 1) * (K - 1)$. As always, any statistical package will provide this information together with the resulting *P*-value which will then enable the decision whether to reject the null hypothesis on the basis of the data collected (i.e. whether or not the *P*-value is less than the chosen significance level of 0.05).

- The chi-squared approximation (to the distribution of the test statistic when the null hypothesis is true) is a good one as long as there is no expected frequency which is 'too small'. A practical rule of thumb is to rely on the chi-squared test only when there is no expected frequency less than 2, although some conservative individuals prefer to use 'less than 5'. If some expected frequencies are considered too small, it is possible to group neighbouring categories together in order to derive new categories that have expected frequencies which meet this requirement.

- In the simplest case of comparing a binary variable across two populations (often referred to as a 2×2 table) it is obviously not possible to group the levels when the expected frequencies are small. However, there is an alternative method: **Fisher's exact test**. In essence, Fisher's exact test evaluates the *P*-value of the observed pattern of data or a more extreme pattern occurring using a basic argument involving permutations and combinations (i.e. the exact distribution is considered as opposed to a large-sample approximation).

9 Investigating within-subject factors: dependent observations

9.1 Introduction

In many studies, it is obvious that the design of the study should involve *multiple* observations of the *same variable* on each subject, perhaps under different 'conditions' or on different body sites or at different times or possibly after each of a number of interventions. (Indeed, some studies might involve all of these.) These are termed **within-subject designs** (see Chapter 2 for discussion). For example, to investigate the usefulness of walking poles for hill walkers, the energy expenditure of a sample of hill walkers could be measured at 5-minute intervals over a simulated 60-minute walking course both *with and without* the use of such poles. Further, the effect of a high-protein diet on physical well-being could be assessed through an appropriate questionnaire at the *start* of, as well as *one* and *three* months into, such a diet.

Clearly, the observations on each subject across the 'conditions' will be more related to one another – to a greater or lesser extent – than they will be to those of any other subject. This provides the basis for the phrase 'dependent observations' since it is often true that the multiple observations on each subject will be interdependent in the sense that a 'good' subject will tend to give, relatively speaking, high values of the variable across all the conditions whereas 'poor' subjects will tend to give 'low' values of the variable. Exploiting this dependence in the analysis of such data often dramatically improves the power of the study and hence allows the investigator to identify small to moderate differences among the conditions that would be missed in a study of similar size but which used separate subjects for each of the conditions.

The simplest situation of this kind is that of *paired data,* where there are two observations (under different conditions, such as before and after some intervention) on each subject in a sample from some target population and interest lies in assessing the population average difference between these two conditions. For example, a sample of strength trainers might be taken and the bench press strength of each measured on a standard test both at the start and at the end of a month long course of creatine supplementation. The aim would be to quantify the average improvement, if any, in strength due to creatine supplementation. Another example would be to take a sample of (right-footed) professional footballers and measure the flexibility of both the right and left hip of each player in order to ascertain by how much, if at all, the right hip is more flexible than the left in general. In such problems, the key interest is in whether there is a 'significant' difference on average between the two conditions, and often this problem can be reduced to a so-called paired-sample problem (introduced in Chapter 4) using only the sample of differences in the response variable between the two conditions (e.g. Strength at End of Month on Creatine minus Strength at Start of Month).

An important extension to this type of problem is when there are three or more observations on each subject, such as measuring the (dominant hand) grip strength of elite rock climbers after each minute of a 3-minute endurance grip test. Here a researcher might be interested in whether the average grip strength of such climbers, in general, is significantly reduced at any stage of the endurance grip test and, if so, when and by how much. This type of situation, where all the three or more conditions (e.g. sites of the body, times into a test or even each of a set of distinct and different stimuli) can be thought of as constituting the **levels** of a single factor, is known as a single repeated measures factor design with the factor such as Time, Site etc. itself known as a **within-subject factor** or a **repeated measures factor**. Again the key element of this type of study is to investigate the differences, if any, among the population averages of the response variable across the different levels of the factor. For example, a sample of endurance runners may have their performance over 5 km measured under low, moderate and high humidity conditions and interest would focus on whether the average 5 km performance of runners would differ at all under these different humidity conditions, and, if so, by how much and in which humidity condition.

The basis of how to analyse any of the data types described above, and indeed any data following under the umbrella of this and the next two chapters, is once again the **general linear model (GLM)**. The GLM for the data from a one within-subject factor design could be written heuristically in the following form:

Observed measurement of the response variable for subject X at level Y of the within-factor = 'Mean' of level Y + Subject X effect + Natural variability/Error

The main interest, of course, is in comparing the means (i.e. the population means) of the different levels of the within-factor by an appropriate hypothesis test but the ideas of 'subject effects' and 'natural variability/error' are essential to the analysis and should be understood for better understanding of the whole procedure.

The 'subject X effect' term is simply how much, on the scale of measurement of the response variable, subject X is above or below the typical subject response to the particular level of the factor. On average across the population of all possible subjects, this would be zero. It is then assumed that this subject effect is constant for all observations on subject X (i.e. at all levels of the within-factor) and all that has to be modelled is the variability across all possible subjects. In the GLM, this variability is assumed to be Normally distributed, and this part of the GLM is referred to as 'the subject being a random effect'.

The 'natural variability/error' term is likely be different for different levels of the within-factor even for the same subject and will also be assumed to be Normally distributed with zero mean. The interpretation of this term depends upon the context, with 'natural variability' relating to variables of interest where there are naturally short-term differences in the same subject (e.g. blood pressure or flexibility), while 'error' may simply refer to a measurement error or indeed some measure of how far the true underlying situation/model is from the assumed GLM.

The remaining sections of this chapter concentrate on the appropriate analyses of data from such studies involving a single sample of dependent observations from some target population. The following chapter will consider studies where there are samples of dependent observations from two or more distinct and different populations (e.g. comparing males to females or contrasting endurance athletes, strength trainers and non-exercisers/controls).

The illustrations of within-factor designs in this chapter comprise the following:

- One-factor designs at two levels and at three levels, respectively.
- Two-factor designs with both factors at two levels, and then with one factor at two levels and the other at three levels.
- Three-factor design with all three factors at two levels.

Note, however, that these should not be thought of as explicit prescriptions for analysing such data but are merely illustrations of how to use some basic techniques to help in understanding data of this general form.

9.2 Analysing dependent observations: paired data

When a dataset involves a response variable being measured under two distinct and different levels/conditions on each of a single sample of subjects, the following steps are often appropriate:

1 Provide a scatter plot of the paired measurements under the two conditions with a line of equality superimposed on the plot.

2 Assuming this plot shows a general pattern of points (i.e. subjects) roughly parallel to the line of equality – but possibly widely spread about such a 'parallel line' – then take the *differences* between the measurements under the two conditions (for each subject) and draw a box plot of these with a 'line' of zero superimposed on the box plot.

3 Assuming these differences appear to have arisen from a single Normal population, then simply produce an *interval estimate for the population average difference* (between the conditions) which will enable the magnitude of the population average difference, if any, between the two conditions to be quantified (the interval will contain zero if no 'significant' average difference between the levels can be identified by the study).

Illustration 9.1   % Body fat in males

Background

The use of underwater weighing is considered by some to be an appropriate method to evaluate (percentage) body fat but it is time consuming, requires expensive equipment and may provoke fear in some subjects who may even refuse to carry out the procedure. If an easily administered, inexpensive and non-threatening substitute for underwater weighing could be found, it would enable more subjects to be tested. However, it is important to establish whether any other method will produce similar results to those from underwater weighing. The measurement of four skinfold sites – the biceps, triceps, subscapular and iliac crest – was recommended by Durnin and Womersley (1974) as the basis of a simple method of 'evaluating' body fat.

Study description

As part of a PhD study at Glasgow University, a student obtained a representative sample of 78 West of Scotland males, aged between 18 and 30 years, and 'evaluated' the % Body Fat of each by Densitometry (underwater weighing) and by using the (sum of) 4-Skinfolds approach of Durnin and Womersley (1974).

Aim

To provide an estimate of the average difference, if any, between two methods of 'evaluating' % Body Fat in males: Densitometry (underwater weighing) and by using the (sum of) 4-Skinfolds approach of Durnin and Womersley (1974).

Data

Name of data file:	*% Body Fat Male*
Response variable:	% Body Fat (%)
Within-subject factor:	Method (2 levels: Densitometry, 4-Skinfolds)

Analysis

First provide a scatter plot (Figure 9.1) of the Densitometry % Body Fat against the 4-Skinfolds % Body Fat, assess from it a sensible range of the variable being covered by both methods (5% to 22% here) and then superimpose a line of equality on the plot across this range.

The points on the scatter plot lie predominantly below the line of equality, suggesting that the 4-Skinfolds method gives (slightly) higher % Body Fats than the Densitometry method in general. However, although this seems to be a fairly consistent pattern across the full range of % Body Fats (i.e. from 5% to 22%), be aware that it is a general pattern and not the case for every subject.

Since Figure 9.1 strongly suggests a 'consistent pattern' across the full range of % Body Fats, it can now be reasonably assumed that there is, on average, a systematic difference between the two methods of 'evaluating' % Body Fat and interest can now be focused on the differences between the two methods by first providing a box plot of the differences for each subject (Figure 9.2).

From these differences (here taken 'naturally' as 4-Skinfolds minus Densitometry since most of these are positive), it can be seen from Figure 9.2 that most of the subjects have a

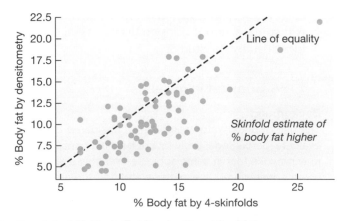

Figure 9.1 Scatterplot of % Body Fat 'evaluations' for Males.

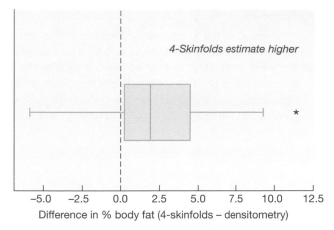

Figure 9.2 Box plot of differences in 'evaluations' of % Body Fat.

positive difference (i.e. a higher 4-Skinfolds % Body Fat than Densitometry) which is very likely to be statistically significant since the 'box' lies entirely in the positive part of the diagram, i.e. just over three-quarters of the sample have positive differences. It is also reasonably obvious from the box plot of Figure 9.2 that the sample of differences is nearly symmetrical with, in particular, the sample median lying near the centre of the sample quartile box. Hence, it seems reasonable to assume the single sample of differences has arisen from a Normal population and then to provide an interval estimate for the average difference of % Body Fat as 'evaluated' by 4-Skinfolds and Densitometry, respectively, for 18–30-year-old males in (at least) the West of Scotland based on the standard one-sample t-interval (Box 9.1).

Box 9.1

```
One-Sample T: 4-Skinfold - Densitometry

Variable          N     Mean    StDev  SE Mean        95% CI
Skin - Den       78  2.04286  2.93666  0.33251  (1.38075, 2.70497)
```

Since the differences were taken as 4-Skinfolds minus Densitometry, and since this interval does not contain zero, it can be concluded not only that there is a significant difference, on average, between the two methods of 'evaluating' % Body Fat but also, more importantly, that the 4-Skinfolds method gives % Body Fat 'evaluations' between 1.4% and 2.7% higher on average than the Densitometry method.

Conclusion

For males in the 18–30-year-old age range in the West of Scotland, % Body Fat as 'evaluated' by the sum of 4-Skinfolds (Durnin and Womersley 1974) is, on average, 1.4% to 2.7% higher than the equivalent 'evaluation' by Densitometry.

References: Durnin, J.V.G.A. and Womersley, J. (1974). 'Body fat assessed from total body density and its estimation from skinfold thickness: Measurements on 481 men and women aged 16–72 years.' *British Journal of Nutrition*, **32**: 77–97.

Maria T. Espinosa-Zepeda (1995). 'Metabolic rate related to body composition in lean muscular humans.' PhD thesis, University of Glasgow.

Additional comments on Illustration 9.1

1 The design of the study simply involved half of the subjects having their % Body Fat 'evaluated' first by Densitometry and then by 4-Skinfolds while the other half had their % Body Fat "evaluated" first by 4-Skinfolds and then by Densitometry. To carry out a simple assessment of whether there was any significant learning or order effect (see Chapter 2), simply carry out a two-sample comparison (i.e. of the two halves of the data) of the differences of the two methods of 'evaluating' % Body Fat (Box 9.2).

Box 9.2

```
Two-sample T for Diff. (4-Skin - Dens)

Sample Half              N   Mean  StDev  SE Mean
First Half Sampl        39   2.51   3.44     0.55
Second Half Samp        39   1.57   2.28     0.36

Difference = mu (First Half Sample) - mu (Second Half Sample)

Estimate for difference:  0.944231
95% CI for difference:  (-0.375002, 2.263464)
T-Test of difference = 0 (vs not =): T-Value = 1.43
                                P-value = 0.158  DF = 65
```

There is no evidence of a significant difference of these two separate samples of differences ($P = 0.158$), hence it can be assumed that the order in which the two methods were used did not influence the results of the study.

2 If there was concern about the validity of the assumption of Normality, then a non-parametric interval estimate (strictly speaking for the median difference between the methods and based on the Wilcoxon signed-ranks procedure) could be used (Box 9.3).

Box 9.3

```
Wilcoxon Signed Rank CI: DiffM (4-Skin - Dens)

                   Estimated    Achieved  Conf.  Interval
               N      Median  Confidence  Lower     Upper
Skin - Den    78        2.04        95.0   1.31      2.68
```

Using this approach produces a marginally wider interval, i.e. 1.3% to 2.7% compared with that produced by the Normality-based approach of 1.4% to 2.7%. Another 'non-parametric' approach here is to use the bootstrap discussed in Section 4.8.

3 To assess the assumption that the differences were Normally distributed, use a Normal probability plot (see Section 5.6) to show that, for these data (Figure 9.3), the assumption is reasonable, with a P-value for the Anderson–Darling (AD) test of the null hypothesis that the differences are Normally distributed being 0.58.

4 If there was concern about taking differences, then this could be investigated by a plot (Figure 9.4) of the differences against the average of the two % Body Fat methods and

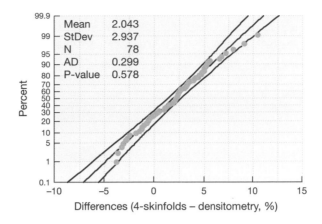

Figure 9.3 **Probability plot of differences for Males (Normal − 95% CI).**

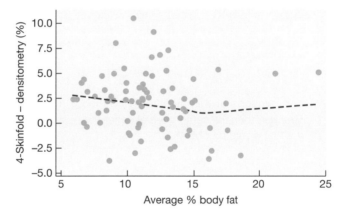

Figure 9.4 **Bland–Altman plot of % Body Fats (Males).**

provide a 'smoothed' version of the dependence of the difference on the magnitude of the % Body Fat (i.e. the average of the two methods here for each subject).

The diagram shows very little trend in the smoothed relationship so the assumption of a 'consistent' systematic difference between the two methods seems reasonable. For more information on this approach, see Chapter 12 on assessing agreement between methods of measurement (and in particular the Bland–Altman method).

5 A general linear model (GLM) could be fitted to these data with one column for all % Body Fat measurements, one column for the method used and one column for a unique subject identifier. Box 9.4 displays the resultant output when the GLM incorporates Method as a fixed effect and Subject as a random effect.

However, this ANOVA table adds little or nothing to the analysis other than to confirm that the Methods are significantly different on average (i.e. Method P-value of 0.000 although this is not actually zero but just less than 0.0005). If a Tukey-based multiple

267

Box 9.4

```
General Linear Model: %Body Fat versus Method, Subject

Factor    Type     Levels  Values
Method    fixed        2   4-Skinfolds and Densitometry
Subject   random      78   1, 2, 3, 4, 5, 6, 7 . . .   to 78

Analysis of Variance for %BF M, using Adjusted SS for Tests

Source    DF     Seq SS     Adj SS    Adj MS      F       P
Method     1    162.758    162.758   162.758   37.75   0.000
Subject   77   1801.905   1801.905    23.401    5.43   0.000
Error     77    332.022    332.022     4.312
Total    155   2296.685

Tukey 95.0% Simultaneous Confidence Intervals
Response Variable %BF M
All Pairwise Comparisons among Levels of Method
Method = Dens   subtracted from:

Method  Lower   Center   Upper   -----+-----+-----+-----+-
4-Skin  1.381    2.043   2.705   (-----------*----------)
                                 -----+-----+-----+-----+-
                                  1.60    2.00   2.40   2.80
```

comparisons of this significant Method effect in this GLM were carried out, as in Box 9.4, then the same interval as for the paired-sample t-analysis above (i.e. 1.38% to 2.71%) would be obtained.

Exercises

9.1 The dataset % *Body Fat Female* consists of the % Body Fat of a sample of 18–30-year-old females from the West of Scotland as 'evaluated' by both 4-Skinfolds and Densitometry. Is there a significant difference, on average, between the two methods of 'evaluating' % Body Fat in such a population? If so, how much of a difference is there?

9.2 Creatine is a natural constituent of the body formed in the liver and kidneys. Some studies have shown that oral creatine supplementation has the potential to enhance performance in repeated high-intensity sprints in some subjects. It is of interest to see whether creatine supplementation would delay fatigue in some way. Twenty female subjects who took part in regular physical exercise, were involved in this study. Each subject carried out a set of ten 10-second sprints (with one-minute rest between sprints) on an exercise bike. These sprints were monitored, and the Power Output (in watts) was recorded. Each subject was then placed on a 4-week course of Creatine supplementation, after which the test was carried out again, and the Power Output recorded as before. By how much, if at all, does Creatine supplementation increase the average Power Output of the subjects in general? This dataset is called *Creatine Supplements*.

Analysing dependent observations: a single within-subject factor at three or more levels

When there are data involving a response variable being measured under three or more (in general K) distinct and different conditions or levels of the within-subject factor on each of a single sample of subjects, the appropriate steps are:

1 Provide scatter plots of all pairwise combinations of the K levels with the same line of equality superimposed on each plot.

2 Draw up *case* profile plots of the response variable across the K levels with the values for each subject connected. Then augment this with the corresponding box plots for the K levels with the sample medians connected.

3 Assuming the profile plots look roughly parallel across subjects and that each box plot looks roughly Normally distributed, then carry out a one-way repeated measures analysis of variance which, as long as a random subject effect is included, allows for the dependence across the observations for each subject and involves a test of the null hypothesis that all K levels have the same population average for the response variable.

4 If the hypothesis test proves non-significant, then stop, and simply conclude that there are no significant differences across the K levels. However, if the test proves significant ($P < 0.05$), then carry out a follow-up pairwise multiple comparison procedure of the K levels to discover which levels are significantly different.

Illustration 9.2 Energy expenditure in step classes

Background
Many individuals wish to lose fat or maintain current fat levels, and regular exercise has a role to play in achieving this. Some people (particularly females) take part in regular step aerobic classes where they perform a range of routines (i.e. a variety of movements including steps and straddles and a number of arm movements) on a step, the height of which can be adjusted. As it seems highly plausible that the higher the step, the greater the energy expenditure, then step aerobic classes should use step heights appropriate to the level of energy expenditure that a particular class targets.

Study description
A sample of 10 (18–22-year-old) females had their Energy Expenditure measured while undergoing the same 30-minute step class on three occasions while using a different Step Height (i.e. 6 or 8 or 10 inch steps) on each occasion. Expired air was collected in Douglas bags for each subject on each occasion for the full step class and Energy Expenditure was calculated using the Weir* method.

*Weir, J.B. de V. (1949). 'New methods for calculating metabolic rate with special reference to protein metabolism.' *Journal of Physiology*, **109**: 1–9.

Aim
To investigate what differences, if any, exist in the average Energy Expenditure for these three different Step Heights in this 30-minute Step class.

Data

Name of data file:	*Step Height*
Response variable:	Energy Expenditure (kilojoules)
Within-subject factor:	Step Height (3 levels: 6, 8, 10 inch steps)

Analysis

The three pairwise plots of Energy Expenditure for the three Step Heights are shown in Figures 9.5 to 9.7 (all on the same scales) with a common line of equality from 750 to 1300 kJ.

From the figures it appears obvious that the Energy Expenditures on the three Step Heights are all different from one another, with the least Energy Expenditure on the 6 inch step and most on the 10 inch step. This is perhaps less obvious in the case profile plots of Figure 9.8 but still appears substantial in the box plots of Figure 9.9.

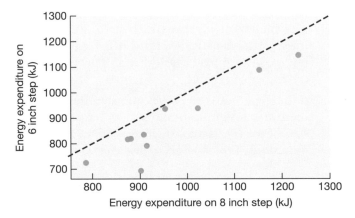

Figure 9.5 Scatter plot of Energy Expenditure 6 inch by 8 inch Step Heights (with line of equality).

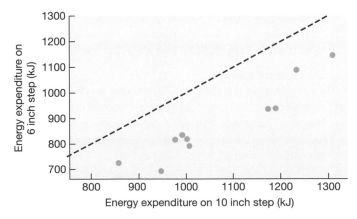

Figure 9.6 Scatter plot of Energy Expenditure 6 inch by 10 inch Step Heights (with line of equality).

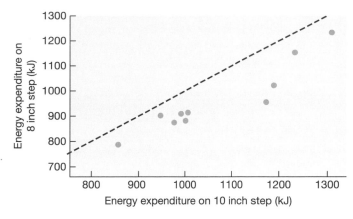

Figure 9.7 **Scatter plot of Energy Expenditure 8 inch by 10 inch Step Heights (with line of equality).**

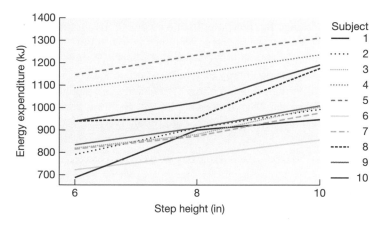

Figure 9.8 **Individual profile plots of Energy Expenditure by Step Height.**

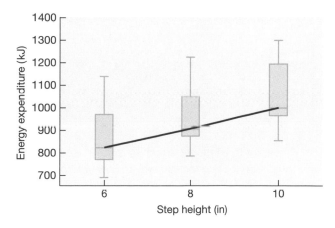

Figure 9.9 **Box plot of Energy Expenditure by Step Height.**

To confirm (or otherwise) that there are 'significant' differences in average Energy Expenditure (EE) for this step class among the three Step Heights, use a GLM with Height as a fixed factor and Subject as a random factor to produce the repeated measures ANOVA table (Box 9.5).

Box 9.5

```
General Linear Model: EE versus HEIGHT, SUBJECT

Factor    Type    Levels  Values
HEIGHT    fixed       3   6, 8, 10
SUBJECT   random     10   1, 2, 3, 4, 5, 6, 7, 8, 9, 10

Analysis of Variance for EE, using Adjusted SS for Tests

Source   DF  Seq SS  Adj SS  Adj MS      F      P
HEIGHT    2  181289  181289   90645  73.00  0.000
SUBJECT   9  537606  537606   59734  48.11  0.000
Error    18   22349   22349    1242
Total    29  741245
```

Virtually the only important element of this output is the P-value of 0.000 (actually not quite zero but very close to it) in the row titled 'Height' in the ANOVA table. Since this P-value is less than 0.05, reject the null hypothesis that all three Step Heights give the same average Energy Expenditure and conclude that there is at least one pair of the three Step Heights where the two Step Heights are significantly different from each other.

Since the ANOVA does not tell which or how many of the three levels (Step Heights) are significantly different, carry out a Tukey pairwise multiple comparison procedure (Box 9.6).

Box 9.6

```
Tukey 95.0% Simultaneous Confidence Intervals
Response Variable EE
All Pairwise Comparisons among Levels of HEIGHT

HEIGHT =  6  subtracted from:
HEIGHT   Lower   Center  Upper   ---+-----+-----+-----+---
 8       43.83    84.06  124.3   (----*----)
10      149.77   190.00  230.2                     (----*----)
                                 ---+-----+-----+-----+---
                                    60    120   180   240

HEIGHT =  8  subtracted from:
HEIGHT  Lower   Center  Upper    ---+-----+-----+-----+---
10       65.71   105.9  146.2       (----*----)
                                 ---+-----+-----+-----+---
                                    60    120   180   240
```

There are three pairwise comparisons in Box 9.6. The first provides an interval estimate for the difference in population mean Energy Expenditure for the 8 inch step minus the 6 inch step in such a 30-minute step class and is 43.8 to 124.3 kJ. Since this interval is entirely positive, conclude that the 8 inch step provides between 44 to 124 kJ more Energy Expenditure, on average, than the 6 inch step on this step class. In a similar vein, the 10 inch step provides, in terms of average Energy Expenditure, between 150 and 230 kJ more than the 6 inch step and 66 to 146 kJ more than the 8 inch step.

Conclusion

The average Energy Expenditure for the step class under consideration in this study is significantly greater using a 10 inch step than an 8 inch step which in turn is significantly greater than a 6 inch step.

Reference: Sutherland, R., Wilson, J., Aitchison, T. and Grant. S. (1999). 'Comparison of physiological and rate of perceived exertion responses to a university step aerobics class.' *Journal of Sports Sciences*, **17**: 495–503.

Additional comments on Illustration 9.2

1 The original design of the study was to use twelve rather than ten subjects but two subjects dropped out prior to the start of the study. The original design was in two sets of two balanced 3×3 Latin squares (see Section 2.2.4) with the intention of allowing for any order (i.e. learning or boredom) effect for subjects doing all three of these different Step Height classes.

2 To assess whether the subjects showed any order effect, include the order of the test (i.e. first, second or third test) as a fixed effect in the ANOVA, as in Box 9.7.

Box 9.7

```
General Linear Model: EE versus SUBJECT, HEIGHT, Order of Test

Factor          Type    Levels  Values
SUBJECT         random      10  1, 2, 3, 4, 5, 6, 7, 8, 9, 10
HEIGHT          fixed        3  6, 8, 10
Order of Test   fixed        3  1st, 2nd, 3rd

Analysis of Variance for EE, using Adjusted SS for Tests

Source          DF   Seq SS   Adj SS   Adj MS      F      P
SUBJECT          9   537606   537606    59734  48.01  0.000
HEIGHT           2   181289   176879    88440  71.08  0.000
Order of Test    2     2440     2440     1220   0.98  0.397
Error           16    19909    19909     1244
Total           29   741245
```

Since the *P*-value for the 'order of test' effect is 0.4, the null hypothesis of 'no order effect' cannot be rejected and hence it is fair to assume that the order in which subjects used the three Step Heights did not influence the results to any great extent. (In addition, remember that the original design attempted to balance out any such effect anyway.)

3 While, to some, it may seem excessive to use all the plots suggested above, there is something different to be seen in each plot. The pairwise scatter plots allow comparisons of each level of the factor (Step Height); the profile plots allow examination of the implicit assumption that the subject effect is 'additive' (e.g. here, the profiles for all subjects are roughly parallel); and the box plots allow a representation of the general or average trend across the levels of the factor (Step Height) as well as an assessment of the assumption of Normality for each level.

4 Since there is a slight positive skewness in the box plots, it might be better to use the logarithms of the Energy Expenditure (since taking logarithms will reduce any positive skewness in data). Indeed, if natural logarithms (i.e. to the base e) were taken here, then exactly the same conclusions would be reached i.e. all three Step Heights give different average (logged) Energy Expenditures based on the corresponding Tukey multiple comparisons (see Box 9.8).

Box 9.8

```
Tukey 95.0% Simultaneous Confidence Intervals
Response Variable loge EE
All Pairwise Comparisons among Levels of HEIGHT
HEIGHT =  6  subtracted from:
HEIGHT    Lower   Center   Upper   ---+------+------+------+---
  8       0.04846 0.09517  0.1419  (----*----)
 10       0.15305 0.19977  0.2465                    (----*----)
                                   ---+------+------+------+---
                                   0.060   0.120   0.180  0.240

HEIGHT =  8  subtracted from:
HEIGHT    Lower   Center   Upper   ---+------+------+------+---
 10       0.05788 0.1046   0.1513     (----*----)
                                   ---+------+------+------+---
                                   0.060   0.120   0.180  0.240
```

While this explicitly produces interval estimates for the average differences in log Energy Expenditure (and hence for the ratio of Energy Expenditures themselves), it is easier to interpret by taking the following approach. Take antilogs (i.e. exponentials) of the end points of these intervals, subtract the value 1 from these and then multiply by 100 to obtain (approximately) the average **percentage change** in Energy Expenditure from one Step Height to another. Here, this works out to be a 5% to 15% increase in Energy Expenditure going from a 6 inch to an 8 inch step, 6% to 16% going from an 8 inch to a 10 inch step, and finally a 17% to 28% increase going from a 6 inch to a 10 inch step.

5 The further assumption that the variability across subjects is the same for all levels of the factor (Step Height) does seem not unreasonable here since all three boxes are roughly the same size. If there was concern about this assumption of equal variability across the different levels of the factor necessary for the ANOVA (or indeed the assumption of constant correlation), then mimic the approach adopted in Section 9.2 on paired data and use all pairwise differences of the levels (i.e. the three Step Heights) with a suitable 'Bonferroni' correction for this version of multiple comparisons. Here that would correspond to providing 98.33% confidence intervals for each of the three pairwise comparisons, as in Box 9.9.

Box 9.9

```
Pairwise Bonferroni intervals (simultaneous 95% i.e. marginal 98.33%)

One-Sample T: Diff 8-6, Diff 10-6, Diff 10-8

Variable    N    Mean    StDev  SE Mean      98.333% CI
Diff 8-6    10   84.0566 51.3981 16.2535  (36.3817, 131.7314)
Diff 10-6   10   189.995 46.138  14.590   (147.200,  232.791)
Diff 10-8   10   105.939 51.762  16.369   ( 57.927,  153.951)
```

These intervals are all slightly wider than the corresponding intervals (based on the Tukey method) for the ANOVA since they do not pool information across the three Step Heights. Basically, though, there is little difference here from the standard approach and the overall conclusions remain unchanged.

9.3.1 The assumptions in repeated measures ANOVA

As discussed briefly in Section 9.2, the GLM, and hence the repeated measures ANOVA for a one within-factor design, is based on the following assumptions:

1 The subject effect in the GLM is additive.

2 The between-subject variability is Normally distributed and is the same for all levels of the factor (e.g. Step Height in Illustration 9.2).

3 The natural variability in measurements of the response variable (e.g. Energy Expenditure) for each subject at each level of the factor (e.g. Step Height) is Normally distributed and is the same for all subjects at all levels.

4 The correlation between any pair of measurements on the same subject is constant across all levels of the factor (e.g. Step Height) and across all subjects. (This is sometimes referred to as **sphericity** or **compound symmetry** and is a consequence of assumptions 1 and 2).

The assumption of sphericity is the one which can attract concern in the analysis of almost any repeated measures dataset. It can only cause problems if a within-factor has three or more levels and can be assessed by a hypothesis test known as **Mauchly's test of sphericity**. If the test can reject the null hypothesis that assumption 4 is true, then there are available a variety of so-called multivariate (repeated measures) tests which assume a much more general structure to the data but are generally much less effective for identifying a significant factor effect (i.e. the multivariate tests are much less powerful than the repeated measures ANOVA).

Another approach that is commonly used, if the test of sphericity proves significant (and hence the assumption unreasonable), is to correct for how far the assumption is from being true by adjusting all the test statistics and hence P-values. The most common of these correction factors is called Greenhouse–Geisser. It is often worth examining these adjusted P-values.

In Illustration 9.2, the assumption of sphericity or compound symmetry can be checked by the appropriate hypothesis test (see Box 9.10) and there is clearly no problem with this (P-value of 0.921 to test the null hypothesis of symmetry being true).

Box 9.10 **Mauchly's test of sphericity**

Within Subjects Effect	Mauchly's W	Approx. Chi-Square	df	Sig.	Epsilon		
					Greenhouse-Geisser	Huynh-Feldt	Lower-bound
StepHeight	.980	.165	2	.921	.980	1.000	.500

Output from SPSS

Correspondingly, the multivariate tests of the effect of Step Height and the corrections for lack of symmetry such as Greenhouse–Geisser (0.98 here) give almost exactly the same P-values, and hence conclusion, as the univariate repeated measures test in Box 9.7 (i.e. confirming the significant differences in average energy expenditure across all three Step Heights).

275

9.3 Major athletic events can be held in cities where high heat and humidity are prevailing weather conditions (e.g. the 1996 Olympics in Atlanta, USA). High heat and humidity have the potential to reduce athletic performance in a number of events. Researchers carried out a study comparing three distinct regimes. One was in effect a Control involving a warm-up and an Intermittent Supramaximal Running Performance Test (ISRPT) test in cool (UK) conditions. The second involved a warm-up in cool conditions but an ISRPT test in hot and humid conditions. The third involved a warm-up and sprint performance test both in hot and humid conditions. Twelve athletes had their Performance in the ISRPT monitored in each of these three regimes. The longer the performance time the better the performance is. The key question is to determine if there are any significant average differences in Performance in an ISRPT among the three Conditions outlined above. The dataset is called *Humidity*.

Reference: Maxwell, N.S., Aitchison, T.C. and Nimmo, M.A. (1996).'The effect of climatic heat stress on intermittent supramaximal running performance in humans.' *Experimental Physiology*, **81**: 833–845.

9.4 As part of a sports science degree, students used four different methods of 'evaluating' % Body Fat on each of a sample of 46 fellow students. These methods were underwater weighing using an Oxygen Dilution technique to measure residual volume (RV), underwater weighing using an electric Spirometer to measure RV, Skinfolds measurements and Bio-electrical Impedance analysis. Which, if any, of these four methods give, on average, significantly different measurements of % Body Fat, and by how much? The data are in the file *%Body Fat Four*.

Reference: Archibald, S., Bibby, C., Henderson, L. (students) and Baxendale, R. (staff) (2006). 'Comparison of different methods of estimating percentage body fat.' University of Glasgow Physiology and Sports Science student project.

9.4 Analysing dependent observations: two or more within-subject factors

A natural extension to the scenarios discussed in the previous two sections is a study that involves combinations of two (or more) distinct and different factors, each of which is at two or more levels. This may involve subjects undergoing exercise tests both before and, say, one month after some form of intervention such as dietary advice, with the performance of the subjects being measured at fixed times into the exercise test; the two within-subject factors would be Intervention Point (with two levels, namely Before/After) and Time (at three levels, namely 30, 60 and 90 minutes into the test). Another example would be measuring the 20 m sprint times of rugby backs either carrying the ball with two hands or in their dominant hand; both of these carried out on either a straight sprint or on a zig-zag sprint. This would therefore involve two within-subject factors each with two levels, namely Hand (i.e. both or dominant hand) and Course (i.e. straight or zig-zag).

In such scenarios, there will be a number of questions to be answered – comparing the levels of each factor separately as well as investigating the 'combination' effect of the two factors. For example, in the rugby study just mentioned, there would be interest in:

1 how much, if at all, the zig-zag course increases the average sprint time compared with a straight course of the same distance;

2 whether, on average, holding the ball with both hands allows quicker short sprints than holding the ball in the dominant hand only;

3 whether, on average, any such difference between sprint times for the different handling options is greater for the zig-zag course than for the straight course?

These questions correspond respectively to the two main effects of the factors and the interaction between the factors discussed for similar studies with no repeated measurements in Section 7.3 (i.e. two-way ANOVA on two between-subject factors).

When there are data involving a response variable being measured on all combinations of *two distinct factors (each at two or more levels)* on each of a single sample of subjects, then the following steps are appropriate:

1 Draw up case profile plots of the response variable across one of the factors (chosen appropriately – for example, Time is an obvious choice), with the values for each subject connected and this repeated across all combinations of the other factor. Augment this with the corresponding box plots with the sample medians connected.

2 If one of the factors has only two levels, then scatter plots of the response variable for these two levels should be drawn for each combination of the other factor.

3 Assuming that a GLM with the assumptions involving additive factors, common variability across all combinations of the factors and underlying Normality of each combination is appropriate, then carry out a full repeated measures ANOVA incorporating Subject as a random factor to allow for the dependence of observations on the same subject;

4 Produce follow-up multiple comparisons for any significant terms, although, if there are significant interactions, be careful about the interpretation not only of these but any main effects as well.

Illustration 9.3   Walking poles

Background

The sight of hill walkers using walking poles has become markedly more common over the past few years. Manufacturers claim that walking poles provide benefits for the (hill) walker, such as enhanced stability, less strain on the lower limbs and a lower rating of perceived exertion.

Study description

A sample of 14 physically active males underwent a simulated short hill walk of 10 minutes, once using walking poles and once without using walking poles, with a 15-minute rest between the two 'hill walks'. Each subject walked at 3.7 km.h^{-1} on a 12.7% gradient and had his $\dot{V}O_2$ measured using Douglas bags over of each of the last 3 minutes of each 'hill walk' (i.e. during the eighth, ninth and tenth minutes).

Aims

To investigate any effect of the use of walking poles on $\dot{V}O_2$ at each of the last 3 minutes into such a 'hill walk'. To be more explicit perhaps, to find out whether any effect of the walking poles is the same for each of the last 3 minutes.

Data

Name of data file:	*Walking Poles*
Response variable:	$\dot{V}O_2$ (ml.kg^{-1}.min^{-1})
Within-subject factors:	Pole Use (2 levels: Yes, No)
	Time (3 levels: 8th, 9th, 10th min. into 'walk')

Analysis

The three pairwise plots (Figures 9.10 to 9.12) of $\dot{V}O_2$ using the walking poles against $\dot{V}O_2$ not using the walking poles for the three Times is the first useful step in this analysis.

These plots clearly suggest that $\dot{V}O_2$ is higher when using the Poles than when a subject is not using the Poles at all three times of the 'hill walk', with only one subject at each time having a lower $\dot{V}O_2$ when walking with the Poles.

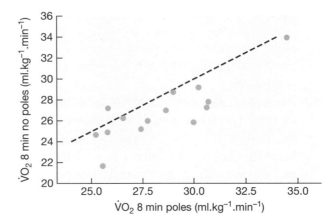

Figure 9.10 Scatter plot of $\dot{V}O_2$ No Poles against Poles, minute 8 (with line of equality).

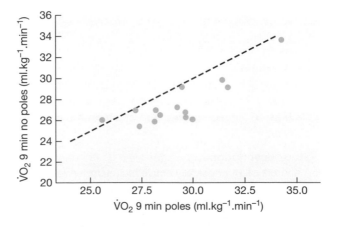

Figure 9.11 Scatter plot of $\dot{V}O_2$ No Poles against Poles, minute 9 (with line of equality).

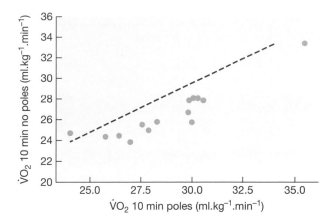

Figure 9.12 Scatter plot of $\dot{V}O_2$ No Poles against Poles, minute 10 (with line of equality).

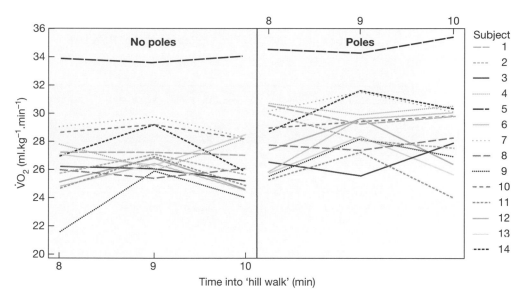

Figure 9.13 Subject profile plots by Time for each level of Pole Use.

This is perhaps almost as obvious as looking at the case profile plots (Figure 9.13) across time for each of the two levels of Pole use (note that the same subject appears in both parts of this plot with the same symbol).

It can be seen in Figure 9.13 that subject 5 has a much higher $\dot{V}O_2$ regardless of Pole Use than any other subject, and that there are some differences in the patterns among the subjects, but, overall, there are only small differences across the Pole Use factor and less convincingly across the three times, as can be seen in the box plots of Figure 9.14.

Now, the output in Box 9.11 is obtained by carrying out a repeated measures ANOVA with a GLM involving two fixed factors, Pole Use and Time, as well as their interaction and a random subject factor.

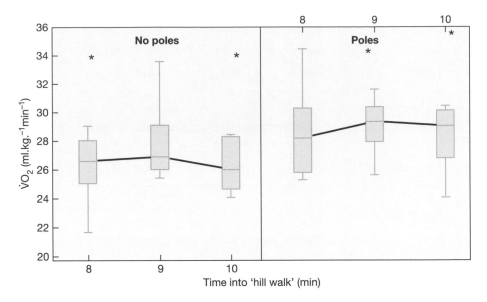

Figure 9.14 Box plot of $\dot{V}O_2$ by Time for each level of Pole Use.

Box 9.11

```
General Linear Model: VO₂ versus Time, Pole Use, SUBJECT

Factor     Type     Levels  Values
Time       fixed         3  1, 2, 3
Pole Use   fixed         2  Yes, No
Subject    random       14  1, 2, 3, 4, 5, 6, . . . .  14

Analysis of Variance for VO₂, using Adjusted SS for Tests

Source            DF    Seq SS   Adj SS  Adj MS       F       P
Time               2    10.547   10.547   5.274    4.17   0.020
Pole Use           1    66.359   66.359  66.359   52.41   0.000
Time*Pole Use      2     0.410    0.410   0.205    0.16   0.851
Subject           13   420.948  420.948  32.381   25.58   0.000
Error             65    82.293   82.293   1.266
Total             83   580.557
```

The first item to note from this ANOVA is the P-value of 0.85 for the interaction between Pole Use and Time. Since this is much greater than 0.05, the (null) hypothesis that there is no interaction between Pole Use and Time cannot be rejected. Hence it can be concluded that the (average) *difference in* $\dot{V}O_2$ *between Pole and No Pole Use* is the *same for all three times*. This makes interpretation of the rest of the results of the ANOVA much more straightforward. Indeed, both of the main effects of Time ($P = 0.02$) and Pole Use ($P < 0.0005$) allow us to conclude not only that are there (some) significant differences in average $\dot{V}O_2$ among the three times but also that there is a clear and significant difference in average $\dot{V}O_2$ between using Poles and not using Poles. However, in order not only to find out the direction of such differences but also to quantify them, perform follow-up multiple comparisons separately on the two factors. For the Pole Use factor, this is equivalent to a standard one-sample *t*-interval based on the averages across the three times, as shown in Box 9.12.

Box 9.12

```
Tukey 95.0% Simultaneous Confidence Intervals
Response Variable V̇O₂
All Pairwise Comparisons among Levels of Pole Use
Pole Use = Yes  subtracted from:

PoleUse Lower  Center   Upper    ---+------+------+------+---
No     -2.268  -1.778  -1.287    (-----*-----)
                                 ---+------+------+------+---
                                 -2.10   -1.40  -0.70   0.00
```

Since this (simple) comparison of the population average $\dot{V}O_2$ for 'No Pole Use minus Pole Use' gives an interval estimate of -2.3 to -1.3 ml.kg^{-1}.min^{-1}, it can be concluded that using Poles significantly increases $\dot{V}O_2$, on average, by between 1.3 and 2.3 ml.kg^{-1}.min^{-1} at all three Times into the 'hill walk'. To put this into perspective, note that without Poles the typical $\dot{V}O_2$ of this sample is around 27 ml.kg^{-1}.min^{-1} so the increase in $\dot{V}O_2$ due to Pole Use is between 5 and 10% (i.e. between roughly 1.3/27 and 2.3/27).

For the Time factor, the set of Tukey-based multiple comparisons can be summarised as:

Time	minus	Time	Interval estimate
9th min		8th min	(0.1, 1.5)
10th min		8th min	(−0.5, 0.9)
10th min		9th min	(−1.3, 0.1)

As only the interval comparing 9th minute and the 8th minute does *not* contain zero, the only significant difference across the three times is between the 8th and 9th minutes with raised levels at 9 minutes. There are not significant differences, however, between the 10th minute and either the 8th or the 9th minute of the 'hill walk'.

Conclusion

The use of walking poles on a simulated hill walk significantly raised $\dot{V}O_2$ on average by between 1.3 and 2.3 ml.kg^{-1}.min^{-1} for all three of the last 3 minutes of a 10-minute 'hill walk'.

Reference: Mills, S., Millott, J. (students), Grant, S., Aitchison, T., Pitt, C. and Watt, I. (staff) (2003). 'The effect of walking poles on physiological and psychological variables.' University of Glasgow Physiology and Sports Science student project.

Additional comments on Illustration 9.3

1 The design of the study was simply that half the subjects used the poles on their first 'hill walk' and half the subjects use the poles on their second 'hill walk'.

2 A formal analysis of whether subjects had a difference in $\dot{V}O_2$ from their first 'hill walk' compared with their second 'hill walk', would use the same repeated measure ANOVA as above but include an 'order of test' factor (coded as poles 1st and poles 2nd). The results are shown in Box 9.13.

   Since the *P*-value for the 'order of test' factor is 0.24, the null hypothesis that the order of Pole use has no effect on average $\dot{V}O_2$ cannot be rejected (i.e. it is reasonable to assume that the order of Pole Use did not significantly affect the results of the study).

3 The repeated measures ANOVA here is based on the assumption of sphericity (i.e. the correlations between all pairs of measurements on the same subject are the same and hence the somewhat unlikely suggestion that minutes 8 and 10 are equally as related as

Box 9.13

General Linear Model: $\dot{V}O_2$ v. Pole Use, Time, Order of Test, Subject

```
Factor          Type     Levels   Values
Pole Use        fixed        2    1, 2
Time            fixed        3    1, 2, 3
Order of Test   fixed        2    Poles 1st, Poles 2nd
Subject         random      14    1, 2, 3, 4, 5, 6, 7, 8 etc.
```

Analysis of Variance for $\dot{V}O_2$, using Adjusted SS for Tests

```
Source             DF   Seq SS    Adj SS   Adj MS      F       P
Pole Use            1   66.359    66.359   66.359   52.73   0.000
Time                2   10.547    10.547    5.274    4.19   0.019
Pole Use * Time     2    0.410     0.410    0.205    0.16   0.850
Order of Test       1    1.752     1.752    1.752    1.39   0.242
Subject            13  420.948   420.948   32.381   25.73   0.000
Error              64   80.541    80.541    1.258
Total              83  580.557
```

minutes 9 and 10 etc., and that this could apply to both Pole and No Pole Use). This is assessed by the appropriate tests presented in Box 9.14, where it appears that the assumption of similar correlations between successive times is reasonable ($P = 0.327$) and that this is true regardless of Pole Use ($P = 0.590$).

Box 9.14 **Mauchly's test of sphericity**

Within-Subjects Effect	Mauchly's W	Approx. Chi-Square	df	Sig.	Epsilon		
					Greenhouse–Geisser	Huynh–Feldt	Lower-bound
Poles	1.000	.000	0	.	1.000	1.000	1.000
Time	.830	2.235	2	.327	.855	.971	.500
Poles * Time	.916	1.056	2	.590	.922	1.000	.500

Output from SPSS

4 If the *P*-value of 0.327 above seems to be too close to significance, indicating that the assumption of sphericity might not be true, then the appropriate corrected tests based on the correction factors in Box 9.14 (e.g. Greenhouse–Geisser correction factor of 0.855 for the test of the main effect of Time) are always worth considering. These are presented in a brief form in Box 9.15. There are minor changes in the *P*-values but only the lower-bound correction seems to have any moderate effect. Moreover, this procedure is far too conservative to be of any importance. Overall, therefore, the effects of any difficulty with the assumption of sphericity in this example are minor at best.

5 The multivariate tests which do not involve any such assumptions as sphericity (but are much less powerful at detecting real effects) are given in Box 9.16 and show some differences, in terms of *P*-values, from those in Box 9.15. For example, the standard univariate repeated measures test of Time has a *P*-value of 0.75 while the corresponding multivariate test has a *P*-value of 0.169. Both, of course, are non-significant,

Box 9.15 **Tests of within-subject effects**

Source		Type III Sum of Squares	df	Mean Square	F	Sig.
Time	Sphericity Assumed	10.547	2	5.274	2.866	.075
	Greenhouse–Geisser	10.547	1.709	6.170	2.866	.085
	Huynh–Feldt	10.547	1.943	5.430	2.866	.077
	Lower-bound	10.547	1.000	10.547	2.866	.114
Poles * Time	Sphericity Assumed	.410	2	.205	.338	.717
	Greenhouse–Geisser	.410	1.845	.222	.338	.700
	Huynh–Feldt	.410	2.000	.205	.338	.717
	Lower-bound	.410	1.000	.410	.338	.571

Output from SPSS

Box 9.16 **Multivariate tests**

Effect		Value	F	Hypothesis df	Error df	Sig.
Poles	Pillai's Trace	.780	46.180	1.000	13.000	.000
	Wilks' Lambda	.220	46.180	1.000	13.000	.000
	Hotelling's Trace	3.552	46.180	1.000	13.000	.000
	Roy's Largest Root	3.552	46.180	1.000	13.000	.000
Time	Pillai's Trace	.257	2.071	2.000	12.000	.169
	Wilks' Lambda	.743	2.071	2.000	12.000	.169
	Hotelling's Trace	.345	2.071	2.000	12.000	.169
	Roy's Largest Root	.345	2.071	2.000	12.000	.169
Poles * Time	Pillai's Trace	.056	.357	2.000	12.000	.707
	Wilks' Lambda	.944	.357	2.000	12.000	.707
	Hotelling's Trace	.060	.357	2.000	12.000	.707
	Roy's Largest Root	.060	.357	2.000	12.000	.707

Output from SPSS

suggesting that there is no difference in average $\dot{V}O_2$ across the three times but, even though the univariate case looks somewhat closer to showing significance, the result of the multivariate test would certainly suggest that this near significance may be based on a slight departure from the assumption of sphericity.

6 If there was concern about the influence of subject 5, who has the consistently very high $\dot{V}O_2$ values in the region of 34 to 36 ml.kg^{-1}.min^{-1}, then redo this analysis without that subject. The conclusions are more or less identical, with a P-value for the interaction of 0.89 (as opposed to 0.85 with all subjects) and the interval estimate for the effect of Pole Use of 1.34 to 2.36 ml.kg^{-1}.min^{-1} (as opposed to 1.29 to 2.27 ml.kg^{-1}.min^{-1} with all subjects).

7 Strictly speaking, the GLM used in the analysis (Box 9.11) is not the most general model that might be considered for these data. It is possible to fit interactions between the random effect of Subject and each of the fixed effects (i.e. Time and Pole Use). The interpretation of such random effect interactions is not always clear but generally could be thought of as allowing for different variability at different combinations of the fixed effects. The output from this GLM is given in Box 9.17.

Box 9.17

```
General Linear Model: V̇O₂ versus Time, Pole Use, Subject

Factor      Type     Levels    Values
Time        fixed         3    1, 2, 3
Pole Use    fixed         2    Yes, No
Subject     random       14    1, 2, 3, 4,  . . ., 13, 14

Analysis of Variance for V̇O₂, using Adjusted SS for Tests

Source              DF      Seq SS      Adj SS     Adj MS      F      P
Time                 2     10.5473     10.5473     5.2736    2.87  0.075
Pole Use             1     66.3585     66.3585    66.3585   46.18  0.000
Subject             13    420.9484    420.9484    32.3806   12.13  0.000 x
Time*Pole Use        2      0.4097      0.4097     0.2048    0.34  0.717
Time*Subject        26     47.8393     47.8393     1.8400    3.03  0.003
Pole Use*Subject    13     18.6802     18.6802     1.4369    2.37  0.030
Error               26     15.7732     15.7732     0.6067
Total               83    580.5567

x Not an exact F-test.
```

The only slight difference in conclusions based on this model is that the significance of the effect of Time changes from a *P*-value of 0.02 (see Box 9.11) to 0.075. The 'random' interactions with Time and Pole Use can perhaps be interpreted here as simply indicating small differences in variability particularly with No Pole Use at 8 minutes into the 'hill walk', but it hardly seems worth commenting on these or making the GLM more complicated by inclusion of these random 'interactions'.

8 There is no simple recipe for handling all the possible scenarios for two (or indeed more than two) within-subject factors, but the basic ideas of displaying data, the appropriate repeated measures ANOVA and any relevant follow-up multiple comparisons procedure should constitute the building blocks for the analysis of such data.

9 However, when *all of the within-subject factors are at two levels only*, it is often possible to use paired/one-sample procedures on appropriate 'differences' within each subject (see Illustration 9.4 below) to obtain an adequate analysis.

10 If the data, and hence analysis, appear to be too complicated, the sensible option is to try to find a tame and comprehensible statistician (there are a few about!).

Illustration 9.4   Altitude illness

Background

High altitude pulmonary oedema (HAPE) is a life-threatening illness. Healthy individuals are susceptible to HAPE at altitudes as low as 2700 m. Calcium antagonists, particularly nifedipine, have been shown to have a preventative and therapeutic role in HAPE. Amlodipine, another calcium antagonist, is known to have very little adverse effect on the force of contraction of the heart at rest. Thus it may be useful to evaluate this drug at altitude during exercise using a range of physiological variables. The results of the study may be of value to high-altitude climbers who have to exercise for long periods in 'thin air'.

Study description

Fourteen male regular exercisers had their Heart Rate measured both on the drug amlodipine and on a placebo both at sea level (Normoxia) and at a simulated altitude of 4500 m

(Hypoxia) during a standardised exercise bout. In Hypoxia, the subjects breathed from a 1000 litre Douglas bag with a gas mixture with a low concentration of oxygen (12.5%) which is approximately equivalent to an altitude of 4500 m.

Aims

To investigate the effect, if any, of Amlodipine on Heart Rate both in Normoxia and in Hypoxia. To discover whether any such effect is different under the two atmospheres.

Data

Name of data file:	*Altitude Illness*
Response variable:	Heart Rate (b.min^{-1})
Within-subject factors:	Drug (2 levels: Amlodipine, Placebo)
	Atmosphere (2 levels: Normoxia, Hypoxia)

Analysis

As always in such examples, a selection of plots tells most of the story. Here plots of Amlodipine against Placebo for each Atmosphere are useful (especially if both plots are on the same scale), as well as the case profile plots and box plots (see Figures 9.15 to 9.18).

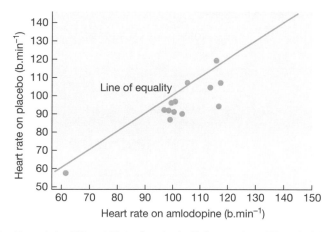

Figure 9.15 Scatter plot of Heart Rate (on Amlodipine and on Placebo) in Normoxia.

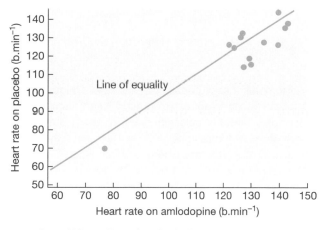

Figure 9.16 Scatter plot of Heart Rate (on Amlodipine and on Placebo) in Hypoxia.

285

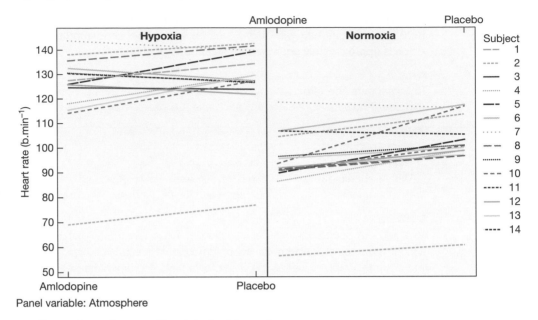

Figure 9.17 **Case profile plots by Atmosphere.**

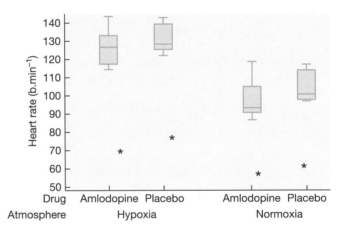

Figure 9.18 **Box plots of Heart Rate by Drug and Atmosphere.**

From all these graphs, but especially Figures 9.15 and 9.16, it can be seen that Amlodipine does appear to reduce Heart Rate but perhaps less so in Hypoxia than in Normoxia. There is a clear increase in Heart Rate in Hypoxia (compared with Normoxia) on both drugs. Although one individual (subject 3 in Figure 9.17) has much lower Heart Rates than the other 13, the changes in his Heart Rate from Placebo to Amlodipine in both Atmospheres are comparable to the changes in the other subjects and so, in terms of the effects of Drug and Atmosphere, he is not an outlier or indeed a particularly influential observation.

The formal analysis could involve a repeated measures ANOVA based on a GLM similar to that of Illustration 9.3 but, in this simpler case, it makes good sense simply to look only at the changes in Heart Rate (say, Placebo minus Amlodipine) for both Normoxia and Hypoxia and produce an interval estimate for each of the population mean changes (Box 9.18).

Box 9.18

```
Variable       N     Mean   StDev SE Mean        95% CI          T      P
Pl-Am Norm   14  7.35714  6.53225  1.74582  ( 3.58553, 11.12875)  4.21  0.001
Pl-Am Hypo   14  4.00000  7.56002  2.02050  (-0.36502,  8.36502)  1.98  0.069
```

Hence it can be deduced that, in Normoxia, Amlodipine reduces Heart Rate on average by between 4 and 11 b.min^{-1} while, in Hypoxia, it cannot quite be concluded that Amlodipine reduces Heart Rate significantly – as the interval estimate only just contains zero, i.e. is from −0.4 to +8.4 b.min^{-1}.

Conclusion

Amlodipine, on average, reduces Heart Rate at sea level (Normoxia) by between 4 and 11 b.min^{-1} but it is uncertain whether this reduction is maintained at altitude (Hypoxia).

Reference: Watt, M., Peacock, A., Aitchison, T., McDonagh., T. and Grant, S. (2000). 'The effects of amlodipine on respiratory and cardiac responses in experimental conditions of hypoxia in healthy regular exercisers.' *European Respiratory Journal*, **15**: 459–463.

Additional Comments on Illustration 9.4

1 This study was originally intended for 16 subjects with a balanced design described below. As often happens, two subjects dropped out before the study got under way. The choice of 16 subjects was based on balancing the order of first the type of Atmosphere (i.e. N or H) and then, within that, the order of Drug (i.e. P or A) where both Drugs were tested immediately after each other in the same Atmosphere. Thus there were two groups of eight subjects as follows:

Subject	Test 1	Test 2	Test 3	Test 4
1	H/A	H/P	N/P	N/A
2	H/P	H/A	N/A	N/P
3	H/P	H/A	N/P	N/A
4	H/A	H/P	N/A	N/P
5	N/P	N/A	H/A	H/P
6	N/A	N/P	H/P	H/A
7	N/P	N/A	H/P	H/A
8	N/A	N/P	H/A	H/P

2 It is sensible to test and here confirm that the order of the four tests did not influence the results of the analysis. This is achieved by running a further GLM with Order as a fixed effect to produce a *P*-value of 0.61 for Order in such a GLM.

3 The standard repeated measures ANOVA based on a GLM adds very little to the understanding of data involving within-factors with two levels. Here the results for the full model are given in Box 9.19.

4 A simpler test of the null hypothesis of 'no interaction between Atmosphere and Drug' could also be carried out by considering the *difference of the differences* in Heart Rate between Placebo and Amlodipine (i.e. the difference between these in Hypoxia and in

Box 9.19

```
Analysis of Variance for HR, using Adjusted SS for Tests

Source              DF    Seq SS    Adj SS    Adj MS      F       P
Atmosphere           1  10587.50  10587.50  10587.50  144.44  0.000
Drug                 1    451.45    451.45    451.45   12.04   0.004
Subject             13  10940.38  10940.38    841.57    8.55   0.000  x
Atmosphere*Drug      1     39.45     39.45     39.45    3.18   0.098
Atmosphere*Subject  13    952.87    952.87     73.30    5.90   0.002
Drug*Subject        13    487.43    487.43     37.49    3.02   0.028
Error               13    161.43    161.43     12.42
```

Normoxia for each subject). A one-sample *t*-analysis of the column of data consisting of the Heart Rates for (Placebo − Amlodipine)$_{Normoxia}$ minus (Placebo − Amlodipine)$_{Hypoxia}$ is all that is needed (Box 9.20).

Box 9.20

```
Variable    N    Mean    StDev  SE Mean      95% CI          T      P
P-A N-H    14  3.35714  7.04772  1.88358  (-0.712, 7.426)  1.78  0.098
```

Since the *P*-value is 0.10 and the interval (just) includes zero, strictly speaking the null hypothesis of 'no interaction' cannot be rejected (i.e. it is reasonable to assume that any difference between the average Heart Rate on the Placebo and on Amlodipine is the same for both Atmospheres, or, put another way, that the effect of the Drug is the same in Normoxia and Hypoxia). However, in this instance since the *P*-value is only a little larger than 0.05, it makes sense to report separate intervals for the effect of the Drug in Normoxia and Hypoxia.

5 It is worth investigating whether subject 3 (with low Heart Rates on all four combinations) has any substantial influence on the results by redoing the analysis missing out subject 3. The interval estimates for the effect of Amlodipine over the Placebo hardly change, being (3.5, 11.6) b.min^{-1} in Normoxia and (−1.0, 8.4) b.min^{-1} in Hypoxia compared with the full data equivalents of (3.6, 11.1) and (−0.4, 8.4) b.min^{-1}, respectively. Hence, subject 3 has no discernible effect on the conclusions.

Exercises

9.5 Two different (types of) treadmill – PowerJog and Woodway – were compared at two different target speeds (3.11 m.s^{-1} and 4.00 m.s^{-1}) with 11 regular runners used as subjects. After suitable familiarisation and warm-ups, $\dot{V}O_2$ was measured during the latter stages of 10-minute session at each speed on each treadmill. Is there any suggestion that these two treadmills produce similar performances in this type of test? The data are in the file *Treadmill Comparison*.

9.6 Anecdotal reports from Norwegian mountain rescue teams suggest that one layer of Bubble Wrap (BW) around a casualty requiring evacuation is useful in preventing loss of body heat. The aim of this study was to compare a BW bag against a previously evaluated casualty bag (CB) currently in use by some Scottish mountain rescue teams. Twelve male subjects each participated in two tests (one for each bag). Tests were carried out lying on a stretcher in a cold ($-10°C$), windy (wind speed 2.7 m.s^{-1}) environment. Reductions in Skin Temperature (assessed and averaged over four body sites) from baseline were recorded at three times (5, 15 and 25 minutes). Is there any difference in this Skin Temperature response between the two bags over the time of this test? The data are in the file *BubbleWrap3*.

The following illustration shows how to analyse a set of data with three within-subject factors.

Illustration 9.5   Drug heart rates

Background

Atenolol is a beta-blocker that is often given to cardiac patients to lower blood pressure and heart rate and thus reduce the oxygen demand of the heart. Verapamil is a calcium channel blocker that is used to help arteries relax and lessen the work of the heart. The use of these drugs has the potential to lower the likelihood of angina attacks. Cardiac patients who have certain other conditions, including asthma, may be prescribed verapamil instead of beta-blockers. Possible differences in a variety of responses to medication may result in the selection of one drug in preference to another. Results gained from 'normal' subjects may provide information that may be applicable to cardiac patients.

Study description

Eleven healthy volunteers had their Heart Rate measured at Rest and in the last minute of a standard Exercise bout on all combinations of two drugs, Atenolol and Verapamil (i.e. there were placebos for both drugs). The combinations were given in an order originally intended for 16 subjects and involved balanced Latin squares.

Aim

To discover what effect, if any, that Atenolol and Verapamil have on Heart Rate at the start and end of a standard treadmill test.

Data

Name of data file:	*Drug Heart Rates*
Response variable:	Heart Rate (b.min^{-1})
Within-subject factors:	Atenolol (2 levels: Amlodipine, APlacebo)
	Verapamil (2 levels: Verapamil, VPlacebo)
	Status (2 levels: Rest, Exercise)

Analysis

As always in such examples, a selection of plots tells most of the story. Here, simple labelled scatter plots in Figure 9.19 show the following:

● As the points in the left-hand panel are generally 'higher' than those in the right-hand panel, Exercise increases the Heart Rate regardless of drug combination.

● As all the points in both panels lie well above the line of equality, there is a marked reduction of heart rate on Atenolol.

● As the labelled points show moderate differences in each panel, there is a moderate effect of Verapamil.

289

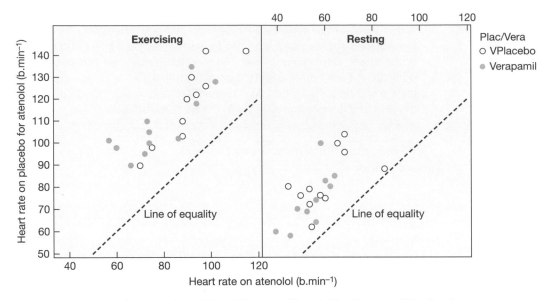

Figure 9.19 **Scatter plot of Heart Rate by Atenolol by Verapamil by Regime.**

- There is a suggestion of an increased effect of Atenolol on Exercise (as compared with its effect while at Rest) as the points in the left-hand panel are generally further from the line of equality than in the right-hand panel.

These main effects of all three factors are evident in the box plots of Figure 9.20 and the plot of the pairwise sample means in Figure 9.21, but in neither is there much suggestion of a possible interaction between Atenolol and Status (i.e. Exercise or Rest).

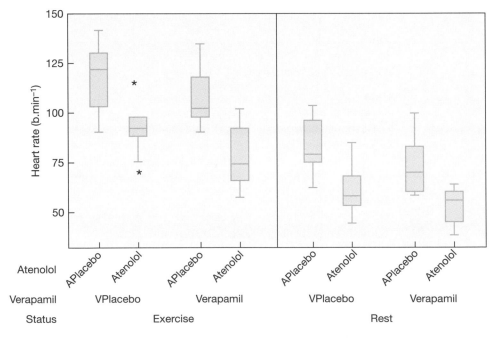

Figure 9.20 **Box plots of Heart Rate by Status, Verapamil and Atenolol.**

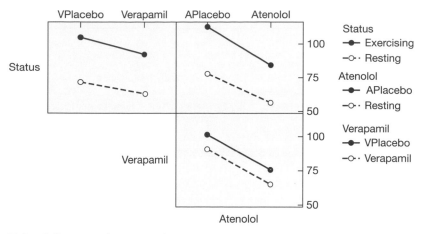

Units of all axes are beats per minute

Figure 9.21 **Sample mean plot for Heart Rate by Factors.**

The formal analysis incorporates fixed effects of these three factors as well as a random effect of subject (i.e. allowing for the fact that eight measurements are taken on each subject). The resulting ANOVA table is given in Box 9.21 and confirms the (highly) significant main effects of all three factors. It also provides the first concrete evidence of an interaction between Atenolol and Status with a *P*-value of 0.02.

Box 9.21

```
Analysis of Variance for Heart Rate, using Adjusted SS for Tests

Source                    DF    Seq SS    Adj SS    Adj MS        F       P
Status                     1   22240.9   22240.9   22240.9   373.68   0.000
Verapamil                  1    2457.1    2457.1    2457.1    41.28   0.000
Atenolol                   1   14280.0   14280.0   14280.0   239.93   0.000
Status*Verapamil           1     106.9     106.9     106.9     1.80   0.184
Status*Atenolol            1     324.6     324.6     324.6     5.45   0.022
Verapamil*Atenolol         1       0.6       0.6       0.6     0.01   0.923
Status*Verapamil*Atenolol  1      23.0      23.0      23.0     0.39   0.536
Subject                   10    9737.7    9737.7     973.8    16.36   0.000
Error                     70    4166.3    4166.3      59.5
Total                     87   53337.1
```

While appropriate interval estimates for the main effects could be provided on the basis of the full repeated measures ANOVA model, it is not really appropriate to do because of the presence of the significant interaction. A better approach is simply to separate out the data into eight columns corresponding to the eight combinations of the three factors and then provide interval estimates of appropriate contrasts of these (i.e. simply add or subtract all the columns in an appropriate manner).

For the main effect of, say, Verapamil, this is simply the sum of the four columns where Verapamil is used minus the sum of the four columns where the Placebo (for Verapamil) was used. Accordingly, from Box 9.22, Verapamil reduces Heart Rate, on average, by between 5 and 16 b.min^{-1}. To quantify the 'interaction' between Atenolol and Status, Box 9.22 provides interval estimates for the 'effects' of Atenolol (compared with its placebo)

Box 9.22

Variable	Estimate	ESE	95% CI
Verapamil Main Effect	10.5682	2.3438	(5.3459, 15.7904)
Variable	Estimate	ESE	95% CI
Atenolol Exercise	21.6364	1.5331	(18.2204, 25.0523)
Atenolol Rest	29.3182	1.8244	(25.2531, 33.3832)

for both levels of Status – by using appropriate sums and differences of the four columns for each level of Status. These intervals do not overlap, which is really what the significant 'interaction' is showing, and, further, show that the reduction in Heart Rate due to Atenolol is between 18 and 25 b.min^{-1} towards the end of the Exercise bout but between 25 and 34 b.min^{-1} at Rest (i.e. significantly more of an 'Atenolol' effect at Rest compared with the end of the steady state Exercise bout). In both cases it is clear that the effect of Atenolol is significantly greater than that of Verapamil, which is around 5 and 16 b.min^{-1} for both Rest and Exercise.

Conclusion

Atenolol and Verapamil both significantly reduce Heart Rates, on average, at Rest and at the end of Exercise. Atenolol has a significantly greater effect than Verapamil especially at Rest.

Additional comment on Illustration 9.5

This study was originally intended for 16 subjects with the design based on four balanced Latin squares but recruitment of subjects proved difficult and only 11 volunteers were eventually used. Disappointing but unfortunately all too common in small studies – beware!

Summary

To cover designed studies with only within-subject factors, the following scenarios were illustrated in this chapter:

- One within-subject factor at two levels.

- One within-subject factor at three levels.

- Two within-subject factors at two and three levels, respectively.

- Two within-subject factors each with two levels.

- Three within-subject factors all at two levels.

Graphical procedures such as case profile plots, box plots and scatter plots with a line of equality were used to obtain subjective impressions of the data.

Formal analysis was generally based on repeated measures ANOVA with subjects identified through a random effect and, where appropriate, a follow-up multiple comparison. For problems involving within-subject factors with two levels, paired-sample t-intervals often turn out to be sufficient, and generally these use differences of observations on the same subject.

Although general approaches to these types of problem can be suggested, always endeavour to be flexible in any analysis in an attempt to reflect the underlying aims of the study.

10 Investigating studies with between-subject and within-subject factors: more on dependent observations

Introduction

Many studies involving within-subject factors are often carried out on samples from different and distinct populations, such as males and females or athletes and non-athletes, i.e. with each subject belonging to one and only one of these between-subject populations. A study may even involve only one population, where subjects from a random sample from the target population are then randomly allocated to receive an intervention or a control, where the intervention may be a method of relaxation, such as meditation, and the target population is club middle distance runners.

It is usually possible to uniquely define a factor to specify such populations, and in such circumstances this is referred to as a **between-subject factor** where subjects can belong to one and only one of the 'levels' (i.e. populations/ treatments, etc.) of this factor. Note carefully the distinction between a **between-subject factor** where subjects are associated with *one and only one level* of the between-subject factor and a **repeated measures/within-subject factor** where each subject has his/her response measured at *every level* of the within-subject factor.

In studies involving one or more between-subject factors and one or more within-subject factors, interest will often lie in comparing the average profile (across the within-factor(s)) among the levels of the between-subject factor(s) and hence there may be a whole series of main effects and interactions to be investigated both among and between between- and within-subject factors. As usual, when any of the factors (between- or within-subject) is at two levels only, then part of the analysis can sometimes be simplified to two-sample and paired-sample *t*-intervals.

The basic model for the standard analysis (a repeated measures ANOVA) for such datasets assumes the usual additive structure for the effect of all between- and within-factors through main effects and interactions with a Normally distributed error/variability term for each individual measurement as well as a further additive random effect term for each subject assumed to be Normally distributed with a zero average across the population of subjects. This so-called *univariate repeated measures model* implies the assumption of sphericity which in effect assumes that all measurements on the same subject have equal correlations with every other measurement on that subject. This really only has consequences for the analysis if the within-factors are at three or more levels, and the ideas of *multivariate tests* and 'lack of sphericity' corrections (such as the Greenhouse–Geisser correction) introduced in the previous chapter can be extended here.

In this chapter, the following combinations of between-subject and within-subject factor studies will be illustrated:

- *One between* at two levels and *one within* at two levels.
- *One between* at two levels and *one within* at $K > 2$ levels.
- *One between* at $K > 2$ levels and *two within* each at two levels.
- *Two between* each at two levels and *one within* at two levels.
- *Two between* each at two levels and *two within* each at two levels.

Obviously, any combination of any number of between- and within-subject factors may be encountered in practice (and at any number of levels of each factor), but it is impossible to give simple recipes to deal with all possibilities. Nevertheless, it is hoped that the analyses introduced through these five illustrations give a reasonable guide to how to approach almost any problem of this type.

10.2 One between-subject factor at two levels and one within-subject factor at two levels

This scenario was introduced in Chapter 4 when it was considered simply in terms of paired-sample and two-sample *t*-problems. Here, it is included as the simplest form of a repeated measures problem with between- and within-subject factors.

When a researcher has data involving a response variable being measured under two distinct and different levels/conditions (within-subject factor) on each of two separate samples of subjects (between-subject factor), the following steps should be carried out:

1 Provide a scatter plot of the two levels of the within-subject factor labelled by the between-subject factor and with a line of equality superimposed on the plot.

2 Assuming this plot shows a general pattern of points (i.e. subjects for both levels of the between-subject factor) roughly parallel to the line of equality – but possibly widely spread about such a parallel line – then take the *differences* between the two levels of the within-subject factor (for each subject at each level of the between-subject factor) and provide box plots of these by the between-subject factor with a line of zero (i.e. no change in the within-subject factor) superimposed on the box plot.

3 Assuming these differences (for each level of the between-subject factor) appear to have arisen from Normal populations, then simply produce an *interval estimate for the difference* (between the levels of the between-subject factor) *in population average differences* (i.e. differences between the levels of the within-subject factor) which will provide quantification of the magnitude of the difference between the relevant population average differences, if any, between the two populations which constitute the two levels of the between-subject factor.

Illustration 10.1 Overweight women and exercise

Background

Obesity is an ever-increasing problem in the western world. Problems associated with obesity include a greater incidence of diabetes and coronary heart disease. One problem often encountered by the obese and substantially overweight is limited mobility. Exercise programmes have the potential to enhance mobility by decreasing body mass and by improving strength and endurance.

Study background

Twenty-six overweight middle-aged females were randomly allocated to be either an Exerciser or a Control. The Exercisers were asked to carry out two (aerobic and strength) exercise sessions per week for 12 weeks. One key variable used to investigate the usefulness of the exercise programme was the time taken for the woman to walk 20 metres from a standing start.

Aim

To investigate whether such an Exercise Regime can significantly improve the short distance walking of overweight women over a 12-week period of this form of Exercise over any 'natural' improvement of Controls.

Data

Name of data file:	*20m Walk*
Response variable:	Walking Time (seconds)
Between-subject factor:	Exercise Regime (2 levels: Exercise, Control)
Within-subject factor	Time (2 levels: Pre-Study, Post-Study)

Analysis

Start by creating a scatter plot (Figure 10.1) of the Pre and Post Walking Times for each woman using a different label for the two levels of the between-subject factor (i.e. Control and Exercise). Assess from this plot a sensible range of the variable being covered in the plot (e.g. 14 to 24 seconds here) and then draw in the line of equality (i.e. the line of no change over the 12 weeks of the study).

Figure 10.1 indicates that the Exercisers do, in general, appear to show a modest improvement over the study (i.e. decrease their 20 m Walking Time) while the situation is less

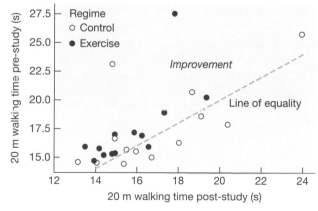

Figure 10.1 Scatter plot of 20 m Walking Times (Pre- and Post-Study) by Exercise Regime.

clear-cut for the Controls. However, there are two subjects (one in each Exercise Regime and in the top left of Figure 10.1) who show quite dramatic improvements over the study. These may have a substantial impact on any analysis and would make a diligent researcher wonder about the authenticity of these subjects' results.

Both Regimes tend to show changes (i.e. Pre-Study 20 m Walking Time minus Post-Study 20 m Walking Time) that are, in general, parallel to the line of equality and thus suggest that there is a consistent and constant change not dependent, in any sense, on the magnitude of the subject's 20 m Walking Time. This ensures that the use of the simple changes (i.e. Pre-Study minus Post-Study 20 m Walking Times) will give an adequate summary of the effect of the Exercise intervention.

Figure 10.2 shows the box plots of these changes by Exercise Regime and, while confirming the general improvement of Exercisers, suggests that there may not be a great difference, if any, between Controls and Exercisers since the box plots overlap considerably regardless of the two possible outliers with very high improvements.

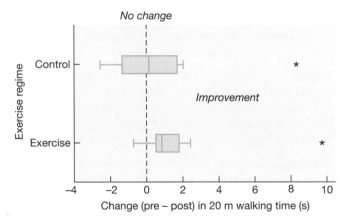

Figure 10.2 **Box plot of change (Pre minus Post) in 20 m Walking Time by Exercise Regime.**

The summary statistics of these changes (Box 10.1) also indicate this degree of overlap as well as the effect of the two potential outliers – note the differences between sample mean and sample median for each Exercise Regime caused by each outlier.

As was seen in Chapter 4, the formal analysis involves a simple two-sample comparison of these changes between the two Exercise Regimes to obtain the output in Box 10.2.

Box 10.1

```
Descriptive Statistics: Change in 20 m Walking Time(secs)

Variable   Regime      N    Mean  StDev  Minimum      Q1  Median      Q3
Change     Control    13   0.594  2.753   -2.540  -1.350   0.130   1.720
           Exercise   13   1.666  2.558   -0.690   0.530   0.850   1.810

Variable   Regime      Maximum
Change     Control       8.320
           Exercise      9.750
```

Box 10.2

```
Two-Sample T-Test and CI: Change (Pre - Post) in 20 m Walk by Exercise
Regime

Regime     N   Mean  StDev  SE Mean
Control   13   0.59   2.75     0.76
Exercise  13   1.67   2.56     0.71


Difference = mu (Control) - mu (Exercise)
Estimate for difference: -1.07
95% CI for difference:  (-3.23, 1.08)
T-Test of difference = 0 (vs not =): T-Value = -1.03 P-value = 0.314 DF = 23
```

Since the *P*-value of 0.314 is not less than 0.05, it must be concluded that Exercise does not produce a significantly different change in 20 m Walking Time on average from Controls over a 12-week period of study.

To understand better why this somewhat discouraging conclusion has been arrived at, provide interval estimates for the average change in 20 m Walking Time for each Regime separately, as in Box 10.3.

Box 10.3

```
One-Sample T: Change in 20 m Walk_Control, Change in 20 m Walk_Exercise

Test of mu = 0 vs not = 0

Variable                N   Mean  StDev  SE Mean      95% CI          T     P
Change for Controls    13  0.594  2.753   0.764  (-1.070, 2.258)  0.78  0.452
Change for Exercisers  13  1.666  2.558   0.709  ( 0.121, 3.212)  2.35  0.037
```

On the basis of these, it can be seen that, on average, Controls do not significantly improve over the study period (since the interval of −1.1 to 2.3 seconds does include zero) whereas the Exercisers do, in general, improve 20 m Walking Time by between 0.1 and 3.2 seconds on average. However, there is a lot of overlap between these two intervals and that is why the two-sample comparison turns out non-significant, as a moderate 'improvement' cannot be ruled out for the Controls.

Conclusion

Overweight women, on average, have not been shown to benefit significantly from a 12-week period of exercise in terms of the time they take to walk 20 metres from a standing start.

Reference: Grant, S., Todd, K., Aitchison, T.C., Kelly, P. and Stoddart, D. (2004). 'The effects of a 12 week group exercise programme on physiological and psychological variables and function in elderly obese women.' *Journal of Public Health*, **118**: 31–42.

Additional comments on Illustration 10.1

1 The assumption of Normality for each sample looks plausible (from the Normal probability plots of the changes for each Exercise Regime separately) but, if the researcher was so inclined, he/she could carry out the equivalent non-parametric procedure, the Wilcoxon–Mann–Whitney test, as displayed in Box 10.4.

Box 10.4

```
Mann-Whitney Test and CI: Change in 20 m Walk_Control, Change in 20 m
Walk_Exercise

                                 N  Median
Change in 20 m Walk_Control     13  0.130
Change in 20 m Walk_Exercise    13  0.850

Point estimate for ETA1-ETA2 is -1.090
95.4 Percent CI for ETA1-ETA2 is (-2.470,0.492)
W = 146.5
Test of ETA1 = ETA2 vs ETA1 not = ETA2 is significant at 0.1439
The test is significant at 0.1438 (adjusted for ties)
```

On this occasion the conclusion of the hypothesis test is the same although the *P*-value of 0.144 is closer to significance than that for the two-sample *t*-test of 0.314. Further, the corresponding interval estimate (albeit for the difference in population medians rather than means) of –2.5 to +0.5 seconds is a little narrower than that for the Normal-based approach (i.e. –3.2 to +1.1 seconds) but still suggesting no significant effect of Exercise.

2 The effect, if any, on the conclusions of the two suspicious subjects with very high improvements must be investigated and this is perhaps best done by simply repeating the formal analysis without these two subjects (see Box 10.5). This does make a substantial difference to the *P*-value for testing 'no difference in average changes between the two Regimes' by reducing it from 0.314 to 0.057. Not quite significant but indicating the effect of both these outliers on the original conclusions and suggesting that it would be worthwhile to increase the sample sizes for both regimes in a further study as well as perhaps increasing the length of such a study from 12 weeks.

Box 10.5

```
Two-Sample T-Test and CI: Change in 20 m Walk, Regime

Regime     N    Mean   StDev   SE Mean
Control    12   -0.05  1.55    0.45
Exercise   12   0.992  0.837   0.24

Difference = mu (Control) - mu (Exercise)
Estimate for difference:  -1.042
95% CI for difference:  (-2.118, 0.033)
T-Test of difference = 0 (vs not =): T-Value = -2.05 P-value = 0.057 DF = 16

One-Sample T: Change in 20 m Walk_Control, Change in 20 m Walk_Exercise

Test of mu = 0 vs not = 0

Variable                  N    Mean StDev SE Mean      95% CI          T     P
Change for Controls       12 -0.050 1.546   0.446 (-1.032, 0.932) -0.11 0.913
Change for Exercisers     12  0.992 0.837   0.242 ( 0.461, 1.524)  4.11 0.002
```

However, from this study with or without the suspicious subjects, it is clear that any improvement is modest as the Pre-Study sample mean for all subjects was around 17 seconds and the potential improvement for the Exercisers gave a 95% CI of around 0.5 to 1.5 seconds (see Box 10.5), i.e. a 5% to 10% increase at most.

10.1 The Osteoporosis and Exercise study used in Illustration 4.5 involved the measurement of other variables such as a measure of Flexibility, the sit-and-reach test. Investigate, using the methods above, whether the Exercise intervention improved this measure of Flexibility significantly more on average than for Controls. If so, by how much more?

10.2 Ankylosing spondylitis (AS) is a debilitating condition which can have wide ranging and varied effects, particularly in restriction of movement of the spinal and thoracic areas. An exercise programme may improve (i.e. increase) cervical rotation in these patients, resulting in enhanced mobility. A sample of 42 AS sufferers were randomised to be either a Control or to undergo an Exercise Intervention for a period of 12 weeks. Is there evidence that the Exercise Intervention, on average, improved Cervical Rotation significantly over Controls? If so, how much of a difference is there? The data are in the file *Ankylosing Spondylitis*.

10.3 One between-subject factor at two levels and one within-subject factor at $K > 2$ levels

When the researcher has data involving a response variable being measured under *three or more* (in general K) distinct and different conditions or levels of the within-subject factor on (hopefully random) samples of subjects at each of the two levels of the between-subject factor, he/she should:

1 Provide scatter plots of all pairwise combinations of the K levels, each plot labelled by the between-subject factor and with the same line of equality superimposed.

2 Draw up individual profile plots of the response variable across the K levels, with the values for each subject connected, separately for each level of the between-subject factor. Augment this with the corresponding box plots for the K levels with the sample medians connected, again separately for each of the between-subject factor levels.

3 Assuming the profile plots look roughly parallel across subjects and that each box plot looks roughly Normally distributed, then carry out a repeated measures ANOVA. This approach is appropriate as long as the researcher includes a random subject factor which allows for the dependence across the observations of each subject. This analysis involves three hypothesis tests, comprising the main effects of each of the between and within subject factors, respectively, and the interaction between them.

4 If all of the hypothesis tests prove *non-significant* (i.e. all three P-values >0.05), then the researcher can stop and conclude that neither the between-subject factor nor the within-subject factor has any (significant) effect on the response variable. However, if the *interaction proves significant*, the researcher has a relatively 'complicated' result in that, the effect of the between-subject factor is to change the response across the levels of the within-subject factor. The best approach then

may be to produce a set of simultaneous comparisons between the two levels of the between-subject factor at each level of the within-subject factor. If the test of *interaction proves non-significant*, but one or other or both of the main effects (of within- and between-subject factors, respectively) does prove significant, then the researcher simply provides either a *follow-up pairwise multiple comparison procedure* of the K levels of the within-subject factor to discover which levels are significant and/or a simple two-sample *t*-interval for the (main) effect of the between-subject factor. Both of these procedures are carried out automatically by most statistical packages and actually involve the averages, for each subject, of the response variable across the 'other factor'.

Illustration 10.2   Exercise in pregnancy

Background

Pregnancy can often result in major psychological trauma for the mother. A midwife in a West of Scotland local hospital believed that regular exercise would benefit expectant (and recent) mothers not only physically but also mentally. Subsequently, she devised a simple questionnaire to 'measure' various aspects of a mother's mental health with respect to how she coped both during and just after the pregnancy. This Coping Assets score ranged from 0 to 50, with high values denoting subjects who were having only a few problems coping with the pregnancy and indeed life in general.

Study description

All expectant mothers, over a three-month period, in the catchment area were invited to take part in the study and, if consenting, were then randomised to be a Control (who carried on with their 'natural' lifestyle) or an Exerciser (who attended twice weekly exercise classes for pregnant women). After drop-outs – none due to 'exercise' problems or non-attendance at exercise classes – there remained 34 Controls and 39 Exercisers. Each mother-to-be completed a questionnaire from which this Coping Assets score was calculated as early as possible on recruitment to the study, as late as possible in the pregnancy (usually around 38 weeks), and then post-pregnancy (usually around 12 weeks after delivery). All mothers in this study delivered healthy singleton babies at around term (approximately 40 weeks).

Aim

To investigate whether Exercise classes of this nature have, on average, a beneficial effect (as measured by the Coping Assets score) on mothers during or after pregnancy compared with Controls.

Data

Name of data file:	*Exercise in Pregnancy*
Response variable:	Coping Assets (score from 0 to 50)
Between-subject factor:	Exercise Regime (2 levels: Exercisers, Controls)
Within-subject factor:	Stage (3 levels: Early, Late, Post pregnancy)

Analysis

It is arguable here whether the Early Coping Assets scores can be considered as baselines since not all subjects provided scores before introduction to the Exercise classes. However, the effect of Exercise may not manifest itself in the early stages and differences between Exercisers and Controls may be found only at the two later stages of pregnancy.

So, at first here, consider all three levels of the within-subject factor (i.e. Early, Late and Post pregnancy) rather than a new within-subject factor of two levels incorporating the changes in Coping Assets score (i.e. Late minus Early and Post minus Early).

The three pairwise plots of the Coping Assets scores for the three stages of pregnancy are plotted in Figures 10.3 to 10.5 labelled by Exercise Regime. From these it looks clear that both in Late and Post pregnancy the Controls seem, in general, to have reduced ability to cope (i.e. Coping Assets score) whereas the Exercisers appear, on average, to remain roughly unchanged from Early to Late pregnancy and seem to increase Post pregnancy (in terms of the Coping Assets score).

Figure 10.6 provides the case profile plots for the effects of Stage in pregnancy separately for the Exercisers and Controls. These show considerable variability among the women and indeed among their responses across the pregnancy. Some women bounce back from severe falls in Coping Assets Late in pregnancy whereas others keep falling Post pregnancy. In general though, the plot shows a general downward trend for the Controls whereas the Exercisers hardly show this at all and, if anything, tend to finish higher Post pregnancy than in Early pregnancy.

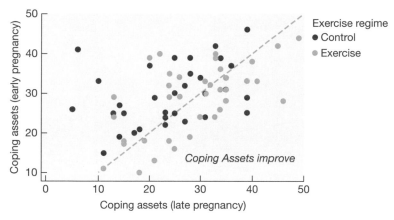

Figure 10.3 Scatter plot of Coping Assets Early by Late Pregnancy by Exercise Regime.

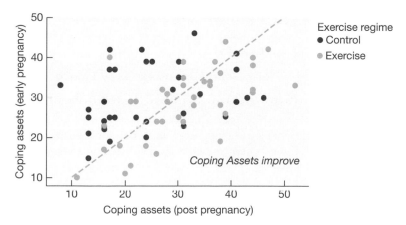

Figure 10.4 Scatter plot of Coping Assets Early by Post Pregnancy by Exercise Regime.

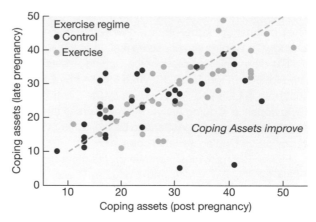

Figure 10.5 **Scatter plot of Coping Assets Late by Post Pregnancy by Exercise Regime.**

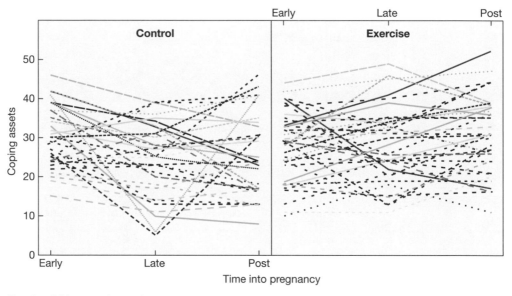

Panel variable: exercise regime

Figure 10.6 **Profile plots of Coping Assets by Time for each Exercise Regime.**

The box plots in Figure 10.7, while not showing the individual trends, do show that although the two samples start roughly equal in terms of distribution of Coping Assets score, the Exercisers tend to maintain their scores Late in pregnancy and indeed increase them Post pregnancy, unlike the Controls whose scores decrease, in general, at both these stages. This is further confirmed by the sample means from each of the combinations of the within- and between-subject factors in Box 10.6.

To formally investigate these data, the researcher should carry out a repeated measures ANOVA with Exercise Regime and Stage in Pregnancy as fixed factors (with two and

Box 10.6

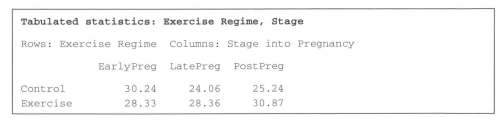

```
Tabulated statistics: Exercise Regime, Stage

Rows: Exercise Regime   Columns: Stage into Pregnancy

             EarlyPreg  LatePreg  PostPreg

Control         30.24     24.06     25.24
Exercise        28.33     28.36     30.87
```

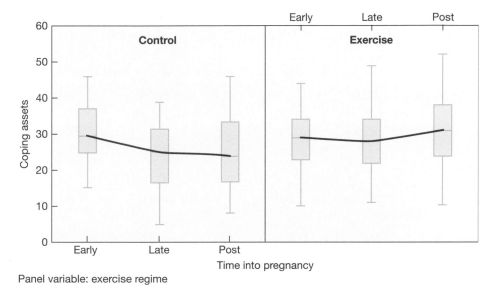

Panel variable: exercise regime

Figure 10.7 **Box plot of Coping Assets by Time for each Exercise Regime.**

three levels, respectively) and with a subject identifier/number as a random factor which, crucially, is **nested** within Exercise Regime, i.e. subjects appear in one and only one Exercise Regime in the study. The resulting ANOVA table is given in Box 10.7.

Box 10.7

```
General Linear Model: Coping by Exercise Regime, Stage, Subject

Factor                      Type   Levels  Values
Exercise Regime             fixed       2  Control, Exercise
Stage                       fixed       3  EarlyPreg, LatePreg, PostPreg
Subject(Exercise Regime) random       73  6, 14, 15, 21, 26, 37, 42, etc.

Analysis of Variance for Coping Assets, using Adjusted SS for Tests

Source                     DF     Seq SS    Adj SS   Adj MS     F      P
Exercise Regime             1     390.87    390.87   390.87  2.19  0.144
Subject(Exercise Regime)   71  12692.69  12692.69   178.77  4.44  0.000
Stage                       2     309.43    348.17   174.08  4.32  0.015
Exercise Regime*Stage       2     587.80    587.80   293.90  7.29  0.001
Error                     142    5721.43   5721.43    40.29
Total                     218  19702.23
```

303

The key element of this ANOVA table is the significant P-value (0.001) for the interaction between Exercise Regime and Stage into pregnancy; the other P-values are of little interest because of this. This significant interaction indicates that the pattern of response across the Stages of pregnancy is significantly different on average for the two Exercise Regimes. So the next step in the formal analysis is to investigate at which Stages these significant differences appear. Here there is the choice of either simply providing a set of intervals comparing the two Regimes at each of the three Stages, or using the Early pregnancy score as a baseline and providing interval estimates comparing the Regimes for the *changes* from Early pregnancy to Late and Post pregnancy, respectively. The latter approach seems the more sensible here and the resulting intervals can be seen in Box 10.8.

Box 10.8

```
Two-Sample T-Test and CI: Coping Assets Late - Early by Regime

Regime        N    Mean   StDev   SE Mean
Control       34   -6.18   9.64     1.7
Exercise      39    0.03   8.11     1.3

Difference = mu (Control) - mu (Exercise)
Estimate for difference:  -6.20211
95% CI for difference:  (-10.40110, -2.00313)

Two-Sample T-Test and CI: Coping Assets Post - Early by Regime

Regime        N   Mean   StDev   SE Mean
Control       34   -5.0   10.9     1.9
Exercise      39   2.54    7.99    1.3

Difference = mu (Control) - mu (Exercise)
Estimate for difference:  -7.53846
95% CI for difference:  (-12.07381, -3.00311)
```

From these intervals, it can be seen that, on average, Exercise significantly benefits mothers-to-be by between 2 and 10 units on the Coping Assets scale Late in pregnancy and between 3 and 12 units Post pregnancy (over their Early pregnancy 'coping level'). Since the typical Early pregnancy Coping Assets score is around 30 units, an improvement of up to 10 or 12 units is more than substantial.

Conclusion

Participation in regular exercise sessions during pregnancy can have a beneficial effect on the ability of expectant mothers to cope in late and post pregnancy in Normal, healthy singleton pregnancies.

Reference: Jeanie Blakely Rankin (1999). 'Primigravid women and the effects of exercise on psychological well-being, pregnancy and birth outcome.' PhD thesis University of Glasgow.

Additional comments on Illustration 10.2

1 The assumptions of Normality for each subject and for the variability at each Stage on each Exercise Regime look quite plausible but should be checked using separate probability plots for subject and error/measurement effects.

2 The assumption of constant correlation, or sphericity, can and should be checked and the corrections for lack of symmetry made, if necessary, since the within-subject factor has three levels. The resultant output is given in Box 10.9 and there is clearly no problem

Box 10.9

Mauchly's Test of Sphericity(b)

Within Subjects Effect	Mauchly's W	Approx. Chi-Square	df	Sig.	Epsilon(a)		
					Greenhouse–Geisser	Huynh–Feldt	Lower-bound
Stage	.987	.933	2	.627	.987	1.000	.500

Tests of Within-Subjects Effects

Source		Type III Sum of Squares	df	Mean Square	F	Sig.
Stage	Sphericity Assumed	348.167	2	174.084	4.321	.015
	Greenhouse–Geisser	348.167	1.974	176.388	4.321	.015
	Huynh–Feldt	348.167	2.000	174.084	4.321	.015
	Lower-bound	348.167	1.000	348.167	4.321	.041
Stage * ExerGroup_1	Sphericity Assumed	587.802	2	293.901	7.294	.001
	Greenhouse–Geisser	587.802	1.974	297.791	7.294	.001
	Huynh–Feldt	587.802	2.000	293.901	7.294	.001
	Lower-bound	587.802	1.000	587.802	7.294	.009
Error(Stage)	Sphericity Assumed	5721.431	142	40.292		
	Greenhouse–Geisser	5721.431	140.145	40.825		
	Huynh–Feldt	5721.431	142.000	40.292		
	Lower-bound	5721.431	71.000	80.584		

Output from SPSS

with the assumption of symmetry as the P-value is 0.627–testing a null hypothesis of the symmetry assumption being true. Further, the corrections, particularly Greenhouse–Geisser, make little or no difference to the P-values of the univariate repeated measures ANOVA.

3 The results of the corresponding multivariate tests are given in Box 10.10 and are clearly not dissimilar from the univariate tests since the assumption of sphericity is not at all unreasonable here.

Box 10.10

Multivariate Tests

Effect		Value	F	Hypothesis df	Error df	Sig.
Stage	Pillai's Trace	.115	4.542(a)	2.000	70.000	.014
	Wilks' Lambda	.885	4.542(a)	2.000	70.000	.014
	Hotelling's Trace	.130	4.542(a)	2.000	70.000	.014
	Roy's Largest Root	.130	4.542(a)	2.000	70.000	.014
Stage* ExerGroup_1	Pillai's Trace	.157	6.526(a)	2.000	70.000	.003
	Wilks' Lambda	.843	6.526(a)	2.000	70.000	.003
	Hotelling's Trace	.186	6.526(a)	2.000	70.000	.003
	Roy's Largest Root	.186	6.526(a)	2.000	70.000	.003

a Exact statistic
b Design: Intercept+ExerGroup   Within Subjects Design: Stage

Output from SPSS

10.3 A sample of 28 recreational distance runners was taken and randomised into a Control and a Treatment sample. In the Treatment sample each subject was further randomised to either Meditation or Progressive Muscular Relaxation (PMR) as a potential way of reducing oxygen cost of running and of lowering exercise Heart Rate. The Heart Rates in the last minute of a standardised (running) exercise bout of all 28 athletes (13 controls, 8 on Meditation and 7 on PMR) were taken both before and after two months of 'treatment' where the appropriate 'treatment' was adhered to by each runner for the two-month period. The reduction in Heart Rate over this period was taken as the response variable. Is there a significant difference, on average, between any of the three methods of relaxation? If so, which methods are different and by how much? The data are in the file *Relaxation*.

10.4 The Exercise in Pregnancy study (see Illustration 10.2) used other measures of the pregnant women's psychological status such as a score of Physical Well-Being. Is there evidence from these data, in the file *Exercise in Pregnancy*, that the Exercise Regime has significantly improved, on average, the measure of Physical Well-Being more than in Controls and, if so, at what times during the pregnancy?

10.5 Each of a sample of Glasgow University sports science students had their Anaerobic Power measured by each of three methods: the Lewis, Margaria and Wingate methods. Also recorded was the Sex of each student. Is there any evidence that the (suspected) Sex difference in Anaerobic Power is significantly different for the three methods of measuring this? If so, which methods are different and by how much? Do the methods appear to measure the same average for Anaerobic Power for both Males and Females? The data are in the file *Anaerobic Power*.

10.4 One between-subject factor at $K > 2$ levels and two within-subject factors each at two levels

When a researcher has data involving a response variable being measured under distinct and different conditions or levels of two within-subject factors on (hopefully random) samples of subjects at each of the three or more levels of the between-subject factor, the following steps are appropriate:

1 Provide scatter plots of any interesting pairwise combinations of the levels of the two within-factors, each plot labelled by the between-subject factor and with, as appropriate, a line of equality superimposed. It often is sensible to put all these plots on the same scales.

2 Draw up individual 'profile' plots of the response variable across each pair of levels of the two within-factors with the values for each subject connected, separately for each level of the between-subject factor. Augment this with the corresponding box plots for the four combinations of the two within-factors with the sample medians connected, again separately for each of the between-subject factor levels.

3 Assuming the profile plots look roughly parallel across subjects and that each box plot looks roughly Normally distributed, then carry out a repeated measures ANOVA

which, as long as the researcher includes a random subject factor, allows for the dependence across the observations of each subject and involves hypothesis tests for the main effects of both the between- and both within-factors as well as all three two-way interactions and the three-way interaction between all three factors (i.e. the between- and both the within-subject factors).

4   If all of the hypothesis tests prove *non-significant* (i.e. all *P*-values >0.05), then the researcher could stop but would be better eliminating one term (i.e. three-way, two-way interactions and main effects) at a time from the ANOVA table (starting with the three-way interaction, then each of the two-way Interactions) until all non-significant terms from the model are removed. It is almost essential (in terms of interpretation) to remove all interactions before starting to remove any main effects.

Once all non-significant terms have been removed, the researcher then has to interpret the remaining (significant) terms, and how to do this depends crucially on what terms remain. If it is *only main effects remaining*, then look at these separately by producing appropriate follow-up multiple comparisons of the levels of each (significant) factor whether it is the between-subject factor or indeed either of the within-factors. Note that, for each within-factor, this is simply a paired comparison between the two levels of that factor. However, if any of the *two-way interactions prove significant*, this is a relatively complicated result where no simple recipe is available and is often best handled by appropriate multiple comparisons across the between-subject factor of the differences between the two levels of the within-factor whose interaction with the between-subject factor is significant. Significant two-way interactions between the within-factors can often be handled by paired-sample *t*-intervals of the difference of the differences of the two within-factors but a significant three-way interaction will have to be interpreted with great care.

Illustration 10.3   Kicking the habit

Background

There is limited information on the physiological characteristics of elite youth soccer players in Scotland. Comparisons, with physiological data from other countries may demonstrate that Scottish players have relatively low fitness levels which could have a detrimental effect on playing performance. For example, some studies have shown that fitter teams have a higher league position than less fit teams. It is reported that many children in Scotland have a relatively sedentary lifestyle which is considered to have an adverse effect on health. Comparison of professional and recreational youth soccer players with non-soccer players may highlight the benefit of taking part in regular physical activity.

Study description

Each subject in samples of 19 Professional soccer players, 19 Recreational soccer players and 10 Non-Soccer players had both legs tested on an isokinetic dynamometer at velocities of 30 and 180 deg.s^{-1}. Four maximal efforts were given for each leg at each Velocity and the highest score recorded as the measurement of interest, i.e. Concentric Knee Extension Peak Torque in newton metres (N·m).

Aim

To investigate differences in Knee Extension Peak Torque (PT) between the Right and Left legs and at different Velocities (using an isokinetic dynamometer) across three populations of soccer players.

Data

Name of data file:	*Kicking the Habit*
Response variable:	Knee Extension PT (newton metres)
Between-subject factor:	Soccer Level (3 levels: Professional, Recreational, Non-Soccer)
Within-subject factors:	Velocity (2 levels: 30, 180 deg.s^{-1})
	Side (2 levels: Left, Right leg)

Analysis

First provide plots (Figures 10.8 and 10.9) of the Knee Extension PT of the Right against the Left leg for each Velocity separately with each plot on the same scale and labelled by the Soccer Level. A suitable choice for the line of equality here (after examination of the plots) is from 70 to 260 N·m.

These plots suggest that:

1 the 30 deg.s^{-1} Knee Extension PT scores are, in general, higher than the 180 deg.s^{-1};

2 there is little or no difference between the Right and Left leg, with only a slight advantage for the Right leg at a Velocity of 30 deg.s^{-1};

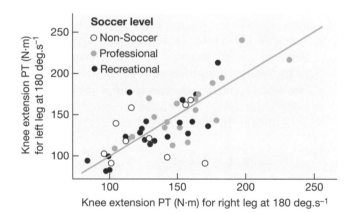

Figure 10.8 Scatter plot of Right vs Left Knee Extension Peak Torque at 180 deg.s^{-1}.

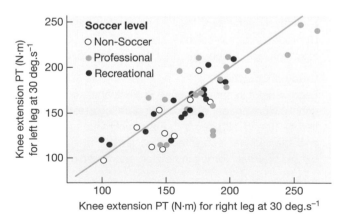

Figure 10.9 Scatter plot of Right vs Left Knee Extension Peak Torque at 30 deg.s^{-1}.

3 Professional Soccer Players appear to have greater Knee Extension PT than either of the other two samples, with Recreational Soccer Players having only a slight advantage over Non-Soccer playing individuals.

Similar impressions can be gained from the case profile plots in Figures 10.10 to 10.12 where the individual variability in response can be more easily identified.

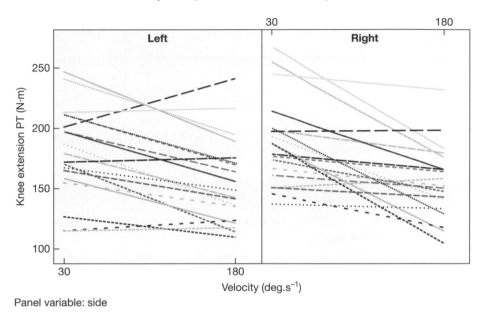

Panel variable: side

Figure 10.10 Scatter plot of Knee Extension Peak Torque by Velocity (Soccer Level = Professional).

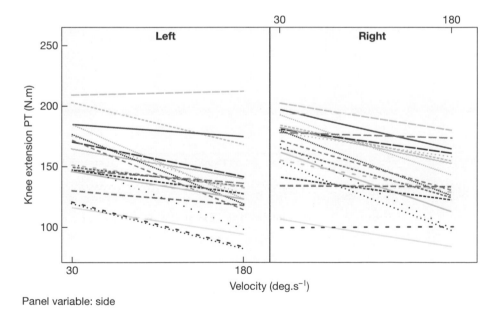

Panel variable: side

Figure 10.11 Scatter plot of Knee Extension Peak Torque by Velocity (Soccer Level = Recreational).

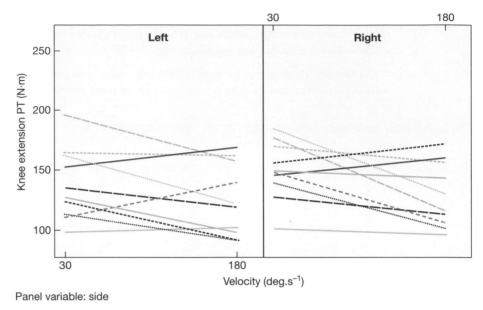

Figure 10.12 **Scatter plot of Knee Extension Peak Torque by Velocity (Soccer Level = Non-Soccer).**

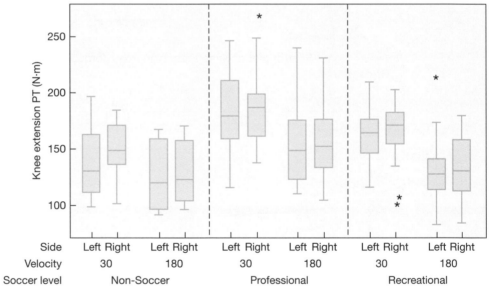

Figure 10.13 **Box plots of Knee Extension Peak Torque by Side, Velocity and Group.**

The overall impressions are confirmed by the box plots in Figure 10.13 which also suggest that the differences among the three Soccer Levels are fairly consistent across each of the four combinations of Velocity and Side.

The sample means for all combinations of the three factors are worth looking at (Box 10.11) and give the same impressions as the diagrams, but it must be remembered that these are subject to considerable variability.

Box 10.11

```
Tabulated statistics: Soccer Level, Velocity, Side

Rows: Soccer Level    Columns: Velocity / Side

                         30          180       All
                    Left Right   Left Right    All

Non-Soccer           138   149    125   129    135
Professional         180   189    156   155    170
Recreational         159   165    129   134    147

All                  163   171    139   141    154

Cell Contents:   Leg PT  :   Mean
```

The next step in the analysis is the formal approach using a repeated measures ANOVA with Soccer Level, Velocity and Side as fixed factors (with three, two and two levels, respectively) and with a subject identifier/number as a random factor which crucially is *nested* within Soccer Level, i.e. subjects are in one and only one Soccer Level. The model must at first incorporate all three two-way interactions and the three-way interaction between the 'fixed effects' factors (i.e. Soccer Level, Velocity and Side) – see Box 10.12.

Box 10.12

```
General Linear Model: Knee Ext. PT versus Soccer Level, Side, ...

Factor                  Type    Levels  Values
Soccer Level            fixed        3  Non-Foot,Professional,Recreational
Side                    fixed        2  Left, Right
Velocity                fixed        2  30, 180
Subject(Soccer Level)  random       48  1, 2, 3, 4, .. . . . 48

Analysis of Variance for Knee Ext. PT, using Adjusted SS for Tests

Source                    DF     Seq SS     Adj SS    Adj MS       F      P
Soccer Level               2    37371.2    37371.2   18685.6    6.25  0.004
Subject(Soccer Level)     45   134468.7   134468.7    2988.2    9.34  0.000
Side                       1     1225.1     1312.0    1312.0    4.10  0.045
Velocity                   1    35452.5    28668.1   28668.1   89.62  0.000
Soccer Level*Side          2      101.9      101.9      50.9    0.16  0.853
Soccer Level*Velocity      2     1334.4     1334.4     667.2    2.09  0.128
Side*Velocity              1      344.0      349.4     349.4    1.09  0.298
Soccer Level*Side*Velocity 2      149.1      149.1      74.5    0.23  0.792
Error                    135    43186.7    43186.7     319.9
Total                    191   253633.6
```

First, note that the three-way interaction is non-significant ($P = 0.79$), as indeed are all three two-way interactions (P-values of 0.85, 0.13 and 0.30, respectively). Further, dropping the three-way followed by each of the two-way interaction leaves none of the interactions as significant, so only main effects are left in the final model presented in Box 10.13.

Clearly, there are highly significant effects of Soccer Level and of Velocity but the Side main effect is borderline with a P-value of 0.052. At this stage (with this main-effects-only model), the researcher should simply produce multiple comparisons of the three Soccer

Box 10.13

```
Analysis of Variance for Leg PT, using Adjusted SS for Tests

Source                   DF    Seq SS     Adj SS    Adj MS       F      P
Soccer Level              2   37371.2    37371.2   18685.6    6.25  0.004
Side                      1    1225.1     1225.1    1225.1    3.86  0.052
Velocity                  1   35452.5    35452.5   35452.5  111.58  0.000
Subject(Soccer Level)    45  134468.7   134468.7    2988.2    9.41  0.000
Error                   142   45116.1    45116.1     317.7
Total                   191  253633.6
```

Levels (which is carried out by averaging across Velocity and Side for each subject) and then a paired comparison of the two velocities (i.e. in effect averaged across Side and across all subjects regardless of Soccer Level) and these are presented in Box 10.14.

Box 10.14

```
Tukey 95% Simultaneous Confidence Intervals
All Pairwise Comparisons among Levels of Soccer Level
Individual confidence level = 98.06%

Group = Non-Soccer subtracted from:

Group           Lower   Center  Upper    ----+------+------+------+------
Professional     8.82    34.72  60.61                 (------*------)
Recreational   -14.38    11.52  37.42          (------*------)
                                          ----+------+------+------+------
                                            -30     0      30     60

Group = Professional subtracted from:

Group           Lower   Center  Upper    ----+------+------+------+------
Recreational   -44.70   -23.20  -1.69    (------*------)
                                          ----+------+------+------+------
                                            -30     0      30     60

Tukey 95.0% Simultaneous Confidence Intervals
Response Variable Knee Ext. PT
All Pairwise Comparisons among Levels of Velocity
Velocity =  30  subtracted from:

Velocity Lower  Center  Upper    ----+------+------+------+------
180     -32.26  -27.18  -22.09   (------*------)
                                  ----+------+------+------+------
                                    -30    -20    -10     0
```

These results confirm that Professional soccer players have, on average, significantly greater Knee Extension PT (on Right and Left legs and at either 30 or 180 deg.s^{-1}) than Non-Soccer individuals by between 9 and 61 N·m and Recreational soccer players by between 2 and 45 N·m. There is not a significant difference, however, in Knee Extension PT between Non-Soccer playing individuals and Recreational soccer players. Further, from the last interval, it can be concluded that subjects in general show significantly greater Knee Extension PT of between 22 and 32 N·m more at a velocity of 30 deg.s^{-1} than at a velocity of 180 deg.s^{-1}.

Conclusion

Knee Extension PT (as measured by an isokinetic dynamometer) is significantly higher in Professional (youth) soccer players than in Recreational soccer players or Non-Soccer playing individuals. This is consistent across both legs/sides and (two) different dynamometer Velocities. Such measurements at a lower Velocity (30 deg.s^{-1}) are significantly higher than at a higher Velocity (180 deg.s^{-1}). There is not (quite) a significant advantage of the Right over the Left leg.

Reference: Murray, A. (2004). 'Comparison of physiological variables in elite youth and recreational soccer players and an age matched control group.' MSc thesis, Glasgow University.

Additional comments on Illustration 10.3

1 Both of the assumptions of Normality for each subject and for the variability at each Velocity/Side combination in each Soccer Level look quite plausible but should be checked using two separate Normal probability plots.

2 The borderline significance of Side is illustrated by the pairwise comparison of the main effect of Side in Box 10.15.

Box 10.15

```
Tukey 95.0% Simultaneous Confidence Intervals
Response Variable Leg PT
All Pairwise Comparisons among Levels of Side
Side = Left subtracted from:

Side       Lower   Center   Upper    +-------+-------+-------+----
Right    -0.03380   5.052   10.14    (-------------*-------------)
                                     +-------+-------+-------+----
                                    0.0     3.0     6.0     9.0
```

Hence the Right leg is between -0.03 N·m lower and 10 N·m higher than the Left leg in terms of average Knee Extension PT (across all subjects and both Velocities). Since this interval (just) contains zero it cannot (quite) be claimed that the Right leg is on average stronger than the Left. Perhaps, though, a slightly larger study may find a significant effect of Side.

3 As neither of the within-factors has three or more levels, there is no need to consider the test of sphericity or, indeed, to carry out subsequent corrections as any such corrections would give exactly the same results as above.

10.5 Two between-subject factors each at two levels and one within-subject factor at two levels

When a researcher has data involving a response variable being measured under two distinct and different levels/conditions (within-subject factor) on each of four separate samples of subjects (each combination of the two between-subject factors), then appropriate steps in the analysis of such data are as follows:

1 Provide a scatter plot of the two levels of the within-subject factor labelled by one of the two between-subject factors but with separate panels for the other

between-subject factor and with a line of equality superimposed on each panel plot. Augment this with the corresponding box plots by all three fixed factors (i.e. the two between- and one within-subject factors).

2 If each of the box plots looks roughly Normally distributed and roughly the same width, then carry out a repeated measures ANOVA with a random subject factor nested within the two between-subject factors (i.e. to allow for the dependence across the observations on the within-subject factor of each subject) included in the model.

3 If all of the hypothesis tests (of the three main effects, three two-way interactions and the three-way interaction) turn out to be non-significant (i.e. all three P-values >0.05), then stop and conclude that none of the between-subject or within-subject factors has any (significant) effect on the response variable. However, if at least some of the tests prove significant, then the necessary further analysis will depend on which terms of the model are significant and it is not really helpful to try to give some general guidelines on how to proceed. The best approach is to develop some experience in such problems and then try to use paired-sample or two-sample t-intervals of either differences or averages of the two levels of the within-subject factor, possibly comparing these across either or both of the between-subject factors. If in doubt, as always try to find a tame and practically minded statistician.

4 Although there is a temptation to carry out a whole series of paired-sample and two-sample t-tests and/or interval estimates on the differences and/or the averages of the two levels of the within-subject factor across the two between-subject factors in place of the repeated measures ANOVA, it is certainly more compact and probably more effective to use the ANOVA.

Illustration 10.4   Youth football (505 agility test)

Background

It is acknowledged that physical fitness and agility are important for soccer players. Quantification of these characteristics is important in being able to identify 'poor' players who can be prescribed appropriate training schedules in an attempt to improve an identified weakness. In addition, regular testing can provide information on the effectiveness of training interventions. There is limited information on the fitness and agility of youth players in Scotland. Quantification of these variables will provide information on current fitness and agility levels, resulting in a database to which coaches can refer. Comparison of scores between soccer clubs may allow differences in recruitment and/or training practices between clubs to be identified.

Study description

Samples of soccer players from the under 13 and under 14 teams of two Scottish professional soccer clubs (W and T) were taken and a battery of physiological tests of fitness and agility carried out on all 42 subjects. One of these tests is the 505 agility test which involves timing a 15 m sprint from a standing start, turn and return sprint to the start to provide an Agility score. Each subject does two such sprints, one turning to the left, the other to the right.

Aim

To investigate whether there was any difference in youth soccer players' performance in the 505 agility test and whether this was different across 13- and 14-year-olds (squads) and indeed different Teams.

Data

Name of data file: *Youth Football Agility*

Response variable: Agility (seconds)

Between-subject factors: Team (2 levels: W, T)

                                  Squad (2 levels: under 13, under 14)

Within-subject factor: Side (2 levels: Left, Right)

Analysis

First provide a scatter plot (Figure 10.14) of the 505 agility test scores of turning to the Left against turning to the Right (the Side factor) labelled by one of the between-subject factors (Team) with separate panels for the other between-subject factor (Squad). First, note that there is little difference between the two Sides in either panel (more or less symmetrical about the line of equality). There is, though, a strong suggestion that Team W have higher scores (slower times) than Team T for both Squads while, the under 13 Squad appear to be slower than the under 14s for both Teams. These impressions are more or less confirmed by the box plots of Figure 10.15. Note also the somewhat unfortunate aspect of the data that the sample sizes range from 7 to 13 across the four combinations of Teams and Squads. Clearly, a more balanced sample would have been preferable.

The summary statistics in Box 10.16 indicate these same subjective impressions but certainly not as clearly as a plot of the sample means (Figure 10.16).

While there may be a temptation to carry out multitudes of paired-sample and two-sample *t*-tests, it is almost certainly more informative and at least more compact to carry out the full repeated measures ANOVA as contained in Box 10.17. Be careful here to use

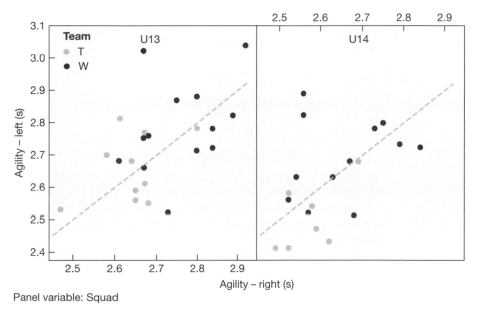

Panel variable: Squad

Figure 10.14 Scatter plot of Agility by Side labelled by Team for each Squad (with line of equality).

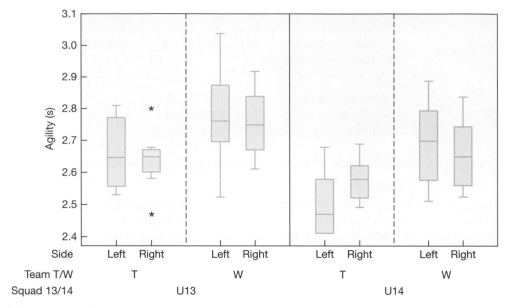

Figure 10.15 Box plot of Agility by Squad, Team and Side.

Box 10.16

```
Tabulated statistics: Team, Squad

Rows: Team    Columns: Squad

        U13     U14     All          U13     U14     All

T      2.658   2.503   2.594    W   2.785   2.689   2.739
       2.642   2.573   2.614        2.759   2.653   2.708
         10       7       1           13      12      25

All    2.730   2.621   2.680
       2.708   2.624   2.670
         23      19      42

Cell Contents:  Agility Left  :  Mean
                Agility Right :  Mean
                Count
```

the fact that subjects are nested within both Team and Squad (i.e. each subject/footballer belongs to only one Squad/Team combination.

There are clearly (and highly) significant main effects of Team and Squad as well as the random effect of subject, with little or no indication of any of the interactions being substantial at all.

Finally, it may be of interest to quantify and compare these main effects of Team and Squad. This is easily done using the average Agility score for each subject, and then providing interval estimates of the main effects as if this was a standard two-way ANOVA. The results are presented in Box 10.18.

In summary, then, Team W are between 0.07 and 0.18 seconds slower than Team T on average, while the under 13s are between 0.05 and 0.16 seconds slower on average than

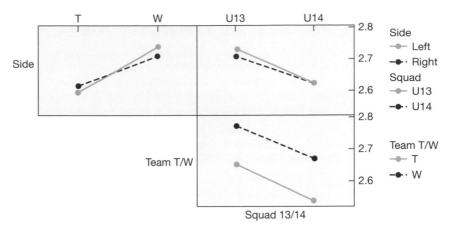

Figure 10.16 **Sample mean plots for Agility by Side, Team and Squad.**

Box 10.17

```
Analysis of Variance for Agility, using Adjusted SS for Tests

Source                    DF    Seq SS    Adj SS    Adj MS      F      P
Team T/W                   1  0.291314  0.324389  0.324389  20.65  0.000
Squad 13/14                1  0.230412  0.225517  0.225517  14.35  0.001
Side                       1  0.002305  0.000079  0.000079   0.01  0.921
Subject(Team T/W
  Squad 13/14)            38  0.597060  0.597060  0.015712   1.97  0.020
Team T/W*Squad 13/14       1  0.000610  0.000610  0.000610   0.04  0.845
Team T/W*Side              1  0.012756  0.016686  0.016686   2.09  0.156
Squad 13/14*Side           1  0.004165  0.007225  0.007225   0.91  0.347
Side*Subject(Team T/W
  Squad 13/14)            38  0.303320  0.303320  0.007982    **
Team T/W*Squad 13/14*Side  1  0.011355  0.011355  0.011355   1.42  0.240
Error                      0         *         *         *
Total                     83  1.453295

** Denominator of F-test is zero.
```

Box 10.18

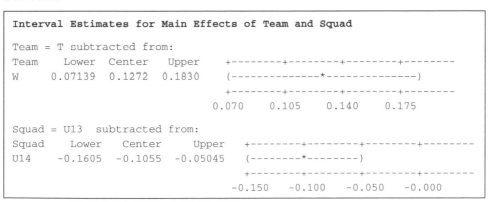

```
Interval Estimates for Main Effects of Team and Squad

Team = T subtracted from:
Team    Lower   Center   Upper    +--------+--------+--------+--------
W     0.07139  0.1272  0.1830    (--------------*--------------)
                                  +--------+--------+--------+--------
                            0.070    0.105    0.140    0.175

Squad = U13  subtracted from:
Squad   Lower   Center   Upper    +--------+--------+--------+--------
U14   -0.1605 -0.1055 -0.05045   (--------*--------)
                                  +--------+--------+--------+--------
                           -0.150   -0.100   -0.050   -0.000
```

317

the under 14s, i.e. more or less comparable differences somewhere between 2% and 7% in magnitude (since a typical 505 agility test score is around 2.6 seconds).

Reference: Doyle, P. (2006). 'Performance assessment in youth soccer: an investigation of reproducibility and measurement error.' MSc thesis, Glasgow University.

Additional comments on Illustration 10.4

1 The assumptions of Normality for each Agility measurement and for each subject (within each combination of Squad and Team) look plausible on the basis of the box plots of Figure 10.15 – as does the assumption of common variability across all four combinations of Squad and Team. However, it would be advisable to check this through relevant Normal probability plots.

2 As there are only two levels for all factors here, there is no assumption of sphericity required and the multivariate tests and Greenhouse–Geisser corrections all result in exactly the same *P*-values as in Box 10.17.

Exercises

10.6 The dataset *Climbers (Male)* consists of measurements of two modes of Finger Strength (Grip and Climbing Specific) for both hands of samples of three different levels of climbing status (Elite, Recreational and non-climbers/Controls). See Illustration 3.9 for more details. Are there any significant differences in Finger Strength in Mode, Hand and/or Climbing Status?

10.7 Knee Flexion Peak Torque was also measured in the *Kicking the Habit* dataset considered in Illustration 10.3. Investigate these data for effects of Soccer Level, Side and/or Velocity. The data are in the file *Kicking the Hamstring*.

10.8 Samples of amateur and professional rugby union players had their 10 m sprint times recorded under three conditions (namely a straight sprint and two zig-zag sprints starting to the left and right, respectively. Are there any significant effects of Status (Amateur or Professional), Position (Back or Forward) and/or Sprint Condition (Straight, Left or Right) in terms of average 10 m Sprint Times? These data are in the file *Rugby Sprints*.

10.6	Two between-subject factors each at two levels and two within-subject factors each at two levels

When there are data involving a response variable being measured under each combination of two distinct and different levels/conditions of each of two within-subject factors for each subject in four separate (and similarly sized) samples of subjects from two between-subject factors, each of two levels, the following steps are appropriate:

1 Provide scatter plots of the two levels of one of the within-subject factors labelled by the between-subject factors for each of the levels of the other within-subject factor with, possibly, the same scale for each plot and axis and with a line of equality superimposed on each plot.

2 Augment this with box plots by all factors and an interaction plot of the sample means of all pairwise combinations of the factors.

3 Carry out a repeated measures ANOVA with the subject nested within both between-subject factors and, depending upon the results of this, carry out any appropriate follow-up comparisons through paired-sample or two-sample *t*-intervals.

4 As all the factors are at two levels, the multivariate tests and the corrections for lack of sphericity (e.g. Greenhouse–Geisser) are unnecessary here (i.e. give exactly the same results as the standard univariate repeated measures ANOVA.

Illustration 10.5 Golf psychology

Background

There has been much written on the mental strength and focus required to play 'good' golf. Nowadays, there is considerable material available intended to aid the club golfer and a package of such material has been compiled at Glasgow University for a study of its practical usefulness in improving golfers' performances.

Study description

Samples of 8 Low (i.e. under 15) and 9 High (i.e. over 20) handicap male golfers were randomised to act as controls or to undergo a 6-week course intended to improve mental aspects of golf performance. Each golfer was tested on his performance at Chip (20 to 30 metres from the hole) and Approach (100 to 120 metres from the hole) shots both before and immediately after this 6-week course. Each golfer on each occasion for each distance hit 20 balls at a target (varied over four similar positions for each Shot) and the measure used here is the median of each of these sets of 20 shots.

Aim

To investigate whether an intervention of a 6-week course focusing on psychological techniques intended to aid golf performance has any significant effect on Chip and Approach shots for Low and/or High Handicap golfers.

Data

Name of data file:	*Golf Psychology*
Response variable:	Distance from Hole (centimetres)
Between-subject factors:	Condition (2 levels: Psycho, Control)
	Handicap (2 levels: Low, High)
Within-subject factors:	Time (2 levels: Pre-Study, Post-Study)
	Shot (2 levels: Chip, Approach)

Analysis

First, produce labelled scatter plots of the (median) Distance from Hole for subjects Pre- against Post-Study labelled by Condition (i.e. whether Psycho or Control). Separate plots for the Chip and Approach shots are given in Figures 10.17 and 10.18. Note that they are on different scales as the accuracy of the Chip shots is much greater than that of the Approach shots, especially for the High Handicap group.

There is little indication of any improvement for either Condition from Pre- to Post-Study attempts but there are clear differences between the Handicap groups with perhaps also more consistency among the High handicappers. This is further substantiated by the box

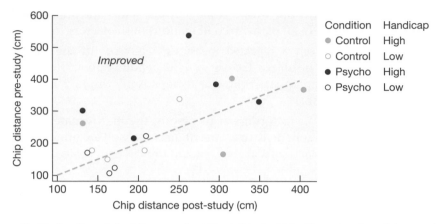

Figure 10.17 Scatter plot of Pre- against Post-Study Chip Shots by Condition and Handicap.

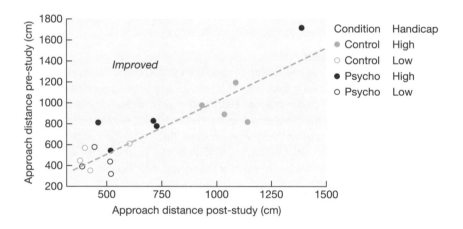

Figure 10.18 Scatter plot of Pre- against Post-Study Appoach Shots by Condition and Handicap.

plots in Figure 10.19 as well as the sample means in Figure 10.20 where there is considerable evidence, in the parlance of ANOVA models, of main effects of Handicap and Shot as well as an interaction between them.

The formal repeated measures ANOVA is given in Box 10.19 where the model involves subjects being nested within both Handicap and Condition, i.e. each golfer/subject belongs to only one Handicap group and was allocated to only one Condition. As suspected from the plots, the key (and significant) effects are one between-subject factor (Handicap) and one within-subject factor (Shot).

Since the only significant terms in the model are the main effects of Handicap and Shot and their interaction (highlighted in Box 10.19), there is clearly no significant and dramatic effect of the psychological intervention although, as always, beware that these are quite small samples (i.e. 4 or 5 subjects per Handicap/Condition combination). However, these data show little indication of the psychological intervention having any effect on performance of either type of shot except that there is at least a slight improvement for the High Handicap group especially on the Chip shots.

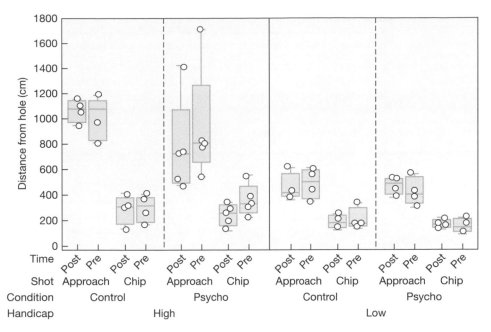

Figure 10.19 Box plots of Distance from Hole by Handicap, Condition, Shot and Time.

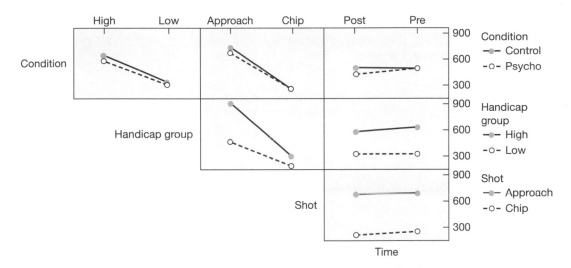

Figure 10.20 Sample mean plots of Distance from Hole by Factors.

If some indication of the significant main effects and interaction is required then paired-sample interval estimates for the difference between Approach and Chip shots for both Handicap levels would be useful as well as two-sample intervals for the difference between Handicap levels for each type of Shot would suffice. These are provided in Box 10.20 by averaging the Pre- and Post-Study shots and ignoring the (non-significant) Condition. From these the greater consistency between the shots for Low Handicap golfers can be seen (a difference, on average, of between 2.39 and 3.16 metres for the Low and between 3.95 and 8.55 metres for the High Handicap samples) as well as the complementary

Box 10.19

```
General Linear Model: Distance versus Condition, Handicap, ...

Factor                     Type    Levels  Values
Condition                  fixed        2  Control, Psycho
Handicap                   fixed        2  High, Low
Shot                       fixed        2  Approach, Chip
Time                       fixed        2  Post, Pre
Subject(Condition Handicap)random     17  1, 2, 3, 4, 5, . . . . . 16, 17

Analysis of Variance for Distance from Hole, using Adjusted SS for Tests

Source                        DF   Seq SS   Adj SS   Adj MS       F      P
Condition                      1    27294    51260    51260    0.71  0.414
Handicap                       1  1450969  1459356  1459356   20.25  0.001
Shot                           1  3619083  3500928  3500928  155.89  0.000
Time                           1    12624     7143     7143    0.32  0.576
Condition*Handicap             1     9560     9560     9560    0.13  0.722
Condition*Shot                 1    17703    26545    26545    1.18  0.284
Condition*Time                 1    20548    15380    15380    0.68  0.413
Handicap*Shot                  1   521685   534488   534488   23.80  0.000
Handicap*Time                  1    12788    10058    10058    0.45  0.507
Shot*Time                      1     1382     2084     2084    0.09  0.762
Condition*Handicap*Shot        1    34743    34743    34743    1.55  0.221
Condition*Handicap*Time        1    57638    57638    57638    2.57  0.117
Condition*Shot*Time            1     4169     3541     3541    0.16  0.693
Handicap*Shot*Time             1      163      336      336    0.01  0.903
Condition*Handicap*Shot*Time 1    11249    11249    11249    0.50  0.483
Subject Number                13   936953   936953    72073    3.21  0.002
  (Condition Handicap)
Error                         39   875826   875826    22457
Total                         67  7614376
```

Box 10.20

```
Differences (Approach minus Chip) for each Handicap Group

Handicap N    Mean    StDev  SE Mean     95% CI
High      9 624.611 299.169  99.723 (394.649, 854.573)
Low       8 277.781  46.300  16.370 (239.073, 316.489)

Differences between Handicap Groups for each Type of Shot

Approach Shots
Difference = mu (Distance High Handicap) - mu (Distance Low Handicap)
Estimate for difference: 463.389
95% CI for difference: (224.676, 702.102)

Chip Shots
Difference = mu (Distance High Handicap) - mu (Distance Low Handicap)
Estimate for difference: 116.559
95% CI for difference: (44.238, 188.880)
```

conclusion that, for each type of shot, Low Handicap golfers get nearer to the target (closer, on average, by between 0.44 and 1.89 metres on Chip shots and by between 2.25 and 7.02 metres on Approach shots).

Conclusions

There is little indication that the 6-week psychological-based course has any impact on Chip or Approach shot performance of Low or High Handicap golfers. The study, perhaps not surprisingly, did show that Low Handicap golfers get closer to the target, on average, than High Handicap golfers, especially on Chip shots.

Reference: Dudley, C., Hill, C.D., Moran S. (students), Penpraze, V. (staff) (2007). 'The effectiveness of cognitive-behavioural intervention in golf.' University of Glasgow Sports Science student project.

Additional comments on Illustration 10.5

1 The assumptions of Normality for each distance measurement and for each golfer (within each combination of Handicap and Condition) look plausible on the basis of the box plots of Figure 10.19. It would be advisable, as always, to check this through the relevant probability plots. However, the assumption of common variability across all eight combinations does look somewhat suspect as the variability of the High Handicap/ Psychology intervention group does appear much larger than the rest, but remember this is based on only five observations and the apparent problem is created by only one subject (subject 15). Further scrutiny of this in Figure 10.17 suggests that the randomisation of the High Handicap sample did not work out well, as the other four golfers on the intervention are clearly all better at Approach shots than any of the corresponding Controls. This, however, is much less evident on Chip shots so perhaps the study was just a little unlucky here.

2 As there are only two levels for all factors here, there is no assumption of sphericity required and the multivariate tests and Greenhouse–Geisser corrections all result in exactly the same *P*-values as in Box 10.19.

Exercises

10.9 The dataset used as Illustration 10.4 involved two complete replicates. The complete dataset is contained in the file *Youth Agility (Replicates)*. By considering replicate as a second within-factor, investigate these data for effects of Replicate, Side, Squad and/or Team.

10.10 The climbing study considered in Exercise 10.6 was carried out on corresponding samples of females and the full dataset is contained in *Climbers (All)*. Are there any significant effects of strength differences in Mode, Hand, Sex and/or Climbing Status for these data?

Summary

To cover designed studies with combinations of both between-subject and within-subject factors, the following scenarios were illustrated in this chapter:

- One between at two levels and one within at two levels.
- One between at two levels and one within at $K > 2$ levels.

- One between at $K > 2$ levels and two within each at two levels.

- Two between each at two levels and one within at two levels.

- Two between each at two levels and two within each at two levels.

Graphical procedures such as case profile plots, box plots and labelled scatter plots with a line of equality were again used to obtain subjective impressions of the data.

Formal analysis was generally based on repeated measures ANOVA with subjects modelled as a random effect and, where appropriate, a follow-up multiple comparisons. For problems involving between-subject and within-subject Factors with two levels, two-sample and paired-sample t-intervals often turn out to be sufficient.

Although it is possible to suggest general approaches for most of these types of problem, the researcher should always endeavour to be flexible with an analysis and tailor the analysis both to the key questions being posed and to the results of each step of the analysis. However, when a within-subject factor has three or more levels which can be 'ordered' naturally, then it is often possible to exploit this and gain better and clearer conclusions by modelling such factors through the techniques of linear mixed-effects models (l.m.e.'s) and random regression, closely related to the analysis of covariance introduced in Section 7.4. These techniques are covered in the next chapter.

11 Handling linear mixed-effects models: more on dependent observations

11.1 Introduction

One common extension to the types of repeated measures designs encountered in the previous two chapters is the inclusion of an **ordered within-subject factor** – over three or more levels – where the response variable may be more appropriately modelled as a *linear* function of this ordered factor (i.e. in effect the factor can be dealt with as a **within-subject covariate**). For example, Age or Time may well be such a covariate. Such contexts will generally involve a random sample of subjects, each of whom has the appropriate response variable measured across each level of this within-subject covariate. For example, a random sample of 10-year-old boys may be taken and their aerobic fitness measured at each of their next five birthdays, or a sample of mountaineers may have their skin temperature taken every two minutes while they are in a cold chamber simulating mountain rescue.

On occasions, a simple random effect for subject may be sufficient to model this linearly with a fixed and constant slope across the within-subject factor (i.e. in effect an analysis of covariance). This is equivalent to modelling the data with different intercepts for each subject but the same slope for all subjects. However, it may well be the case that the *slopes may be different for different subjects* (e.g. different boys growing at different rates) and this must be incorporated into the model. A clear example of this is given in Figure 11.1 where, based on *individual subject* linear regressions, the two (thickly) highlighted subjects have considerably different Sprint Time decay rates (i.e. slopes) as they sprint 10 metres pulling increasing sledge masses – the continuous line subject sprinting much less quickly as the larger the mass he pulls whereas the 'dashed line subject may be a slower sprinter but his sprint speed decreases substantially less than the 'continuous line' subject – for more details of this study see Illustration 11.1. Overall, though, it is clear from Figure 11.1 that it would be foolish to model all subjects as having a common slope (i.e. a common Sprint Time decay rate).

The type of model which includes the possibility of different slopes for different subjects is known as a **linear mixed-effects (lme) model** (sometimes abbreviated as lmm) or as a **random regression** model where, in the simplest context, a random sample of subjects is taken and the response variable modelled on the within-subject covariate as linear with different intercepts and different slopes for each subject.

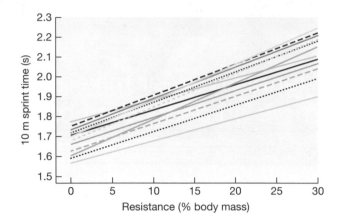

Figure 11.1 **Individual subject regression lines.**

These are then assumed to have arisen from some underlying (bivariate) Normal distribution whose means will be the *population average intercept* and *population average slope* from whatever target population the subjects are sampled from, while the population standard deviations and correlation will reflect the spread and relationship of the intercepts and slopes across subjects.

The key step in analysing these problems is often to determine and interpret the simplest model which adequately describes the underlying process. This is the philosophy used throughout this book where the primary aim of modelling data is to describe what is going on with the data in as simple and parsimonious a final form as possible without compromising the fit of the model to the data. It is also important to plot this final, fitted model for the 'average subject', i.e. a plot of

population average intercept + population average slope ∗ within-subject covariate

against the within-subject covariate across the range of the within-subject covariate covered by the observed data.

The design of such studies may include other between-factors (e.g. sex) and/or other within-subject factors (e.g. control/intervention applied to the same subject) in addition to the within-subject covariate modelled by an lme model. The interest in such situations may well be to compare the different population average intercepts and slopes across the between- and/or within-subject factors.

The illustrations of within-subject covariate designs in this chapter are:

- One within-covariate design.
- One within-factor and one within-covariate design.
- One between-factor and one within-covariate design.
- Two between-factors and one within-covariate design.

As always, think of these not as explicit prescriptions for analysing such data but merely as guidance on how to use some basic techniques to help understand data of this form.

11.2   One within-subject covariate

The first few sections in Chapter 10 involved a one within-subject factor design at only two or three levels. When the within-subject factor has say four or five or more levels and there is a natural ordering in these levels (e.g. time or percentage of Body Mass), then it can make sense to model the data to exploit any underlying relationship between the response variable and this within-subject covariate. Often, this relationship may be of a linear nature, but not necessarily. This section illustrates such a linear model, but the ideas can be extended to any polynomial or other relationship. The following steps are often appropriate in such circumstances:

1   Draw up individual profile plots of the response variable across the within-subject covariate for each subject in the sample in separate panels, although sometimes a single panel plot of all subjects together might suffice. Augment this with the corresponding box plots for the sample.

2   Assuming the profile plots look linear for each subject, then, as in Chapters 9 and 10, any model will include a random subject factor which allows for the dependence across the observations of each subject as in effect a separate intercept for each subject. The additional aspect of the lme model is to allow for another random term which allows, if necessary, for separate 'slopes' for each subject. These random intercepts and slopes are assumed to have arisen from underlying Normal distributions and therefore there are two parameters for each random term: the population mean and standard deviation (as well as the population correlation between the random intercept and slope). The method used in this chapter for choosing the most appropriate model (i.e. the simplest model which still adequately describes the data) is called Akaike's Information Criterion (AIC) and involves the residual sum of squares (or, strictly speaking, the log-likelihood) of any model (a measure of how well the model fits the data) and the number of parameters in the model (i.e. a measure of how complicated the model is). The AIC is similar in nature to Mallow's Cp used for variable selection in multiple regression in Section 6.5.* The final model is chosen to be that which minimises the AIC across all potential models, but be careful always to use the maximum likelihood (ML) method of estimating parameters to compare models with different fixed-effect structures.

3   Often in such problems, one key aim is simply to summarise the final model (chosen by AIC), and this would involve plotting the linear relationship defined by the (estimated) population intercept and (estimated) population slope across the range of the within-subject covariate in the sample. Suitable interval estimates for this population average line can be constructed and could be added to such a plot.

---

*More detailed discussion of AIC and l.m.e. models in general can be found in B.T. West, K.B. Welch and A.T. Galecki, *Linear Mixed Models: A Practical Guide Using Statistical Software* (London: Chapman & Hall, 2006).

Illustration 11.1 **Resistance training**

Background

Sprinting involves generating high forces while moving at speed. It is acknowledged that training for many activities should involve replication of the specific movement patterns and actual competition velocities so that neuromuscular learning can take place. Some coaches have recognised this and asked their athletes, including rugby players, to carry out some sprint training while pulling sledges. While athletes have pulled sledges with varying resistances, there is no consensus on what is the most appropriate resistance to pull. There may be a linear relationship between the Resistance (% Body Mass pulled) and Sprint Time. At some % Body Mass there may be a breakdown in the supposed linear relationship, which might shed light on an appropriate range of Resistances for training purposes. For example, the Resistance becomes so heavy that there is a marked decrease in running speed, which is allied to a change in running mechanics and thus a loss in training specificity.

Study description

Thirteen amateur rugby union players underwent a series of seven 20 m sprints while pulling sledges with a range of Resistances of 0 to 30% of their Body Mass in steps of 5% (i.e. 0, 5, 10, 15, 20, 25 and 30%). The order of Resistance was determined using balanced Latin squares designs (the study was originally intended for 14 players but one failed to turn up). Each player had his mid-sprint 10 m time recorded under each Resistance.

Aims

To model the (average) linear relationship between 10 m Sprint Time and Resistance. To investigate whether, at some stage in the relationship, there is a key % Body Mass where the linear relationship breaks down which might identify a (maximum) 'training-specific' Resistance.

Data

Name of data file:	*Resistance*
Response variable:	10 m Sprint Time (seconds)
Within-subject covariate:	Resistance (7 levels: 0, 5, 10, 15, 20, 25, 30% Body Mass)

Analysis

The individual panel plots of the 13 subjects are given in Figure 11.2 and the box plot across Resistance is given in Figure 11.3.

While the plots show a few minor exceptions, most of the subjects do appear to have a reasonably linear relationship adequately describing the link between 10 m Sprint Time and Resistance. It also appears that there is reasonable variability not only in the 10 m Sprint Times at zero Resistance (i.e. the subjects' 'intercepts'), but also in the rate of increase of 10 m Sprint Time with increasing Resistance (i.e. the subjects' slopes – compare, for example, subjects 2 and 38). Thus a linear mixed effects model with variability in slopes and intercepts across subjects appears plausible for these data.

On the secondary aim of a breakdown in such linearity it does appear that subjects 1, 4 and 41 have non-linear increases from 25% to 30% whereas subjects 3 and 29 have these at 20% to 25%. There is certainly no clear and consistent Body Mass percentage

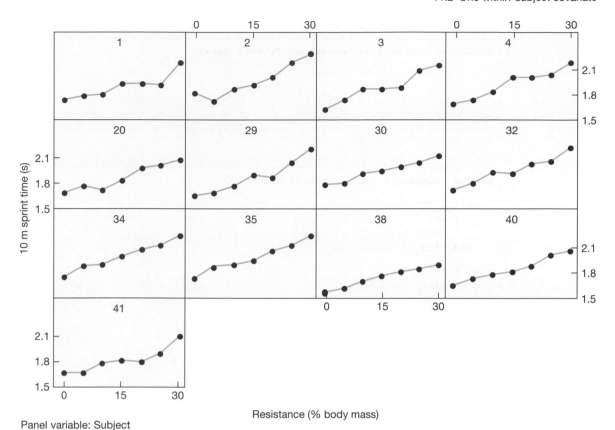

Panel variable: Subject

Figure 11.2 **Scatter plot of 10 m Sprint Time by Resistance per subject.**

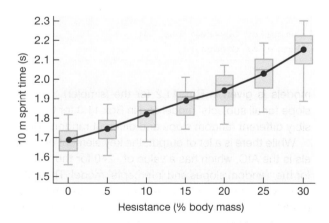

Figure 11.3 **Box plot of 10 m Sprint Time by Resistance.**

where the relationship breaks down, although the sample means (Box 11.1) do make a slight case for the jump from 25% to 30% being greater than any of the other consecutive jumps.

Now, two competing (linear) models are fitted here using an appropriate computing package (in this case the freeware known as R) and the resulting output summarising the

329

Box 11.1

```
Tabulated statistics: Resistance (% Body Mass)

        0      5     10     15     20     25     30    All

    1.689  1.745  1.819  1.888  1.943  2.026  2.152  1.895

Cell Contents:   10m   :   Mean
```

Box 11.2

```
Random Intercepts (and Common Slope) Model

Linear mixed-effects model fit by maximum likelihood
 Data: ans
       AIC        BIC     logLik
 -240.1729  -230.1295  124.0865

Random effects:
 Formula: ~1 | Subject
        (Intercept)    Residual
StdDev:  0.07027764  0.05120181

Fixed effects: Time10m ~ Resistance
                Value    Std.Error  DF   t-value   P-value
(Intercept)  1.6726923  0.022004318  77  76.01655        0
Resistance   0.0148022  0.000542738  77  27.27318        0
  Correlation:
             (Intr)
Resistance  -0.37

Standardized Within-Group Residuals:
       Min          Q1          Med          Q3         Max
-2.63651657  -0.60881118  -0.01920249  0.71227877  2.21805657

Number of Observations: 91
Number of Groups: 13
```

models is given in Box 11.2 for the (simpler) 'different random Intercepts but common slope for all subjects' model and in Box 11.3 for the model with each subject having a possibly different random slope and different random intercept.

While there is a lot of output, the key element of comparison of the two competing models is the AIC, which has a value of –240 for the 'random intercepts only' model and –241 for the 'random slopes and intercepts' model. Thus, the second model has to be preferred as its value of AIC is less (i.e. more negative) than that for the simpler model. Hence the model with random slopes and random intercepts is required to adequately describe this dataset in spite of this model being 'more complicated'. Note also from the output in Box 11.3 that the population average slope is estimated as 0.014802 (in seconds per unit of % Body Mass) with estimated standard error (e.s.e.) of 0.00063 and is clearly highly significant as the corresponding P-value is <0.0001. This confirms that Resistance does significantly influence 10 m Sprint Time.

This final model can be summarised as a 'population average' relationship of

$$10 \text{ m Sprint Time} = 1.6727 + 0.014802 * \text{Resistance}$$

Box 11.3

```
Random Slopes and Random Intercepts Model

Linear mixed-effects model fit by maximum likelihood
Data: ans
      AIC        BIC    logLik
 -241.4081 -226.3429 126.7040

Random effects:
 Formula: ~Resistance | Subject
 Structure: General positive-definite, Log-Cholesky parametrization
            StdDev       Corr
(Intercept) 0.051806146 (Intr)
Resistance  0.001260898 0.982
Residual    0.049357312

Fixed effects: Time10m ~ Resistance
                Value     Std.Error DF  t-value  p-value
(Intercept) 1.6726923 0.017322002 77 96.56461       0
Resistance  0.0148022 0.000631482 77 23.44041       0
 Correlation:
            (Intr)
Resistance 0.086

Standardized Within-Group Residuals:
         Min           Q1          Med           Q3          Max
-2.65874983  -0.66804322   0.01795170   0.58642274   2.25828344

Number of Observations: 91
Number of Groups: 13
```

with random components whose estimated standard deviations are 0.0518 for the distribution of intercepts, 0.00126 for the distribution of slopes (with correlation 0.982 between intercept and slope) and 0.0494 for the distribution of error/natural variability about a subject's regression line. The final model is plotted in Figure 11.4 and, from this, the general pattern of increase in 10 m Sprint Times with Resistance (as a function of Body Mass) can be seen.

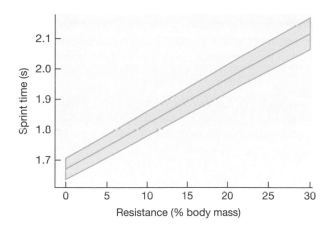

Figure 11.4 Estimated average regression of Sprint Time on Resistance with pointwise 95% interval estimates.

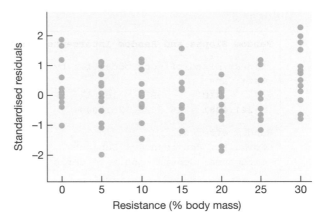

Figure 11.5 Residual plot for 10 m Sprint Time.

As always in linear models (see Chapter 6), it is essential to investigate how well the various assumptions of the model are adhered to by the data. The various assumptions of Normality in this model can be considered by producing Normal probability plots for the intercepts, slopes and errors, respectively. A plot of the standardised residuals in this example is given in Figure 11.5 and, although in general it is reasonably satisfactory, there are slight suspicions at Resistances of 0% and 30% of some bias, with most of the residuals at these values being positive – whereas, with the perfect model, roughly half would be positive which, in fact, is clearly the case for Resistances from 5% to 25% inclusive. Now, this may be due to a departure from linearity at, possibly, both the start and end of the range of Resistances considered in this study and this is investigated in the Additional Comments below.

A simple approach to investigate any departures from linearity is to consider the population average increases between Resistances (i.e. in steps of 5% Body Mass) without assuming linearity at all. This is best carried out using a (Bonferroni-based) multiple comparison procedure (to guard against any contradictions with the overall hypothesis test – of all Resistances having the same average sprint speed – when producing so many intervals). These pairwise adjacent intervals are presented in Box 11.4 and Figure 11.6. These intervals all overlap with each other although the last interval (10 m Sprint Times compared at Resistances of 30% and 25%) does appear to be slightly, but not significantly, greater than any of the other comparisons. Hence, there is not sufficient evidence to suggest that the increase in population average 10 m Sprint Time is any different at the end of the Resistance range considered in this study.

Box 11.4

```
Pairwise Adjacent Intervals for Population Average 10 m Sprint Times
95% Multiple Comparisons (i.e. 99.2% Individual Intervals)

Comparison  N    Mean      StDev     SE Mean        99.2% CI
   5-0     13  0.056154  0.065643  0.018206  (-0.001644, 0.113952)
  10-5     13  0.073846  0.059377  0.016468  ( 0.021565, 0.126127)
  15-10    13  0.069231  0.056489  0.015667  ( 0.019492, 0.118969)
  20-15    13  0.054615  0.055320  0.015343  ( 0.005907, 0.103324)
  25-20    13  0.083077  0.073642  0.020424  ( 0.018236, 0.147918)
  30-25    13  0.125385  0.068144  0.018900  ( 0.065384, 0.185385)
```

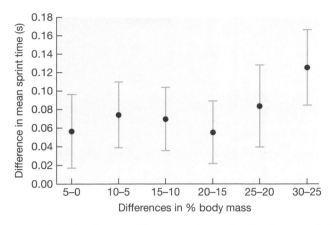

Figure 11.6 Interval plot of adjacent differences for rugby Resistance (95% CI for the mean).

Conclusions

There appears to be a linear relationship between 10 m Sprint Times and Resistance (as % Body Mass between 0% and 30%) while pulling sledges in resistance training among amateur male rugby players. This relationship varies across (male) subjects in terms of both their speed (i.e. intercept) and their rate of increase of 10 m Sprint Time per unit increase in Resistance (i.e. slope).

Reference: Murray, A., Ross, G., Sutherland, K. (students), McLean, D. and Grant, S. (staff) (2004). 'Towing a range of relative resistances and sprint performance in rugby players.' Physiology and Sports Science student project, University of Glasgow.

Additional comments on Illustration 11.1

1   There are three assumptions of Normality involved in the full model here: Normality of the between-subject intercepts and the between-subject slopes (each consisting of one per subject) as well as Normality of the errors/residuals for all observations on all subjects. Consequently, three separate Normal probability plots are necessary here. For the Resistance data, these plots are given in Figures 11.7 and 11.8. All three plots appear roughly linear in nature and hence all three assumptions appear reasonable.

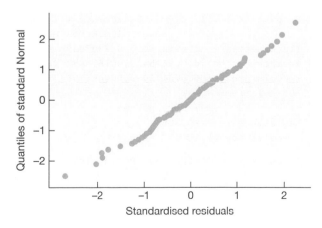

Figure 11.7 Probability plot of residuals for 10 m Sprint Time.

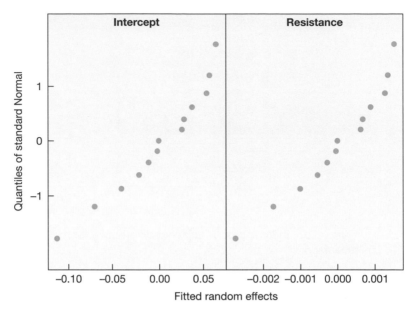

Figure 11.8 **Probability plots of random effects for 10 m Sprint Time.**

Box 11.5

```
Quadratic Model

Linear mixed-effects model fit by maximum likelihood
 Data: ans
       AIC       BIC    logLik
  -248.3733 -230.7973 131.1867

Random effects:
 Formula: ~Resistance | Subject
 Structure: General positive-definite, Log-Cholesky parametrization
            StdDev       Corr
(Intercept) 0.053193929 (Intr)
Resistance  0.001427635 0.756
Residual    0.046068273

Fixed effects: Time10m ~ Resistance + I(Resistance^2)
                    Value    Std.Error DF  t-value  p-value
(Intercept)     1.6943040 0.018807039 76 90.08882   0.0000
Resistance      0.0096154 0.001815852 76  5.29525   0.0000
I(Resistance^2) 0.0001729 0.000056706 76  3.04894   0.0032
 Correlation:
                (Intr) Rsstnc
Resistance      -0.325
I(Resistance^2)  0.377 -0.937

Standardized Within-Group Residuals:
       Min          Q1         Med         Q3        Max
-2.80119692 -0.55039838 -0.03174106  0.57451998  2.04982372

Number of Observations: 91
Number of Groups: 13
```

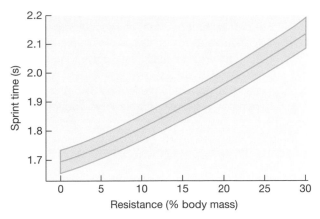

Figure 11.9 Estimated quadratic regression of Sprint Time on Resistance with point-wise 95% interval estimates.

2 To investigate one aspect of any departure from linearity it would be useful to fit a quadratic effect of Resistance on 10 m Sprint Time. The results of the full model for this are presented in Box 11.5 and there is strong evidence that the quadratic term is worth including in the model for these data ($p = 0.0032$) and, since the AIC is -248, compared with -241 for the linear model (based on the ML method of parameter estimation here), the quadratic term should be included in the final model.

A plot of the estimated average quadratic model is given in Figure 11.9 and shows the slight curvature in the relationship.

3 While it is obvious in this example that there are substantial differences in intercepts and slopes among the subjects, it is worth considering the estimates of the population averages and standard deviations (s.d.) in such to roughly quantify the effects of these. From Box 11.2, the intercepts have an estimated population average of 1.67 and estimated population s.d. of 0.052, so the variability in the population would be around 3% to 4% (i.e. 0.052/1.67 as a percentage) with the subjects' intercepts ranging roughly from 1.57 to 1.78 (i.e. $1.673 \pm 2 * 0.052$). Correspondingly, the slopes have a population average estimated as 0.0148 with population s.d. estimated as 0.00126 (roughly 10%), and so exhibit more variability than the intercepts. The residual or error s.d. is estimated as 0.049 which is around the same value as the population intercept s.d. (0.052), suggesting that the variability in the linear model for any subject is of the same magnitude as the variability in the intercepts across the population.

Exercises

11.1 Fourteen subjects had their End Tidal CO_2 (PETCO$_2$) measured at one-minute intervals while they breathed through a mouthpiece into a closed-circuit system attached to a Douglas bag containing 12 litres of 100% O_2. (See Illustration 4.9 for more details of this study.) All subjects were still 'breathing' after 9 minutes into the closed-circuit system. By modelling the pattern of PETCO$_2$ across time for the first 10 minutes of subjects' breathing in an airtight space, describe the average such pattern and investigate whether a linear-based l.m.e. model is appropriate for such data. The data are in the file *Soda Lime Controls*.

11.2 The dataset *Bubble Wrap Temperature* gives the change from baseline Skin and Core Temperatures of 12 subjects 'covered' in Bubble Wrap (as is reputedly used in mountain rescue in Norway) while lying for 30 minutes in a cold ($-10°C$), windy (wind speed 2.7 m.s^{-1}) environment. By fitting l.m.e. models, investigate and summarise the (population) effect on Skin and Core Temperature, respectively, across 30 minutes of lying in Bubble Wrap under such severe weather conditions.

11.3　One within-subject factor and one within-subject covariate

Studies involving a within-subject covariate often involve the comparison of the population average profile of this factor across two or more levels of another factor. The design of the study may be such that the levels of the additional factor are investigated on the same subjects (i.e. another within-subject factor design) or on different subjects (i.e. a between-factor design). This section considers the former case, where a sample of subjects is drawn from the target population and their response measured at each of the levels of the within-subject covariate for each of the levels of the other within-subject factor, e.g. paraplegic subjects had their oxygen uptake measured at four specific work rates (the within-subject covariate), both in a sitting and in a standing posture (the other within-subject factor). The following steps are often appropriate to analyse data in such circumstances:

1　Draw up individual profile plots of the response variable across the within-subject covariate for each subject in the sample with all the levels of the other factor plotted in the same panel for each subject separately. Augment this with either the corresponding box plots for the sample and/or profile plots with all subjects in the same panel but separate panels for each level of the within-subject factor.

2　Assuming that a linear model reasonably represents the relationship between the response variable and the within-subject covariate (for every level of the within-subject factor), proceed to fit a selection of potential l.m.e. models to investigate the effects of both the factor and covariate in terms of population means and in terms of population standard deviations (i.e. allowing for random slopes or effects across subjects). The range of such a selection of models will in effect be the same for both the fixed (i.e. population mean) terms and the random (i.e. population standard deviation) terms and each of these will cover the customary choice of five models in a two-factor situation (i.e. no effect, effect of one factor only, effect of the other factor only, the additive effects of both factors and the full model with both factors and their interaction).

3　The choice of final model, for both fixed and random terms, will again be based on AIC (Akaike's Information Criterion) and will be the minimum AIC value achieved across all possible models here with all these fitted by the maximum likelihood (ML) method. As always, plotting and interpreting the final model are key stages in the complete analysis.

Illustration 11.2 Ice baths

Background

Ice baths are sometimes used in aerobic sports after training and competition. One of the supposed benefits of this practice is a reduction in blood lactate. There is little, if any, direct evidence that the use of ice baths really does lower blood lactate.

Study description

Ten club-standard oarsmen had their Blood Lactate profiles recorded at regular intervals after successfully completing a 2 km row in less than 7 minutes on two separate occasions 3 days apart. On one occasion each rower cooled down 'normally' (Control) while, on the other occasion, the oarsman was immersed in an ice bath.

Aim

To investigate whether ice baths significantly reduce, on average, Blood Lactate build-up at any stage in a 25-minute period after exercise compared with not using an ice bath.

Data

Name of data file:	*Ice Baths*
Response variable:	Blood Lactate Concentration (mmol.L^{-1})
Within-subject factor:	Condition (2 levels: Control, Ice Bath)
Within-subject covariate:	Time (6 levels: 0, 5, 10, 15, 20, 25 minutes post exercise)

Analysis

The within-subject covariate is Time and the within-subject factor is Condition. The first step is to produce adequate plots of the data such as the individual profile plots (Figure 11.10) comparing Control (i.e. no ice bath) to Ice Bath Blood Lactate profiles across Time for each

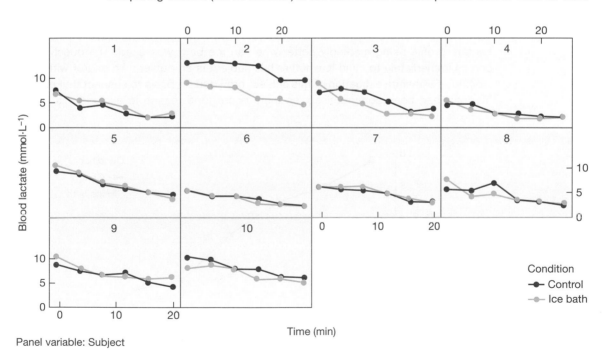

Panel variable: Subject

Figure 11.10 Blood Lactate profiles for each Condition by Subject.

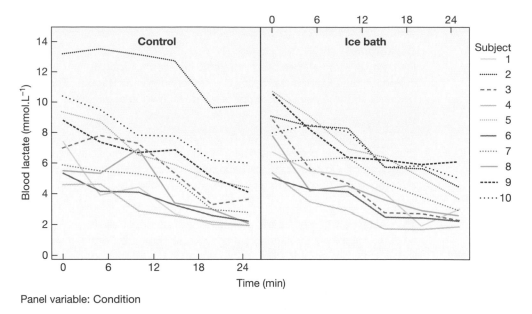

Panel variable: Condition

Figure 11.11 **Blood Lactate profiles by Condition.**

subject separately in a different panel. Figure 11.11 provides the same plots but with all Control profiles in the same panel and all Ice Bath profiles in a different panel. Finally, Figure 11.12 provides a plot of the sample mean profiles for each level of Condition (i.e. Control/Ice Bath).

Possibly the most outstanding aspect of the first two figures is that Subject 2 behaves differently from all other nine subjects with the only clear case of the Blood Lactate profile being markedly better when an ice bath was used. The question that comes immediately to mind is whether this subject is an outlier with and/or without an ice bath. Further investigation of this subject provided no basis to suspect that either of his trials had been compromised, so there is no good reason to exclude this subject

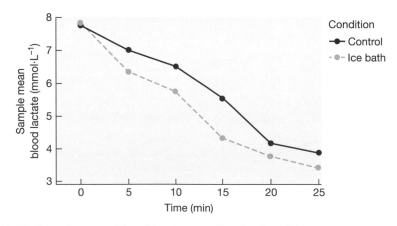

Figure 11.12 **Sample mean Blood Lactate profiles by Condition.**

from the analysis although considerable care must accordingly be exercised in interpreting these data.

Using all available data therefore, Figure 11.10 suggests that it is reasonable to assume that the Blood Lactate profiles are linearly related to Time, and so a selection of l.m.e. models can be fitted allowing for the combinations of all the usual* different structures of both population mean (fixed effects) and population s.d. (random effects) for the effects of the two factors, i.e. Condition (two levels each applied to each subject) and Time (modelled linearly for each subject on each Condition). The results for these, in terms of the AIC are given in Table 11.1.

*This would involve the five models constituting no effects of either factor, effects of each factor only, an additive effect of both factors and the full model with main effects and an interaction of the two factors (i.e. Time and Condition here although Time is modelled as a linear covariate).

Table 11.1

Model terms		Random/Popn s.d. terms				
		Common s.d.	C.S.D. + T	C.S.D. + C	C.S.D + T + C	C.S.D. + T * C
Fixed/Popn mean terms	Common mean	528	451	521	384	390
	Time (T)	419	422	355.0	355.2	362
	Condition (C)	528	445	521	386	392
	T + C	414	416	356	356	363
	T * C	415	418	357	357	364

Choosing as the best model that with the smallest AIC, in this case 355.0 (Table 11.1), gives the resulting output in Box 11.6 for the model with only Time linearly affecting the population mean but having random terms for different Subjects and for different Conditions in addition to the usual random error/natural variability term.

It is essential to write down and interpret the final (estimated) model both in its population mean and in its population s.d. aspects. First, the population mean Blood Lactate is simply estimated as:

$$7.244 - 0.1718 * \text{Time}$$

The population s.d. is made up of additive terms consisting of the *subject effect under each condition* with estimated s.d.'s of 2.61 and 1.51, respectively, for Control and Ice Bath (with an estimated correlation of 0.81 between the random intercepts of the two Conditions for the same subject), and an *error* with estimated s.d. of 0.77. Basically this involves a subject random effect which is constant across all observations of Blood Lactate for that subject (i.e. all Times and both Conditions), while the Condition random effect is different for each Condition even on the same subject but is then constant across all measurements of Blood Lactate on that Condition. Finally, the error random effect generates a different value/error for each measurement on each condition on each subject.

Here, it is clear first that Condition has *no (significant)* fixed effect on Blood Lactate (i.e. no difference in Blood Lactate population profiles with or without ice baths). However, it does appear that there is a random mechanism underlying the data whereby there is additional variability between the different Condition profiles even on the same subject.

Box 11.6

```
Final Model - Chosen by AIC

 Linear mixed-effects model fit by maximum likelihood
 Data: ans
       AIC      BIC      logLik
  355.0169 371.7419 -171.5085

Random effects:
 Formula: ~Condition - 1 | Subject
 Structure: General positive-definite, Log-Cholesky parametrization
                StdDev    Corr
ConditionControl 2.6113582 CndtnC
ConditionIceBath 1.5121168 0.805
Residual         0.7712975

Fixed effects: Lactate ~ Time
                Value Std.Error  DF   t-value p-value
(Intercept)  7.243904 0.4814216 109  15.04690       0
Time        -0.171800 0.0083151 109 -20.66120       0
 Correlation:
     (Intr)
Time -0.216

Standardized Within-Group Residuals:
       Min          Q1         Med          Q3         Max
-1.82565189 -0.65393550 -0.07633264  0.45331001  2.79805481
Number of Observations: 120
Number of Groups: 10
```

Conclusion

The effect of Ice Baths on club-standard oarsmen appears to be minimal at best. While Blood Lactate profiles clearly decrease with Time following exercise, the use of Ice Baths appears only to introduce a random component to the profile.

Reference: 'Comparison of the effect of different cool-down procedures on the decrease in blood lactate after exercise.' University of Glasgow student project, 2005.

Additional comments on Illustration 11.2

1 The whole analysis was repeated without Subject 2. Missing out this apparent outlier made no difference to the selected final model so there is really no need in this particular example to exclude this apparently anomalous subject.

2 The assumption of Normality – for the subject random effect/intercept – for each *Condition* looks plausible from the Normal probability plots of Figures 11.13 and 11.14 where only Time is modelled as a fixed effect for each Condition separately. The effect of the potential outlier in the Control sample (i.e. all six values for Subject 2) can be seen as the top right end of Figure 11.13.

3 To further emphasise the variability of each Condition separately, approximate 95% prediction bands (see Chapter 4 for more information on the statistical concept of prediction) are provided for a future Blood Lactate profile for each Condition in Figure 11.15 based on the final model. Clearly, the Control profiles are wider than the Ice Bath profiles. Also, slight inadequacies of the linear model appear as the Blood Lactate approaches

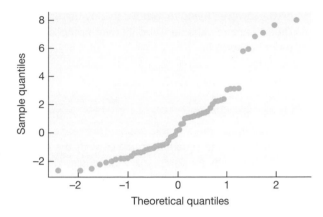

Figure 11.13 **Probability plot of Residuals (Controls).**

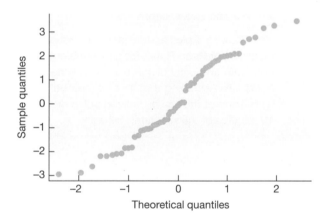

Figure 11.14 **Probability plot of Residuals (Ice Bath).**

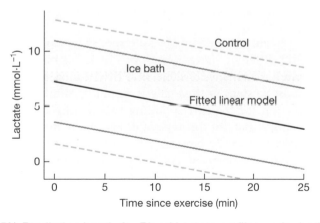

Figure 11.15 **95% Prediction bands for Blood Lactate profiles under both Conditions.**

zero. However, trying to remove this by using quadratic terms or trying to transform the Blood Lactate variable will only over-complicate the model with little, if any, improvement in overall fit.

Exercises

11.3 Determination of cardio-respiratory responses to arm exercise in paraplegic subjects has the potential to assist with the development of wheelchair design and walking aids for paraplegic individuals. The posture of the subjects may influence cardio-respiratory responses as there may be an increase in blood pooling with some postural positions compared with others. In addition, the effect of posture may vary depending on exercise intensity. The *Paraplegic Posture* dataset gives the results of a study of a sample of nine paraplegic subjects each of whom had their $\dot{V}O_2$ and heart rate measured at each of four separate work rates (0, 12, 23 and 35 watts) and in two postures (sitting and standing). What effects, if any, do work rate (modelled linearly) and/or posture have on each of the two responses (i.e. $\dot{V}O_2$ and Heart Rate)?

11.4 The Walking Poles study (see Illustration 9.3) involved the minute-by-minute recording of Heart Rates for all 14 subjects on their 10-minute simulated hill walk both with and without the use of walking poles. The data are in the file *Walking Poles HR*. Assuming that an l.m.e. model is appropriate here, investigate the effect, if any, of the use of walking poles on the (linear) heart rate 'profile' across the 10 minutes of the simulated hill walk.

11.4   One between-subject factor and one within-subject covariate

A design with one between-subject factor and one within-subject covariate is very similar to that considered in Section 11.3 except that, instead of the within-subject covariate being measured for the same subject across different levels of the within-subject factor, there are separate samples for each level of the between-subject factor.

When a dataset involves a response variable being measured under $K > 2$ distinct and different *ordered* conditions or levels of a within-subject factor on (hopefully random) samples of subjects at two or more levels of a between-subject factor, then sensible steps in the analysis would be similar to those described in the preceding section for the corresponding two within-subject factor design with the one real change that, for this type of design, there may be different variability for the different levels of the between-subject factor rather than, as in the previous section, an extra component of variability to allow for the other within-subject factor. Overall, model fitting and choice can be quite a complicated procedure and, although illustrated here in a relatively straightforward manner, is best carried out in collaboration with a practical statistician.

Illustration 11.3 **Resistance training by sport**

Background
See Illustration 11.1.

Study description
Samples of 13 rugby union and 20 soccer players underwent a series of resistant sprint training pulling a sledge with resistances comprising seven different percentages, from 0 to 30%, of their Body Mass. All subjects were club-standard amateurs. Sprint times over 10 metres were recorded.

Aim
To investigate whether the relationship of 10 m Sprint Time on Resistance is different for Soccer and Rugby Union players and, if so, whether any difference varies with Resistance.

Data
Name of data file:	*Sport Resistance*
Response variable:	10 m Sprint Time (seconds)
Between-subject factor:	Sport (2 levels: Rugby Union, Soccer)
Within-subject covariate:	Resistance (7 levels: 0, 5, 10, 15, 20, 25, 30% Body Mass)

Analysis
First provide case profile plots of Sprint Time against Resistance (i.e. the within-subject covariate) for each subject with separate panels for the two levels/sports of the between-subject factor (on the same scale) (see Figure 11.16). Individual profile plots for each subject in each sport are worth considering for detailed inspection of the data, particularly with respect to the assumption of linearity but are not included here.

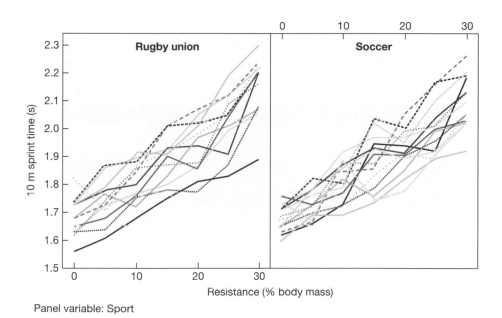

Panel variable: Sport

Figure 11.16 **Profile plots of Sprint Time by Resistance for each sport.**

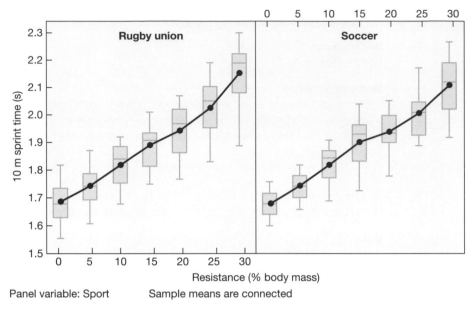

Figure 11.17 Box plots of Sprint Times by Resistance by Sport.

Linear relationships between Sprint Time and Resistance look perfectly plausible for these data but the intercepts and, possibly, slopes appear quite different across individuals both between and within each sport. There is also a suggestion that the Soccer players, in general, have lower profiles (i.e. are faster – at least towards the end of this resistance range). This interpretation is given a little credibility by the box plots (Figure 11.17) and sample mean plot (Figure 11.18).

As a first step it is worth fitting the full l.m.e. model with different standard deviations in both intercepts and slopes for the two sports. The output for this is provided in Box 11.7.

Although this is clearly not the final model since there is no significant difference in slopes at least ($P = 0.26$ here), it is worth plotting the fitted model in terms of the difference in population average linear relationships between the two sports, and this is portrayed in Figure 11.19.

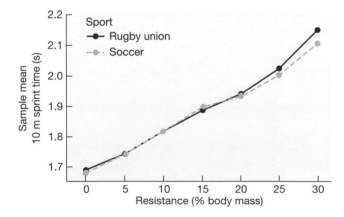

Figure 11.18 Sample means plot of Sprint Times by Sport.

Box 11.7

```
Full Model Output for Sport Resistance Study

Linear mixed-effects model fit by maximum likelihood
 Data: ans
       AIC       BIC    logLik
 -622.7802 -584.9136 322.3901

Random effects:
 Formula: ~ 1 + (Sport - 1) * (Resistance - 1) - Resistance | Subject
 Structure: General positive-definite
                    StdDev      Corr
    SportRugbyU 0.051389525 SprtRU SprtSc
    SportSoccer 0.025414930 -0.693
Sport:Resistance 0.001598208 -0.840  0.926
       Residual 0.050418391

Fixed effects: Time10m ~ Sport * Resistance
                    Value    Std.Error  DF   t-value p-value
     (Intercept)  1.675427 0.009899828 196 169.2379  <.0001
           Sport  0.002734 0.009899828  31   0.2762  0.7842
      Resistance  0.014296 0.000446919 196  31.9874  <.0001
Sport:Resistance -0.000506 0.000446919 196  -1.1332  0.2585

Standardized Within-Group Residuals:
      Min         Q1        Med        Q3       Max
 -3.152591 -0.6206636 0.02664923 0.5533893 2.405137
Number of Observations: 231
Number of Groups: 33
```

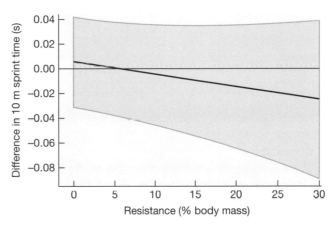

Figure 11.19 **Estimated difference in 10 m Sprint Time for Soccer minus Rugby Union with pointwise 95% interval estimates.**

It is therefore clear from this plot that there is no significant difference in population average relationships since the pointwise 95% confidence intervals easily include the value zero across the full range of Resistance – even at around 25% to 30%.

Finally, using the AIC to compare a full range of potential models, the final model turns out to have random components for intercepts and slopes but no effect of Sport whatsoever in either fixed or random terms. This final model is displayed in Box 11.8 and consists of the population (*of amateur Soccer and Rugby Union players*) estimated average relationship of

$$10 \text{ m Sprint Time} = 1.676 + 0.01419 * \text{Resistance}$$

with a distribution of random intercepts with an estimated s.d. of 0.0379, a distribution of random slopes with an estimated s.d. of 0.00167 (with an estimated correlation on any subject of 0.731) and a distribution about any subject's linear relationship with estimated s.d. of 0.0504.

Box 11.8

```
Final model output for Resistance by Sport data

Linear mixed-effects model fit by maximum likelihood
 Data: ans
       AIC        BIC     logLik
  -628.6854  -608.0309  320.3427

Random effects:
 Formula: ~Resistance | Subject
 Structure: General positive-definite, Log-Cholesky parametrization
             StdDev        Corr
(Intercept) 0.037944557  (Intr)
Resistance  0.001673091  0.731
Residual    0.050418379

Fixed effects: Time10m ~ Resistance
                Value     Std.Error   DF   t-value   p-value
(Intercept) 1.6760065  0.008949169  197  187.28068        0
Resistance  0.0141883  0.000443363  197   32.00155        0
 Correlation:
            (Intr)
Resistance -0.062

Standardized Within-Group Residuals:
          Min           Q1          Med           Q3          Max
 -3.1846152952  -0.6289562827  0.0007879376  0.5391985163  2.5337507331

Number of Observations: 231
Number of Groups: 33
```

Conclusions

There is no significant difference in the distribution of the linear relationship of 10 m Sprint Time and Body-Mass-determined Resistance between amateur Soccer and Rugby Union players. However, it is clear that there is a random distribution not only of the basic sprint speed of such populations but also in the rates (slopes) at which their sprint speed declines with increasing Resistance as applied by sledge-pulling.

Reference: Murray, A., Ross, G., Sutherland, K., Watt, I., McLean, D., Aitchison, T. and Grant, S.J. (2005). 'The effect of towing a range of relative resistances on sprint performance.' *Journal of Sports Sciences*, **23**: 927–935.

Additional comments on Illustration 11.3

1 The plot of the (estimated) random effects (i.e. intercept against slope) for all subjects, labelled by Sport, is given in Figure 11.20 (note that these are all relative to the estimated fixed effects, i.e. deviations from 1.676 and 0.0142, respectively). There is little

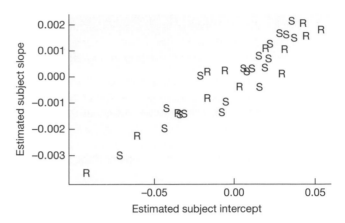

Figure 11.20 **Plot of subject effects by Sport.**

evidence here of any differences in the regression parameter distributions for the two sports. As is natural in linear regressions, the estimated intercepts and slopes are highly correlated.

2 Prediction bands for any (future) athlete of this type (i.e. high standard amateur soccer or rugby player) undergoing such testing are given in Figure 11.21 and could be used to identify whether any future recruit followed the same pattern of Resistance/Sprint response. Indeed, perhaps, the estimated subject/athlete profiles could be used to order athletes in terms of their pulling/sprinting power. This information may be of value to rugby coaches and players.

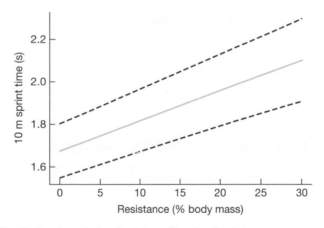

Figure 11.21 **Prediction bands for Sprint profiles by Resistance.**

Exercises

11.5 The *Physio Pain* dataset comes from a study of the effect of a mental distraction intended to reduce ischaemic pain. A sample of 20 volunteers were randomised as Controls or to the Distraction (see Illustration 4.4 for details) and each subjected to ischaemic pain until she could tolerate it no longer. A visual analogue scale (VAS) of perceived pain was recorded at each of the first 4 minutes after onset of pain (all subjects lasted at least 4 minutes in the study). Is there any evidence that the pattern of VAS across the first 4 minutes is different, in general, for those to whom the distraction is applied compared to those who do not have the distraction?

11.6 Improvements in running economy (defined as the steady-state oxygen uptake ($\dot{V}O_2$) for a particular running velocity) have the potential to enhance performance. It is often assumed that an individual's chosen cadence is the most economic. Measurement of $\dot{V}O_2$ at a range of cadences may reveal that the individual's chosen cadence is not the most economic. Cadence is defined as the number of complete steps taken in one minute. Ten males and ten females underwent five separate running tests at different running speeds (i.e. –10%, –5%, 0%, 5% and 10% of their natural/preferred Cadence). Each subject had his/her average $\dot{V}O_2$ measured for each test at each Cadence. Assuming that suitable l.m.e. models describe this dataset, investigate the effects of Sex and Cadence on $\dot{V}O_2$ for this dataset in the file *Cadence and Sex*.

11.5 More complicated designs involving within-subject covariates

In theory, a study could involve any number of between- and within-subject factors with, in addition, one or more within-subject covariates to be modelled linearly. The complexity of potential models to be compared in any such design can often be daunting, and considerable care should be employed when tackling such problems. The general points illustrated in this chapter should always be applied: plot the data sensibly (and in different ways) and use Akaike's Information Criterion (AIC) as a device to choose the best and simplest model which adequately describes the dataset. The following illustration involves two between-subject factors and one within-subject covariate and should give some insight into the complexities and difficulties involved with analysing even a relatively simple extension to the designs covered in earlier sections of this chapter.

Illustration 11.4 Knee extensor peak torque and velocity

Background

In isokinetic tests the maximum velocity at which a lever (attached to a limb – in this example the lower leg) can move is predetermined. In a knee extension test, the subject sits on a chair with his/her lower leg in a vertical position. The subject is asked to kick as hard and as fast as possible so that the entire leg finishes in a horizontal position. When a subject makes a maximum effort, the limb accelerates until it reaches the predetermined velocity set on the lever. Thus, after the initial acceleration the angular velocity of the knee joint is held constant at the predetermined velocity. Normally, peak torque decreases as angular velocity increases, but some studies have shown that there is a plateau in peak torque over a range of slow angular velocities. Measuring knee extensor peak torque across a range of angular velocities for different age groups in young girls and boys provides profiles of overall knee extension strength for each category of subject.

Study description

Samples of 10 children of each of the eight combinations of both Sexes and four Age groups (i.e. 5, 8, 11 or 14 years) were recruited. Their Knee Extensor Peak Torque was measured at each of four Angular Velocities (30, 120, 210 and 300 deg.s^{-1}) on a Cybex isokinetic dynamometer.

Aim

To investigate the effect of Angular Velocity on Knee Extensor Peak Torque across Sex and Age in children.

Data

Name of data file:	*Cybex*
Response variable:	Knee Extensor PT (newton metres)
Between-subject factors:	Sex (2 levels: Male, Female)
	Age (4 levels: 5, 8, 11, 14 years)
Within-subject covariate:	Velocity (4 levels: 30, 120, 210, 300 deg.s^{-1})

Analysis

There are two between-subject factors (Age and Sex) and one within-subject covariate (Velocity). First, provide profile plots of Peak Torque against Velocity for each subject across each of the eight combinations of the two Sexes and four Ages (Figure 11.22). It is clear from Figure 11.22 that the relationship between Peak Torque and Velocity is not linear, nor indeed does it exhibit constant variability across either Velocity or combinations of Sex and Age.

The simple way out of such a situation in many biological problems is to transform the data. In this example, taking the (natural) logarithm of Peak Torque removes all of these problems (Figure 11.23).

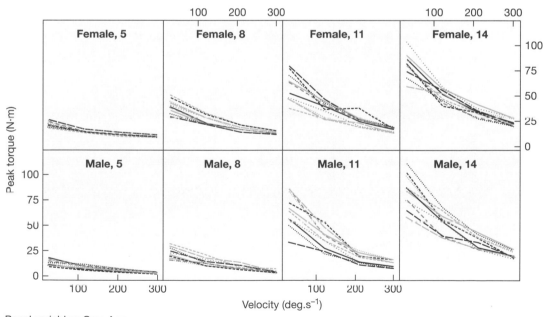

Panel variables: Sex, Age

Figure 11.22 Case profile plots of Peak Torque by Sex and Age.

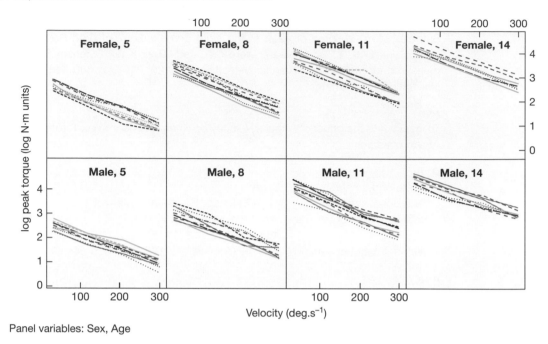

Panel variables: Sex, Age

Figure 11.23 **Case profile plots of log Peak Torque by Sex and Age.**

Indeed, the plots in Figure 11.23 look remarkably similar across all eight combinations of Sex and Age, with only the increasing effect of Age standing out in a dominant fashion. These suggestions are consolidated in the appropriate box plots in Figure 11.24 and the sample mean plots in Figure 11.25 with the clear differences across Age for both Sexes although

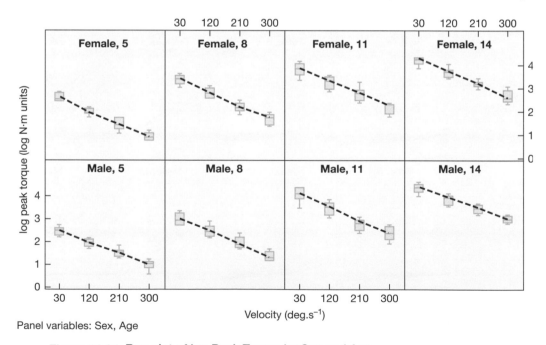

Panel variables: Sex, Age

Figure 11.24 **Box plot of log Peak Torque by Sex and Age.**

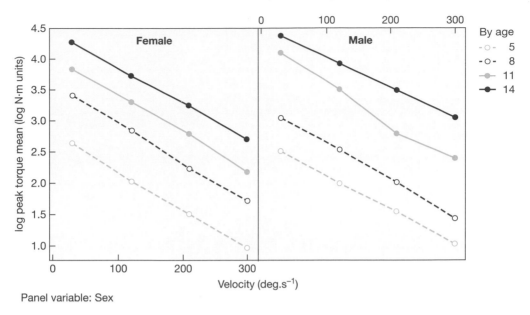

Panel variable: Sex

Figure 11.25 **Sample means plots of log Peak Torque.**

there appears to be a rise in Knee Extension Peak Torque for Females between 5 and 8 years of age while, for Males, it is between 8 and 11 years. On careful inspection, some slight differences in the rate of (log) Peak Torque decay with Velocity are apparent across individuals of the same Age and Sex as well as, on average, between Ages for the Males at least.

Even with only three factors here, Sex and Age as between-subject factors and Velocity as a within-subject covariate, there is still a considerable range of potential l.m.e. models. It is difficult to carry out a full search of all these possible models although a backwards stepwise approach to the random effects structure followed by a similar approach to the fixed effects structure would be reasonable (but complicated). However, as a first step in the analysis, Box 11.9 provides the output from the l.m.e. model with the full factorial structure for the effects of Sex, Age and Velocity (linearly) as well as random slopes for Velocity and different variability in all the combinations of Age and Sex about the appropriate population regressions.

High-order interactions here generally appear to be non-significant and some of these can be dropped from the model (but be careful doing this – see the first Additional Comment below). In addition, it appears that there are differences in variability across the Age/Sex combinations, with the 11-year-old Males showing most variability about their 'population' regression (i.e. about 1.3 times that of 14-year-old Males). Further, the estimated population s.d. (0.000019) of the slopes is small even when compared to the estimated overall population slope (−0.0059), suggesting that there is little or no real variability in slopes across all subjects regardless of Age or Sex.

Dropping the non-significant fixed effects in turn from the higher-order interactions and considering the inclusion of random slopes and different variabilities across Age and/or Sex, the final model based on AIC has the output given in Box 11.10.

The key elements of this final model are:

1 No evidence of random slopes for the effect of Velocity (i.e. variability is defined entirely by the intercepts).

Box 11.9

```
Full l.m.e. model for Cybex data

Linear mixed-effects model fit by maximum likelihood
 Data: ans
       AIC       BIC    logLik
 -257.0797 -155.335 155.5399

Random effects:
 Formula:  ~ Velocity | Subject
 Structure: General positive-definite
                  StdDev    Corr
(Intercept) 0.19281362246 (Inter
   Velocity 0.00001944505 -0.999
   Residual 0.10788393518

Variance function:
 Structure: Different standard deviations per stratum
 Formula:  ~ 1 | Sex * Age
 Parameter estimates:
 Male*14 Female*14 Male*11 Female*11   Male*8 Female*8    Male*5 Female*5
       1  1.036579 1.31405  1.122625 1.241899 0.906417 0.7161395 0.7865215
Fixed effects: logPT ~ Sex * Age * Velocity
                    Value  Std.Error  DF   t-value p-value
     (Intercept)  3.687414 0.02530289 232  145.7309  <.0001
             Sex -0.023976 0.02530289  72   -0.9476  0.3465
            Age1  0.340202 0.03500251  72    9.7194  <.0001
            Age2  0.363493 0.02114919  72   17.1871  <.0001
            Age3  0.260188 0.01457383  72   17.8531  <.0001
        Velocity -0.005911 0.00006364 232  -92.8955  <.0001
         SexAge1 -0.059721 0.03500251  72   -1.7062  0.0923
         SexAge2  0.079325 0.02114919  72    3.7507  0.0004
         SexAge3  0.021123 0.01457383  72    1.4493  0.1516
    Sex:Velocity  0.000207 0.00006364 232    3.2543  0.0013
    Age1Velocity -0.000175 0.00008135 232   -2.1451  0.0330
    Age2Velocity -0.000119 0.00005699 232   -2.0816  0.0385
    Age3Velocity  0.000183 0.00003637 232    5.0338  <.0001
 SexAge1Velocity -0.000076 0.00008135 232   -0.9390  0.3487
 SexAge2Velocity -0.000148 0.00005699 232   -2.6046  0.0098
 SexAge3Velocity  0.000072 0.00003637 232    1.9832  0.0485

Standardized Within-Group Residuals:
       Min         Q1        Med        Q3       Max
 -2.322131 -0.5382011 0.08459506 0.609112 3.023817

Number of Observations: 320
Number of Groups: 80
```

2 Different variabilities in the population intercepts among the Age groups, with higher variability in the 8- and 11-year-olds (and of course across Subjects within each Age group).

3 Different population slopes for Males and Females (i.e. significant Sex * Velocity interaction).

4 Different population intercepts for (at least some) combinations of Sex and Age groups (i.e. significant Sex * Age interaction).

Box 11.10

```
Final l.m.e. model for Cybex data

Linear mixed-effects model fit by maximum likelihood
 Data: ans
        AIC        BIC      logLik
  -238.2464 -181.7216 134.1232

Random effects:
 Formula: ~1 | Subject
         (Intercept)   Residual
StdDev:    0.1873535 0.1250497

Variance function:
 Structure: Different standard deviations per stratum
 Formula: ~1 | Age
 Parameter estimates:
        14         11          8          5
1.0000000 1.2179585 0.9798458 0.6552846
Fixed effects: logPT ~ Sex * Age + Velocity * Sex
                   ·    Value  Std.Error  DF   t-value p-value
(Intercept)        2.7828306 0.06333837 238  43.93594  0.0000
SexMale           -0.1001551 0.08957398  72  -1.11813  0.2672
Age8               0.7674673 0.08835980  72   8.68571  0.0000
Age11              1.2509877 0.08954686  72  13.97020  0.0000
Age14              1.7023029 0.08845087  72  19.24575  0.0000
Velocity          -0.0061285 0.00008889 238 -68.94642  0.0000
SexMale:Age8      -0.2893044 0.12495962  72  -2.31518  0.0235
SexMale:Age11      0.1843549 0.12663838  72   1.45576  0.1498
SexMale:Age14      0.2292018 0.12508842  72   1.83232  0.0710
SexMale:Velocity   0.0005423 0.00012571 238   4.31400  0.0000

Standardized Within-Group Residuals:
        Min         Q1         Med         Q3         Max
-2.67185333 -0.62833597  0.03091913  0.61320704  2.47752936

Number of Observations: 320
Number of Groups: 80
```

A plot of this final model in terms of the estimated population means is given for the logarithm of Peak Torque in Figure 11.26 and for Peak Torque itself in Figure 11.27. The changing of the 'Sex differences' through the Age groups is clearly visible, with little difference among 5-year-olds, the Females ahead at 8 years but the Males overtaking and stretching ahead through 11 and 14 years of age.

Conclusion

The relationship between the logarithm of Peak Torque and Velocity for Cybex-based knee extensor measurements is, in general, linear but differs across 5- to 14-year-olds, with the pattern of difference being dissimilar for Males and Females. There is no real suggestion that the rates of (log) Peak Torque change with Velocity are different for subjects within any of the Age or Sex populations.

Reference: Ommer, J. (1987). 'Motor ability in children.' MSc thesis, Glasgow University.

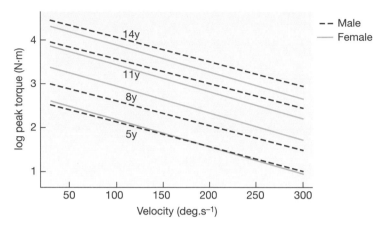

Figure 11.26 **Estimated population regressions for Ages and Sexes.**

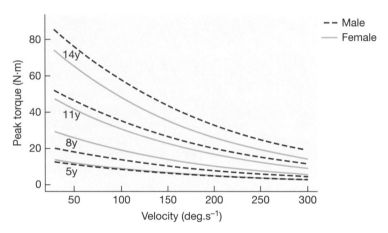

Figure 11.27 **Estimated population regressions of Peak Torque for Ages and Sexes.**

Additional comments on Illustration 11.4

1 Care has to be taken in dropping fixed effects terms from a full model as, for example, apparently non-significant two-way interactions may have their *P*-value dramatically altered when corresponding three-way interactions containing these two factors are dropped from the model. For example, the Sex * Velocity interaction *P*-value changes from 0.08 to 0.03 when one compares the models in Boxes 11.9 and 11.10 − note though that the Sex * Velocity interaction here is really a difference in the slopes of the effects of Velocity between the populations of Males and Females.

2 The possibility that the effect of Age was itself linear (and possibly different between the Sexes) was investigated here and given little credibility (corresponding AIC = 68.8 for the model equivalent to that in Box 11.10 but with Age as linear compared with AIC = 38.3 with Age simply as a factor).

3 Treating Velocity as a fixed effect, the full repeated measures ANOVA (with an additive, random effect for Subject) is given in Box 11.11.

Box 11.11

```
General Linear Model: LogPT versus Velocity, Sex, Age, Subject

Factor              Type    Levels  Values
Velocity            fixed        4  30, 120, 210, 300
Sex                 fixed        2  Female, Male
Age                 fixed        4  5, 8, 11, 14
Subject(Sex Age)    random      80  1, 2, 3, 4, 5, 6, 7, 8,

Analysis of Variance for LogPT, using Adjusted SS for Tests

Source               DF     Seq SS     Adj SS     Adj MS        F       P
Velocity              3   113.2370   113.2370    37.7457  3036.52   0.000
Sex                   1     0.0332     0.0332     0.0332     0.19   0.665
Age                   3   153.2462   153.2462    51.0821   290.17   0.000
Velocity*Sex          3     0.1555     0.1555     0.0518     4.17   0.007
Velocity*Age          9     0.5002     0.5002     0.0556     4.47   0.000
Sex*Age               3     3.3272     3.3272     1.1091     6.30   0.001
Velocity*Sex*Age      9     0.3725     0.3725     0.0414     3.33   0.001
Subject(Sex Age)     72    12.6748    12.6748     0.1760    14.16   0.000
Error               216     2.6850     2.6850     0.0124
Total               319   286.2317
```

Virtually all the terms in this model are significant, even the three-way interaction of Velocity, Age and Sex. Instead of trying to interpret and explain all these significant terms, now try to fit Velocity as a covariate (i.e. model its effect on log Peak Torque in a linear fashion) but with the same slope for all subjects regardless of Sex and Age (i.e. a form of analysis of covariance). The output is in Box 11.12.

Box 11.12

```
Analysis of Variance for LogPT, using Adjusted SS for Tests

Source               DF     Seq SS     Adj SS     Adj MS        F       P
Sex                   1     0.0332     0.0499     0.0499     0.87   0.352 x
Age                   3   153.2462    39.8301    13.2767   232.62   0.000 x
Velocity              1   113.2241   113.2241   113.2241  8824.86   0.000
Sex*Age               3     3.3272     1.0896     0.3632     6.36   0.001 x
Sex*Velocity          1     0.1389     0.1389     0.1389    10.83   0.001
Age*Velocity          3     0.4435     0.4435     0.1478    11.52   0.000
Sex*Age*Velocity      3     0.1671     0.1671     0.0557     4.34   0.005
Subject(Sex Age)     72    12.6748    12.6748     0.1760    13.72   0.000
Error               232     2.9766     2.9766     0.0128
Total               319   286.2317
```

This does not reduce the complexity of the resulting final model (i.e. that with all significant terms) and both of these approaches have considerably more terms/ interactions than the final l.m.e. model which is anyway to be preferred as it allows for random slopes and different variances among each of the various sub-populations.

Exercises

11.7 High levels of finger endurance are considered to be a very important attribute for elite rock climbers. Climbing is sometimes carried out in a high altitude environment. To date, there has been no published study examining the effects of altitude-induced hypoxia on rock-climbing-specific finger endurance. Ten elite climbers and 10 non-climbers/controls carried out Climbing Specific Endurance tests at 40% of maximum voluntary contraction in both Normoxia and Hypoxia (first test randomly assigned). Surface electromyographic (EMG) was recorded in the flexor digitorum superficialis (a muscle which contributes to finger flexion) throughout each of the endurance tests. The Median Frequency of the EMG power spectrum was used as an index of fatigue. The *Climbing Fatigue* dataset provides the data from the Median Frequency of the EMG power spectrum across three points (First, Middle and Last Muscle Contraction). Is there any evidence that the Fatigue profile differs, on average, between the Climbers and Non-Climbers and/or the type of Atmosphere (i.e. Normoxia and Hypoxia)?

11.8 Studies of the thermal protective properties of three Arctic survival suits were carried out at −6°C and −10°C in a cold chamber. Ten subjects underwent the −6°C study and had their skin temperature reduction from baseline recorded at 15-minute intervals while they remained for one hour in the chamber for each of the three suits. Eight different subjects underwent the same procedure in the −10°C study. Assuming that the Reduction in Skin Temperature is linearly dependent on time in the cold chamber, carry out a suitable l.m.e. analysis to investigate the effects of Suit, Study and Time (in the cold chamber). The data are in the file *Cold Suits*.

Summary

To cover designs with within-subject covariates the following scenarios were illustrated in this chapter:

- One within-subject covariate.
- One between-subject factor at two levels and one within-subject covariate.
- One within-subject factor at two levels and one within-subject covariate.
- Two between-subject factors and one within-subject covariate.

The key elements of all analyses were appropriate plots of the data, including panel plots, linear mixed-effects or random regression models incorporating variability in slopes of the linear relationship with the within-subject covariate and a choice of model among the many possible based on Akaike's Information Criterion.

These are just a few of the many general scenarios where linear mixed-effects models can be usefully applied. These techniques are being used more and more in sports science and many other biomedical disciplines, so a basic understanding is essential in the many areas of research where such within-subject covariates apply (growth is an obvious general area).

12 Measurement error and method agreement studies

12.1   Introduction

An essential ingredient in any study is that measurements on all the variables, and especially the response variables, are 'reliable' in the sense that, if they were measured again on the same subjects under effectively identical conditions, then the results would be 'similar'. The words 'reliable' and 'similar' here are not well defined but the key element is that repeat (or replicate) observations within the same subject under effectively identical conditions should be much closer to each other than observations between different subjects. In the statistical jargon introduced in Section 2.3 of Chapter 2, this is saying that the within-subject variability should be much less than the between-subject variability or the variable is likely to be useless in identifying either differences in population means or even individual subject changes due to an exercise regime or, indeed, over time.

The difficulty in measuring even the simplest variable should not be underemphasised. For example, measuring a subject's height seems straightforward, even trivial. However, lack of care by the measurer could result in a poor observation if the measurer does not ensure that the subject is standing straight, has nothing on his/her feet, ignores the question of the subject's hair (bald or afro would make a difference) and even discounts the time of day which adds to the variability in a subject's height as humans reduce in height over the course of a day due to shortening of the vertebral column. All in all, therefore, it is not a simple matter to 'measure a variable'. The measurement of height of any specific subject can at least be easily repeated almost simultaneously either by the same observer a number of times (replicates) or by different observers. This is quite unlike more complicated variables such as $\dot{V}O_2$ max or blood lactate markers, a single measurement of which might require a considerable time on the part not only of the subject but also of the observer and involve fairly complex measurement procedures. It would be almost impossible to take replicates of such variables by the same observer under effectively identical conditions or by different observers or using different apparatus.

There are different **sources of variability** for different variables and, while some researchers may be interested in identifying and measuring the contributions to overall variability of the specific sources, most researchers will be concerned only that the results of his/her study are **Repeatable** and **Reproducible**. What do these words mean? While there are no universally accepted definitions of these terms, repeatability refers to ensuring that the variability of measurements of a random variable on the same subject by the same observer under effectively identical conditions is less than some predetermined value. Reproducibility, however, refers to whether the results of the study can be replicated to an acceptable degree by another observer or research team. A pilot study with replicate observations on the same subjects (covering a wide range of the target population) by the same observer is often a good idea before carrying out the full study. If possible, repeat observations on the same subjects by different observers and/or by different set-ups of the measuring apparatus can give key information (sometimes frightening) on the reproducibility of a study.

If possible, any variable should be assessed for its most important sources or components of variability. For many variables, there will almost certainly be variability across *observers* as well as variability due to the measuring apparatus/regime (e.g. different callipers for skinfolds and different positioning of timing gates for sprint trials). Each different component of variability has associated a standard deviation (based on a Normal distribution assumption) quantifying the likely spread of error due to that component about the true value of any measurement (i.e. plus or minus twice the standard deviation about the measurement). The basic assumption for modelling these components of variability is that errors are additive, are independent of each other and are all Normally distributed. Having a measurement where the standard deviations from all acknowledged sources of variability (estimated from a suitably designed study) are relatively small compared with the between-subject variability is a basic requirement for any study.

The other key ingredient of this chapter is the situation where the characteristic underlying the variable of interest can be measured by two or more different methods or measuring techniques and the problem is which method to use. There are really two distinct scenarios here for so-called **method agreement** or **Method Comparison** studies:

1 A new method is compared with a gold standard (i.e. an unbiased reliable method) to see if the new method is an adequate alternative to the gold standard.

2 Two different methods, neither of which is a gold standard for the characteristic under consideration, are compared with each other where a key question is the level of agreement between the methods.

In the context of comparing a new method to an established or direct method (i.e. a gold standard), consider the measurement of $\dot{V}O_2$ max. The gold standard for this is a direct measurement of $\dot{V}O_2$ max carried out on a treadmill, say, while a simple (and considerably cheaper) alternative is available through an 'estimate' of $\dot{V}O_2$ max using a multi-stage shuttle test. In the context of comparing two methods, both of which are indirect measures of the characteristic, consider the 'estimation' of % body fat through the use of skinfolds or through the application of electrical impedance. Neither of these is a direct method (impossible without boiling down a subject to separate out bones, fat etc. – not to be recommended). The questions for the researcher, though, are which of these is more reliable and is either measuring the true underlying characteristic? This is the problem of the **validity** of a method or measuring technique, i.e. is the new method, at least on average, measuring the true, underlying quantity of interest or does it have some in-built systematic bias?

Section 12.2 introduces and illustrates some of the simplest aspects of assessing measurement error for reliability studies using the same observer and for reproducibility studies involving more than one observer. The remainder of the chapter (Section 12.3) introduces and illustrates the statistical ideas used in method agreement or method comparison problems.

12.2   Measurement error

There are two potential types of error possible in any physiological measurement: namely a systematic bias due, perhaps, to a flaw in the design of the study, and random components such as natural variability within subjects as well as variability across observers, measuring apparatus etc.

Systematic bias is error in a particular direction which applies itself to every observation in the study. For example, if time gates are not set accurately on a sprint test there will be a systematic bias, e.g. the distance being timed may be shorter than the target of 20 metres so the sprint times will all appear faster than they really are because the sprinters have not covered the required distance. Systematic bias could also arise when a blood lactate analyser is wrongly calibrated and consistently provides a higher reading than the real value. These types of systematic bias can only be assessed by redoing the study.

Such systematic biases can be due to the 'order of the replicates', such as 'learning effects' where a subject improves his/her score simply through repeating and becoming familiar with the test (Counter Movement Jumps could be greater on the third trial), or fatigue effects where a subject cannot perform as well on, say, the third maximal sprint as on the first. The first step in analysing data from any reliability study is to assess whether there is any systematic bias across the replicates of the study, i.e. whether the first measurement is producing measurements which are significantly different on average from those of the second trial and so on. The key phrase here is on average as the systematic bias will apply to all subjects' measurements.

Components of variability are assumed to be **random** in nature (i.e. the error is just as likely to increase or decrease the estimate of the true underlying characteristic). Hence the overall mean of a measurement is not changed but the variability is increased. Every measurement is prone to error and good studies are needed to quantify all (suspected) sources of variability. If the overall random error from all the sources of variability is too large, then the usefulness of the measuring system and hence the study must be in doubt. How large depends upon the context and largely relates to the between-subject variability in the target population. A key summary of any reliability study is to quantify the (suspected) sources of variability through estimating their corresponding standard deviations having corrected, if necessary, for any systematic biases due to the order of replicates.

The illustrations in this section cover such studies, from simple ones involving two replicates per subject through to another involving three replicates per subjects and finally to a reproducibility study involving variability across observers.

Illustration 12.1   Anthropometric measurement error

Background

A sports dietician was interested in estimating the measurement error inherent in measuring a youth player's foot length. This measurement may be of value in the monitoring of maturational status.

Study description

Foot Length measurements were taken twice on a sample of 19 male soccer players in a professional youth academy. The two measurements were taken on successive days (to the nearest centimetre).

Aim

To assess the repeatability of a Youth Player's Foot Length measurement.

Data

Name of data file:	*Anthropometric Error*
Response variable:	Foot Length (centimetres)
Within-subject factor:	Measure (2 levels: Measure 1, Measure 2)

Analysis

The initial analysis needed is identical to that used for paired data, and indeed this is nothing more than paired data with a slightly different emphasis. As always, a plot of the data is essential. Here this should be a scatter plot of the Foot Length measurements using the same scales for each axis and including the line of equality (Figure 12.1).

The figure shows perfect agreement between most of the pairwise measurements. It might appear obvious to include the correlation coefficient here as a useful summary of agreement but this is not appropriate. Recall that the correlation coefficient provides a measure of the scatter about the *line of best fit* and not the *line of equality* which is the more important comparison in this context.

Clearly if there was no measurement error, the individual differences should be zero. A box plot of the differences in the first and second Foot Length measurements (Figure 12.2) suggests that the sample median difference is zero (as is the upper quartile). One difference is flagged as a potential outlier and there is a slight suggestion of a lack of symmetry

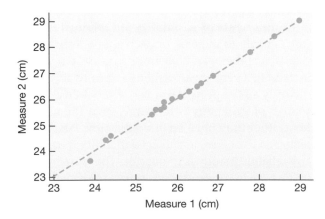

Figure 12.1 **Scatter plot of Foot Length measurements (with line of equality superimposed).**

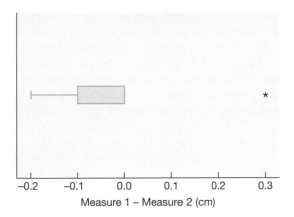

Figure 12.2 **Box plot of differences in Foot Length measurements.**

due to the longer tail in the 'negative' direction. Note also that the median is not high-lighted as it happens to be identical to the upper quartile.

A clearer indication is provided by the individual values plot (Figure 12.3) where six sub-jects (out of nineteen) are identified as not having perfect agreement.

The next step is to use a paired-sample *t*-test to investigate the population mean change across the two measurements. The results (Box 12.1) suggest that despite the second measurement being slightly larger than the first, on average the mean difference did not reach statistical significance (at the 0.05 significance level).

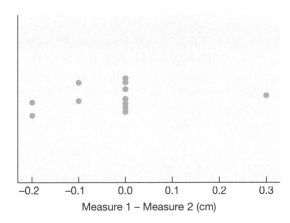

Figure 12.3 **Individual value plot of differences in Foot Length measurements.**

Box 12.1

```
Paired T for Measure 1 - Measure 2

            N      Mean    StDev   SE Mean
Measure 1   19    26.242   1.460    0.335
Measure 2   19    26.263   1.461    0.335
Difference  19    0.0211   0.1032   0.0237

95% CI for mean difference: (-0.0708, 0.0287)
T-Test of mean difference = 0 (vs not = 0): T-Value = -0.89
P-value = 0.385
```

Although six subjects were identified as having measurement error (i.e. non-zero differences between the two recordings of Foot Length), the measurements do not appear to be biased on average, i.e. there is no significant systematic error present. Any concerns about the Normality (of the sample of differences) can be checked by providing an interval estimate for the population mean difference using the bootstrap or by concentrating on the median instead. Rather than summarising the mean change, a more useful summary would be to estimate the dietician's measurement error for a single observation, i.e. what is the estimated random error in any single Foot Length measurement?

The random error is quantified as the sample **within-subject standard deviation** (s_{within}). It might appear obvious that an average of each individual's standard deviation would suffice, but this would also contain the systematic error component (if present). One appropriate estimate of s_{within} is calculated by dividing the standard deviation of the differences by $\sqrt{2}$ – the value 2 is used here since each subject is measured twice.

The resulting quantity is sometimes referred to as the **typical error**, which is simply an estimate of the within-subject variability. The estimated typical error for the Foot Length measurement is $0.1032/\sqrt{2} = 0.0729$ cm (see Box 12.1). Any subject's Foot Length measured by this dietician (using an identical protocol) is likely to vary about the actual Foot Length of the subject by plus or minus twice this (i.e. ± 0.14 cm). As the sample mean Foot Length is around 26 cm, this ± 0.14 is miniscule and the measurement of Foot Length can be relied upon to the nearest centimetre.

The within-subject variability is an important component of variability in any such study but it should be compared with the between-subject variability in order to get a feel for their relative magnitude. If, for example, the within-subject variability (i.e. the overall random error) is larger than the other sources of variability the measurement system is highly dubious.

Estimates of the variance components are available by using the GLM to fit a repeated measures ANOVA with Foot Length as the response and Subject as a random between-subject factor representing individuals (as these are assumed to constitute a random sample from a population of such footballers). The results are shown in Box 12.2.

Box 12.2

```
General Linear Model: Foot Length versus Subject

Factor    Type     Levels   Values
Subject   random      19    1, 2, 3,...

Analysis of Variance for Foot Length, using Adjusted SS for Tests

Source    DF    Seq SS    Adj SS   Adj MS        F       P
Subject   18   76.7147   76.7147   4.2619   809.77   0.000
Error     19    0.1000    0.1000   0.0053
Total     37   76.8147

S = 0.0725476  R-Sq = 99.87%  R-Sq(adj) = 99.75%

Variance Components, using Adjusted SS

          Estimated
Source      Value
Subject   2.12833
Error     0.00526
```

There is a significant subject effect ($P < 0.001$ in Box 12.2) highlighting that individuals differ significantly. The largest variance component is that across subjects (2.128) which is considerably larger than that of within-subject variability/random error (0.005). This result validates the measuring system as the dominant source of variability is due to the subjects differing from each other in terms of Foot Length (i.e. between-subject is the largest source of variability).

A useful summary here is to form the ratio of the between-subject variability over the total variability (i.e. between plus within plus any other sources), and express as a percentage (i.e. $2.128/(2.128 + 0.005) = 0.997$ or, as a percentage, 99.7%). This **reliability coefficient** measures the relative size of the between-subject variability to the total variability and can be thought of as similar to the R^2 statistic, i.e. the larger the better.

Conclusion

There was no significant ($P = 0.39$) difference in successive Foot Length measurements. An estimate of the typical error of Foot Length is 0.07 cm, the dietician should assess whether this is within the recommended acceptable measurement error for such. The reliability coefficient was estimated to be 99.7%, indicating near perfect agreement between measurements on the same subject.

Source: Sports Performance Unit, Scottish Premier League Club.

Additional comments on Illustration 12.1

1. An estimate of the typical error (s_{within}) is given in the output of Box 12.2 as S, the standard deviation of the error, and here turns out to be 0.07. This is actually just the square root of the variance component due to error (i.e. $\sqrt{0.00532} = 0.07$).

2. As the units of measurement error are in the same units as the measurement itself, the magnitude of the error depends on the magnitude of the variable of interest, e.g. the measurement error in measuring a thigh circumference will be larger than when measuring upper arm girth. In order to make measurement error comparable across different variables it is common practice to express measurement error as a percentage of the mean, i.e. 100 * measurement error divided by the sample mean across all replicates on all subjects. This **within-subject coefficient of variation** for Foot Length measurements is $100 * 0.07/26.25 = 0.27\%$.

3. In this same study, an interesting result arises when comparing the Heights of the soccer players over the two days in question. There is evidence of a significant mean difference (highlighted in Box 12.3), such that the players appear to be significantly taller, on average, on the second day. However, a quick look at the relevant 95% confidence

Box 12.3

```
Paired T for height (cm)_1 - height (cm)_2

                 N     Mean    StDev   SE Mean
height (cm)_1   19    177.59    6.91      1.59
height (cm)_2   19    177.64    6.91      1.59
Difference      19   -0.0526   0.0612   0.0140

95% CI for mean difference: (-0.0821, -0.0231)
T-Test of mean difference = 0 (vs not = 0): T-Value = -3.75
P-value = 0.001
```

interval reveals that this significant increase is between 0.2 and 0.08 cm, hardly more than a hair's breadth.

A slight change is needed when estimating the variance components for this analysis as a significant difference has been identified across the two measurements. The GLM needed has Height as the response, Measurement as a fixed effect (to account for the change in Height across the measurements) and Subject as a random effect (Box 12.4).

Box 12.4

```
General Linear Model: Height versus Measurement, Subject

Factor        Type     Levels  Values
Measurement   fixed        2   Measure 1, Measure 2
Subject       random      19   1, 2, 3, ...

Analysis of Variance for Height, using Adjusted SS for Tests

Source   DF    Seq SS     Adj SS   Adj MS         F       P
Measure   1     0.026      0.026    0.026     14.06   0.001
Subject  18  1719.531   1719.531   95.529  51048.56   0.000
Error    18     0.034      0.034    0.002
Total    37  1719.591

S = 0.0432590  R-Sq = 100.00%  R-Sq(adj) = 100.00%

Variance Components, using Adjusted SS

            Estimated
Source        Value
Subject      47.7638
Error         0.0019
```

Although a significant measurement effect was identified and quantified as between 0.2 and 0.08 cm, the typical error is miniscule (0.04 cm) and the between-subject variance component is massive relative to this error.

The next example illustrates the case where three replicates of a measurement process are taken by the same observer on a random sample of children. First, investigate for systematic biases across the three replicates and then, allowing for this if necessary, estimate the within-subject and between-subject variability to assess the reliability of the measurement process.

Illustration 12.2   BMI repeatability

Background

Measurement of anthropometric and physiological variables in young children is necessary in order that changes can be monitored. It is important that these variables can be measured accurately. While it may seem simple to weigh and to measure the height of children it should be remembered that children find it difficult to remain still for any length of time. Body mass index (BMI) is determined by dividing a person's body mass (in kilograms) by the square of a person's height (in metres). BMI is used to provide some indication of the degree of fatness.

Study description

Thirteen 4-year-old children took part in the study. Height and Body Mass were measured on three occasions (each two days apart) by the same researcher.

Aim

To assess the repeatability of the Body Mass Index in pre-school age children.

Data

Name of the data file: *BMI Agreement*
Response variable: BMI (kg.m^{-2})
Within-subject factor: Measure (3 levels: Measure 1, Measure 2, Measure 3)

Analysis

Start by creating a matrix scatter plot of the three variables using the same scales for each axis and including the line of equality in each plot (Figure 12.4).

In this study, the same researcher measured the same quantity (i.e. BMI) three times on each individual. If there was no measurement error whatsoever, then all the points in Figure 12.4 would fall exactly on the line of equality. Clearly, they do not. A case profile plot (Figure 12.5) does not suggest that there is any consistent change across the three measurements as some tend to rise, some drop, and a few individuals exhibit no real difference across the measurements.

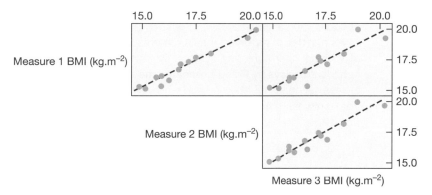

Figure 12.4 **Matrix plot of BMI measurements (with line of equality superimposed).**

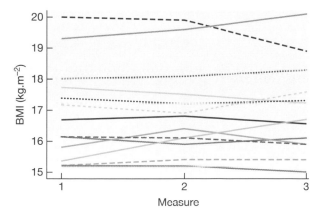

Figure 12.5 **Case profile plot of BMI by Measure.**

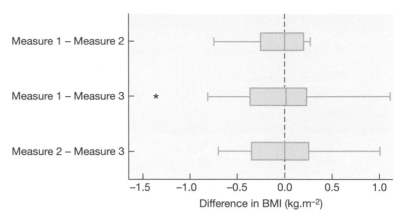

Figure 12.6 Box plot of pairwise differences in BMI by Measure.

Box plots of the differences in the each pair of BMI measurements (Figure 12.6) suggest that, in general, the median difference is close to zero for each comparison and that most of the differences are between ± 1 kg.m^{-2}. There is a suggestion of a larger range in differences when comparing the first and third BMI measurements and one difference has been deemed an outlier (by Minitab). As the three measurements were taken longitudinally it is important to test whether there is any evidence of systematic error present due to a learning/observer fatigue (or whatever) effect.

As a series of repeated measurements were made by the same observer a formal test of whether there are any systematic biases across the three measurements taken on consecutive days by fitting a repeated measures one-way ANOVA. The ANOVA is fitted, as always, using the GLM command while specifying BMI as the response variable and a random between-subject factor representing subjects. The resulting output is presented in Box 12.5.

Box 12.5

```
Factor    Type     Levels   Values
Subject   random        13   1, 2, 3,...

Analysis of Variance for BMI, using Adjusted SS for Tests

Source    DF    Seq SS    Adj SS   Adj MS       F       P
Subject   12   76.4310   76.4310   6.3692   59.39   0.000
Error     26    2.7885    2.7885   0.1073
Total     38   79.2195

S = 0.327492     R-Sq = 96.48%     R-Sq(adj) = 94.86%

Variance Components, using Adjusted SS

          Estimated
Source       Value
Subject     2.0873
Error       0.1073
```

The test of whether there is a difference in the population mean BMI across subjects was significant ($P < 0.001$), which is not surprising given the variability across subjects

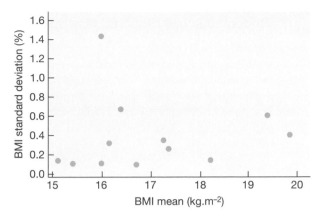

Figure 12.7 **Scatter plot of within-subject BMI mean and standard deviation.**

evident in Figure 12.5. More importantly an estimate of the typical error is given by the estimated standard deviation of the unexplained variability in the model (highlighted in bold in Box 12.5). On the basis of this, the typical error for any child's BMI is 0.33 kg.m^{-2}. Given that BMI in this sample tends to be around 17, this error is fairly minimal.

The variance components are dominated by the between-subject variability, with, in effect, zero contribution from the within-subject variability. The reliability coefficient is $2.0873/(2.0873 + 0.1073) = 95\%$, suggesting excellent repeatability.

Before concluding, it is important to check that the measurement error is the same across all subjects, i.e. across the full range of BMI values observed. This can be checked quite easily by plotting the sample mean against the sample standard deviation for *each subject* (Figure 12.7). The absence of any noticeable trend in Figure 12.7 suggests that the measurement error can be assumed constant regardless of the actual value of BMI being observed in the population of such children.

Conclusion

There was no evidence of a systematic change in the mean BMI across the three measurements ($P = 0.84$). The researcher for this study could measure BMI with an estimated measurement error of 0.33 kg.m^{-2} (e.g. given a BMI of a 4-year-old measured by this researcher as 18, one would believe that child's BMI would really be between $18 - 2 * 0.33$ and $18 + 2 * 0.33$). Given that the range of BMI values (from Test 1 for example) is 15.2 to 20 kg.m^{-2}, a measurement error of 0.33 kg.m^{-2} appears quite small. The repeatability coefficient was estimated to be 95%, suggesting excellent repeatability.

Reference: Jamieson, L. (student), Grant, S., Reilly, J. and Paton, J. (staff) (2003). 'Appropriateness and reproducibility of coronary disease risk factor tests in pre-school age children.' Wellcome Trust Summer Vacation project.

Additional comment on Illustration 12.2

The assumptions underlying each analysis should, of course, be checked before making any formal conclusions. Techniques needed for the GLM are identical to those outlined in Chapter 9.

A further example is now given where the interest is in estimating the measurement error in a blood lactate endurance marker. A different method for estimating measurement error is introduced.

Illustration 12.3 Repeatability of blood lactate markers

Background

Blood lactate testing is commonly used to determine the training status of endurance athletes. Blood lactate endurance markers have been reported to be a sensitive indicator of training status. For such markers to be of value they must be shown to be repeatable. There is a need to determine how reliable blood lactate markers are in order to be able to distinguish real changes in aerobic fitness from changes representing nothing but random error.

Study description

Fourteen female subjects performed two identical incremental tests, one week apart, consisting of at least six 4-minute stages. Blood lactate concentrations were recorded at the end of each stage from which each individual's Lactate Threshold was calculated for each test.

Aim

To investigate the repeatability of the Lactate Threshold endurance marker.

Data

Name of the data file: *Lactate Markers Reliability*
Response variable: Lactate Threshold (km.h^{-1})
Within-subject factor: Measure (2 levels: Measure 1, Measure 2)

Analysis

A scatter plot of the Lactate Threshold (LT) for each Female at the two tests is given in Figure 12.8. The level of agreement between the two measurements is quite poor given that there should not have been any meaningful change in aerobic fitness (i.e. no systematic error component). Although there is no clear indication of a bias across the two measurements, there appears to be a considerable lack of agreement (i.e. within-subject variability) between the two measurements.

A paired-sample *t*-test (Box 12.6) confirms this subjective impression as there is no evidence of a significant change in mean LT across the two measurements ($P = 0.578$).

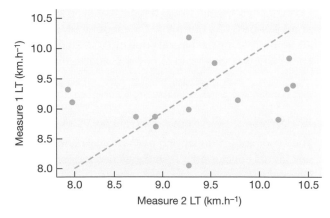

Figure 12.8 Scatter plot of Lactate Threshold by Measure (with line of equality superimposed).

Box 12.6

```
Paired T for Measure 1 - Measure 2

            N     Mean   StDev   SE Mean
Measure 1   14    9.176  0.540    0.144
Measure 2   14    9.307  0.806    0.216
Difference  14   -0.131  0.862    0.230

95% CI for mean difference: (−0.629, 0.366)
T-Test of mean difference = 0 (vs not = 0): T-Value = −0.57
P-Value = 0.578
```

The GLM (Box 12.7) did not identify a significant subject effect ($P = 0.193$) where the athletes are not deemed different, on average, in terms of LT.

Box 12.7

```
General Linear Model: LT versus Subject

Factor      Type     Levels  Values
Subject     random      14   1, 2, 3, ...

Analysis of Variance for LT, using Adjusted SS for Tests

Source   DF   Seq SS   Adj SS   Adj MS     F      P
Subject  13   7.4112   7.4112   0.5701   1.61   0.193
Error    14   4.9523   4.9523   0.3537
Total    27  12.3635

S = 0.594757    R-Sq = 59.94%    R-Sq(adj) = 22.75%

Variance Components, using Adjusted SS

          Estimated
Source      Value
Subject     0.1082
Error       0.3537
```

The variance components in Box 12.7 highlight an interesting fact: they are dominated by the within-subject variability (in bold). This suggests that the variability due to measurement error (i.e. the typical error) is huge in comparison with the variability between athletes. The estimated typical error in an LT measurement is 0.59 km.h^{-1} (highlighted in bold in Box 12.7) and suggests that a female athlete would need to change her LT by more than twice 0.59 (= 1.2 km.h^{-1}) before it is possible to state that she has produced a real change in aerobic fitness level. The reliability coefficient for this dataset is 23%, suggesting poor repeatability.

An alternative approach to quoting the typical error is to quantify the level of agreement between two measurements. The **limits of agreement**, proposed by the British statisticians Bland and Altman, aim to quantify the level of agreement between two measurements. The approach is very simple and intuitive. It builds on the idea of estimating measurement error in paired studies through analysing the simple differences but goes a step further by providing limits of agreement for the likely differences between the two measurements in the population. These limits are similar to tolerance limits (see Section 4.7 in Chapter 4) and provide an estimate of a range of values in which a specified percentage of the differences between the two measurements for future subjects (from the same population) are likely to lie. Wide limits of agreement indicate large discrepancies between the measurements and therefore a lack of agreement.

The (approximate) 95% limits of agreement are calculated as:

> Mean difference between the two measurements
> $\pm 2 *$ Standard deviation of the differences

The limits of agreement are interpreted as follows: it is expected that 95% of the population will have differences between their measurements in this range. The limits of agreement in this case are $-0.131 \pm 2 * 0.862 = -1.86$ to 1.60 km.h^{-1} (Box 12.6), i.e. successive Lactate Thresholds for Female runners in the population could drop by up to 1.86 km.h^{-1} or increase by up to 1.60 km.h^{-1} despite there being no meaningful change in the athlete's aerobic fitness. These values are quite large. Thus, the use of this lactate marker would result in a limited ability to detect changes in aerobic fitness in the selected population.

It has become common practice to include the limits of agreement on a plot of the differences in the two measurements against the mean of the two measurements (Figure 12.9), and indeed such a plot is now typically called the Bland–Altman plot. The justification for this plot is that the difference provides a useful estimate of the standard deviation in paired data while the mean provides an estimate of the 'true' value for this individual. A useful addition is to include an interval estimate for the mean bias on the plot allowing a graphical summary of both the paired-sample t-test and limits of agreement (LoA) results.

It is worth noting that the limits of agreement are sample estimates of the actual limits of agreement in the population. As with all statistics it is important to provide interval estimates for the corresponding parameters. For completion, the limits of agreement and their corresponding 95% CIs for this context are displayed in Box 12.8. The results suggest that the limits of agreement could be as wide as -2.58 to 2.84 km.h^{-1}. This result highlights that the Lactate Threshold has a limited ability to detect changes in aerobic fitness in the selected population.

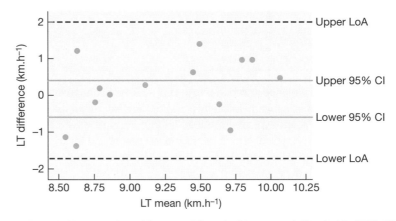

Figure 12.9 Bland–Altman plot of Lactate Threshold repeatability (with 95% CI for mean bias and LoA superimposed).

Box 12.8

	Estimate	Lower 95% CI	Upper 95% CI
Lower LoA	-1.73	-2.58	-0.88
Upper LoA	1.99	1.14	2.84

Conclusion

Although there was no evidence of a significant mean bias between the two measurements ($P = 0.58$), the estimated reliability coefficient of 23% suggests very poor repeatability when measuring successive Lactate Thresholds on the same female, with an estimated typical error of 0.59 km.h^{-1}. The limits of agreement indicate that considerable changes (up to a possible magnitude of 2.5 km.h^{-1}) in observed Lactate Thresholds on the same female are plausible without there being any change in aerobic fitness. These findings cast doubt on the sensitivity to change of the Lactate Threshold in this population as the range in the sample is only just over 2.5 km.h^{-1} itself.

Reference: Eustace, A., Scott, L., Paton, M., Thomas, L. (students), Grant, S., Moug, S. and Aitchison, T. (2001). 'Reproducibility of the lactate threshold, 3 mmol L^{-1} marker, heart rate and ratings of perceived exertion during incremental treadmill exercise in highly trained female endurance athletes.' University of Glasgow Physiology and Sports Science student project.

Additional comment on Illustration 12.3

The assumptions necessary to use limits of agreement are as follows:

1 The observations are independent (i.e. subjects are independent and the methods on the same subject are independent).

2 The differences are Normally distributed.

3 The differences between the measurements are not dependent on the magnitude of the measurement.

The first assumption implies that the observer should be unaware of their previous measurement which, although unlikely, is hoped not to bias the results. The Normality assumption can be checked in the usual manner, and the third assumption can be checked by plotting the pairwise difference in the observations against the mean of the two measurements (Figure 12.9 above). If the observations flare out or narrow across the range then the variability of the measurements is not constant. This would mean that the limits of agreement are dependent on the actual value of the variable of interest, and hence summarising the overall agreement using one limit of agreement is not valid. The pattern in Figure 12.9 does not provide any suggestion that the mean is any way related to the variability as the values are spread quite uniformly across the range of measurements.

The final example in this section is a reproducibility study where, unlike the Illustrations presented so far, more than one observer was used and variability between observers is of interest in addition to measurement error.

Illustration 12.4   Reproducibility of a motor co-ordination score in children

Background

Regular physical activity has been shown to enhance a wide range of health variables. An added benefit of regular physical activity may be the development of motor skills. There is limited information on the effects of physical activity on gross motor co-ordination in pre-school children. Before this effect can be investigated, it is necessary to produce a reliable measure of gross motor co-ordination.

Study description

A local nursery school teacher, using the instructions given in a flipbook (produced after a pilot study by the researchers) administered the Charlop–Atwell test (CAT) on eight 4-year-old

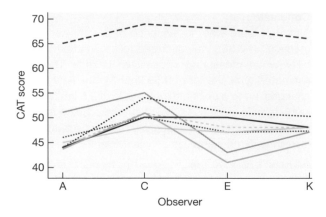

Figure 12.10 Case profile plot of CAT Score by Observer.

female children. The subjects performed the activities individually where each child was assessed simultaneously by all four observers independently.

Aim
To investigate the reproducibility of the CAT motor coordination score in children.

Data
  Name of the data file: *Motor Coordination Reproducibility*
  Response variable: CAT Score
  Between-subject factor: Observer (4 levels: A, C, E, K)

Analysis
A case profile plot of CAT Score by Observer (Figure 12.10) immediately identifies one child as having a considerably higher CAT Score than her peers. There is a suggestion that the Observers are in reasonable agreement in ranking the children in CAT Score. Observer E tends to assign lower CAT Scores than the other Observers, for example.

If the CAT Score is reproducible, then there should be no significant observer effect, while if it is useful, then the typical error should be negligible relative to the average magnitude of the CAT Score in such children. Both of these can be assessed by fitting a GLM with CAT Score as the response, and Subject and Observer as random effects as described in Chapter 10. See Box 12.9 for the resulting output.

The model has identified a significant observer effect ($P = 0.001$) and subject effect ($P < 0.001$). The subject effect is not of any great interest as it is expected that children of this age will differ in motor co-ordination. This is further highlighted by the massive between-subjects variance component (highlighted in bold). The typical error is 2, which, expressed as a percentage of the sample mean of around 50, is about 4% and therefore not insubstantial.

Conclusion
The CAT Score does not appear to be ideally reproducible as a significant observer effect ($P = 0.001$) was present. The significant observer effect, although undesirable, is similar in magnitude to the within-subject variability (typical error), but both are much smaller than the between-subject variability. This suggests that in future studies the same observer should be used if the same child has repeated CAT Score measurements.

Box 12.9

```
General Linear Model: CAT Score versus Subject, Observer

Factor     Type    Levels  Values
Subject    random      8   1, 2, 3, 4, 5, 6, 7, 8
Observer   random      4   A, C, E, K

Analysis of Variance for MC Score, using Adjusted SS for Tests

Source    DF   Seq SS   Adj SS   Adj MS      F      P
Subject    7  1346.97  1346.97  192.42   32.94  0.000
Observer   3   136.59   136.59   45.53    7.80  0.001
Error     21   122.66   122.66    5.84
Total     31  1606.22

S = 2.41677    R-Sq = 92.36%    R-Sq(adj) = 88.73%

Variance Components, using Adjusted SS

          Estimated
Source      Value
Subject    46.646
Observer    4.961
Error       5.841
```

Reference: Malcolmson, E., Laybourne, A., Hanan, K., Anderson K. (students), Grant, S., Paton, J.Y., Aitchison, T.C. and Reilly, J.J. (staff) (2002). 'Reproducibility of a motor coordination score in children using four independent observers.' University of Glasgow Physiology and Sports Science student project.

Exercises

12.1 Provide evidence of whether there has been a change in the mean in the Triceps Skinfolds measurement across the two tests in the *Anthropometric Error* data (introduced in Illustration 12.1). In addition estimate the typical error associated with this variable.

12.2 Blood lactate data were collected from 13 female endurance trained runners while completing two treadmill tests (one week apart). Each test continued until a blood lactate of at least 3 mmol.L^{-1} was attained. Quantify the typical error associated with the 3 mmol.L^{-1} lactate marker. The dataset is *Lactate Endurance Markers*.

Sports scientists often wish to compare *different methods* of measuring the same characteristic of subjects where interest focuses on studying the level of agreement between the methods. However, there is considerable disagreement among statisticians regarding how to measure agreement. Indeed, most methods presented in the literature are concerned with detecting disagreement rather than agreement. The statistical techniques needed for formally testing for agreement are extensions of many of the techniques already presented when analysing paired data and in simple linear regression problems.

12.3 Testing for agreement

There are two different types of 'agreement' problem. A researcher may be interested in comparing a new method of measurement with a gold standard where, typically, the new method has some advantage (e.g. speed, cost of measurement) over the gold standard. Evidence must be provided that the new method can be thought of as interchangeable before it can be adopted. The second type of agreement is where there are two methods to compare (in terms of agreement), neither of which is a gold standard.

12.3.1 Comparing a new method with a gold standard

The first example of a study which aims to compare a new method for estimating $\dot{V}O_2$ max with a gold standard in order to determine whether the two methods might be interchangeable.

Illustration 12.5 $\dot{V}O_2$ max agreement

Background
The direct measurement of maximal oxygen uptake ($\dot{V}O_2$ max) is considered to be the gold standard measurement for cardio-respiratory fitness. A direct measurement of $\dot{V}O_2$ max, however, is expensive, time consuming and requires highly trained and experienced personnel to carry this out properly. Thus, it would be of value to find a simpler method which was able to predict $\dot{V}O_2$ max reasonably accurately. Such a method may be a sub-maximal cycle ergometer test.

Study description
Twenty-six physically active males took part in the study. The subjects ran on a treadmill to volitional exhaustion to provide a direct measurement of $\dot{V}O_2$ max. Subjects also carried out sub-maximal bouts at a range of work rates on a cycle ergometer. Steady-state heart rate was used to predict $\dot{V}O_2$ max by extrapolating the heart rate/work rate relationship to each subject's measured maximum heart rate. This method is referred to as Lin Exp in the following analysis.

Aim
To investigate the level of agreement between the $\dot{V}O_2$ max predicted from a sub-maximal test with a direct measurement of $\dot{V}O_2$ max during treadmill running.

Data
Name of the data file: $\dot{V}O_2 Test$
Response variable: $\dot{V}O_2$ max (ml.kg^{-1}.min^{-1})
Within-subject factor: Method (2 levels: Treadmill, Lin Exp)

Analysis
Start by plotting the Treadmill $\dot{V}O_2$ max against the Lin Exp (always put the gold standard, here the Treadmill value, on the horizontal axis) using the same scale for both axes and including the line of equality (Figure 12.11).

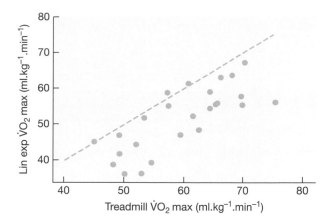

Figure 12.11 **Scatter plot of Treadmill and Lin Exp $\dot{V}O_2$ max (with line of equality superimposed).**

It is immediately apparent from Figure 12.11 that there is poor agreement between the Lin Exp and the gold standard. There is evidence that, in general, $\dot{V}O_2$ max returned by the Lin Exp tends to be lower than that returned by the Treadmill.

A natural estimate of the population mean bias is available by analysing the simple differences. In general, the gold standard should be subtracted from the new test (i.e. Lin Exp − Treadmill in this example) as the differences have a natural interpretation: positive differences represent observations where the new test has overestimated the gold standard, negative values where the new test has underestimated the gold standard.

In this example, there is evidence of a significant population mean bias (Box 12.10) as the 95% CI for the mean difference is strictly negative and the corresponding P-value is less than 0.05.

Box 12.10

```
Paired T for Lin Exp - Treadmill

            N    Mean   StDev   SE Mean
Lin Exp    25   51.58    8.84     1.77
Treadmill  25   59.59    8.24     1.65
Difference 25   -8.01    5.85     1.17

95% CI for mean difference: (−10.43, −5.60)
T-Test of mean difference = 0 (vs not = 0): T-Value = −6.85
P-Value = 0.000
```

The Lin Exp test tends to underestimate the Treadmill by between 5.6 and 10.4 ml.kg^{-1}.min^{-1} on average. This result relates to average bias when in fact the difference at the individual level is of more practical importance. The estimated mean bias (8.0 ml.kg^{-1}.min^{-1}) could be added to the Lin Exp score for each individual as a form of recalibration but this serves only to correct the average bias and gives little indication of the level of agreement on the individual level.

Indeed, a simple linear regression model can be used to assess the level of agreement by regressing the new method on the gold standard. Recall that one of the assumptions in regression is that the explanatory variable should be error-free and the only variability

375

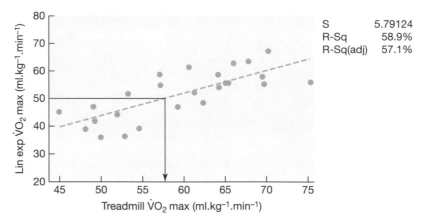

Figure 12.12 **Scatter plot of Treadmill and Lin Exp with line of best fit (Lin Exp = 2.51 + 0.82 Treadmill).**

of interest is in the response variable. It is for this reason that the gold standard is used as the explanatory variable when fitting the regression model. The line of best fit and other summaries from fitting the simple linear regression model as outlined are given in Figure 12.12.

The R^2 is 59%, suggesting that there is considerable variability about the line of best fit. Typically in regression problems, values of the explanatory variable are used to predict the response variable. What is required in this example, however, is the opposite: a mechanism to predict what the gold standard would have been given the recorded Lin Exp value. Such an 'inverse prediction' is demonstrated in Figure 12.12 where a Lin Exp test value of $\dot{V}O_2$ max 50 ml.kg^{-1}.min^{-1} has been recorded and the corresponding Treadmill score is estimated to be around 58 ml.kg^{-1}.min^{-1} – Lin Exp has underestimated the actual gold standard measure.

Inverse prediction techniques are commonly used in chemistry typically when calibrating a concentration against a gold standard. Indeed, freely available Minitab macros and R code exist for precisely this purpose. The results of running the inverse prediction Minitab macro (available in the Macros folder on the website) for selected Lin Exp values gave the output in Box 12.11.

Box 12.11

```
95.00% Confidence Interval(s) for the Predicted Values of X

Y    Pred_X   Lower CI   Upper CI    Width
30   33.3864   15.7998   50.9729    35.1732
40   45.5312   29.8526   61.2097    31.3571
50   57.6760   42.8222   72.5298    29.7076
```

An individual with a Lin Exp $\dot{V}O_2$ max of 30 ml.kg^{-1}.min^{-1} corresponds to an estimated Treadmill score of 33.39 ml.kg^{-1}.min^{-1} with an accompanying wide **inverse prediction** (or Calibration) **interval** of 15.80 to 50.97 ml.kg^{-1}.min^{-1}. The point predicted values for the three Lin Exp $\dot{V}O_2$ max values do at least rise proportionally with increasing Lin Exp $\dot{V}O_2$, however.

Conclusion

There is evidence of a significant mean bias ($P < 0.001$) when using the Lin Exp method to predict Treadmill $\dot{V}O_2$ max where the Lin Exp method tends to underestimate Treadmill $\dot{V}O_2$ max by between 6 and 10 ml.kg^{-1}.min^{-1} on average. The use of the Lin Exp method to predict Treadmill $\dot{V}O_2$ max is very limited as the calibration interval estimates are very wide.

Reference: Grant, S., Corbett, K., Amjad, A., Wilson, J. and Aitchison, T. (1995). 'A comparison of methods of predicting maximum oxygen uptake.' *British Journal of Sports Medicine*, **29**: 147–152.

12.3.2 Comparing two methods neither of which is a gold standard

A different approach is needed when neither method can be considered a gold standard as it is then inappropriate to use simple linear regression as it would be unclear which of the two methods should act in place of the gold standard. There is variability in both methods and neither would qualify as a 'natural' gold standard. The limits of agreement are, however, appropriate, as evidenced in the following illustration.

Illustration 12.6   Densitometry comparison

Background

There are several (indirect) methods of 'estimating' percentage body fat in humans (such as skinfold thicknesses and bioelectrical impedance). Some methods are more time consuming than others and some require expensive equipment. If there are several methods which give virtually the same score, the choice of method may be made based on convenience and cost. However, differences between methods may have a meaningful effect on an individual's reported % body fat.

Study description

Twenty-five male subjects aged between 18 and 25 years volunteered for the study. They underwent two methods to estimate body fat: skinfolds measurement using four body sites and underwater weighing using the Cranlea method.

Aim

To compare two different methods of estimating body fat in young healthy males.

Data

Name of data file:	*Densitometry Males*
Response variable:	% Body Fat (%)
Within-subject factor:	Method (2 levels: Skinfolds, Cranlea)

Analysis

A scatter plot of % Body Fat by the two methods (Figure 12.13) suggests that the methods do not have perfect agreement and there may not be a systematic difference between the two methods.

This subjective impression is confirmed through a paired-sample *t*-test as the interval estimate for the population mean difference contains zero (Box 12.12).

As neither variable can be considered a gold standard it is inappropriate to use simple linear regression. There is variability in both variables and neither would qualify as a 'natural' explanatory variable.

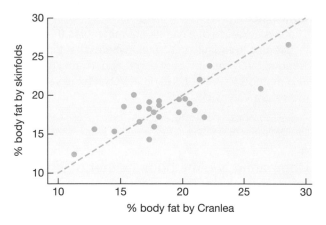

Figure 12.13 **Scatter plot of % Body Fat by Method (with line of equality superimposed).**

Box 12.12

```
Paired T for Skinfolds - Cranlea

            N    Mean  StDev  SE Mean
Skinfolds  25  18.541  2.926    0.585
Cranlea    25  18.652  3.778    0.756
Difference 25  -0.111  2.325    0.465

95% CI for mean difference: (-1.071, 0.849)
```

Using the output from Box 12.12, the sample mean difference in % Body Fat (i.e. the sample mean bias) is −0.111 with a standard deviation of 2.325. The approximate 95% limits of agreement are therefore −0.111 ± 2 * 2.325 = −4.761 to 4.53 (Figure 12.14).

The limits of agreement should be interpreted as follows: it is likely that 95% of the population will have differences between their Skinfolds and Cranlea test measurements (i.e. Skinfolds minus Cranlea) in this range. Some individuals in the population could have a Skinfolds % Body Fat as much as 4.76 below the Cranlea-based % Body Fat whereas

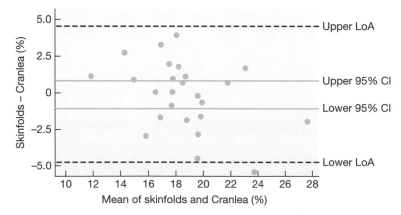

Figure 12.14 **Bland–Altman plot of densitometry repeatability (with 95% CI for mean bias and LoA superimposed).**

some could return a Skinfolds % Body Fat of up to 4.53 higher than the Cranlea-based % Body Fat.

The pattern evident in Figure 12.14 does not raise any concerns regarding the assumption that the mean is related to the variability, hence the limits of agreement approach is applicable. For completion, the limits of agreement and their corresponding 95% CIs for this context are provided in Box 12.13.

Box 12.13

```
          Estimate  Lower 95% CI  Upper 95% CI
Lower LoA   -4.67      -6.31        -3.09
Upper LoA    4.44       2.80         6.09
```

Conclusion

There was no evidence of a significant mean difference ($P = 0.81$) between the Skinfolds and Cranlea measurements of % Body Fat. The 95% limits of agreement are estimated as -4.67 to 4.44 % Body Fat. The magnitude of the difference detectable is quite large. Thus it is inappropriate to compare the % Body Fat of two individuals whose measurements have been made using the two different methods.

Reference: Archibald, S., Bibby, C., Henderson, L. (students) and Baxendale, R. (staff) (2006). 'Comparison of different methods of predicting percentage body fat.' University of Glasgow Physiology and Sports Science student project.

This chapter concludes with an example where the mean and standard deviation of the differences are related, necessitating an extension to the limits of agreement method.

Illustration 12.7 $\dot{V}O_2$ max agreement (revisited)

Background
See Illustration 12.5 for details.

Study description
Twenty-six physically active males took part in the study. In the Cooper walk/run test the subjects were asked to cover as much distance as possible in 12 minutes by walking or running on an indoor track. The distance covered was converted into a predicted $\dot{V}O_2$ max. In the shuttle test the subjects ran between two lines 20 metres apart. The running speed was determined by an audible metronome. Running speed was increased every minute and the test was terminated when the subject could no longer maintain the speed dictated by the metronome. The level (distance) attained during the test was converted into a predicted $\dot{V}O_2$ max.

Aim
To assess the level of agreement between the Shuttle and Cooper methods for the prediction of $\dot{V}O_2$ max.

Data
Name of the data file:	$\dot{V}O_2Test$
Response variable:	$\dot{V}O_2$ max (ml.kg^{-1}.min^{-1})
Within-subject factor:	Method (2 levels: Shuttle, Cooper)

Analysis

There is evidence of a relationship between the mean and standard deviation of the differences (Cooper − Shuttle), where the variability tends to increase with increasing mean as evidenced by the line of best fit in Figure 12.15.

It is not sensible to calculate limits of agreement directly here as agreement appears to depend on the magnitude of the $\dot{V}O_2$ max. Several alternative approaches have been suggested. One approach is to generate limits of agreement for the difference as a percentage of the mean, where the limits of agreement now corresponds to *percentage difference* rather than to *difference*.

Create a new variable by dividing each subject's sample difference by the subject's sample mean, multiply this by 100 to turn it into a percentage and plot this percentage difference against the mean (Figure 12.16).

Figure 12.16 shows that there has been a slight improvement in the overall pattern in that the increasing variability is now not as evident. The limits of agreement on the percentage difference scale are calculated using the sample (i.e. across all subjects) mean

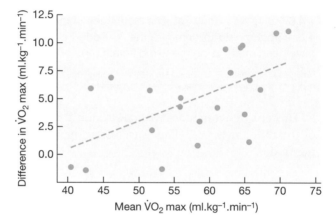

Figure 12.15 Scatter plot of $\dot{V}O_2$ max Mean and Difference (with line of best fit superimposed).

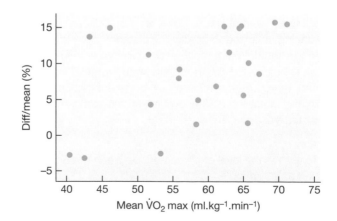

Figure 12.16 Scatter plot of Diff/Mean and Mean (Cooper and Shuttle method comparison).

and standard deviation for this new variable in the usual manner, i.e. $8.26 \pm 2 * 6.35 = -4.44\%$ to 20.96%. The limits of agreement are interpreted as most individuals are likely to have a *percentage* difference in $\dot{V}O_2$ max of at most 4% higher in the Shuttle test than in the Cooper or up to 21% higher in the Cooper test compared with the Shuttle test.

A second approach involves generating limits of agreement in the original units while adjusting for the variability increasing with magnitude. This approach involves using simple linear regression to model the relationship between the standard deviation and the mean in order to predict the level of agreement across the range of $\dot{V}O_2$ max readings while incorporating for the increased variability. Details of the procedure are given in the software guide relating to this example and accompanying R code is available on the book's website for generating these 'proportional' limits of agreement. The required proportional limits of agreement for the Cooper and Shuttle test of agreement are displayed in Figure 12.17, in which the limits of agreement increase with increasing $\dot{V}O_2$ max, as required.

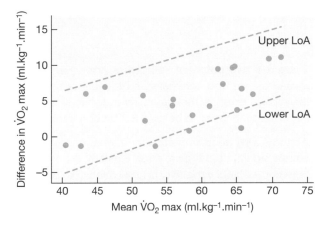

Figure 12.17 Bland–Altman plot with proportional limits of agreement (Cooper and Shuttle method comparison).

Conclusion

There is evidence that the level of agreement between the Cooper and the Shuttle $\dot{V}O_2$ max predictions depends on the $\dot{V}O_2$ max of the individual. For example, subjects with a $\dot{V}O_2$ max of 60 ml.kg^{-1}.min^{-1} have estimated limits of agreement between -5.1 and -6.1 ml.kg^{-1}.min^{-1}, respectively. Hence predicted $\dot{V}O_2$ max from the Shuttle method is estimated to be between 5 and 6 ml.kg^{-1}.min^{-1} lower compared with that of the Cooper method. These data indicate that it is inappropriate to compare any predicted $\dot{V}O_2$ max on the Cooper method with any measured on the Shuttle method whether on the same or on different subjects.

Exercises

12.3 Treadmills are commonly used in exercise science laboratories for exercise tests. They often differ in size, power of motor, and surface. This study aimed to compare Woodway or Powerjog treadmills using physiological responses during submaximal exercise. Eleven regular exercisers were tested on both Woodway and Powerjog treadmills using a balanced design. Each individual's $\dot{V}O_2$ was measured using the same protocol, speed and gradient. Estimate the level of agreement in $\dot{V}O_2$ between the two treadmills (at each speed separately). The dataset is called *Treadmill*.

12.4 Investigate the level of agreement between the Lin Exp2 ($\dot{V}O_2$ max prediction was made by extrapolating sub-maximal heart rates to each subject's predicted maximum heart rate (220 minus age) and the Treadmill for $\dot{V}O_2$ max values of 30, 40 and 50 ml.kg^{-1}.min^{-1} in Illustration 12.5. The dataset is called *$\dot{V}O_2$ Max Agreement*.

12.5 Calculate proportional limits of agreement for comparing the Skinfolds and Cranlea 'estimates' of % Body Fat in Illustration 12.6 and compare with those presented in Figure 12.14.

Summary

There are two potential sources of error (i.e. variability) present in any physiological measurement: the between- and the within-subject variability. The within-subject (i.e. the typical error) is the variability in a measure within any subject and is of particular importance in order to be able to detect meaningful changes.

A study with good repeatability is one where the between-subject variability is large compared with the typical error. Similarly, a good reproducibility study is one where the between-subject variability is large relative to both the between-observer variability and the typical error.

A related problem involves comparing two methods purporting to measure the same characteristic. Techniques were presented, initially for the scenario where one of the methods is a gold standard, and then for assessing the agreement between methods neither of which can be considered a gold standard. Analysing simple differences is often sufficient to quantify the level of agreement in such scenarios.

Technical appendix

Simple linear regression

- Simple linear regression is inappropriate in method agreement studies that do not involve a gold standard. Extensions are available, however; these are 'error in variable' models to perform method comparisons in the absence of a gold standard. Examples include the Deming regression model and the Passing and Bablok model; however, the limits of agreement method presented in this chapter is considered more practical.

Measurement error

- If it can be assumed that no significant difference in the means occurred an alternative estimate of the within-subject standard deviation is calculated by summing up the squared differences, dividing this by the number of differences and taking the square root. The corresponding measurement error is calculated by dividing this within-subject standard deviation by $\sqrt{2}$. This version of the measurement error for the Foot Length data of Illustration 12.1 is $0.103/1.414 = 0.073$ cm, which is virtually identical to that presented in the illustration.

● Another measurement error statistic often quoted is the **technical error of measurement** (**TEM**). The TEM may or may not correct for a mean change across the measurements as so desired. If an adjustment to the mean is not needed, the TEM for the Foot Length measurements (introduced in Illustration 12.1) is identical to the S statistic in the GLM in Box 12.2. If, however, an adjustment is needed for a change in the mean, the TEM is calculated by using the GLM to fit a repeated measures ANOVA with Foot Length as the response, Measure and Subject as random factors and reading off the S statistic (highlighted in bold in Box 12.14).

Box 12.14

```
General Linear Model: Foot Length versus Measure, Subject

Factor    Type     Levels  Values
Measure   random      2     Measure 1, Measure 2
Subject   random     19     1, 2, 3, ...

Analysis of Variance for Foot Length, using Adjusted SS for Tests

Source   DF    Seq SS    Adj SS   Adj MS        F       P
Measure   1    0.0042    0.0042   0.0042     0.79   0.385
Subject  18   76.7147   76.7147   4.2619   800.87   0.000
Error    18    0.0958    0.0958   0.0053
Total    37   76.8147

S = 0.0729496     R-Sq = 99.88%     R-Sq(adj) = 99.74%
```

Limits of agreement

● Limits of agreement can be used to compare a method to a gold standard. For completeness, the limits of agreement for the Lin Exp Treadmill comparison of Illustration 12.5 are -19.71 to 3.69 ml.kg^{-1}.min^{-1}: it is expected that 95% of the population will have differences between their Lin Exp and Treadmill test measurements in this range. Some individuals in the population could have a difference as high as 19.71 ml.kg^{-1}.min^{-1} (i.e. Lin Exp reads 19.71 ml.kg^{-1}.min^{-1} below the Treadmill), whereas some could return a Lin Exp score of up to 3.69 ml.kg^{-1}.min^{-1} higher than the Treadmill.

● Points that fall outside the limits of agreement are often incorrectly interpreted as providing evidence of potential lack of agreement. This is not necessarily the case, as the limits of agreement represent the likely range of differences between the two methods for approximately 95% of the individuals in the population of interest. In any sizable sample it would be expected that approximately 5% of the observations will fall outside the intervals.

- All of the contexts relating to method agreement studies in this chapter had a within-subject factor (with two levels) for each of the response variables in question. More complicated designs could involve more than two measurements taken on more than two methods, possibly involving more than one observer. Such studies involve the need to extract the variability due to the difference in the mean, the observers and any possible interaction, and are beyond the scope of this text. Your now overworked statistician should be consulted again. Be nice to him or her and bring gifts.

13 Speculating on the sample size required

13.1 Introduction

For much of the twentieth century, sample sizes used for studies across the scientific world were often based on convenience and accessibility of subjects, but this has gradually changed through the past thirty years or so with the realisation that small samples can be misleading either by missing an important finding or by throwing up a spurious positive result. Almost all journals and funding agencies now require the researcher to defend his/her choice of sample size in clear and unambiguous terms. The key here is to make sure that the sample size was derived before the study was carried out and that it is based on sensible and justifiable assumptions about the population parameters of the underlying statistical model. Pilot studies can be of considerable value not only in laying down good design and procedures for a full study but also in eliciting ball-park values for population parameters used in assessing an adequate sample size.

This chapter provides some guidance for and illustrations of determining or, in truth, speculating on sample size not only from the viewpoint of a conventional approach based on hypothesis testing but also from that of interval estimation. Astute readers will realise that the approach based on hypothesis testing is endemic in the scientific world and, accordingly, is widely available through software packages. The approach based on interval estimation, though less commonly used, has much to commend it and, although requiring more effort on the part of the researcher, is well worth consideration.

13.2 Using interval estimation

13.2.1 The basic idea

As this book has continually stressed the merits of interval estimation over hypothesis testing for formal statistical inference, this section provides a rationale for sample size determination based on the former. The simple idea here is that the *width of the interval estimate* is the key to choosing an adequate sample size by deciding in advance of the study just how precise the estimate of the key population parameter has to be – often to ensure a minimum requirement for the study, e.g. to ensure that a parameter is estimated to within a specified minimum precision or that the difference between two parameters is estimated to ensure that a specified minimum difference is not missed.

Many interval estimates, particularly 95% confidence intervals (CIs) found throughout this book, are of the form:

Estimate (of the Population Parameter) ± *Twice its estimated standard error*

This result is true for almost all important contexts involving Normal models and indeed for population means of large samples regardless of the underlying model, thanks to the so-called central limit theorem. Note also that most estimated standard errors (e.s.e.'s) are inverse functions of the sample size (i.e. as the sample size increases, the e.s.e. decreases), and are often inversely proportional to the square root of the sample size.

These interval estimates are *four e.s.e.'s* wide (i.e. two e.s.e.'s on either side of the point estimate). So, if the researcher decides in advance that he/she would like a sample size to fulfil the requirement that the resulting interval estimate has a required width, called RW say, then the appropriate (minimum) sample size will be the solution of the equation *'RW = 4 times the e.s.e.'*. This tries to ensure that the sample size is sufficiently large to measure the required parameter within a range corresponding to that required width, RW. This idea is now illustrated across various contexts in the next few subsections.

13.2.2 A single sample

If the data consist of a single sample of a continuous response variable from a Normal population where the interest lies in the population mean, then the relevant e.s.e. of the sample mean is, from Chapter 4, Section 4.3:

$$\frac{sample\ standard\ deviation}{square\ root\ of\ the\ sample\ size}$$

This implies, after a little algebra, that the solution for the **required sample size** is obtained by squaring the result of

$$\left[\frac{four\ times\ the\ standard\ deviation}{required\ width}\right]$$

In practice, the true/population standard deviation will not be known and, before the study, the sample standard deviation will not have been measured. So the problem arises as to where a guesstimate of the standard deviation should come from. The value then of a pilot study is obvious but, if not practical, then historical data may be available. Failing that, the researcher has to make an educated guess with all the potential for error that that implies.

Illustration 13.1   Soda lime canisters

Background

Asphyxiation is a common cause of death in avalanche burial. This is often due to the accumulation of expired CO_2 in the immediate air supply, leading to the displacement of available oxygen. Recent studies have indicated that the incorporation of a CO_2 scrubbing agent into a breathing apparatus may improve survival prospects in such circumstances. Soda lime is one of the most commonly used CO_2 removal agents in anaesthetic practice.

Study description

Healthy subjects will breathe through a mouthpiece into a closed-circuit system attached to a Douglas bag containing 12 litres of 100% O_2. Each subject is to continue for as long as he/she can tolerate breathing from the system (i.e. his/her Tolerance Time) incorporating a canister of Soda Lime.

Aim

To provide a sensible choice of sample size in order to estimate the population mean Tolerance Time for such a closed-circuit system with subjects breathing from a canister of Soda Lime to within a range of 5 minutes.

Data

    Response variable: Tolerance Time (minutes)

Sample size

The relevant assumptions/prerequisites before an indication of an adequate sample size can be deduced are as follows:

1 From previous studies, the between-subject variability in Tolerance Time would consist of a standard deviation of around *5 minutes* (i.e. the likely width of the Normal range of Tolerance Times would be around 20 minutes).

2 The researchers would like to be able to estimate the population mean Tolerance Time to a range of 5 minutes (i.e. an interval estimate width of *5 minutes* or, put another way, 2.5 minutes either side of the sample mean).

  Based on these assumptions/prerequisites, the sample size should be **16 subjects**, i.e. squaring the result of

$$(4 * 5)/5$$

Conclusion

To estimate the population mean Tolerance Time using a canister of Soda Lime, the study should involve a minimum of 16 (healthy) subjects to achieve the required precision, i.e. to provide an interval estimate around 5 minutes in width.

13.2.3 Two-sample problems

If the data consist of two independent samples of a continuous response variable from Normal populations (e.g. a design with one between-subject factor at two levels) where the interest lies in the difference of the population means, then the relevant e.s.e. of the difference in sample means – if the sample sizes from both populations are taken, as seems natural, to be the same – is the square root of the result of

$$\frac{\textit{first sample standard deviation}^2 + \textit{second sample standard deviation}^2}{\textit{common sample size}}$$

This sounds a bit complicated but Section 4.4 of Chapter 4 provides some explanation. This implies that the solution for the required common sample size from both populations is obtained from:

$$\frac{16 \times (\textit{first sample standard deviation}^2 + \textit{second sample standard deviation}^2)}{\textit{required width squared}}$$

This may seem rather complicated, but the following illustration may illuminate. Again, in practice, the required standard deviations will have to be plucked out of thin air or estimated from a pilot study.

Illustration 13.2 Physiotherapy pain relief

Background
Ischaemic pain is induced by applying a tourniquet to the arm just above the elbow to obstruct the flow of blood and then squeezing a hand-exercising device for a short time (e.g. 2 minutes). When the exercising stops, pain begins to mount and typically becomes unbearable after about 8 minutes. It is used in experimental studies of pain because it causes no permanent tissue damage.

Study Description
A sample of young healthy females is to be taken to investigate the effect of a mental distraction task on induced ischaemic pain. Sub-maximal effort tourniquet technique (SETT) is to be used to induce ischaemic pain on a subject's non-dominant arm while she performs sets of 20 repetitions of hand-gripping exercises at 75% of her maximal grip strength over a 100 second period. The Intervention/Distraction is a colour word Stroop test. This mental task consists of a pencil and paper Stroop task modified to cover 160 words typed in red, yellow, blue or green in a randomised order. Each word is coloured in a different colour from its meaning. While the method of Pain Relief (i.e. Control/Distraction) is being carried out, each subject will record her perceived pain levels using a visual analogue scale (VAS) from the moment she acknowledges pain (i.e. her Pain Threshold) until she can tolerate the pain no longer (i.e. her Pain Tolerance). It is assumed that equal numbers of subjects should be (randomly) allocated to the two methods of Pain Relief (i.e. Control and Distraction).

Aim
To provide adequate sample sizes to be able to estimate the difference in population mean Pain Tolerance for induced ischaemic pain between the Distraction and Control within an interval estimate 30 seconds.

Data:
    Response variable: Pain Tolerance *(seconds)*
    Between-subject factor: Pain Relief (2 levels: Control, Distraction)

Sample size
A priori, it seems natural to take equal-sized samples from both populations – from a statistical viewpoint because it is advisable to estimate both population means with the same precision, and from an ethical viewpoint as there was only anecdotal evidence of the distraction being successful in reducing pain tolerance. The relevant assumptions/prerequisites before an indication of an adequate common sample size from both populations (i.e. Distraction and Control) can be deduced are as follows:

1 The physiotherapist, from extensive research and experience of ischaemic pain, suggests that the between-subject variability in Pain Tolerance without the Distraction would consist of a standard deviation of around *30 seconds* – since she suggested a 'Normal range' of around 2 minutes (i.e. 4 times 30 seconds).

2 In the light of no information to the contrary, she is prepared to assume that the standard deviation in Pain Tolerance with the Distraction will also be around *30 seconds*.

3 Further, she suggested that the typical Pain Tolerance without the Distraction would be around 300 seconds (but this is not required for the calculation).

4 She has decided that she would like to be able to estimate the difference in population mean Pain Tolerance to a range of 30 seconds (i.e. an interval estimate width of *30 seconds*). She justifies this as being the minimum worthwhile reduction (i.e. around 10%) of mean Pain Tolerance from her assessment of the typical Control Pain Tolerance of 300 seconds.

Based on these assumptions/prerequisites, the sample size should be **32 subjects for each sample** (i.e. 32 Controls and 32 on the Distraction) since

$$\{16 * (30^2 + 30^2)\}/30^2 = 32$$

Conclusion

To estimate the difference in population mean Pain Tolerance to an interval of width 30 seconds, the study should involve a minimum of 32 subjects on each method of Pain Relief.

Additional comment

In some studies there may be ethical or good practical reasons why the sample sizes for the two populations should not be equal. For example, in a study of exercise in elderly, obese women, the authors recruited and assigned subjects in randomly permuted blocks of five with three exercisers and two controls, simply in order to compensate for the potentially high drop-out rate in such a target population. The formula for choice of sample size above can be easily adapted to allow for this but that is probably best done with the aid of a statistician. For example, in the Physiotherapy Pain Relief example above, the physiotherapist may feel from an ethical standpoint that she should use twice as many subjects on the intervention than as controls. Then, based on appropriate calculations similar to those above, she should use 24 subjects as controls and 48 on the intervention based on the same choices for standard deviations and interval width as in the Illustration (i.e. an increase from 64 to 72 subjects in the whole study because the Control population mean Pain Tolerance is being less well estimated in this second study).

13.2.4 Paired-sample problems

The simplest paired-sample problem is a single sample of paired data for a continuous variable, and this is dealt with in exactly the same way as in Section 13.2.2 but applied to the sample of differences (i.e. differences between the two levels of the within-subject factor). The only additional difficulty in determining sample size for such problems is guesstimating the standard deviation of the differences.

The context of one between- and one within-subject factor, each at two levels, has been illustrated well throughout this book (see Section 10.2). The determination of sample size for such a problem turns out to be exactly the same as that illustrated in Section 13.2.3 but involves the two samples of differences. Again, the only additional difficulty is providing sensible choices for the standard deviations of the differences in the two populations (i.e. the levels of the between-subject factor).

One aspect of paired data that has the potential to cause problems is the reporting in published work of only summary statistics for the before and after data separately rather than the summary statistics of the differences that are essential for the choice of sample size. If previous studies do this, then the current study will have to come up with a sensible value for the correlation between the before and after values to allow calculation of the difference summary statistics, whether it be a simple paired problem or a one between- and one within-subject factor design.

13.2.5 Categorical response variables

When the response variable is categorical in nature (see Chapter 8), then the approach introduced here can be easily extended to any of the two- and paired-sample problems for such variables, but at a heavy price! When dealing with categorical variables, the minimum sample sizes are much greater than for continuous variables, often by a factor of ten or more.

For example, in a one-sample problem where the researcher would like to estimate a population proportion by an interval estimate whose width is 10% (i.e. an e.s.e. of the sample proportion of 2.5%), the required sample size will be around 400. For an interval width of 1%, then he/she would require 40,000 subjects – a bit of an effort. (Perhaps, the researcher will now have some sympathy with opinion polling organisations where sample sizes are typically around 1000 but have to be satisfied with errors of around 2% to 3%, i.e. the corresponding intervals will be 8% to 12% wide.)

A conservative formula for the appropriate sample size for a single sample of a categorical variable is the square of

two divided by the required width

with the required width (RW) expressed as a fraction.

For example, if the required width of the interval estimate for the population proportion is taken as 0.01 (i.e. 1%), then the required sample size will be around $(2/0.01)^2 = 40,000$. If a wider interval was sufficient for the researcher (say 0.05 wide), then the sample size would be around $(2/0.05)^2 = 1600$.

For the two-sample binary problem, to provide an interval estimate for the difference in two population proportions will require 800 subjects for each sample to ensure an interval 10% wide and 80,000 subjects in each sample for an interval 1% wide. The moral is clear: use categorical or binary variables only if an almost limitless supply of subjects and resources is available.

A conservative formula for the appropriate sample size from each of the two populations is two times the square of

two divided by the required width

with the required width (RW) expressed as a fraction.

For example, if the required width of the interval estimate for the difference in population proportions is taken as 0.05 (i.e. 5%), then the study will require around $2 * (2/0.05)^2 = 3200$ subjects from each of the populations.

Exercises

13.1   Many people aspire to climb Mont Blanc (4807 m), the highest mountain in western Europe. A key component in planning a climb of Mont Blanc is the likely time for a successful ascent. Physiological tests are to be performed on climbers passing through the Gouter Hut as they prepare to climb Mont Blanc and the climbers intercepted on their descent to record their success/failure in the climb and, if successful, their Ascent Time. How many (successful) climbers have to be intercepted in order to estimate the typical Ascent Time Mont Blanc (in good summer conditions) to an interval estimate of width 15 minutes if the standard deviation of Ascent Times is assumed to be around 30 minutes? (See Illustrations 3.1 and 4.2 for details of the analysis of this study.)

13.2   Ice baths are sometimes used in aerobic sports after training and competition. One of the supposed benefits of this practice is a reduction in blood lactate. There is little, if any, direct evidence that the use of ice baths really does lower blood lactate. Club-standard oarsmen are needed for a study where each will have their blood lactate levels (over a 25-minute cool-down after exercise) recorded at regular intervals after successfully completing a 2 km row in under 7 minutes on two separate occasions three days apart. On one occasion each rower will cool down normally (i.e. a control) while, on the other occasion, the oarsman will be immersed in an ice bath. Assuming the key variable of interest is the Reduction in Blood Lactate 10 minutes after exercise ceases, then how many oarsmen should be used in the study to provide an interval estimate of width 2 mmol.L^{-1} for the difference in mean Reduction between Use of Ice Baths and Control if the standard deviation of such changes/reductions is assumed to be around 2 mmol.L^{-1}? (See Illustrations 2.2 and 11.2 for details of the design and analysis of this study.)

13.3   Ankylosing spondylitis (AS) is a debilitating condition which can have wide-ranging and varied effects, including restriction of movement of the spinal and thoracic areas. An exercise programme may improve (i.e. increase) cervical rotation in these patients, resulting in enhanced mobility. Each of a sample of AS sufferers is to be randomised to be either a Control or to undergo an Exercise Intervention for a period of 12 weeks. Assuming the key variable of interest is the Improvement in Cervical Rotation over these 12 weeks and that it is reasonable to assume that the standard deviation of such improvements is around 3% for both Exercise and Control, how many AS sufferers are required to produce an interval estimate for the mean Improvement in Cervical Rotation of Exercise over Control to be of width 4%? (See Exercise 10.2 for analysis of the actual study.)

13.4   A sample of Glasgow University (GU) students are to be questioned regarding whether they are regular exercisers, defined as taking part every week in a minimum of three sessions per week of at least 20 minutes aerobic activity at, or above, 65% of maximum heart rate. How many students must be sampled to obtain an interval estimate of width 10% for the GU student population proportion who regularly exercise? How many GU male and female subjects would be required to estimate the difference in population proportions who regularly exercise between the sexes to an interval of width 10%? (See Exercise 8.1 for analysis of the actual study.)

Power and sample size determination

13.3.1 The basic idea

Chapter 5 introduced the concept of hypothesis testing where the decision of whether to reject the null hypothesis depends upon whether the observed *P*-value (from the data) is less than the chosen significance level, conventionally taken as 0.05. The use of a *P*-value can cause concern when the size of the sample chosen is not large enough to detect a significant effect even though there is an effect present in the population. For example, a sports dietician is interested in estimating the difference in the mean height of professional male basketball players and professional male jockeys. She records the heights of a random sample of three males from each sport and performs a two-sample *t*-test to compare the population means. The resulting *P*-value turns out to be 0.28. Since this is greater than her chosen significance level of 0.05, she is forced to conclude that there is no significant difference in the mean of the response variable (i.e. height) in the two populations of interest (i.e. basketball players and jockeys). She is astounded and makes derogatory remarks about the discipline of statistics, claiming that 'everyone knows such a difference in heights exists'. What has gone wrong? The answer is simple. The samples obtained, albeit random and independent, were too small. The test lacked **power** – the (prob)ability of a hypothesis test to detect correctly a difference actually present between the population means.

The idea that the required sample size can be *determined* with any real certainty is untrue in general – unless there have been many studies in the area and these are in good agreement with one another. Even then, the current target population must also have been covered by such studies before any degree of conviction can be attached to the determination of sample size. All in all, the process is a bit like gazing into a crystal ball or consulting the Sibylline Books of Ancient Rome.

The conventional approach is to use the concept of the power of the relevant hypothesis test for the context involved to ensure that this power, *the probability of correctly rejecting the null hypothesis*, is at an acceptably high level (e.g. preferably 0.95 or 95% but at least 0.80 or 80%, which is often taken simply in order to reduce the sample size). Even having chosen this acceptably high level, the researcher is still forced to provide other guesstimates of some of the relevant population parameters (unknown in reality) before the prophecy of sample size can be extracted from the dark, misty mind of the mathematical haruspex. There is always a high price to pay for 'words from the gods'!

The rationale behind sample size determination based on hypothesis testing is to provide values for all of the population parameters for the full probability model under both the null and alternative hypotheses as well as specifying the choice of significance level (the probability of correctly not rejecting the null) and the power (the probability of correctly rejecting the null) – these are conventionally taken as 0.05 and at least 0.80, respectively, although the latter choice of 0.80 should be treated with caution as providing at best an absolute minimum sample size. To get some idea of the required calculations in the case of a two-sample *t*-test problem the avid reader can consult the oracle otherwise known as the technical appendix. The remainder of this chapter provides illustrations of the use of the power and sample size commands in Minitab across the simplest and most common contexts in sports and exercise science.*

*A more than adequate starting point for the ideas involved in sample size 'determination' is R.V. Lenth's article 'Some practical guidelines for effective sample size determination' in *The American Statistician,* **55** (2001): 187–193, with accompanying website http://www.stat.uiowa.edu/~rlenth/Power/index.html.

13.3.2 Two-sample problems

For the standard problem of comparing two population means, the two-sample *t*-test is appropriate if the underlying distributions of the continuous variable being investigated are adequately modelled as Normal distributions (see Chapter 5, Section 5.3 for details). To guesstimate the required sample sizes the following prerequisites are relevant:

1 Unless there is good reason to do otherwise, assume that the sample sizes are to be made *equal* for the two populations.

2 Provide a reasonable choice for the *(minimum) difference* in population means that should not be missed by the study (some software packages ask for both population means to be provided but this is not essential).

3 Produce adequate choices for the *standard deviations* of both populations from either a previous study, a pilot study or the researcher's knowledge.

4 Some software packages ask for a common choice of standard deviation but this assumption should be treated with care and an informed decision is needed on whether or not it is valid.

5 The *significance level* must be specified; 0.05 or 5% is more than adequate.

6 The required *power* for the study must be pre-specified and is often set low at 0.80 or 80%, but the careful researcher should consider setting this at 0.95 or 95% to give him/herself a much more solid possibility of not missing an important significant result.

All in all, then, quite a lot of information is required before the sample sizes can be speculated on. Again, the value of a pilot study cannot be overestimated in getting realistic values for these prerequisites rather than simply depending upon the researcher's experience (and/or ego!).

Illustration 13.3   Physiotherapy pain relief (almost revisited)

Background
See Illustration 13.2.

Study description
While the Distraction is being carried out, subjects record their perceived pain levels using a VAS from the moment they acknowledge pain (i.e. their Pain Threshold) until they can tolerate the pain no longer (i.e. their Pain Tolerance). It is assumed that equal numbers of subjects should be (randomly) allocated to the two methods of pain relief (i.e. Control and Distraction).

Aim

To provide adequate sample sizes to be able to estimate the difference in population mean Pain Threshold for induced ischaemic pain between the Distraction and Control based on appropriate assumptions and a power of 0.95.

Data

Response variable: Pain Threshold (seconds)

Between-subject factor: Pain Relief (2 levels: Control, Distraction)

Sample size

As in Illustration 13.2, it seems natural to take equal-sized samples from both populations – from a statistical viewpoint because it is advisable to estimate both population means with the same precision, and from an ethical viewpoint as there was only anecdotal evidence of the Distraction being successful in reducing pain tolerance. The relevant prerequisites before an indication of an adequate common sample size from both populations (i.e. Distraction and Control) can be deduced from power calculations are as follows:

1 The physiotherapist, from extensive research and experience of ischaemic pain, suggests that the between-subject variability in Pain Threshold without the Distraction would consist of a standard deviation of around 20 seconds – since she suggested a Normal range of around 2 minutes width (i.e. 4 times 30 seconds).

2 In the light of no information to the contrary, she is prepared to assume that the standard deviation in Pain Threshold with the Distraction will also be around 20 seconds.

3 Further, she suggested that the typical Pain Threshold without the Distraction would be around 300 seconds (but this is not required for the calculation).

4 She believes that the minimum worthwhile reduction in mean Pain Threshold caused by the Distraction should be 30 seconds (i.e. around a 10% improvement on the typical Control Pain Threshold of 300 seconds).

5 She is prepared to work with a power of 0.80 (or 80%), i.e. the probability that *'her study will correctly reject the null hypothesis of no difference in population mean Pain Threshold between Control and Distraction'* will be 0.80. As usual, the significance level would be taken as 0.05 or 5%.

Based on these assumptions/prerequisites, the results of the power calculation are given in Box 13.1 and hence the sample size should be **9 subjects in each sample** (i.e. 9 Controls and 9 on the Distraction).

Box 13.1

```
Power and Sample Size
2-Sample t Test

Testing mean 1 = mean 2 (versus not =)
Calculating power for mean 1 = mean 2 + difference
Alpha = 0.05 Assumed standard deviation = 20

              sample  Target
Difference    Size    Power   Actual Power
        30      9     0.8         0.847610

The sample size is for each group.
```

Conclusion

To ensure a power of at least 80% so that a minimum difference in population mean Pain Threshold of 30 seconds would not be missed, the study should involve a minimum of 9 subjects on each method of Pain Relief. *Remember, though, that this is highly dependent on the reliability of the relevant prerequisites specified above, as is illustrated in the following comments.*

Additional comments on Illustration 13.3

Figure 13.1 provides plots, called **power curves**, of the achieved power against the true difference in population means for choices of sample size 5, 10, 15 and 20 in each sample assuming a common standard deviation of 20 seconds. From this it can be seen, among many other things, that if the true difference in population mean Pain Threshold is only 10 seconds then the power of the study is only just under 40% even for sample sizes of 20, i.e. it is almost a waste of time carrying out even such an enlarged study of 40 rather than 18 subjects if the mean difference is around 40 seconds.

If the researcher had considerably underestimated the standard deviation of Pain Threshold distributions and, in fact, this was 40 seconds rather than 20 seconds, then the resulting impact on the power can be seen in Figure 13.2. The resulting sample size to

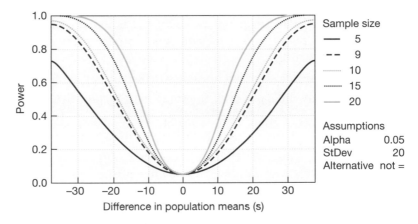

Figure 13.1 **Power curve for two-sample *t*-test (SD = 20).**

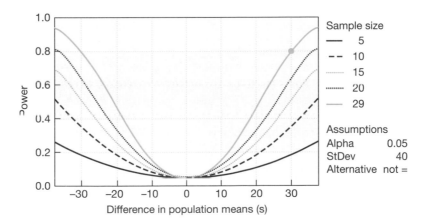

Figure 13.2 **Power curve for two-sample *t*-test (SD = 40).**

achieve a power of 0.80 would be 29 subjects in each sample – virtually a tripling of the required sample size if the true difference in population means was 30 seconds. The maxim is, therefore, to be very careful, if not highly conservative, in making informed choices, a priori, on the possible true values of population parameters.

13.3.3 One between-subject factor designs (at *K* levels)

For the problem of comparing *K* (three or more) population means, the one-way ANOVA is appropriate if the underlying distributions of the continuous variable being investigated are adequately modelled as Normal distributions (see Chapter 7 for details). To guesstimate the required sample sizes the following prerequisites are relevant:

1 Unless there is good reason to do otherwise, assume that the sample sizes are to be the same from all *K* populations.

2 Provide a reasonable choice for the *(minimum) difference* in the smallest and largest of the *K* population means that should not be missed by the study. (Some software packages ask for all *K* population means to be provided but this is not essential.)

3 Produce an adequate choice for the assumed *common standard deviation* of all *K* populations from a previous study, a pilot study or the researcher's 'knowledge/ experience'.

4 The *significance level* must be specified at, say, 0.05 or 5%.

5 The required *power* for the study must be pre-specified at, say, 0.95 or 95%.

Yet again, then, quite a lot of information is required before the sample sizes can be speculated on. At the risk of sounding like a good old-fashioned rote teacher, remember that the value of a pilot study cannot be overemphasised in getting realistic values for these prerequisites rather than simply depending upon an educated guess.

Illustration 13.4 **Chronic low back pain (revisited)**

Background
See Illustration 2.1.

Study description
Patients referred to orthopaedic clinics with chronic low back pain are to be recruited from Glasgow hospitals. Each subject will be allocated to one of three treatments: usual outpatient physiotherapy (OP), spinal stabilisation classes (SC), or physiotherapist-led pain management classes (PM). Compliance to each of the three treatments will then be monitored over the period of the study. The Time Off-Work for the six months after the end of treatment will be taken as the response variable.

Aim
To provide adequate sample sizes to be able to estimate the differences, on average, in Time Off Work among the three treatments (for chronic low back pain patients for the six months after the end of treatment) in order to ensure that a difference in means among the three treatments of *at least* 14 days has a high probability (95%) of not being missed.

Data

Response variable: Time Off Work (days)

Between-subject factor: Treatment (3 levels: OP, SC, PM)

Sample size

As usual, it seems natural to take equal-sized samples from all three populations – from a statistical viewpoint because it is advisable to estimate all population means with the same precision and, from ethical considerations, there is no real difference in cost across the three treatments in NHS terms. The relevant prerequisites before an indication of an adequate common sample size from all three populations (i.e. OP, SC and PM) can be deduced (based on power calculations) are as follows:

1 The researchers suggest that the between-subject variability in Time Off Work over a six-month period would consist of a standard deviation of around 14 days for each of the three treatments (i.e. the variability seen in Time Off Work for any treatment would range around the appropriate population mean by plus or minus 28 days, i.e. covering roughly a two-month period in the six months.

2 They are interested only in ascertaining that the minimum difference in population mean Time Off Work among the three treatments should be at least 14 days (i.e. they assume that any differences less than 14 days would be of no practical interest).

3 They would prefer a Power of 0.95 (or 95%), i.e. the probability that 'the *study will correctly reject the null hypothesis of no differences among the three treatments in population mean Time Off* Work' should be 0.95. As usual, the significance level would be taken as 0.05 or 5%.

Based on these assumptions, the results of the power calculation are given in Box 13.2 and hence the sample size should be **32 subjects in each sample** (i.e. 32 on outpatient physiotherapy, 32 in spinal stabilisation classes, and 32 in physiotherapist-led pain management classes.

Box 13.2

```
Power and Sample Size
One-way ANOVA

Alpha = 0.05 Assumed standard deviation = 14 Number of Levels = 3

   SS      Sample    Target                      Maximum
 Means      Size      Power   Actual  Power     Difference
   98        32        0.95       0.950573           14
The sample size is for each level.
```

Figure 13.3 (page 398) illustrates the achieved power for a selection of sample sizes plotted against the actual minimum difference in population means (but all of these power curves are based on assuming a common standard deviation of 14 days for each treatment). This plot suggests that the choice of sample size is adequate as long as the true minimum difference in population means is not less than 10 days.

Conclusion

To ensure a power of at least 95% so that a minimum difference in population mean Time Off Work of 14 days among the three treatments would not be missed, the study should

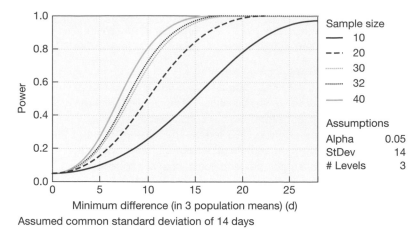

Figure 13.3 **Power curves for one-way ANOVA (three levels).**

involve a minimum of 32 subjects on each method of relieving chronic low back pain. *Remember, though, that this is highly dependent on the reliability of the assumed prerequisite values of a minimum difference of 14 days among the population means, a common standard deviation of 14 days and a power of 95%.*

13.3.4 Paired-sample problems

For the problem of comparing two population means based on a single sample of paired data, the paired-sample *t*-test is appropriate if the underlying distribution of the *differences* of the continuous variable being investigated is adequately modelled as a Normal distribution (see Section 5.4 for details). To guesstimate the required sample size the following prerequisites are relevant:

1 Provide a reasonable choice for the *(minimum) difference* in population means that should not be missed by the study.

2 Obtain a ball-park figure for the *standard deviation of the differences*.

3 The *significance level* must be specified at, say, 0.05 or 5%.

4 The required *power* for the study must be specified, preferably around 0.95 or 95%.

Illustration 13.5   Walking poles (revisited)

Background
See Illustration 9.3.

Study description
A sample of physically active males are to undergo a simulated short hill walk of 10 minutes, once using walking poles and once without using walking poles and with a 15-minute rest between the two 'hill walks'. Each subject will walk at 3.7 km.h^{-1} on a 12.5% gradient and have his $\dot{V}O_2$ measured (in ml.kg^{-1}.min^{-1}) using Douglas bags over each of the last 3 minutes of each 'hill walk' (i.e. during the 8th, 9th and 10th minutes). The key variable of interest here is to be the $\dot{V}O_2$ in the final (10th) minute of the 'hill walk'.

Aim

To provide an adequate number of males to be able to estimate the difference, on average, in $\dot{V}O_2$ in the final (10th) minute of the 'hill walk' due to using Walking Poles. This is to be such that a difference in population means due to use of the Walking Poles of around 5% (i.e. *at least* 1.3 ml.kg^{-1}.min^{-1}) has a high probability (95%) of not being missed.

Data

Response variable:	$\dot{V}O_2$ at 10 minutes (ml.kg^{-1}.min^{-1})
Within-subject factor:	Pole Use (2 levels: Yes, No)

Sample size

Under the assumptions for paired data described in Section 5.4 and the Chapter 5 technical appendix, the relevant variable of interest will be the *difference* in the 10th minute $\dot{V}O_2$ not using and using the Walking Poles – better to take 'Using minus Not Using the poles' as this would tend to be positive if the pole use really does increase energy cost. The relevant prerequisites, before an indication of an adequate sample size can be obtained, are:

1 The researchers are interested only in ascertaining that the minimum difference in mean $\dot{V}O_2$ due to the use of Walking Poles should be at least 1.3 ml.kg^{-1}.min^{-1} (i.e. any difference less than 1.3 ml.kg^{-1}.min^{-1} would be of no practical interest). This is 5% of the typical $\dot{V}O_2$ seen at 10 minutes for such a 'hill walk' (i.e. 26 ml.kg^{-1}.min^{-1}) obtained from previous studies.

2 These previous studies also suggested that the *standard deviation* of the differences (i.e. $\dot{V}O_2$ Not Using the poles minus $\dot{V}O_2$ Using the poles) would be approximately 1.35 ml.kg^{-1}.min^{-1}.

3 The study group decided that they would be satisfied with a power of 0.90 (or 90%), i.e. the probability that *'the study will correctly reject the null hypothesis of no difference in 10 minute $\dot{V}O_2$ due to Pole Use'* should be 0.90. As usual, the significance level would be taken as 0.05 or 5%.

Based on these assumptions, the results of the power calculation are given in Box 13.3 and hence the sample size should be **14** males who would carry out the study twice, once using poles and once not using poles. For good design, 7 of the subjects would use the poles on their first trial and 7 the poles on their second trial (the allocation of subjects to this order would of course be done in a random fashion – see Chapter 2).

Box 13.3

```
Power and Sample Size
1-Sample t Test

Testing mean = null (versus not = null)
Calculating power for mean = null + difference
Alpha = 0.05 Assumed standard deviation = 1.35

              Sample   Target
Difference     Size    Power     Actual Power
     1.3         14     0.9        0.914125
```

The effects on the power of the study of any changes in the choice of the true difference in means and sample size are illustrated in the power curves of Figure 13.4. From this, it can be seen that the suggested sample size of 14 males is adequate as long as the true

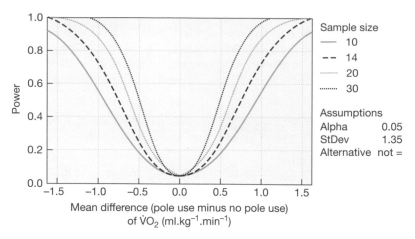

Figure 13.4 **Power curves for Walking Poles study.**

mean difference does not fall below 1 ml.kg^{-1}.min^{-1}. If the true mean difference were below 0.5 ml.kg^{-1}.min^{-1} then the required sample size would have to be over 30 males to stand even a 50/50 chance (i.e. 50% power) of being detected.

Conclusion

To ensure a power of at least 90% so that a minimum difference in population 10th minute $\dot{V}O_2$ of 1.3 ml.kg^{-1}.min^{-1} due to use of the Walking Poles in the simulated hill walk would not be missed, the study should involve a minimum of 14 males all tested with and without using the Walking Poles. *Remember, though, that this is highly dependent on the reliability of the assumed prerequisite values of a minimum difference of 1.3 ml.kg^{-1}.min^{-1} due to the use of the poles, a standard deviation of the difference for each subject of 1.35 ml.kg^{-1}.min^{-1} and a power of 90%.*

Reference: Mills, S., Millott, J. (students), Grant, S., Aitchison, T., Pitt, C. and Watt, I. (staff) (2003). 'The effect of walking poles on physiological and psychological variables.' University of Glasgow Physiology and Sports Science student Project.

13.3.5 One within-subject factor designs (at *K* levels)

For the problem of a single within-subject factor design comparing *K* (three or more) population means (i.e. with each subject being measured under all *K* levels), the one-way repeated measures ANOVA is appropriate under certain assumptions (see Section 9.3 for details).

To guesstimate the required sample size for such a context, the following prerequisites are relevant:

1 Provide a reasonable choice for the *(minimum) difference* in the smallest and largest of the *K* population means that should not be missed by the study. (Some software packages ask for all *K* population means to be provided but this is not essential.)

2 Produce an adequate choice for the assumed *common standard deviation* for all *K* levels from a previous study, a pilot study, or the researcher's knowledge/experience (as always, a dangerous source).

3 Suggest a reasonable choice for the (positive) *correlation* between any pair of observations on the same subject, i.e. the correlation between the responses for any

two of the *K* levels of the within-factor on the same individual. Such a correlation is assumed common across all pairs of levels of the within-factor.

4 The *significance level* must be specified at, say, 0.05 or 5%.

5 The required *power* for the study must be specified at, say, 0.95 or 95%.

Illustration 13.6 Humidity

Background

Major athletic events can be held in cities where high temperatures and humidity are prevailing weather conditions (e.g. the 2008 Olympics in Beijing, China). High temperatures and humidity have the potential to reduce athletic performance in some events, particularly distance running and games where repeat sprints are common, as in soccer and hockey. Single sprint performance may also be adversely affected as athletes have to live, train and warm up in very hot and humid conditions. Athletes and players may have the choice of warming up either indoors in an air-conditioned environment or outdoors in the high heat and humidity where he/she will perform (see Exercise 2.4).

Study description

To investigate the effects of heat and humidity on intermittent supra-maximal running performance, a group of sports scientists would like to carry out a study comparing three distinct Conditions. The first condition is in effect a Control (CC) involving a warm-up and an intermittent supramaximal running Performance Test (ISRPT) in cool (i.e. British) conditions. The second (CH) involves a warm-up in cool conditions but an ISRPT in hot and humid conditions. The third (HH) involves a warm-up and an ISRPT both in hot and humid conditions. Healthy male students who regularly exercise would have their Performance in an ISRPT monitored under each of these three Conditions. The order in which each subject would undergo the three Conditions will be balanced across subjects using 3×3 Latin squares as described in Chapter 2, Section 2.2.4.

Aim

To provide an adequate sample size for a one within-subject factor design to be able to estimate the differences, on average, in Performance among the three Conditions. This should be done in order to ensure that a difference between the largest and smallest of the three population mean Performances of *at least* 4 ml.kg^{-1}.min^{-1} has a high probability (95%) of not being missed. This corresponds roughly to a range in mean Performance of 4% across the three Conditions.

Data

Response variable: Performance (ml.kg^{-1}.min^{-1})
Within-subject factor: Condition (3 levels: CC, CH, HH)

Sample size

This is an example of a repeated measures design with one within-subject factor at three levels. The relevant prerequisites before an indication of an adequate sample size can be obtained are:

1 The researchers are interested only in ascertaining that the minimum difference in mean Performance across the three Conditions should be at least 4 ml.kg^{-1}.min^{-1} (i.e. any difference less than 4 ml.kg^{-1}.min^{-1} would be of no practical interest). This corresponds to a pre-study belief of the researchers that the population mean Performances would range from 108 to 112 ml.kg^{-1}.min^{-1}.

2 These previous studies also suggested that the standard deviation of Performance would be approximately 4 ml.kg^{-1}.min^{-1} for each Condition and that the correlation between any two performances for any subject would be around 0.6.

3 The researchers would like to use a power of 0.90 (or 90%), i.e. the probability that 'the study will correctly reject the null hypothesis of no difference in Performance across the three Conditions' should be 0.90. As usual, the significance level would be taken as 0.05 or 5%.

Based on these assumptions, the results of the power calculation from the software PASS (Power Analysis and Sample Size software for Windows) are given in Box 13.4 and hence the sample size should be **12** sprinters who would carry out the running test three times, once under each of the three Conditions. For a good design, the subjects would be divided into sets of 6 and two balanced 3×3 Latin squares used for each set to determine the order in which each subject was tested under the three Conditions (see Chapter 2, Section 2.2.4).

Box 13.4

Advanced Repeated Measures ANOVA Power Analysis

Results for Factor Condition (Levels =3)

Test	Power	n	N	Multiply By	SD of Means Effects (Sm)	Standard Deviation (Sigma)	Effect size	Alpha	Beta	Power
GG F	0.8987	12	12	1.00	1.63	1.46	1.12	0.0500	0.1013	0.90
Wilks	0.8131	12	12	1.00	1.63	1.46	1.12	0.0500	0.1869	0.81

Summary Statements
A repeated measures design with 0 between factors and 1 within factor has 1 groups with 12 subjects each for a total of 12 subjects. Each subject is measured 3 times. This design achieves 90% power to test factor *Condition* if a Geisser–Greenhouse Corrected F Test is used with a 5% significance level and the actual effect standard deviation is 1.63 (an effect size of 1.12).

Output from PASS

To gain an impression of the effect of changing the sample size on the power of the repeated measures one-way ANOVA, consider Figure 13.5 where a sample size of at least 10 sprinters looks reasonable as long as the assumed prerequisites are sensible.

Conclusion

To ensure a power of at least 90% so that a minimum difference in population mean intermittent supra-maximal running performance of 4 ml.kg^{-1}.min^{-1} among the three Conditions (i.e. CC, CH and HH) would not be missed, the study should involve a minimum of 12 subjects being tested under all three Conditions.

Remember, though, that this is highly dependent on the reliability of the assumed prerequisite values of a minimum difference of 4 ml.kg^{-1}.min^{-1} among the population means, a common standard deviation of 4 ml.kg^{-1}.min^{-1}, a within-subject correlation of 0.6 and a power of 90%.

Reference: Maxwell, N.S., Aitchison, T.C. and Nimmo M.A. (1996). 'The effect of climatic heat stress on intermittent supramaximal running performance in humans.' *Experimental Physiology*, 81: 833–845.

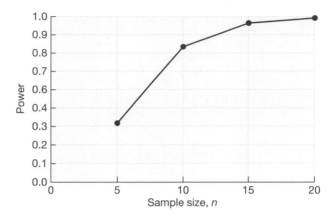

Figure 13.5 **Power vs sample size with Terms = 1, *K* = 1.00, Geisser–Greenhouse *F*-test.**

13.3.6 One between-subject and one within-subject factor designs

The most common design in many areas of research is that with one between- and one within-subject factor, each at two levels. The appropriate analysis often boils down to a two-sample *t*-test (across the levels of the between-factor) on the differences of the response variable across the two levels of the within-factor (see Section 10.2 for details). Correspondingly, therefore, the sample size problem corresponds exactly to that of the two-sample *t*-test scenario discussed in Section 13.3.2 but this time with the response variable being the *difference* across the within-subject factor in the response variable. Basically the same prerequisites as in Section 13.3.2 are then necessary except that they should be based on the *standard deviations of the differences* and the *difference* (across the between-factor) *of the mean differences* (across the within-factor). Perhaps, this is more easily understood through the following illustration.

Illustration 13.7 **Osteoporosis and exercise (revisited)**

Background
See Illustration 4.5.

Study description
A sample of middle-aged osteoporotic women are to be randomised either to a twice-weekly physiotherapist-led Exercise regime or to be a Control. Physiological assessments, including a functional reach test measuring *Balance*, will be conducted on all women both before and after two months of the intervention (i.e. Exercise or Control).

Aim
To suggest how many osteoporosis sufferers need to be included in a study of whether such an exercise regime can significantly improve, on average, the Balance of osteoporotic women over a two-month period of exercise relative to any natural improvement of Controls.

Data

Response variable	Balance (centimetres)
Between-subject factor:	Regime (2 levels: Exerciser, Control)
Within-subject factor:	Time (2 levels: Pre-Study, Post-Study)

Table 13.1

Regime	Balance Pre-Study (cm)	Balance Post-Study (cm)	Difference Post − Pre (cm)	Sample mean (s d)
Exercise	34.3	35.6	1.1	5.9 cm (5.3)
	26.7	31.8	5.1	
	19.0	30.5	11.5	
Control	26.2	24.5	−1.7	0.9 cm (3.1)
	30.5	30.5	0	
	15.2	19.5	4.3	

Sample size

As usual, it seems natural to take equal-sized samples from both populations (i.e. Exercisers and Controls) – from a statistical viewpoint because it is advisable to estimate all population means with equal precision and on ethical grounds becasue physical exercise is not guaranteed to improve any aspect of osteoporosis. Gathering suitable information to meet the necessary requirements to guesstimate the sample sizes can be more problematical than for a simple two-sample problem. Here, some indication of the population mean and standard deviation of the differences (i.e. Post-Study Balance score minus Pre-Study Balance score) must be plucked from an appropriate source. Again, the value of a pilot study even with as few as three Exercisers and three Controls is well worth the effort and, unless the pilot study throws up changes in the protocol, these same subjects may be included in the full study. In this case, a small pilot study resulted in the data presented in Table 13.1.

Based on this pilot study, the prerequisites chosen for this study are as follows:

1 The analysis is likely to be carried out on the differences, so a mean difference of around 5 cm may be plausible (i.e. 5.9 – 0.9 cm).

2 Assuming a common standard deviation of the differences for both Exercisers and Controls, then a value for this around 4 cm seems reasonable (i.e. roughly half-way between 5.3 and 3.1 cm).

3 The researcher would prefer a power of 0.95 (or 95%), i.e. the probability that 'the study will correctly reject the null hypothesis of no difference in mean Balance due to the Exercise Regime (over Controls)' should be 0.95. As usual, the significance level would be taken as 0.05 or 5%.

For this study, the researcher decided in advance of the study that she was interested only in rejecting the null hypothesis of no effect of the Exercise Regime on Balance in favour of the alternative hypothesis that the Exercise in fact increased the population average Balance measurement. A decision of this sort always has a definite effect on the calcuation of sample size as it reduces the sample size, in this instance from 18 subjects in each sample based on a two-sided hypothesis test, to 15 subjects in each sample based on this choice of a one-sided test (see Box 13.5). See also the technical appendix to Chapter 5 for more on one-sided and two-sided hypothesis tests.

As always, it is worthwhile having a look at power curves across a range of possible sample sizes and true differences in the population means (Figure 13.6). From Figure 13.6 it appears that a sample size of around **15 for each regime** should in fact be sufficient to

Box 13.5

```
Power and Sample Size
2-Sample t Test

Testing mean 1 = mean 2 (versus >) i.e. a One-Sided Test
Calculating power for mean 1 = mean 2 + difference
Alpha = 0.05 Assumed standard deviation = 4

                Sample    Target
Difference       Size     Power      Actual Power
         5         15     0.95           0.954863

The sample size is for each group.
```

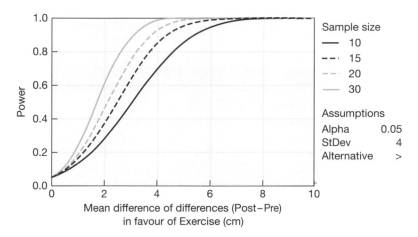

Figure 13.6 **Power curves for Osteoporosis (Balance) study.**

stand a reasonable chance (i.e. over 50%) of identifying correctly a true difference in excess of 3 cm in favour of the Exercise Regime.

Conclusion

To ensure a power of at least 95% so that a minimum difference in improvement of population mean Balance score of 5 cm in favour of Exercisers over the two months of the study would not be missed, the study should involve a minimum of 15 osteoporotic sufferers being allocated to each Exercise Regime.

Remember, though, that this is highly dependent on the reliability of the assumed prerequisite values of a minimum difference of 5 cm between the population mean improvements, a common standard deviation of the improvements of 4 cm and a power of 95%.

Reference: Mitchell, S., Aitchison, T. and Grant, S. (1998). 'Physiological effects of a structured 12 week exercise programme on post-menopausal osteoporotic women. Physical activity and health in the elderly.' *Physiotherapy,* **84**: 157–163.

13.3.7 Categorical variables

As was seen in Section 13.2.5, studies with categorical response variables generally require much greater sample sizes than those with continuous variables. This is true regardless of whether sample size calculations are based on interval estimation or on hypothesis testing. In the use of hypothesis testing for guesstimating categorical

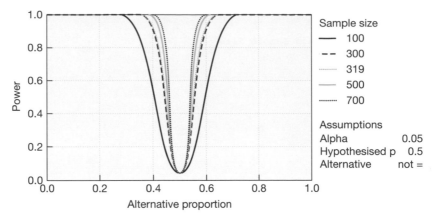

Figure 13.7 **Power curves for test of one proportion.**

study sample sizes, the true population proportions are in fact needed as prerequisites in what seems to be a rather convoluted and over-prescribed procedure. For example, if a study using a single sample of a binary variable was intended to be used to carry out a hypothesis test of whether the true population proportion was 0.5 (or 50%) against the alternative hypothesis that it was in fact 0.6 (i.e. 60%), then, to achieve a power of 0.95, a sample of 319 subjects would be necessary (see Box 13.6).

Box 13.6

```
Power and Sample Size
Test for One Proportion

Testing proportion = 0.5 (versus not = 0.5)
Alpha = 0.05

Alternative    Sample    Target
 Proportion      Size     Power   Actual Power
        0.6       319      0.95       0.950056
```

Figure 13.7 shows the appropriate power curves against different values of the true proportion and, among other things, it can be seen there that a sample size of 100 will have a good chance (a power of, say, >80%) of correctly rejecting the null hypothesis of 0.50 only if the true population proportion is over 0.65 or under 0.35.

For a study involving two distinct populations and a binary response variable, interest usually lies in comparing the population proportions (e.g. whether the proportion of a target population who will take up active commuting based on an intervention package is significantly greater than the natural take-up among controls). Again, the relevant prerequisites will involve specifying the true population proportions in both populations. For example, if it seemed to the researcher that controls had (around) a 50% (0.5) likelihood of taking up active commuting but she thought the intervention economically worthwhile only if this improved by at least 10% to 60% (0.6), then her study would require just 641 controls and 641 on the intervention for a power of 0.95 (see Box 13.7).

Box 13.7

```
Power and Sample Size
Test for Two Proportions
Testing proportion 1 = proportion 2 (versus not =)
Calculating power for proportion 2 = 0.6
Alpha = 0.05

                 Sample      Target
Proportion 1      Size       Power      Actual Power
        0.5        641        0.95          0.950212

The sample size is for each group.
```

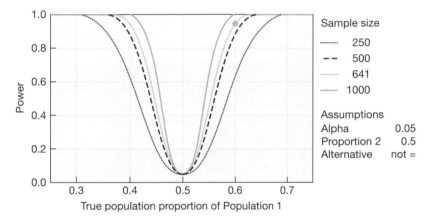

Figure 13.8 **Power curves for comparing two different population proportions.**

Again, it is worth looking at an appropriate power curve which shows various aspects of the worth of the study. Figure 13.8 shows that taking, say, 250 subjects in each sample would only be likely to show up (as significant) differences of the order of 0.15 or 15% (i.e. be able to reject one population proportion of 0.50 in favour of 0.65 or greater for the other population).

All in all, sample sizes for binary and categorical response variables in general are only likely to frighten off all but the dedicated and extremely well-funded researcher.

Exercises

13.5 There is a paucity of knowledge concerning climbing-specific performance in response to altitude-induced hypoxia and there is a need to examine the underlying mechanisms related to changes in performance in hypoxia. The aim of this study is to compare the effect of hypoxia on performance in a climbing-specific task in advanced climbers and non-climbers. Male rock climbers who can climb at least 7a on the French sport scale are to be used so they can be described as being of advanced ability. The controls are to have no previous rock climbing experience and are not to participate in any sports where forearm and finger strength are important. The response variable is to be the Endurance Time in a climbing-specific endurance test in hypoxia. How many climbers and controls should be recruited to this study to achieve a power of 95% for the appropriate two-sided two-sample hypothesis test? The researcher believes that both population standard deviations of Endurance Time will be around 50 seconds and that the minimum difference of interest in population means will be 25 seconds.

13.6 In a study of three nutritional supplements for 1–2-year-old children in Third World rural communities, a sample of such children are to be randomised to one of three supplements (i.e. a High Energy (H) or a Mineral (M) or a Placebo (P) supplement. The key response variable to be analysed is the (log of the) total motor activity (TMA) score of the child after 6 months of daily supplementation. Previous studies have suggested that the (log)TMA is likely to have a standard deviation around this age of 0.1 units and the minimum mean difference likely to be of interest is around 0.2 units. How many children should be randomised to each of the three supplements to achieve a power of 0.95 for the appropriate one-way ANOVA? (See Exercise 2.6 for details of the design of this study.)

13.7 Creatine is a natural constituent of the body formed in the liver and kidneys. Some studies have shown that oral creatine supplementation has the potential to enhance performance in repeated high-intensity sprints. A sample of female subjects, each of whom took part in regular physical exercise, would be involved in this study. Each subject would carry out a set of ten 10-second sprints (with one minute rest between sprints) on an exercise bike and her median Power Output (in watts) recorded. Each subject would then be placed on a 4-week course of creatine supplementation, after which the same procedure would be repeated. Assuming that the standard deviation of the *changes* in Power Output over the 4 weeks of this study will be around 12 watts and that the researchers would like to make sure that they have a good chance of picking up an average improvement of at least 2% on the typical Power Output for this procedure of 500 watts, how many subjects should be used in this study to achieve a power of at least 0.95 for a two-sided paired-sample *t*-test here? (See Exercise 9.2 for analysis of this study.)

13.8 Deep water running (DWR) is performed by some athletes who wish to reduce the number of training sessions on land where the high impact of foot strikes may result in injury over time. Despite the fact that lactate threshold (LT) is sometimes used to provide training intensity guidance, no comparison has been made between LT in DWR and during track and treadmill running. As some athletes use DWR, track and treadmill training, it would be useful to compare, say, the heart rate at LT for DWR and track and treadmill running. Information relating to the above will help the athlete to adjust his/her training heart rate (if necessary) for a given exercise setting. A sample of well-trained male endurance runners is to be recruited to perform incremental tests using 3-minute stages once for each of DWR, track running and treadmill running. These running tests will take place at the same time of day at least one week apart. The order of these three tests for each subject is determined by a series of balanced Latin squares (see Chapter 2). The key response variable is to be the Heart Rate at Lactate Threshold. The coach carrying out this study believes the range of likely means across the three running environments to be from 130 to 160 b.min^{-1}, the standard deviation of each measurement to be around 12 b.min^{-1} and the correlation between any two measurements on the same subject around 0.6. How many subjects should be used in the study to ensure a power of at least 0.95? (See Exercise 2.7 for details of the design of this study.)

13.9   Being overweight, if not obese, is an ever-increasing problem in the western world. Problems associated with obesity include a greater incidence of diabetes and coronary heart disease. One problem often encountered by the obese and substantially overweight is limited mobility. Exercise programmes have the potential to enhance mobility by decreasing body mass and by improving strength and endurance. A sample of overweight (i.e. BMI > 25) middle-aged females are to be randomly allocated to be either an Exerciser or a Control. The Exercisers are to be asked to carry out two (aerobic and strength) exercise sessions per week for 12 weeks. A key variable used to investigate the usefulness of the exercise programme is the improvement in the time taken for such a woman to walk 20 metres from a standing start over a 12-week period. The researchers believe that the least improvement in mean 20 m Walking Time that would be of practical value is 1 second and that the standard deviation of such improvements is likely to be around 2 seconds. How many females would be required for such a study to ensure a power of 0.95 for an appropriate two-sample t-test of the improvements between Exerciser and Control? (See Exercise 2.1 and Illustrations 3.8 and 10.1 for design and analysis of the study, which was in fact grossly under-sampled.)

13.10 A sample of Glasgow University (GU) students are to be questioned regarding whether they are regular exercisers, i.e. those who take part regularly in a minimum of three sessions per week of at least 20 minutes aerobic activity at, or above, 65% of maximum heart rate. How many students must be sampled in order to carry out a hypothesis test that 40% of GU students 'regularly' exercise against an alternative that this is in fact at least 50% with the hypothesis test having a power of 95%? How many GU male and female subjects would be required to provide a hypothesis test, with power of 95%, that there is no difference in population proportions who regularly exercise between the sexes against an alternative hypothesis that the true proportions are 40% for Males and 50% for Females? Compare these sample size choices to those in Exercise 13.4 based on interval estimation. (See Exercise 8.1 for analysis of the actual study.)

Summary

Although every researcher wants to make a sensible choice of sample size before carrying out a study, doing so is a difficult and almost thankless task unless, of course, the conclusions of the study are known in advance! Then, what would be the point of the study? This doesn't stop many people from trying to use available software or to badger a tame statistician into giving them an official, sanctified required number of subjects. Without a lot of input from the researcher, who has often to make quite a few assumptions about the true, unknown population parameters (such as population means, standard deviations or proportions), this is impossible and, even when such assumptions are made, the resulting numbers should still be thought of, at best, as simple, very rough guides to the general ball-park of an adequate sample size and not as guaranteed, mathematical solutions.

This chapter provides ideas and illustrations of how to speculate on sample size for a variety of contexts from two different perspectives, one based on interval estimates and the other, more common approach, based on hypothesis testing. Both methods depend on moderately complicated mathematics but this should not hide the fact that they are based on a number of assumptions whose justification is tenuous, to say the least. The watchword throughout is to take considerable care in any attempt to come up with an 'adequate' sample size for any study and, if in any doubt, to double the number first thought of! Far too many studies turn out to be a waste of time as they are too small to have a reasonable chance of picking up (i.e. concluding significant) even a moderately large effect.

One last thought is always to remember that any study will one day be the previous study on which someone else will be basing their own study.

Technical appendix

The power calculations required for any hypothesis test can be heuristically described as follows.

Solve the following two (simultaneous) equations:

the probability of rejecting H_0 when H_0 is actually true = SL

and

the probability of rejecting H_0 when H_1 is actually true = P

where SL is the assumed significance level, P the assumed Power and H_0 and H_1 are the null and alternative hypotheses, respectively. The assumed prerequisites ensure that both these probabilities can be fully evaluated.

These two equations are functions of the (common) *sample size* and the *numerical value* which will be used to conclude that the difference in sample means is such that H_0 must be rejected. The latter equation is of only limited interest until the hypothesis test is carried out, but the former is the key result here and should always be rounded up. The procedure may seem complicated and reassuringly mathematical but its results are only as good as the assumptions used in the specification of these two probabilities.

Chapter 2 Designing a study

Illustrations

Illustration	Context (sample size)	Design	Response variable
2.1	Chronic low back pain (30)	Between-subject factor (3 levels) – randomised	Time Off Work
2.2	Ice baths (10)	Within-subject factor (2 levels) – balanced	Blood Lactate Concentration
2.3	Rugby ball carrying (12)	Within-subject factor (4 levels) – balanced	20 m Sprint Time
2.4	Golf psychology (24)	Randomly permuted blocks (2 levels – blocks of 4 for each of 4 strata by Handicap Group)	Distance from Hole
2.5	Zig-zag sprinting (24)	Balanced 3×3 Latin squares (2 for each of 4 factor combinations)	Sprint Time

Exercises

Exercise	Context (sample size)	Design	Response variable
2.1	Overweight women and exercise (20)	Between-subject factor (2 levels) – randomised	20 m Walking Time
2.2	Relaxation (30)	Between-subject factor (3 levels) - randomised	Heart Rate
2.3	Walking poles (14)	Within-subject factor (2 levels) – balanced	$\dot{V}O_2$
2.4	Humidity (12)	Within-subject factor (4 levels) – balanced	Performance
2.5	Exercise in pregnancy (32)	Randomly permuted blocks (2 levels {Exer/Control} – 2 blocks of 4 for each of 3 strata by Age)	Coping Ability/Assets
2.6	Indonesian study (24)	Randomly permuted blocks (3 levels {HE/M/P} – blocks of 6 for each of 4 strata by Age)	Motor Activity Level
2.7	Deep water running (12)	Balanced 3×3 Latin squares (2 sets of 2)	HR at Lactate Threshold
2.8	Rugby resistance (32)	Balanced 4×4 Latin squares (2 for each of 4 factor combinations)	10 m Sprint Time

Chapter 3 Summarising and displaying data

Illustrations

Illustration	Context (sample size)	Technique	Response variable
3.1	Mont Blanc ascent time (285)	Summary statistics, Box plot One-sample	Ascent Time

Illustration	Context (sample size)	Technique	Response variable
3.2	Soccer fitness (37)	Summary statistics, Box plot One between-subject factor (2 levels)	CMJ Height
3.3	Relaxation and running performance (28)	Summary statistics, Box plot One between-subject factor (3 levels)	Heart Rate Reduction
3.4	Exercise and well-being (285)	Summary statistics, Box plot Two between-subject factors (each at 2 levels)	Well-being
3.5	Exercise and the elderly (12)	Scatter plot, Box plot One within-subject factor (2 levels)	Relative Intensity
3.6	Deep water running (18)	Case profile plot One within-subject factor (3 levels)	Heart Rate
3.7	Bubble wrap (12)	Case profile plot Two within-subject factors (2 levels, 5 levels)	Reduction in Skin Temperature
3.8	Overweight women and exercise (26)	Scatter plot, Box plot One between-subject factor (2 levels) One within-subject factor (2 levels)	Walking Time
3.9	Grip strength (30)	Labelled scatter plot One between-subject factor (3 levels) One covariate	Grip Strength
3.10	Physical activity in children (76)	Scatter plot (correlation)	Midweek PA, Weekend PA
3.11	3 km Running times (16)	Scatter plot (regression)	3 km Running Time
3.12	Power and body mass (30)	Scatter plot (regression)	Anaerobic Power
3.13	Maximum heart rate and age (26)	Scatter plot (regression)	Maximum Heart Rate

Exercises

Exercise	Context (sample size)	Technique	Response variable
3.1	Popmobility (10)	Summary statistics, Box plot One-sample	Energy Expenditure
3.2	Haemoglobin (50)	Summary statistics, Box plot One-sample	Haemoglobin Concentration
3.3	Soccer fitness (37)	Summary statistics, Box plot One between-subject factor (2 levels)	Squat Strength
3.4	Basal metabolic rate (24)	Summary statistics, Box plot One between-subject factor (2 levels)	Basal Metabolic Rate
3.5	Training intervention (18)	Scatter plot, Box plot One within-subject factor (2 levels)	$\dot{V}O_2$ max
3.6	Bubble wrap (12)	Case profile plot Two within-subject factors (2 levels, 5 levels)	Core Temperature
3.7	Basal metabolic rate (24)	Labelled scatter plot One between-subject factor (2 levels) One covariate	Basal Metabolic Rate
3.8	$\dot{V}O_2$ max and body mass (19)	Labelled scatter plot One between-subject factor (2 levels) One covariate	$\dot{V}O_2$ max

Exercise	Context Sample Size	Technique	Response
3.9	$\dot{V}O_2$ test (26)	Scatter plot (correlation)	Cooper $\dot{V}O_2$ max, Treadmill $\dot{V}O_2$ max
3.10	3 km Running times (16)	Scatter plot (regression)	3 km Running Time

Chapter 4 Estimating parameters

Illustrations

Illustration	Context (sample size)	Technique	Response variable
4.1	5 m Sprint time in soccer players (43)	One-sample (interval estimation)	5 m Sprint
4.2	Mont Blanc ascent time (285)	One-sample (interval estimation)	Ascent Time
4.3	Soccer fitness (37)	Two-sample (interval estimation)	CMJ Height
4.4	Physiotherapy pain relief (29)	Two-sample (interval estimation)	Pain Threshold
4.5	Osteoporosis and exercise (30)	Two-sample (interval estimation)	Balance
4.6	Training intervention (18)	One-sample paired data (interval estimation)	$\dot{V}O_2$ max
4.7	Osteoporosis and exercise (30)	Two-sample paired data (interval estimation)	Balance
4.8	Exercise and the elderly (12)	Two-sample paired data (interval estimation)	Relative Intensity
4.9	Avalanche survival (14)	One-sample (prediction interval)	Tolerance Time
4.10	Mont Blanc ascent time (285)	One-sample (tolerance interval)	Ascent Time
4.11	Walk In to Work Out (14)	One-sample (transformations and bootstrap)	Walking Time
4.12	Walk In to Work Out (26)	Two-sample (transformations and bootstrap)	Walking Time
4.13	Soccer fitness (37)	Two-sample (transformations and bootstrap)	CMJ Height

Exercises

Exercise	Context (sample size)	Technique	Response variable
4.1	Popmobility (10)	One-sample (interval estimation)	Energy Expenditure
4.2	Haemoglobin (25)	One-sample (interval estimation)	Haemoglobin Concentration
4.3	Haemoglobin by sex (50)	Two-sample (interval estimation)	Haemoglobin Concentration
4.4	Soccer fitness (37)	Two-sample (interval estimation)	Knee Extension
4.5	Osteoporosis and exercise (30)	Two-sample (interval estimation)	$\dot{V}O_2$ max
4.6	Training intervention (18)	One-sample paired data (interval estimation)	Squat Jump
4.7	Exercise and the elderly (12)	Two-sample paired data (interval estimation)	Relative Intensity
4.8	Osteoporosis and exercise (30)	Two-sample paired data (interval estimation)	Flexibility
4.9	Ankylosing spondylitis (42)	Two-sample paired data (interval estimation)	Forced Vital Capacity
4.10	Exercise and the elderly (12)	One-sample (tolerance interval)	Relative Intensity
4.11	Soccer fitness (18)	One-sample (tolerance interval)	% Body Fat
4.12	Soccer fitness (54)	Two-sample (transformations and bootstrap)	% Body Fat

Chapter 5 Testing hypotheses

Illustrations

Illustration	Context (sample size)	Technique	Response variable
5.1	Soccer fitness (37)	Two-sample (*t*-test)	CMJ Height
5.2	Osteoporosis and exercise (30)	Two-sample (*t*-test)	Balance
5.3	Training intervention (18)	One-sample paired data (*t*-test)	$\dot{V}O_2$ max
5.4	Osteoporosis and exercise (30)	Two-sample paired data (*t*-test)	Balance
5.5	Exercise and the elderly (12)	Two-sample paired data (*t*-test)	Relative Intensity
5.6	Walk In to Work Out (14)	Test for Normality	Walking Time

Exercises

Exercise	Context (sample size)	Technique	Response variable
5.1	Haemoglobin (50)	Two-sample (*t*-test)	Haemoglobin Concentration
5.2	Soccer fitness (37)	Two-sample (*t*-test)	Knee Extensor Strength
5.3	Osteoporosis and exercise (30)	Two-sample (*t*-test)	$\dot{V}O_2$ max
5.4	Youth soccer (18)	Two-sample (*t*-test)	Squat Score
5.5	Training intervention (18)	One-sample paired data (*t*-test)	Squat Jump
5.6	Avalanche survival (14)	One-sample paired data (*t*-test)	Tolerance Time
5.7	Osteoporosis and exercise (30)	Two-sample paired data (*t*-test)	Flexibility
5.8	Ankylosing spondylitis (42)	Two-sample paired data (*t*-test)	Forced Vital Capacity
5.9	Popmobility (10)	Test for Normality	Energy Expenditure
5.10	Avalanche survival (14)	Test for Normality	Tolerance Time

Chapter 6 Modelling relationships: regression

Illustrations

Illustration	Context (sample size)	Technique: explanatory variable(s)	Response variable
6.1	3 km Running times (16)	Simple linear regression: v-4mM	3 km Running Time
6.2	$\dot{V}O_2$ max and body mass (23)	Simple linear regression: Body Mass	$\dot{V}O_2$ max
6.3	Rowing performance 5000 m (18)	Simple linear regression: Peak Power	5000 m Rowing Time
6.4	Rowing performance 5000 m (18)	Multiple regression: Peak Power, Stroke Length	5000 m Rowing Time
6.5	Body fat and anthropometry (78)	Multiple regression: Height, Weight, Age	% Body Fat
6.6	3 km Running times (16)	Multiple regression: v-4mM, v-Tlac	3 km Running Time
6.7	Power output prediction in cycling (24)	Variable selection techniques: v-4mM, v-Tlac, v-Tlac.ll, DMax, Rise.1PB	Endurance
6.8	Power and body mass (30)	Multiple regression: Body Mass, Sex	Anaerobic Power (Wingate)
6.9	Power and body mass (30)	Multiple regression: Body Mass, Sex	Anaerobic Power (Margaria)
6.10	Mont Blanc ascent time (194)	Regression tree: Age, Sex, Maximum Altitude Climbed	Ascent Time

Exercises

Exercise	Context (sample size)	Technique: explanatory variable(s)	Response variable
6.1	3 km Running times (16)	Simple linear regression: v-Tlac	3 km Running Time
6.2	Cycling power (24)	Simple linear regression: v-4mM	Endurance
6.3	Maximum heart rate and age (26)	Simple linear regression: Age	Maximum Heart Rate
6.4	3 km Running times (16)	Multiple regression: v-4mM, $\dot{V}O_2$ max	3 km Running Time
6.5	Rowing performance 2000 m (18)	Simple linear regression: Peak Power, Stroke Length	2000 m Rowing Time
6.6	Rowing performance 2000 m (18)	Simple linear regression: Peak Power, Stroke Length, Height, Body Mass, Sit and Reach	2000 m Rowing Time
6.7	3 km Running times (16)	Variable selection techniques: v-4mM, v-Tlac, Rel.14.5, Rel.16.1, v-$\dot{V}O_2$ max	3 km Running Time
6.8	Power and body mass (30)	Multiple regression: Body Mass, Sex	Anaerobic Power (Lewis)

Chapter 7 Investigating between-subject factors: independent observations

Illustrations

Illustration	Context (sample size)	Technique: between-subject factors (levels)	Response variable
7.1	Grip strength (30)	One between-subject factor: Climber Type (B3)	Grip Strength
7.2	Relaxation and running performance (28)	One between-subject factor: Treatment (B3)	Reduction in Heart Rate
7.3	Sprint speed in rugby (24)	Two between-subject factors: Status (B2), Position (B2)	Sprint Time
7.4	Electrical muscle stimulation (28)	Two between-subject factors: Device (B2), Sex (B2)	Isometric Abdominal Strength
7.5	Grip strength (30)	One between-subject factor and one covariate: Climber Type (B3), Body Mass	Grip Strength
7.6	Grip strength (30)	Allometric scaling One between-subject factor and one covariate: Climber Type (B3), Body Mass	Grip Strength

Exercises

Exercise	Context (sample size)	Technique: between-subject factors (levels)	Response variable
7.1	Grip strength (30)	One between-subject factor: Climber Type (B3)	Climbing Specific Finger Strength
7.2	Mont Blanc ascent time (194)	One between-subject factor: Maximum Altitude Climbed (B3)	Ascent Time
7.3	Exercise and well-being (285)	Two between-subject factors: Regular Exercise (B2), Sex (B2)	Well-being
7.4	Electrical stimulation (28)	Two between subject factors: Device (B2), Sex (B2)	Abdominal Endurance

Exercise	Context (sample size)	Technique: between-subject factors (levels)	Response variable
7.5	Basal metabolic rate (24)	One between-subject factor and one covariate: Diet (B2), Body Mass	Basal Metabolic Rate
7.6	Grip strength (30)	Allometric scaling: One between-subject factor and one covariate: Climber Type (B3), Body Mass	Grip Strength
7.7	$\dot{V}O_2$ max and body mass (19)	Allometric scaling: One between-subject factor and one covariate: Sex (B2), Body Mass	$\dot{V}O_2$ max

Chapter 8 Modelling categorical data

Illustrations

Illustration	Context (sample size)	Technique	Response variable
8.1	Mont Blanc ascent (285)	Interval estimation for population proportion	Ascent Success
8.2	Gaelic football injuries (323)	Interval estimation for multinomials	Injury (Hamstrings/Quadriceps)
8.3	Hamstring injuries in Gaelic football (323)	Interval estimation for comparison of population proportion (Training vs Game)	Injury (Hamstring)
8.4	Health promotion poster campaign (Females 895)	Comparison of 3 binary population proportions	Stair/Escalator Use
8.5	Back pain at work (2498)	Comparison of 2 multinomials	Severity of Back Pain
8.6	Higher PE and sex (151)	Test of association (2 by 2)	Higher PE by Sex
8.7	Satisfaction with variety and length of exercise classes (424)	Test of association (2 by 2)	Length by Variety
8.8	GAA injuries – footwear by pitch condition (267)	Test of association (3 by 3)	Footwear by Pitch Conditions
8.9	Walk In to Work Out (93)	Test of (marginal) symmetry – Controls	Stage of Change
8.10	Post-natal depression, coping and Exercise (39)	Simple linear logistic regression	PND (Moderate/Low)
8.11	Personal trainer (1654)	Logistic regression with 2 between-subject factors – Sex and Membership (2 and 3 levels)	PTS (Yes/No)
8.12	Active commuting (192)	Variable selection in logistic regression	SOC Change (Improved/Not)

Exercises

Exercise	Context (sample size)	Technique	Response variable
8.1	Well-being (285)	Interval estimation for population proportion and between Sexes	Regular Exerciser
8.2	GAA injuries (323)	Interval estimation for multinomials/comparisons	Ankle Injuries

Exercise	Context (sample size)	Technique	Response variable
8.3	Walk In to Work Out (337)	3 level multinomial (Intervention/Control)	Alteration in Journey SOC
8.4	Poster campaign (males)	Comparison of 3 binary population proportions	Stair/Escalator Use
8.5	Walk In to Work Out (337)	Comparison of 2 multinomials (3 levels)	Alteration in Journey SOC
8.6	Head PE teachers (87)	Test of association (2 by 2)	Sex by Years Teaching
8.7	Use of sports facilities (1710)	Term usage (3) and vacation usage (3)	Use of Sports Centre
8.8	Walk In to Work Out (99)	Test of marginal symmetry – Intervention	Stage of Change (Before by 3 months)
8.9	Shivering (12)	Casualty Bag vs Bubble Wrap – marginal symmetry	Shivering (No/Slight/Severe)
8.10	Elderly mobility (105)	Logistic regression – EMS and Location	Fell in 3 months (Yes/No)
8.11	Variety in classes (1654)	Logistic regression with 2 between-subject factors – Sex and Membership (2 and 3 levels)	Satisfied (Yes/No)

Chapter 9 Investigating within-subject factors: dependent observations

Illustrations

Illustration	Context (sample size)	Technique: within-subject factors (levels)	Response variable
9.1	% Body fat in males (78)	One within-subject factor: Method (W2)	% Body Fat
9.2	Energy expenditure in step classes (10)	One within-subject factor: Step Height (W3)	Energy Expenditure
9.3	Walking poles (14)	Two within-subject factors: Pole Use (2) and Time (W3)	$\dot{V}O_2$
9.4	Altitude illness (14)	Two within-subject factors: Drug (W2) and Atmosphere (W2)	Heart Rate
9.5	Drug heart rates (11)	Three within-subject factors: Status (W2), Verapamil (W2) and Atenolol (W2)	Heart Rate

Exercises

Exercise	Context (sample size)	Technique: within-subject factors (levels)	Response variable
9.1	% Body fat female (78)	One within-subject factor: Method (W2)	% Body Fat
9.2	Creatine supplements (20)	One within-subject factor: Time (W2)	Power Output
9.3	Humidity (12)	One within-subject factor: Conditions (W3)	Performance
9.4	% Body fat four (46)	One within-subject factor: Methods (W4)	% Body Fat
9.5	Treadmill comparison (11)	Two within-subject factors: Treadmill (W2) and Speed (W2)	$\dot{V}O_2$
9.6	Bubble wrap (12)	Two within-subject factors: Bag (W2) and Time (W3)	Change in Skin Temperature

Chapter 10 Investigating studies with between-subject and within-subject factors: more on dependent observations

Illustrations

Illustration	Context (sample size)	Technique: between/within-subject factors (levels)	Response variable
10.1	Overweight women and exercise (26)	One between-subject and one within-subject factor: Exercise Regime (B2) and Time (W2)	20 m Walking Time
10.2	Exercise in pregnancy (73)	One between-subject and one within-subject factor: Exercise Regime (B2) and Stage (W3)	Coping Assets
10.3	Kicking the habit (48)	One between-subject and two within-subject factors: Football Group (B3), Speed (W2) and Side (W2)	Knee Extension Strength
10.4	Youth football (505 agility test) (42)	Two between-subject and one within-subject factor: Team (B2), Squad (B2) and Side (W2)	Agility
10.5	Golf psychology (17)	Two between-subject and two within-subject factors: Handicap (B2), Condition (B2), Shot (W2) and Time (W2)	Distance from Hole

Exercises

Exercise	Context (sample size)	Technique: between/within-subject factors (levels)	Response variable
10.1	Osteoporosis (30)	One between-subject and one within-subject factor: Regime (B2) and Time (W2)	Flexibility
10.2	Ankylosing spondylitis (42)	One between-subject and one within-subject factor: Regime (B2) and Time (W2)	Cervical Rotation
10.3	Relaxation (28)	One between-subject and one within-subject factor: Regime (B3) and Time (W2)	Heart Rate
10.4	Exercise in pregnancy (73)	One between-subject and one within-subject factor: Exercise Regime (B2) and Stage (W3)	Physical Well-Being
10.5	Anaerobic power (30)	One between-subject and one within-subject factor: Sex (B2) and Method (W3)	Anaerobic Power
10.6	Climbers (male) (30)	One between-subject and two within-subject factors: Level (B3), Aspect (W2) and Side (W2)	Strength
10.7	Kicking the hamstring (48)	One between-subject and two within-subject factors: Football Group (B3), Speed (W2) and Side (W2)	Hamstring Strength
10.8	Rugby sprints (39)	Two between-subject and one within-subject factors: Status (B2), Position (B2) and Direction (W3)	Sprint Time
10.9	Youth agility (replicates) (42)	Two between-subject and two within-subject factors: Team (B2), Squad (B2) and Side (W2), Replicate (W2)	Agility
10.10	Climbers (all) (60)	Two between-subject and two within-subject factors: Sex (B2), Level (B3), Aspect (W2) and Side (W2)	Strength

Chapter 11 Handling linear mixed-effects models: more on dependent observations

Illustrations

Illustration	Context (sample size)	Technique: between/within-subject factors (levels)	Response variable
11.1	Resistance training (13)	One within-subject covariate: % Body Weight* (W7)	10 m Sprint Time
11.2	Ice baths (10)	One within-subject covariate: Time* (W6)	Blood Lactate Concentration
11.3	Resistance training by sport (33)	One between-subject factor and within-subject covariate: Sport (B2) and % Body Weight* (W7)	10 m Sprint Time
11.4	Knee extensor peak torque and velocity (40)	Two between-subject factors and within-subject covariate: Sex (B2), Age (B4) and Velocity* (W4)	Leg Strength

Exercises

Exercise	Context (sample size)	Technique: between/within-subject factors (levels)	Response variable
11.1	Soda lime controls (14)	One within-subject covariate: Time* (W10)	PETCO$_2$
11.2	Bubble wrap temperature (12)	One within-subject covariate: Time* (W7)	Skin or Core Temperature (change from base)
11.3	Paraplegic posture (9)	One within-subject factor and one within-subject covariate: Work Rate* (W4), Posture (W2)	$\dot{V}O_2$ and Heart Rate
11.4	Walking poles HR (14)	One within-subject factor and one within-subject covariate: Time* (W10), Pole Use (W2)	Heart Rate
11.5	Physio pain (20)	One between-subject factor and one within-subject covariate: Time* (W4), Intervention (B2)	VAS Pain
11.6	Cadence and sex (20)	One between-subject factor and one within-subject Covariate: %Cadence* (W5), Sex (B2)	$\dot{V}O_2$ average
11.7	Climbing fatigue (20)	One between-subject factor, one within-subject factor and one within-subject covariate: Group (B2), Atmosphere (W2), Time* (W3)	Fatigue
11.8	Cold suits (18)	One between-subject factor, one within-subject factor and one within-subject covariate: Suit (W3), Study (B2), Time* (W4)	Skin Temperature (Change from Baseline)

*Denotes within-covariate (i.e. linear factor)

Chapter 12 Measurement error and method agreement studies

Illustrations

Illustration	Context (sample size)	Technique	Response variable
12.1	Anthropometric measurement error (19)	Repeatability study	Foot Length
12.2	BMI repeatability (13)	Repeatability study	BMI
12.3	Repeatability of blood lactate markers (14)	Repeatability study	Lactate Threshold
12.4	Reproducibility of a motor co-ordination score in children (8)	Reproducibility study	CAT Score
12.5	$\dot{V}O_2$ max agreement (26)	Test of agreement (2 methods, one Gold Standard)	$\dot{V}O_2$ max
12.6	Densitometry comparison (25)	Test of agreement (2 methods, no Gold Standard)	% Body Fat
12.7	$\dot{V}O_2$ max agreement (26)	Test of agreement (2 methods, no Gold Standard)	$\dot{V}O_2$ max

Exercises

Exercise	Context (sample size)	Technique	Response variable
12.1	Anthropometric measurement error (19)	Repeatability study	Triceps Skinfolds
12.2	Lactate endurance markers (13)	Repeatability study	$3mmol.L^{-1}$ Blood Lactate
12.3	Treadmill comparison (11)	Test of agreement (2 methods, no Gold Standard)	$\dot{V}O_2$
12.4	$\dot{V}O_2$ max agreement (26)	Test of agreement (2 methods, no Gold Standard)	$\dot{V}O_2$ max
12.5	Densitometry comparison (25)	Test of agreement (2 methods, no Gold Standard)	% Body Fat

Chapter 13 Speculating on the sample size required

Illustrations

Illustration	Context (sample size)	Technique	Response variable
13.1	Soda lime canisters	One-sample (interval estimation)	Tolerance Time
13.2	Physiotherapy pain relief	Two-sample (interval estimation)	Pain Tolerance
13.3	Physiotherapy pain relief	Two-sample	Pain Threshold
13.4	Chronic low back pain	One between-subject factor (3 levels)	Time Off Work
13.5	Walking poles	Paired-sample	$\dot{V}O_2$ at 10 minutes
13.6	Humidity	One within-subject factor (3 levels)	Performance
13.7	Osteoporosis and exercise	One between-subject and one within-subject factor (each at 2 levels)	Balance Difference

Exercises

Exercise	Context (sample size)	Technique	Response variable
13.1	Mont Blanc	One-sample (interval estimation)	Ascent Time
13.2	Ice baths	Paired-sample (interval estimation)	Lactate Reduction
13.3	Ankylosing spondylitis	Two paired-samples (interval estimation)	Cervical Rotation
13.4	Well-being	Binary (interval estimation)	Regular Exerciser
13.5	Climbers in hypoxia	Two-sample	Endurance Time
13.6	Indonesian study	One between-subject factor (3 levels)	Total Motor Activity
13.7	Creatine supplements	Paired-sample	Power Output
13.8	Deep water running	One within-subject factor (3 levels)	HR at Lactate Threshold
13.9	Overweight women and exercise	One between-subject and one within-factor (each at 2 levels)	20 m Walking Time
13.10	Well-being	Binary one- and two-sample	Regular Exerciser; Sex

Index

agreement
  levels of   373, 382
  limits of   369–71, 379, 383–4
  testing for   374–82
aims of statistical enquiries   11
Akaike's Information Criterion (AIC)   327,
    336, 348, 356
allometric scaling   202, 206–7, 212
alternative hypothesis   117, 121, 133
Altman, D.G.   369–70
analysis of covariance (ANCOVA)   197,
    200–1, 207, 211–12, 325
analysis of variance (ANOVA)   175–201,
    208–12, 246
  assessment of adequacy of   183–5
  assumptions for   210–11
  correction for covariates in   197–201
  multiple-comparison procedure in
    181–3, 186, 209, 211, 222
  one-way   176–85, 209–10, 222, 396
  two-way   185–97
Anderson–Darling Normality test   128
antilog function   251
association
  and categorical variables   229–37
  measures of   231
  tests of   229

balance across subjects   15–17, 33
best subsets of explanatory variables
    159, 174
between-subject factors and designs
    5–6, 12–13, 21–3, 33, 42–7, 57,
    60–4, 92–7, 123–7, 293–4, 342–8,
    396, 403
bias, systematic   359
binary recursive partitioning   257
binary variables   213, 234

Bland, J.M.   369–70
blinding   19
blocks (subgroups of samples)   23
Bonferroni, Carlo   181
Bonferroni procedure   181–2, 196
bootstrap procedure   105–6, 109–12,
    115, 211
box plots   76–7, 127, 184, 190

carryover effects   19
case profile plots   51
categorical variables   4–5, 34, 163–9,
    213–46, 259, 390
  and association   229–37
  formal analyses for   214
  and hypothesis testing   222–8
  interval estimation for   214–21
  modelling relationships with   241–6
  and paired data   237–41
  and sample size   405–7
  summaries for   213–14
causal relationships   64
central limit theorem   386
chi-squared (χ^2) test   222, 229, 231, 260
classification trees   257–8
coefficient of determination   173; see also
    R^2 statistic
coefficient of variation,
    within-subject   363
comparative studies   12 17, 33
comparison of multinomials 222
compound symmetry   275
conditions   15
confidence coefficient   113
confidence intervals (CIs)   80, 97–8, 102,
    114–15, 130, 136, 211, 215
  simultaneous   181–2
contingency tables   229, 234

continuous variables   3, 11, 34, 387
  graphical methods for   37–8
  in multiple regression   169
  numerical summaries for   35–7
control samples   13
controls (baseline conditions)   20
convenience samples   12
correlation and correlation coefficients
    64–6
correlation problems   64
covariates   60–4
  in ANCOVA   200–1
  in ANOVA   175, 197–201
  within-subject   325–56
Cramer's V   231

data analysis   2
data checking and storage   30
data collection   12–21
  learning about   28–9
  system and simplicity in   20
data-snooping   192
degrees of freedom (DF)   222, 260
dependent observations
  analysis of   263–92
  with between- and within-subject
    factors 293–324
  with linear mixed-effect models
    325–56
dependent-samples problems   16
discrete variables   5
double-blinds   19

error in sample statistics   79; see also
    measurement error
estimated standard error (e.s.e.)   79–80,
    113–14, 117, 131, 136, 215,
    259–60, 386
experimental design   31, 42, 84–7
explained variability   130–40
explanatory variables   5, 7, 64
  best subsets of   159, 174
  categorical   163–9
  selection of   157–63, 173–4
  in simple and multiple regression   149

factors   5, 7, 13
familiarisation with statistical
    procedures   29
fatigue effects   359

Fisher, Sir Ronald   175, 208
Fisher's exact test   260
fitted values in regression   140
F-test   152, 157, 175, 208–11

general linear model (GLM)   175–6, 184–5,
    207–11, 262
  assumptions of   275–6
generalisability of findings   174
gold standard methods   358, 374, 377, 382
graphical methods   37–8
Greenhouse–Geisser test   275

histograms   72–7
Hosmer–Lemeshow test   245, 251, 256–7
hypothesis testing   116–34, 174–5, 184,
    209, 262, 385
  and categorical variables   222–8
  and paired data   122–3
  see also null hypothesis; power in
    hypothesis testing

independent data   38
inference   3, 6, 11, 112
  in regression   136
intention to treat   30
interactions between factors   185, 211
interquartile range (IQR)   36–9
interval estimation   79–80, 113, 118, 121,
    127, 130, 134, 175, 385–91, 410
  for categorical variables   214–21
  for paired data   90–2
  for a population mean   80–3
  required width in   386, 390

Kruskal–Wallis test   211

Latin squares and Latin rectangles
    17, 402
learning effects   259
levels of factors   5
limitations on statistical studies   30–1
limits of agreement (Bland and Altman)
    369–71, 379, 383–4
linear mixed effects (l.m.e.) models   325–6,
    355–6
linear regression see multiple linear
    regression; simple linear regression
logarithmic transformation   107–11,
    242–3

logistic regression   241–57
  in complex problems   246–57
longitudinal designs   53, 60

McNemar's test   237
Mallow's *Cp*   327
Mann–Whitney procedure   110–12, 211
marginal symmetry, tests of   237, 240
match statistics   7
mathematical models   6–7, 10
Mauchly's test of sphericity   275
means *see* population means; sample means
measurement error   359–73, 382–3
measurement methods, comparisons
  of   373
measurement problems   357
medians *see* population medians;
  sample medians
method of agreement/method of
  comparison studies   358
mixture distributions   76
modelling of relationships   64–72
  with categorical response variables
  241–6
multinomial variables   213, 259; *see also*
  comparison of multinomials
multiple-comparison procedure *see* analysis
  of variance
multiple linear regression   149–57,
  171–2, 246
  assessment of adequacy of   152
  assumptions for   153–4
  compared with ANCOVA   211
  incorporating categorical explanatory
  variables in   164–9
  interpretation of coefficients in   151
  predictions from   152–3
multiple observations of the same
  variable 261–3
multivariate repeated measures tests   275

natural variability   262
nominal variables   4, 213
non-linear relationships   172–3
Normal distribution   6–7, 10, 36, 73–8, 80,
  83, 92, 98, 131, 140–1, 183–4, 211,
  213, 259, 262, 293, 297, 337, 396, 398
  departures from   102–15, 132
  general properties of   74
  tests for applicability of   127–30, 134

Normal probability plots   127, 153
normal range of observations   34, 98, 101
null hypothesis   116–19, 127, 130, 222,
  229, 392
  acceptance of   133
numerical summaries for continuous
  variables   35–7

observational studies   12, 33, 42, 84
odds and odds ratios   242, 251
one-sample problems   3
one-sided tests   121, 132–3
order effects   19
ordered within-subject factors   325–6
ordinal variables   5, 213
outliers   7, 102, 107

P-values   117–18, 130–3, 152, 186, 235,
  256–7, 260, 392
  interpretation of   133
  misuse of   130
paired data   48, 50, 57, 261
  and categorical variables   237–41
  and dependent observations   263–8
  and hypothesis testing   122–3
  interval estimation for   90–2
paired-sample problems   4, 15, 33, 261–2,
  389–90, 398
pairwise comparisons in ANOVA   181
  subsets of   210–11
parallel lines assumption   200–1
parameters   11, 78, 127
  definition of   3
PASS software   402
pilot studies   28–9, 385, 388, 393, 396
population distributions   38
population means   7, 11, 78–9
  comparison of   83–9, 106–7, 118–23
  interval estimation for   80–3
population medians   114–15
populations, definition of   3
power curves   395, 406–7
power in hypothesis testing   130
  and sample size   392–410
power law equations   202
prediction   135, 171, 174
  from multiple regression   152–3
  from simple linear regression   145–8
prediction intervals (PIs)   98, 113, 114
probability models   6

qualitative and quantitative variables   4–5
quartiles   36–7

R² statistic   140
R²-adjusted statistic   152
random error   359
random regression models   325–6
random sampling   12, 131–4
   stratified   23
randomly-permuted blocks   23
randomness and randomisation   7, 13, 20,
   89, 119
range of a sample   36
regression   135; *see also* logistic regression;
   multiple linear regression; random
   regression models; simple linear
   regression; stepwise regression
regression coefficients, interpretation of   151
regression trees   169–71
reliability studies   31
repeat studies   22
repeatable experiments   357–8, 382
repeated measures factors and tests   183,
   262, 275, 293
replication   26–9, 33
representative samples   6, 12
reproducible findings   357–8, 382
required width in interval estimation
   386, 390
re-sampling   114
residual plots   153, 172–3, 184
residuals in regression   140–2
response variables   5–7, 11, 31, 42, 64
   categorical   390
   explanation of   135
   prediction of   135, 171, 174
   transformation of   172–3
rogue observations   26

sample maxima and minima   36–7
sample means   35–9, 79, 113
sample medians   35–9
sample size   29, 114, 130–4, 174, 214–15,
   385–410
   and the power of a given hypothesis
   test   392–410
sample spread   35–6
sample statistics   79, 136
   uses of   37

samples
   definition of   3
   representativeness of   6, 12
scaling   201–7
scatter plots   61–71
significance levels   117
significance tests   116–18
significant main effects   186
simple linear regression   135–44,
   171–2, 382
   assumptions for   140–2
   interpretation of coefficients in   151
   predictions from   145–8
single-blinded studies   19
single repeated measures factor
   design   262
single-sample problems   38–9
skewness   102, 107, 114
smoothers   172
sphericity   275, 293–4
splitting of data   174, 257
spuriously-declared differences in sample
   means (from ANOVA)   181
standard deviation   36–9, 75, 172, 358,
   386–8
   differences in   183–4, 190, 209–11
standardisation of residuals   141–2,
   153–4
statistic (singular), definition of   3
statistical significance   117–18
statistics (plural), definition of   1–2
stepwise regression   159–60, 174
stratified random sampling   23
Student's *t*-distribution   80, 106
subject effects   262
summarisation of data   34
summary statistics   78
symmetrical distributions   36, 39

t-distribution *see* Student's *t*-distribution
t-test   117, 131–4, 175, 209, 393, 398
technical error of measurement
   (TEM)   383
tolerance intervals (TIs)   98, 101,
   113, 114
transformation of data   107–11, 114,
   172, 211
Tukey, John   182
Tukey procedure   181–2, 195

2 × 2 tables   260
two-sample problems   4, 13, 15, 33, 44
two-sided tests   132

uniform distributions   76–7
univariate repeated measures model   293

V-statistic *see* Cramer's V
validity of measurement techniques   358
variability   1
   components of   359
   explained   130–40
   in sampling   79
   sources of   21–8, 33, 357–8, 382

within and between subjects   21–3, 357,
      363–4, 382
   see also natural variability
variables   3–6
   definition of   3
variance-stabilising transformation   172

Wilcoxon–Mann–Whitney test   114, 297
within-subject covariates   325–56
   with complex designs   348–56
within-subject factors and designs   5–6,
      15, 22, 25–8, 33, 57, 48–57, 92–7,
      122–7, 261–2, 269–93, 325–6, 336–42,
      348, 400–3